Women and Power in Postconflict Africa

The book explains an unexpected consequence of the decrease in conflict in Africa after the 1990s. Analysis of cross-national data and in-depth comparisons of case studies of Uganda, Liberia, and Angola show that postconflict countries have significantly higher rates of women's political representation in legislatures and government compared with countries that have not undergone major conflict. They have also passed more legislative reforms and made more constitutional changes relating to women's rights. The study explains how and why these patterns emerged, tying these outcomes to the conjuncture of the rise of women's movements, changes in international women's rights norms, and, most importantly, to gender disruptions that occur during war. This book will help scholars, students, women's rights activists, international donors, policy makers, nongovernmental organizations (NGOs), and others better understand some of the circumstances that are most conducive to women's rights reform today.

Aili Mari Tripp is Professor of Political Science and Gender and Women's Studies at the University of Wisconsin–Madison. She is the author of several award-winning books, including *Museveni's Uganda: Paradoxes of Power in a Hybrid Regime* (2010) and *Women and Politics in Uganda* (2000). She is coauthor of *African Women's Movements: Transforming Political Landscapes* (2009). Professor Tripp is the coeditor of the book series *Women in Africa and the Diaspora*. She has served as president of the African Studies Association and as vice president of the American Political Science Association.

Cambridge Studies in Gender and Politics

CAMBRIDGE STUDIES IN GENDER AND POLITICS (CSGP) publishes empirical and theoretical research on gender and politics. The Series advances work that addresses key theoretical, normative, and empirical puzzles concerning sex and gender and their mutual impacts, constructions, and consequences regarding the political, comprehensively understood.

General Editors:

Karen Beckwith (Lead)
Case Western Reserve University

Lisa Baldez
Dartmouth College

Christina Wolbrecht
University of Notre Dame

Editorial Advisory Board:

Nancy Burns
University of Michigan

Matthew Evangelista
Cornell University

Nancy Hirschmann
University of Pennsylvania

Sarah Song
University of California at Berkeley

Ann Towns
University of Gothenburg

Aili Mari Tripp
University of Wisconsin at Madison

Georgina Waylen
University of Manchester

Women and Power in Postconflict Africa

By

AILI MARI TRIPP

University of Wisconsin–Madison

CAMBRIDGE
UNIVERSITY PRESS

CAMBRIDGE
UNIVERSITY PRESS

32 Avenue of the Americas, New York, NY 10013-2473, USA

Cambridge University Press is part of the University of Cambridge.

It furthers the University's mission by disseminating knowledge in the pursuit of education, learning, and research at the highest international levels of excellence.

www.cambridge.org
Information on this title: www.cambridge.org/9781107535879

First published 2015

Printed in the United Kingdom by Clays, St Ives plc

A catalog record for this publication is available from the British Library.

Library of Congress Cataloging in Publication Data
Tripp, Aili Mari, author.
Women and power in post-conflict Africa / by Aili Mari Tripp.
    pages   cm – (Cambridge studies in gender and politics)
Includes bibliographical references and index.
ISBN 978-1-107-11557-6 (Hardcover : alk. paper)
    1. Women–Political activity–Africa.   2. Women's rights–Africa.   3. Women's rights–Uganda–
Case studies.   4. Women's rights–Liberia–Case studies.   5. Women's rights–Angola–Case
studies.   6. Africa–Politics and government–21st century.   I. Title.   II. Series: Cambridge
studies in gender and politics.
HQ1236.5.A35T75 2015
305.42096–dc23   2015027392

ISBN 978-1-107-11557-6 Hardback
ISBN 978-1-107-53587-9 Paperback

Advance Praise for *Women and Power in Postconflict Africa*

"In this book Aili Mari Tripp yet again sets the standard for excellence in comparative feminist scholarship. Through rigorous research, she carefully unpacks and explains why some countries emerging from conflict are able to transform the gender order while others are not. Her careful analysis captures the causal mechanisms that together produce change – gender disruptions, women's movements activism and international norms. As is usual with her pioneering work, her skillful illumination of gender change processes in Africa will provide the template for other scholars seeking to explain the conditions under which transformation is possible in other regions of the world. The book is a must-read for anyone interested in Africa, in post-conflict transitions, and in gender transformation."

Louise Chappell,
University of New South Wales

To three remarkable men:
My father, Lloyd Swantz; my husband, Warren Tripp;
and my son, Lloyd Tripp

Contents

Tables

Figures

Map of Africa

FIGURE O.I   Credit: Eva Swantz

Acronyms

AAD	Acção Angolana para o Desenvolvimento
ADRA	Action for Rural Development and the Environment (Angola)/Acção para o Desenvolvimento Rural e Ambiente
AIDS	acquired immune deficiency syndrome
AFL	Armed Forces of Liberia
AFELL	Association of Female Lawyers of Liberia
AU	African Union
CEDAW	Convention on the Elimination of All Forms of Discrimination against Women
CIDA	Canadian International Development Agency
COEIPA	Comité Inter-Eclesiastico para a Paz em Angola
CPA	comprehensive peace agreement
CSOs	civil society organizations
DANIDA	Danish International Development Agency
DFID	Department for International Cooperation (UK)
DPKO	Department of Peacekeeping Operations
DRC	Democratic Republic of Congo
ECCAS	Economic Community of Central African States
ECOMOG	Economic Community of West African States Monitoring Group
ECOWAS	Economic Community of West African States
EMBs	electoral management bodies
FAA	Armed Forces of Angola/Forças Armadas de Angola
FAS	Femmes Africa Solidarité
FESA	Eduardo dos Santos Foundation/Fundação Eduardo dos Santos
FIDA	Women Lawyer's Association

FIND   Foundation for International Dignity (Liberia)
FLEC   Front for the Liberation of the Enclave of Cabinda
FNLA   National Liberation Front of Angola/Frente Nacional
                de Libertaçao de Angola
FONGA   Forum of the Angolan Non-Governmental Organizations
FRELIMO   Mozambique Liberation Front/Frente de Libertação
                de Moçambique
GBV   gender-based violence
GDP   gross national product
GTZ   German Agency for Technical Cooperation
HIV   human immunodeficiency virus
ICD   Inter-Congolese Dialogue
ICTR   International Criminal Tribunal for Rwanda
IDP   internally displaced person
IPU   Inter-Parliamentary Union
IGNU   Interim Government of National Unity (Liberia)
INPFL   Independent National Patriotic Front of Liberia
LGBT   Lesbian Gay Bisexual Transgendered
LIMA   Independent League for Angolan Women/Comité
                Nacional da Liga da Mulher Angolana
LRA   Lord's Resistance Army (Uganda)
LURD   Liberians United for Reconciliation and Democracy
LWI   Liberian Women's Initiative
MARWOPNET   Mano River Women Peace Network
MENA   Middle East and North Africa
MPD   Development Workshop run by Women Peace and
                Development/Movimento Angolano Mulheres Paz
                e Desenvolvimento
MODEL   Movement for Democracy in Liberia
MPLA   People's Movement for the Liberation of Angola/
                Movimento Popular de Libertação de Angola
NAWOU   National Association of Women's Organisations in
                Uganda
NEC   National Electoral Commission (Liberia)
NCW   National Council of Women (Uganda)
NGO   nongovernmental organization
NORAD   Norwegian Agency for International Cooperation
NOVIB   Netherlands Organisation for International Development
                Cooperation
NPFL   National Patriotic Front of Liberia
NPP   National Patriotic Party (Liberia)
NRA   National Resistance Army (Uganda)
NRM   National Resistance Movement (Uganda)
OAU   Organisation of African Unity

ODA	overseas development assistance
OECD	Organisation for Economic Co-operation and Development
OMA	Organization of the Women of Angola/Organização da Mulher de Angola
PRIO	Peace Research Institute Oslo
RCD	Rally for Congolese Democracy/Rassemblement Congolais pour la Démocratie
RENAMO	Mozambican National Resistance/Resistência Nacional Moçambicana
SACC	South African Council of Churches
SADC	Southern African Development Community
SCA	Angolan Civic Association/Sociedade Civil Angolana
SIDA	Swedish International Development Cooperation Agency
SIPRI	Stockholm International Peace Research Institute
SNV	Netherlands Development Organisation
UCW	Uganda Council of Women
ULIMO	United Liberation Movement of Liberia for Democracy
ULIMO-K	United Liberation Movement of Liberia for Democracy – Kromah faction
ULIMO-J	United Liberation Movement of Liberia for Democracy – Johnson faction
UN	United Nations
UNIFEM	United Nations Development Fund for Women
UNOMIL	United Nations Observer Mission in Liberia
UNMIL	United Nations Mission in Liberia
UNICEF	United Nations Children's Fund
UNITA	União Nacional para a Independência Total de Angola/ National Union for the Total Independence of Angola
UNAIDS	United Nations Programme on HIV/AIDS
UNDP	United Nations Development Programme
UNESCO	United Nations Educational, Scientific and Cultural Organization
UNHCR	United Nations High Commissioner for Refugees
UPDF	Uganda People's Defense Forces
USAID	United States Agency for International Development
UNSC	United Nations Security Council
UNSCR	United Nations Security Council Resolution
UPC	Uganda People's Congress
WACC	Women and Children Affairs Coordination Unit (Liberia)
WDC	Ward Development Committees (Sierra Leone)
WIPNET	Women in Peacebuilding Network (Liberia)
WONGOSOL	Women Nongovernmental Organizations' Secretariat of Liberia
YWCA	Young Women's Christian Association

Acknowledgments

This book has been a remarkable journey on which I have met many extraordinary people who have assisted me in myriad ways through interviews, logistical support, feedback on drafts, serving as an audience to my ideas, guiding the book through the editorial process, and providing encouragement. A book like this cannot be written without the input of many hundreds of individuals. I thank them all – including those not mentioned by name – for their crucial assistance, both in large and small ways.

I could not have finished this book without the patience and support of my dear family, foremost my husband, Warren Tripp, as well as my daughter Leila and son Lloyd. My father, Lloyd Swantz, died just before the final manuscript was submitted, but in his own way he contributed to the book, as did my mother, Marja-Liisa Swantz, by giving me the courage to work in unfamiliar countries and be open to the many diverse people and experiences I encountered. My father lived a rich and full life as a result of his open heart to everyone he encountered.

A huge thank you goes to my sister, Eva Swantz, who is a graphic artist by profession, and drew the beautiful maps in this manuscript.

The friendship, encouragement, and input of Stanlie James, Florence Ebila, Grace Thomsen, Myra Marx Ferree, Sandra Barnes, Ulrike Anderssen, Päivi Takala, and Suzanne Moyer Baazet were especially important to me in this process.

Dionisio Lamba served as an intrepid translator and research assistant in Angola. Eveline Viegas, executive director of the Centro para Desenvolvimento e Parcerias de Angola in Luanda, provided incredible logistical assistance. I especially appreciated being able to come to the Centro for espresso coffee breaks in between interviews. In Liberia, the Hon. Amelia Ward, Hon. Florence Chenoweth, and Kevin Gorlator provided important assistance and insights. The late Marie-Ange Bunga conducted interviews for me in Kinshasa,

Democratic Republic of Congo, and enthusiastically engaged with some of the most brave and outstanding women leaders I have encountered. I am only sorry she was not able to see the project come to fruition because of her untimely death. In northern Uganda, Loyce Allen Asire provided critical support, both as a translator and research assistant. I am indebted to Marissa Moorman, Richard Strickland, Laura Singleton, Ladan Affi, Miriam Kelberg, Michael Burns, Sara Burnes, and Tasneem Amro for their help at crucial points in the process of writing and carrying out research.

Many have provided feedback on parts of this work over the years, and I owe them an enormous debt of gratitude. I can't thank Melanie Hughes enough for her persistence in collaborating with me and for believing in the importance of this project. She provided the conceptual and methodological rigor that went into the *Social Forces* article we coauthored that forms the quantitative basis for this book. I am also particularly indebted to Anne Marie-Goetz, Gretchen Bauer, Alice Kang, Rachel Ellett, and the two reviewers of the book who helped shape the final draft of the manuscript. Christine Scheidegger and Simanti Lahiri provided incisive comparative insights at key moments in the writing.

I would like to thank the Woodrow Wilson International Center for Scholars in Washington, DC, and the Center for Research on Gender and Women at the University of Wisconsin–Madison for providing me with fellowships. The University of Wisconsin System granted me a semester-long sabbatical to work on the book.

And finally, I am thrilled that this book is the first in the new book series, Cambridge Studies in Gender and Politics. I am especially grateful to the series editors, Karen Beckwith, Lisa Baldez, and Christina Wolbrecht, and to the Cambridge editor, Lewis Bateman, for helping shepherd the book to publication.

Preface

When I went to Uganda in 1992 to carry out research, I was interested in why Uganda, which had just come out of years of major conflict, had so many women in top government positions and why the country had the highest rates of representation of women in parliament in Africa at the time. What I did not know then – and could not have known – was that this was the beginning of a pattern that became especially evident after 2000: that post-conflict countries had higher rates of female representation in politics, and that they were making more women's rights reforms in their constitutions and legislation compared with non-postconflict countries. In my 2000 book, *Women and Politics in Uganda,* I attributed the changes to shifts in gender relations during the war, but primarily to the emergence of autonomous women's organizations, supported by international donors. Subsequently, fifteen other countries have emerged from major conflict, exhibiting similar patterns.

This book shows how the trends I noticed in Uganda in the early 1990s are now evident in other parts of Africa. It asks two main questions: What accounts for this somewhat curious by-product of war that has resulted in higher political leadership rates for women and more constitutional and legislative changes regarding women's rights in postconflict countries? This book also asks: How were postconflict countries able, in a relatively short span of time, to advance women's status in key areas and in some of the most challenging areas for women? They not only accomplished what the Nordic countries had done over the course of 100 years in increasing legislative representation, but, in some cases, exceeded their rates almost overnight. Moreover, the changes were not simply in the area of politics, they extended into multiple arenas.

What happened in Uganda and in many other postconflict states was a major shift in social and gender relations and in the gender regime, to borrow a concept developed by Raewyn Connell. The changes have been far from linear and are, in fact, quite uneven and messy. To activists in these countries, the changes have been all too slow and halting, but even the impatience with the slowness in the pace of change is an indication of the way in which expectations have been transformed. In nondemocratic countries, the changes are compromised by a lack of political rights and civil liberties. Taking a step back and looking at the big picture, however, these shifts represent a gender regime change in political institutions. This book focuses on transformations in the political arena, but to fully appreciate the magnitude of the changes, one has to look at the various dimensions of gender regime change, which include increased political power, but also involve women taking on new leadership roles in business, civil society, academia, religious institutions, and other institutions in which women had previously not been visible. Often attitudes toward women and women's leadership changed throughout society. In some countries the changes were more extensive than others, where sometimes one saw change only along a few dimensions.

I argue in this book that these patterns can be accounted for by (1) disruptions in gender relations that are unique to countries experiencing conflict. However, this explanation is insufficient because not all wars result in changes in women's status. Timing is critical. These shifts also occurred at a time when domestic and international norms were changing regarding women's rights. Thus, they took place in the context of (2) a rise in domestic women's mobilization, which was facilitated by an opening of political space, even if limited, and (3) changes in international gender norms along with pressures and encouragements primarily from United Nations agencies as well as other multilateral and bilateral donors. Although other countries may have experienced similar reforms, the postconflict trajectory sped up these developments.

It is an understatement to say that there is still a long way to go until equality is fully realized. Nevertheless, there has been too little attention paid to the accomplishments and too little credit given to the African women and men who brought about these changes. Too much of the credit has been given to donors and to other external actors, as well as to government leaders, who have their own agendas in all this. It is essential, however, to look at how these developments were tied to conjunctures of events that occurred at multiple levels.

Many scholars who focus on constitutional or legislative change, or the introduction of electoral quotas, look more narrowly at institutional change and what makes these institutions work for women. This study looks at what institutional change tells us about society and politics more broadly. In particular, I am interested in institutional change in periods of transition and the opportunity structures that facilitate or limit change.

The study also highlights the importance of looking at regional dynamics in the adoption of quotas and women's political representation. Although cross-national global studies are important in highlighting overall trends, there are regional specificities, such as a decline of many conflicts during the same time period in Africa, that would not describe contemporary Nordic or European dynamics, for example. By the same token, the fact that there are fewer new conflicts emerging and less reversal back into conflict in Africa is also positively influencing these trends because they require a certain amount of stability.

It goes without saying that the claims about the link between the decline of conflict and women's rights and representation are not in any way a normative prescription for or glorification of civil conflict and all its horrors, but rather an analysis of the opportunities that such ruptures may have presented to women's rights advocates.

The study builds on a cross-national quantitative and longitudinal study using latent growth curve analysis, which I carried out with Melanie Hughes (Hughes and Tripp 2015), that explains the factors influencing female representation in Africa. We found postconflict impacts to be highly significant and independent of other factors such as the introduction of quotas and proportional representation electoral systems when examined longitudinally. These postconflict patterns of women's new political leadership are particularly visible in countries that have had conflicts long in duration or high in intensity (high rates of death).

However, all of this requires explanation. Even the adoption of quotas by itself does not explain why governments introduced quotas in the first place any more than the decline of conflict explains why women were able to take advantage of this moment in certain countries to advance themselves. This book attempts to explain the causal mechanisms and opportunity structures that influenced gender regime change.

Part I provides an overview of the main arguments in the manuscript. Chapter 1 introduces the project and sets the stage by discussing the decline of conflict in Africa after the 1990s. It looks at several alternative arguments that potentially challenge the claims made in this book. It engages the literature on backlash to show that it is largely inapplicable to postconflict countries after the 1990s in Africa. It examines similar trends in earlier periods in history, namely the period after World War I, when women gained suffrage in many parts of the world. The chapter outlines the main arguments in the manuscript, including reasons for the distinct trajectory adopted by postconflict countries in bringing about changes in the gender regime in political institutions. This is followed by an explanation of the opportunity structures the women's movements were able to take advantage of to assert their interests, specifically peace negotiations and constitutional reform processes. At the heart of these changes is a transformation in elite configurations as older elites and coalitions are dislodged by new political institutions, making way for new leaders like women.

Chapter 2 outlines the causal mechanisms or explanations of how civil conflict influences women's rights policy adoption and some of the alternative arguments. The chapter then elaborates on the broad argument of the book, linking the rapid changes in postconflict women's rights reforms to the three aforementioned factors (disruptions in gender relations, domestic women's mobilization, and changes in international norms).

Part II of the book involves case studies of Uganda, Liberia, and Angola. Uganda, which is examined in Chapter 3, was the first country in Africa where postconflict influences on women's status described in this book became evident. They became apparent with the takeover of Yoweri Museveni and his National Resistance Movement (NRM) in 1986 after a five-year guerrilla war. The chapter details the three key factors described in Chapter 1 that help explain why postconflict countries have been more ready to promote women's rights and representation. The international factors became more salient after 1995, which was long after Uganda had already adopted women's rights in policy making, thus highlighting the importance of domestic actors, even if international considerations were beginning to become relevant.

Liberia, which is the subject of Chapter 4, is one of the more recent countries to emerge from conflict in Africa. The chapter discusses the evolution of the women's peace movement, which grew after the outbreak of conflict in 1989 and continued until the end of the second war in 2003. The peace movement was transformed into postconflict women's mobilization for political power and women's rights. As in the Uganda case study, the chapter systematically elaborates on all three factors and shows how they were present in the Liberian case.

The case of Angola (Chapter 5) is contrasted with the Ugandan, Liberian, and other African postconflict cases to show how the *absence* of key causal mechanisms made it less likely that Angola would adopt woman-friendly policies, in particular, the absence of an independent women's movement and the withdrawal of most donors after the war, especially those funding civil society. Also, the lack of democratization as a structural precondition, and the lack of a peace process in ending the war all served to limit the extent to which gender policy change could occur in Angola. The same political elites remained in power during and after the war as did the ruling party, similarly constraining gender regime change. The country's leaders did increase female political representation through the adoption of quotas, and they introduced a few woman-friendly policies, but not on the same scale or at the same pace found in other postconflict countries. Angola thus shares many of the same characteristics as other postconflict countries that did not see much significant change (e.g., Chad and Eritrea).

Part III of the book looks at the opportunity structures more closely, in particular peace agreements and constitutional reforms. Chapter 6 on peace agreements explains the importance of how the war ends, demonstrating that conflicts that ended with a comprehensive peace agreement provided significant opportunities for women activists to assert their demands for representation and set goals for a postconflict political order. They were not always able to gain a voice in the peace negotiations, but where they were successful, peace negotiations provided an important opportunity structure, influencing later constitutional and legislative outcomes and processes.

Chapter 7 looks at the stark difference between constitutions in countries coming out of conflict and countries that had not experienced major conflict, but which also reformed their constitutions at the same time. The differences are especially pronounced in the areas of customary law, discrimination, citizenship of children, labor rights, positive measures, violence against women, and the adoption of quotas. The chapter goes into depth regarding the constitution-making process in Uganda and how the women's movement influenced its strong gender-related outcomes.

Part IV looks at outcomes for gender regime change in political institutions. Chapter 8 focuses on women's legislative representation as well as women's leadership roles in the executive and in local government. It engages the literature on representation to show why postconflict influences are among the most important factors explaining female legislative representation in Africa. It also explores the role of women's mobilization in bringing about electoral reforms more generally. Chapter 9 provides an overview of the differences between countries that came out of major conflict and those that did not in adopting legislative reforms, particularly in the areas of violence against women, land and property rights, customary law, and quota adoption.

Chapter 10, the final chapter in Part V, takes the main findings of the book to show how new and unexplored issues emerge from this study and what implications they have for future research.

Throughout this book, I attempt to demonstrate the importance of women to the processes of peace, not in some idealistic way, but rather from a social science perspective. I was quickly disabused of any romantic notions of peacemaking while carrying out fieldwork. The deeper I delved into the stories of people's lives, the more I learned that peace is not always made by Mother Teresa-like characters, although I encountered a large number of unsung heroines and heroes. I also discovered women in the peace movements who had helped start and fuel wars, who supported warlords, who had sabotaged fellow activists, who sought the limelight, and who fought internal demons, in addition to their political foes.

I learned that war is not only gruesome on the battlefield. It is ugly because it distorts the lives of individuals, families, and communities in unimaginable ways and makes people do things that they would never have contemplated doing under normal circumstances. It forces people to make distasteful choices one would not wish on anyone, choices that are often incomprehensible to someone who has not experienced war firsthand. It would be easy to whitewash these realities, but they are part of the story. This book takes a hard look at some of these ambiguities of peacemaking.

Having said that, it astounds me that the very people in civil society and in women's movements who are best equipped to contribute to peace and who have been courageously fighting for it in their communities end up systematically excluded from peace talks. Meanwhile, war criminals and warlords sit around the negotiating table to divide up the spoils of war, that is, government positions and the trappings of power. It is not just a question of fairness and equity that women be included in positions of power, although that argument certainly can be made. It is so clear from the studies in this book that it is at the crux of ending war and of rebuilding society. Studies have shown that where civil society actors are included in talks, peace is less likely to fail (Nilsson 2012). Having interviewed hundreds of women leaders in Liberia, Uganda, Angola, Democratic Republic of Congo, and Kenya, I can say with absolute certainty that there is no shortage of women of high caliber who are more than capable of engaging in peace talks and in leading their countries. The argument that there is a dearth of women leaders never was a credible argument and needs to be retired once and for all.

Women peace activists are largely left out of journalistic accounts of war, and similarly they are absent from academic studies. Galtung (1993, xi) noted that "not only do the media have this perverse fascination with war and violence; they also neglect the peace forces at work. As the media work, they amplify the sound of guns rather than muting them." The same could be said of scholarship, even feminist scholarship, which focuses on war, conflict, and fighters rather than on peacemakers. This study, therefore, seeks to amplify the voices of women pursuing peace and power to show how these pursuits became connected after the 1990s in African civil wars.

PART I

SETTING THE STAGE

1

Introduction

It is not difficult to hurt, but it is difficult to repair.

– South African proverb

Since roughly the early 1990s and especially after 2000, some of the most dramatic changes in women's political engagement have occurred in countries that came out of major conflict. This is especially evident in Africa, where sixteen countries have ended major civil wars since 1986. Postconflict countries in Africa are making more constitutional and legislative changes related to women's rights compared with nonpostconflict countries. They have considerably higher rates of female legislative representation when compared with nonpostconflict countries, and they have more women in executive leadership positions. Postconflict Liberia, for example, had the first elected woman president in Africa; postconflict Uganda had a woman vice president for ten years; and postconflict Rwanda has the highest rates of female legislative representation in the world. The dominant party in postconflict Namibia is in the process of adopting a Gender Zebra Policy in which men and women share governance so that women and men both have 50 percent of positions in government, parliament, and state-owned enterprises.

This study asks: Why do countries that have experienced major civil conflict appear to be following a distinct and faster trajectory than nonpostconflict countries when it comes to adopting women's rights reforms and promoting female leadership?

I am using the term "postconflict" to describe countries where there has been a significant decline in the number of deaths related to conflict and where there has been a decline in hostilities. For purposes of generalization, I am focusing in this book on postconflict African countries that engaged in sustained and high-intensity conflict that ended after 1985. All of these countries had at least one year – and on average eight years of conflict – with over 1,000 recorded deaths per year, according to data collected by the Uppsala Conflict Data Program (UCDP) and the Peace Research Institute Oslo (PRIO). I am certain that most of these conflicts experienced considerably more deaths than what UCDP and PRIO report in their Armed Conflict dataset, but I take these measures simply to be rough indicators and a means by which to distinguish between levels of conflict. Thus, for the purposes of this study, countries experiencing high-intensity conflicts that ended after 1985 include Algeria, Angola, Burundi, Chad, Congo Brazzaville, Ethiopia (Eritrea), Liberia, Morocco (Western Sahara), Mozambique, Rwanda, Sierra Leone, Sudan, South Africa (Namibia), and Uganda. Separatist movements resulted in the creation of new independent states in Eritrea and South Sudan, whereas a national liberation movement resulted in Namibian independence from South Africa. Countries that are treated as experiencing ongoing conflict as of 2014 include Democratic Republic of Congo, Central African Republic, Libya, Nigeria, Somalia, and South Sudan.

My characterization of a decline in conflict does not imply that violence has ended, nor does it imply, as Page Fortna (2004) claims, that peace is "the absence of war." Numerous forms of violence continue in postconflict contexts, particularly for women, who continue to face heightened insecurity in their homes or communities. Sometimes, the forces that are supposed to be "protecting" civilians, like peacekeeping troops, have themselves been sources of insecurity and gender-based violence. Recent research suggests that the death rate for women is higher than for men after the conflict is over (Ormhaug, Meier, and Hernes 2009).

In the postconflict period, we witnessed the beginnings of transformations of various gender regimes within key institutions like the state. Gender regimes in political institutions pertain to gender relations of power and the way politics is organized hierarchically along gender lines in political institutions like legislatures, the executive branch, local government, and other such institutions. Gender regimes can also refer to the gender division of labor and the ways in which occupations are arranged along gender lines. They can refer to the gendered nature of human relations and feelings of prejudice toward women. And finally, they refer to a gendered culture and symbolic system. These regimes operate within a whole system or gender order (Connell 2002).

Change between gender regimes can be uneven. Thus, we have sometimes seen women gaining political power through quotas in legislatures, judiciaries, and government positions, with less change in other spheres such as the military and police. It appears that women found it easier to make inroads into key political and economic institutions, but much harder to gain a foothold in religious and traditional institutions outside the state and market. Nevertheless, there were significant changes in the gender regimes, particularly in political institutions, but also in other institutions in countries affected by major conflict, and some progressed further than others. The case studies in this book examine the regime changes along a variety of dimensions.

Women took on new roles in society and in the labor force in many post-conflict countries. What is less clear is the extent to which men took on more domestic roles in the home, although there is evidence of this in some of the case studies. Women gained more positions of political and economic power. Norms changed regarding acceptable treatment and portrayal of women in the media. People's visions of what was possible for women expanded, sometimes quite dramatically; thus women's symbolic power increased. Transformations in legal frameworks, which this book examines, reflect these normative changes, and they served as a first and necessary step toward fundamentally altering the gender regime. The extent to which legal changes translate into real-world impacts is an empirical question that has to be answered on a country-by-country basis, but there is also evidence of some change in this regard, and it is presented in the three case studies. I am more guarded about making major conclusions about such overall outcomes at this time for the majority of postconflict countries because the constitutional and legislative changes are so new in many of the countries in question.

Some of the aforementioned postconflict changes in Africa, for example, women's legislative representation, are also evident in Southeast Asia (East Timor), South Asia (Nepal), and Central America (Nicaragua). This study focuses on Africa because the trends are most pronounced on this continent. The number of countries embroiled in conflict in Africa has been greater than in any other part of the world in the postindependence period. Also the number of countries coming out of conflict has been the greatest. The increase in the resolution of conflicts in Africa in the 1990s and especially after 2000 was due to such factors as the end of the Cold War, the increased importance of international and regional peacekeeping forces, greater efforts regarding diplomacy and peace negotiations, and the increase in influence of peace movements.

Postconflict Rwanda claimed the world's highest ratio of women in parliament in 2003, and by 2007, Rwandan women held 56 percent of the country's legislative seats, rising to 64 percent in the 2013 elections.[1] Similar trends are evident in other postconflict countries: Women hold on average 28.5 percent of the parliamentary seats in postconflict countries compared with 18 percent in nonpostconflict countries. Liberia's Ellen Johnson Sirleaf became the first elected woman president in Africa in 2005, as more women in postconflict countries began running for the presidency after 2000.

This study explores why we have seen such dramatic increases in female political representation in postconflict countries, especially since around 2000. It looks specifically at why postconflict countries have been more likely to make constitutional and legislative changes advancing women's formal status.

---

[1] All data on national women's legislative representation in this book is derived from the Inter-Parliamentary Union in 2014, www.ipu.org/wmn-e/classif.htm.

The book focuses primarily on three case studies, Uganda, Liberia, and Angola, which are examined against cross-national comparative data pertaining to women's rights influences on opportunity structures (peace agreements and constitutional reforms) as well as outcomes (numbers of female political leaders and women's rights legislation). It traces their evolution, documenting the commonalities and differences in causal mechanisms that gave rise to these developments. It looks at these cases against the backdrop of structural changes in Africa, including the end of conflict and political liberalization. Uganda and Liberia were more successful than Angola in advancing women's rights. The contrast between these countries allows us to identify crucial factors that explain the causal mechanisms at work in postconflict countries.

This chapter starts by outlining the key arguments of the book. It sets the stage by discussing the decline in conflict in Africa and globally as well as the concomitant political liberalization that occurred in Africa. The chapter then details some patterns that have accompanied these trends; it discusses the literature on backlash against women after conflict and on changes in gender relations; and it explores the historical antecedents of present-day trends with the adoption of female suffrage after World War I. The chapter concludes with a description of the research design, methodology, and methods employed in this study.

EXISTING APPROACHES

Beyond the issue of female representation, there have been very few studies that connect the decline of conflict to broader changes in women's rights in Africa, and to the extent that this has been mentioned in the literature, it has been primarily in the context of individual postconflict countries like Mozambique (Disney 2008), Uganda (Tripp 2000), Sudan (Abbas 2010; Tønnessen 2011), and Rwanda (Burnet 2012). Together with Alice Mungwa, Isabel Casimiro, and Joy Kwesiga, I began to explore this relationship between women's rights outcomes and conflict comparatively in a coauthored book; however, the chapter was still fairly speculative (Tripp et al. 2009). Some have mentioned, but not explored, the connection between women's legislative representation and conflict through comparative analysis (Bauer and Britton 2006; Luciak 2006; Muriaas et al. 2013; Zuckerman and Greenberg 2004). Others have examined women parliamentarians' impact on legislation in postconflict countries (Pearson and Powley 2008; Luciak and Olmos 2005).

A few cross-national studies posit a connection between conflict and women's representation. Melanie Hughes (2009) shows how long-lasting and major civil war during the 1980s and 1990s positively impacted female legislative representation in low-income nations. Kathleen Fallon, Liam Swiss, and Jocelyn Viterna (2012) found that the effects of conflict on representation in countries transitioning to democracy are no longer evident after 1995. However, they are only examining countries that have transitioned to democracy. Most postconflict countries in Africa are not democratic.

This study builds on a quantitative cross-national study I carried out with Melanie Hughes (2015) of the relationship between electoral institutions, democratization, and armed conflict. We discovered, using a longitudinal statistical method of latent growth curve analysis, that postconflict African countries follow a trajectory of women's representation that is distinct from that of countries that have not gone through major conflict, and that major civil conflict becomes more important rather than less after 1995 in this correlation. We found that conflict had a significant and independent impact on women's political representation in sub-Saharan Africa and correlates strongly with the sharp increase in female legislative representation in sub-Saharan Africa, which tripled between 1990 and 2010. We also found that incremental changes in civil rights result in increases in women's legislative presence further down the road.

ALTERNATIVE CLAIMS

Backlash against women after conflict?

Much of the literature to date has focused on backlash against women as a consequence of conflict (de Watteville 2002; Kelly 2000; Meintjes et al. 2002; Pankhurst 2003, 2007; Pankhurst and Pearce 1997). I define backlash as a tangible and measurable pattern of undoing the gains made in women's rights, such as the erosion of women's rights legislation and/or replacing them with laws that undermine women's status. Donna Pankhurst has argued: "Rather than receiving support at the end of wars, women usually suffer a backlash against any new-found freedoms, and they are forced 'back' into kitchens and fields. Where governments and/or warring parties establish new constitutions or peace processes, they often neglect the needs of women or outwardly limit or restrict the rights of women" (2003, 161). Indeed this was borne out in earlier periods, globally and within Africa.

Events in Algeria after independence in 1962 were a forerunner of what was to come in other parts of sub-Saharan Africa in the postindependence era. Women first broke gender barriers during the Algerian war of independence against France (1954–1962), when large numbers of women served as freedom fighters, fighting side by side with men in what was considered one of the most brutal liberation wars on the continent. Other women served as civilians who provided food and shelter for the insurgents (Daoud 1996, 138; Salhi 2010). Yet after the war, women found themselves abruptly pushed out of public life (Ahmed 1982).

Women subsequently fought in the armed liberation struggles in Mozambique, Guinea Bissau, Angola, and Rhodesia (Zimbabwe). The changes described in this book did not occur after the end of the aforementioned wars of liberation prior to 1985. As in Algeria, women found themselves sidelined after independence in these countries. Even in struggles where women's concerns were addressed by the liberation movement, they did not necessarily benefit after the struggle was over. In Mozambique and Guinea Bissau, women's liberation was seen as part and parcel of the liberation movement (Ranchod-Nilsson 2006; Urdang 1978). Leaders of the Frente de Libertação de Moçambique (Mozambique Liberation Front), or FRELIMO, envisioned creating a non-patriarchal society after winning independence from Portugal. As the late Mozambican President Samora Machel said in a speech to the First Conference of the Organização da Mulher Moçambican (Mozambican Woman's Organization), or OMA, in 1975: "Woman's liberation is a necessity of the revolution, a condition of its triumph, and a guarantee of its continuity" (Urdang 1978). During the war, women had their own military contingents and played key support roles during the fighting; however, after independence, women were told to put their demands on hold in the interests of development.

Similarly, in Zimbabwe, women had made up one-third of the fighters in the guerrilla movement that led to the end of white minority rule, and they had played supporting roles. Zimbabwean President Robert Mugabe acknowledged that the war would not have been won without the help of women (Mugabe 1984). Nevertheless, Zimbabwean women activists were incensed when they were told to wait for an indefinite time until their rights could be fully addressed in the interests of national development (Staunton 1990; Sylvester 1989). Leaders of women's organizations in Zimbabwe explicitly told women's organizations in South Africa to avoid this predicament when South Africa emerged out of apartheid. I witnessed this sentiment in discussions with Zimbabwean women's organizations as South Africa was transitioning to independence (see also Jirira 1995; Lueker 1998). Janet Place wrote at the time about these feelings of political exclusion in Zimbabwe:

Women still complain that only limited strides have been made in changing the legal and cultural barriers to women's advancement and participation in government. In fact, Zimbabwean women were quick to advise the women of other emerging democracies that the liberation of women must go hand in hand with the political liberation of the country. There was a sense of betrayal among the women of Zimbabwe at the time of independence, who found that the country's call for equality for all did not include them. (Sinclair and Place 1990)

As a former research associate of the John D. and Catherine T. MacArthur Foundation, I visited numerous women's nongovernmental organizations in Harare, Zimbabwe, in 1990. At the time, the frustration was palpable among leaders and activists working with the Association of Women's Clubs of Zimbabwe, Women in Law and Development in Africa (WILDAF), Zimbabwe Women's Resource Centre and Network, Zimbabwe Women's Bureau, and Women's Action Group.

Tanya Lyons (2004) described an Operation Clean-Up carried out in 1983 in which police and soldiers beat and harassed women found traveling alone or in groups on the grounds that they were prostitutes. The majority of the 6,000 women targeted in these humiliating campaigns were ordinary housewives, workers, and even former combatants. Zimbabwean feminist activist Shereen Essof (2005) wrote about how by the late 1990s the state was undermining key women's rights legislation and denying women property and inheritance rights.

Although such disappointments had characterized earlier conflicts, this changed a few years later around the time that the Ugandan civil war ended in 1986. The timing of the end of conflict was critical. A new breed of women activists became visible after the Third United Nations Conference on Women held in Nairobi in 1985 and especially after 1995, the year that the Fourth UN Conference on Women was held in Beijing. By 1985, the norms regarding women's rights were rapidly changing throughout the world, and Africa was about to move into a period of political liberalization in the 1990s. However fraught some of the political openings were, as countries shifted from authoritarian to hybrid regimes (neither fully democratic nor fully authoritarian), they were sufficient to create enough political space to allow autonomous women's movements to mobilize and put pressure on governments for gender-based change. Women's organizations were key actors in the process of political liberalization, but they also were prime beneficiaries of the political opening, which was accompanied by an increase in freedom of association and freedom of the press, as well as an increase in civil liberties and political rights more generally. Since 1995, forty-nine constitutions were rewritten in Africa, and twenty-three of these were in postconflict countries or countries with ongoing conflict. Only four countries did not rewrite their constitutions in this period.

The lack of backlash was evident with the end of conflict in Uganda in 1986, and it has continued to be evident after other conflicts. Liberia came out of conflict in 2003, and there was no major backlash. In part, this was because the country had a long history of women leaders at the local and national levels. Not only did women claim the presidency, key ministerial, and local government positions, but the popularity of the women's movement was at an all-time high, starting with the interim government and continuing into the presidency of Ellen Johnson Sirleaf, who assumed office in 2005. The movement had been credited with speeding up the process of peacemaking and was benefiting from that boost. In a study of the media between 2000 and 2012, for example, Lisa Kindervater (2013) found that the gap between the number of positive and negative articles about women and gender equality increased seven-fold between 2003 and 2006. There were no virtually no antimovement articles between 2000 and 2009, but there was a slight increase between 2010 and 2012. Nevertheless, the number of positive articles remained twice as high. Although there was a drop in the number of positive articles because the movement itself died down after the war, there was not a significant increase in negative articles either. Had there been a backlash, one would have expected an increase in negative press.

In recent years, in countries like Kenya, Uganda, South Africa, and Zimbabwe, mobs have publically stripped individual women who were deemed to be dressed indecently. In several cases, the attacks were caught on video and went viral on YouTube. A South African journalist, Sisonke Msimang (2015), claimed that this was a reflection of backlash in the face of so many women in top positions and the fact that "churches, traditional leaders and politicians are forming powerful coalitions that are seeking to challenge decades of progress." Although one can point to such incidents, I believe they do not reflect a new reaction but, rather, a conservative undercurrent that never went away. These types of attacks on women's bodies are not new and have taken place in earlier periods, as in Uganda under Idi Amin, at a time when women were not gaining positions of power but were adopting Western-style attire (see Chapter 3). I would still contend that one ought to see more such reactions if there were a true backlash, and there would need to be similar new patterns of reversal of gains in multiple arenas. More important, one would expect to see a pullback of women in positions of power and a revocation of quotas as well as an undoing of the legal framework.

Thus, although backlash may have described some outcomes, the dominant trend has been an increase in women's rights at the formal level in most postconflict countries. After 1990, postconflict countries generally did not experience the type of backlash evident in earlier conflicts in Africa because the international norms had changed by the mid-1990s, and there were new pressures, especially from multilateral actors like the United Nations but also from bilateral donors, from regional bodies like the Southern African Development Community (SADC), as well as from domestic women's movements to pursue women's rights reforms. Also countries that had longer traditions of female leadership were less resistant to women in power. Thus, the conjuncture of these factors was critical to setting in motion a distinct path for postconflict countries when it came to a women's rights agenda. After the end of major conflicts from Uganda to Namibia, South Africa, Mozambique, Rwanda, Burundi, and Liberia, women's organizations vigorously pressed for increased representation, often in the form of quotas. Women's rights language was included in 78 percent of the peace agreements in Africa between 2000 and 2011 – more than any other region of the world (see Chapter 6).

Women demanded seats at the peace talks, on electoral commissions, on constitutional commissions that drafted new constitutions, and in interim and newly formed governments. As a result, in Liberia women were represented in all transitional institutions. A woman, Frances Johnson-Morris, headed the Electoral Commission, and three of the six participants were women. Another woman, Elizabeth Nelson, succeeded Johnson-Morris. Gloria Musu Scott headed up the constitutional review committee, and three out of six participants on the commission were women. Four out of the nine commissioners on the Truth and Reconciliation Commission were women. Ruth Ceasar was appointed deputy executive director for operations at the National Commission on Disarmament, Demobilization, Rehabilitation, and Reintegration between 2006 and 2009 and oversaw the implementation of programs affecting 101,000 ex-combatants.

Saying that there is no backlash is not to say that there are no concerns. There is still very little awareness, for example, about UN Security Council Resolution 1325, even 15 years after it was passed. UNSCR 1325 stipulates that all peacekeeping activities need to incorporate women (Anderlini 2011). Only forty-six countries have a UN Security Council–mandated National Action Plan for the implementation of UNSCR 1325. In Africa, the countries with these plans include Burundi (2011), Côte d'Ivoire (2007), DRC (2010), Gambia (2014), Ghana (2010), Guinea (2011), Guinea Bissau (2011), Liberia (2009), Nigeria (2013), Rwanda (2010), Senegal (2011), Sierra Leone (2010), and Uganda (2008). It is noteworthy that the main countries with these plans globally are OECD and African countries. Of our three case studies, it is also telling that Uganda and Liberia were among the first to develop a plan, whereas Angola does not have such a plan. At the international level, however, the awareness is not much better. A Global Summit to End Sexual Violence in Conflict, hosted by the UK and involving 123 governments with sixty to seventy participants at the ministerial level, failed to incorporate civil society actors, with two exceptions, in its deliberations and failed to make links between gender inequality, militarism, and violence against women (Williams 2014).

Changes in sex ratio

Another alternative argument to my study relates to how one evaluates changes in the sex ratio that occur during war. There is a popular and often repeated claim in the literature that women in Rwanda gained political power because there was a change in the sex ratio as a result of male deaths and absence due to war (see, for example, Bennett 2014; Gogineni 2013). It is based on a statistic first advanced by a Human Rights Watch report (1996) that 70 percent of the population was female after the genocide. Sometimes the figure goes as high as 80 percent (Macauley 2013). There was indeed a sizeable 0.4 percent change in the sex ratio in Rwanda right after the genocide, when the female percentage of the population jumped from 51.1 percent in 1993 to 51.5 percent in 1996. But by 2013 it was back to 51.2 percent, according to World Bank data.[2] By all accounts there was enormous displacement of men in the immediate aftermath of the conflict, and the number of female-headed households increased. A large number of men were also incarcerated for their role in the genocide. But it is unlikely that the demographics had changed so dramatically that 70 percent of the actual population was female or that the sex imbalance would have driven the rise in female representation.

This overall aforementioned change of 0.1 percent in women is not enough to drive a 47 percent jump from 17 percent of women in parliament in 1993 to 64 percent in 2014. Instead, this correlation between the change in sex ratio

---

[2] http://data.worldbank.org/indicator/SP.POP.TOTL.FE.ZS.

and changes in female representation in Rwanda is more likely capturing a change in gender relations that occurred as a result of major disruptions of genocide and war rather than simply the absence of men. Were the absence of men to have such an impact on women's representation, one would expect similar changes under other circumstances where men are absent (e.g., work-related migration).

Melanie Hughes and myself (2015) found a strong and independent statistical correlation between women's legislative representation and the length and intensity of conflict. We did not, however, find strong statistical significance for the effects of a change in the sex ratio. When we controlled for changes in the sex ratio, the impact of the end of a major civil conflict remains strong and significant. This further suggests that it is not so much the demographic absence of men, but rather the higher the death rates and the longer the conflict, that cause disruptions in gender roles and relations. This also explains why smaller rebellions and election-related violence generally have not resulted in major changes in women's legal status.

Prolonged and major conflict dislodged gender roles by thrusting women into new activities in the absence of men. In many cases, they ran businesses and sought new sources of livelihood, supported the household, learned how to drive, and played more active roles in communities. In Rwanda, for example, Jennie Burnet (2011) describes how women became entrepreneurs, gained local positions beyond those reserved for women, spoke in public meetings in ways they had not done before, were increasingly gaining an education, participated more in household decision making, and reported having gained respect. These transformations continued in the postconflict period.

Changes in gender relations?

A third alternative argument to my proposition has to do with the extent of the changes that occur during conflict. Bouta et al. (2005) argue that gender roles change in conflict but not gender relations. El-Bushra also does not believe gendered ideologies change as a result of conflict. She writes that: "Conflict may create some space to make a redefinition of social relations possible, but in so doing it seems to rearrange, adapt, or reinforce patriarchal ideologies rather than fundamentally alter them" (2003, 269). Nevertheless, El-Bushra admits that gendered power structures have changed in Somalia as a result of conflict and that women's increased economic power has allowed them to assert greater influence in the household and community, even at the national level.

Based on the case studies of Liberia, Angola, and Uganda, I found changes in gender roles *and* in gender relations, or what I would call gender regime change. I also found that some of the most important changes were, in fact, changes in ideologies and in the normative landscape. These normative changes, which by definition are aspirational, were embodied in the many constitutional changes we find in postconflict countries (see Chapter 7), and they have been quite profound. On the one hand, major social and cultural transformations are slow, and for activists they are always unsatisfying, but such major change never happens in one fell swoop. The fact that countries that once refused to acknowledge women's political representation was important now have large numbers of women in politics is a massive shift in awareness. Practices that used to be upheld such as wife beating, child marriage, and female genital cutting, or denying education for girls, are no longer considered acceptable to defend in public discourse in most countries discussed in this book. Clearly, there is a long road ahead to ensure equality in gender relations, but the fact that there are few institutions or cultural assumptions regarding gender that have remained untouched in these postconflict countries suggests that the changes are more extensive than simply changes in gender roles.

DECLINE IN CONFLICT

The decline of conflict and political liberalization are structural transformations that frame the gender regime change described in this book. The precipitating factor that shaped advancements in women's rights was the increase in the resolution of conflicts after 1990. Since the end of the Cold War, there has been a global decline in the incidence of conflict (Goldstein 2011, Human Security Report Project 2006, Mueller 2009). These patterns are particularly salient in Africa, where the absolute number of countries affected by this trend was among the highest in the world. There has been both a decline in the number of conflicts starting and resuming as well as an increase in the number of conflicts ending, which is evident from data derived from several databases, including those of PRIO and Stockholm International Peace Research Institute (SIPRI) (see Figures 1.1 and 1.2 and Table 1.1). Analysis of the data shows that the number of conflicts ending increased in the 1990s, but because the number of conflicts starting also increased, overall the number of conflicts remained high. By the 2000s, a sharp increase in conflicts ending, alongside a decline in conflicts starting, resulted in the overall downward trend of conflict in Africa. It bears pointing out that even though numerically Africa has the longest and highest number of wars, when one averages out the number of countries, Africa has less armed conflicts than Asia and shorter conflicts than the Middle East and Asia (Straus 2012). It is also worth noting that despite a continued drop in the numbers of conflicts globally between 2008 and 2014, there has, in fact, been an increase in the number of war-related fatalities and in the numbers of refugees and internally displaced peoples. However, these increases have been primarily in the Middle East, according to the IISS Armed Conflict Survey (2015).

Several factors have contributed to the decline in conflict, including the end of the Cold War; the increased importance of international and regional peacekeeping forces, peace diplomacy, and peace negotiations globally; and the greater influence of domestic peace movements. The expansion of conflict

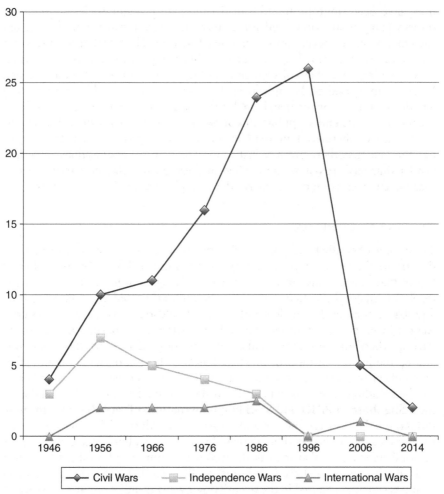

FIGURE 1.1 Number of Major Armed Conflicts, 1990–2009
Sources: Gleditsch (2004), Mueller (2009); PRIO www.pcr.uu.se/gpdatabase/search.php.

resolution initiatives was related to an increase in UN and regional peace-making and peacebuilding efforts, from preventative and behind-the-scenes diplomacy to negotiations, UN sanctions, peacekeeping interventions and the disarmament, demobilization, and rehabilitation of soldiers. Although the UN has generally taken the lead in peacekeeping operations, other actors have played supporting roles through diplomacy, including regional peacekeeping organizations (Fortna 2004; Stedman et al. 2002), the World Bank, foreign donors, and other actors within international and domestic civil society. International awareness has heightened around issues relating to child soldiers,

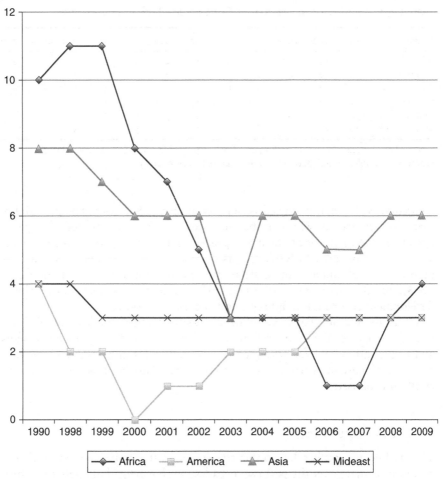

FIGURE 1.2 Number of Major Armed Conflicts by Region, 1990–2009
Source: The Uppsala Conflict Data Project.

blood diamonds, small arms trade, and violence against civilians, resulting in additional pressure to end conflicts (Collier et al. 2003, Human Security Report 2006).

Although conflict resolution is one part of the equation, the other is the drop in the numbers of new wars starting or reigniting. It has been well established that countries coming out of war are most at risk for returning to conflict. Between 1944 and 1997 at least half the civil wars that ended returned to conflict (Quinn, Mason, and Gurses 2007). Countries that have been engaged in war have a 44 percent chance of returning to conflict within five years and are ten times more likely to return to war right after the war ended when

TABLE 1.1 *Number of Major Armed Conflicts by Region, 1990–2009*

Region	1990	1998	1999	2000	2001	2002	2003	2004	2005	2006	2007	2008	2009
Africa	10	11	11	8	7	5	3	3	3	1	1	3	4
America	4	2	2	0	1	1	2	2	2	3	3	3	3
Asia	8	8	7	6	6	6	3	6	6	5	5	6	6
Europe	-	1	2	1	1	1	1	1	1	1	1	0	0
Mideast	4	4	3	3	3	3	3	3	3	3	3	3	3
Total	26	26	25	18	18	16	12	15	15	13	13	15	16

Source: The Uppsala Conflict Data Project, SIPRI 2009 (Table 2A.2, p. 62). www.sipri.org/yearbook/2010/files/SIPRIYB201002A.pdf Accessed April 6, 2015.

compared with when it started (Collier et al. 2003, 83, 104). The probability that they revert to war can be mediated, some have argued, by peace agreements (Walter 2002), the use of peacekeeping forces (Doyle and Sambanis 2000), economic growth (Quinn, Mason, and Gurses 2007), better implementation of rebel-military integration agreements (Glassmyer and Sambanis 2008), and the introduction of foreign aid, resulting in local-level institutional development (Fearon, Humphreys, and Weinstein 2009).

Of all the factors that have influenced these changes, the least studied has been the role of civil society and, in particular, peace and women's movements and organizations, which have played important roles in helping end conflicts and prevent new ones from arising or reigniting. This book is one attempt to rectify this omission.

POLITICAL OPENING

The decline in conflict has occurred alongside the improved political and economic climate over the past two decades that has helped mitigate the return to conflict. Between 1989 and 1999, one saw in Africa almost a tripling of new democracies. Many African countries experienced a shift toward greater political liberalization and democratization, a move from military to civilian rule and from one-party states to multiparty states. They also introduced contested elections. Almost all African countries experienced greater freedom of expression and association and an increase in political and civil liberties, even if constrained. Civil society, which contributed to the political opening, also began to flourish in this environment. This occurred particularly where political freedoms were expanded alongside economic growth, which resulted in a rise of a larger middle class than had been the case in the past. These contexts provided fertile ground in which women activists could press demands for more rights.

At the same time, despite the greater openness, most of the liberalization occurred in autocratic systems, which became hybrid regimes that were neither fully authoritarian nor fully democratic (sometimes referred to as electoral democracies, competitive authoritarian regimes, or illiberal democracies). These regimes are fickle in that freedom of speech and association can be arbitrarily constrained, and elections, which are technically open to multiple parties, are subject to manipulations by those in power (see Levitsky and Way 2002; Schedler 2006; Tripp 2010a; Zakaria 1997).

The end of conflict itself often gave way to political opening, even if it was ever so slight. But often it was sufficient to foster an incipient civil society and women's movement as well as to pave the way for constitutional changes, electoral reforms, and eventually legislative changes. Most important, it generally led to a shift in elite configurations, which allowed for new leaders, including women, to assert themselves. In countries like Liberia, the peace movement that emerged during the conflict transformed itself into a women's movement that pressed for continued changes in women's rights after the war. Some postconflict countries were especially eager to shed the mantle of the one-party state and its stifling effects on civil society and independent mobilization. Quite a few of them even became democracies (e.g., South Africa, Namibia, Sierra Leone), whereas Mozambique and Liberia became semidemocratic countries.

The extent to which authoritarian countries provided such an opening is an important one because authoritarian legacies are much stronger in postconflict states than nonpostconflict states. Based on 2015 data, two postconflict countries were democratic (13 percent), five were hybrids (31 percent), and the largest percentage, nine, were authoritarian (56 percent).[3] This is in contrast to nonpostconflict countries, which had higher representation in democratic (28 percent) and hybrid regimes (40 percent), and relatively less in authoritarian regimes (31 percent). Countries with limited conflict are pretty much equally divided between authoritarian and hybrid regimes.

Even though the political space has been constrained in many postconflict countries, women nevertheless have been able to make limited gains in nondemocratic contexts, and these gains are of consequence. Even a small political opening has been important in allowing for advances in such postconflict countries. Nevertheless, the overall lack of human rights and freedom of expression and mobilization in countries like Rwanda and Sudan constrains how far women can assert themselves even when they are represented at higher rates than in the past.

KEY PATTERNS

There are several major corollaries to the claim that the end of conflict is connected to changes in gender regimes. Two have already been alluded to.

---

[3] The figures here are based on analysis of Freedom House data, www.freedomhouse.org. Accessed in 2015.

First, the relationship between the end of conflict and women's increased rights and representation in Africa was temporally confined to the post-1990 period. The end of earlier armed conflicts in Africa did not have the same kinds of implications for women's rights and representation. *Second, the relationship between conflict and women's representation is especially apparent after intense conflicts high in battle-related deaths and conflicts long in duration. Third, the patterns linking postconflict dynamics to women's representation are found primarily after civil wars or wars of national liberation, but not as often after international war, proxy war, coup d'état, or localized war.* This is because these changes come about as a result of a reordering of institutions and of leadership of a kind that is generally not required after an interstate conflict or these other types of conflict. An armed incursion by an external power or a proxy war puts the focus on ousting the external aggressor and does not necessarily require the reestablishment of new institutions or leaders, although it can. A coup d'état generally does not create enough disruption deep within society to give rise to women leaders. Similarly, the end of localized conflicts like the one in Western Sahara in Morocco, Bakassi Peninsula in Cameroon, Casamance in Senegal, and Cabinda in Angola, do not necessarily result in changes in the overall elite structures and therefore do not necessitate changes in women's leadership or in institutions. The case of Uganda illustrates this pattern.

When Yoweri Museveni and his National Resistance Movement took over Uganda in 1986, the country experienced a change not only in leadership but also in political institutions. These changes allowed for women leaders to rise to national power (and local leadership) in a significant way for the first time. It also allowed for a change in women's rights policy. However, the later proxy war between Uganda and Sudan in northern Uganda (1987–2006) did not result in any changes in national gender policy (see Chapter 3). The conflict in northern Uganda was a localized conflict that had its origins in an uprising of the Holy Spirit Movement led by a spirit medium, Alice Lakwena. Thus, when the northern Uganda conflict ended around 2006, it did not result in a change in national leadership, nor did it necessitate significant institutional transformations, and consequently, there were no visible changes in women's leadership. This is, in part, because the conflict was localized and because it was a proxy war between Uganda and Sudan.

My case studies do not include regions that secede and become new nations like Eritrea and South Sudan. This is a relatively rare occurrence in Africa, but these new countries theoretically should have reordered their polity. However, Eritrea's lack of political opening coupled with nonexistent autonomous women's mobilization and South Sudan's continued civil conflict have meant that neither country has embarked on significant policy changes affecting women's status, apart from the adoption of quotas.

Fourth, *the way war ends matters for women's rights. Civil wars that end in peace negotiations have a greater chance of creating possibilities for negotiating women's rights.* The holding of peace talks, constitutional reform processes, and truth and reconciliation tribunals are all postconflict institutional *opportunity structures* through which women are able to assert their demands. The absence of such processes of national reconciliation and healing deny women and other civil society actors the ability to champion their interests. The lack of initiatives for national reconciliation makes it even harder for women to articulate their agendas. Thus, where conflicts end with the government vanquishing a rebel force, there is little if any impetus for peace talks, hence less opportunities for women to assert their interests.

This was the case in Angola (see Chapter 5), when in 2002, insurgent leader Jonas Savimbi was killed by government troops, and the government threatened to decimate his rebel movement, União Nacional para a Independência Total de Angola (National Union for the Total Independence of Angola), or UNITA. Had it not been for civil society organizations, which tempered the leadership of the ruling party, Movimento Popular de Libertação de Angola (People's Movement for the Liberation of Angola), or MPLA, the government would have annihilated UNITA.[4] Similarly in Sri Lanka, the civil war ended with the victory of government forces and the almost total suppression of the rebel Tamil Tigers. Both the Angolan and the Sri Lankan situation did not allow for a peace process to unfold that would have permitted women advocates to press their demands. Subsequently, both countries have done relatively little to address women's rights concerns compared with other postconflict countries. Angola adopted gender quotas in 2005, and they included in their 2010 constitution a fairly weak provision that traditional authorities should respect the constitution and the law (Article 224). However, in general, the Angolan engagement of gender issues has been fairly anemic relative to other postconflict countries in Africa.

Fifth, *ongoing conflicts do not allow actors enough political space to mobilize to change the status quo because leaders and militia are too preoccupied with conflict to be interested in gender reform.* They don't care about appeasing various constituencies at the ballot box or in polishing their international image. This may explain, in part, why the Democratic Republic of Congo – which continued to be plagued by conflict in the east long after a comprehensive peace agreement was signed – made some policy reforms affecting women, yet women in politics continued to be marginalized.

Sixth, *women's perceived noninvolvement in creating conflict afforded them greater legitimacy as leaders during and after the conflict* (see Chapter 8). Women were often accepted as leaders in postconflict contexts, and sometimes even during conflict, because they were perceived, rightly or wrongly, as outsiders to politics and therefore untainted by corruption, patronage, and the factors that may have led to conflict. The fact that they were often very active in

---

[4] Interview with 3.1, Luanda, 27 June 2008.

peace movements gave them added credibility as new political actors. There is also a recognition that women have not always been as strongly tied to older patronage structures that fueled conflict. Women's outsider status has been linked to women's advancement even in nonpostconflict contexts of political turmoil where women have claimed executive positions (Bauer 2014; Beckwith 2009; Jalalzai 2008; Wiliarty 2008).

In patrilineal societies, women have a different relationship to ethnicity and clan than men because they marry outside their natal homes. Although they are expected to untether relations with their natal home when they marry, their allegiance to their husband's marital home is regarded as uncertain (Kamau-Rutenberg 2008). This can make it difficult for them to gain full acceptance in their husband's clan or ethnic group, which can be problematic when women seek political influence, for example. But it can also afford women a certain capacity to remain aloof from ethnically based conflicts and may make it easier for them to seek alliances that cut across contentious societal divisions.

Thus, the perception of women as outsiders often gave them greater credibility in the newly reconstituted postwar political order. Nevertheless, this argument is too weak to stand alone as an explanation for the changes we have seen, especially because women fought in all three wars discussed in my case studies and even helped incite conflict in the case of Liberia.

HISTORICAL ANTECEDENTS

Although I have made an argument for the temporality of the trends I am describing, it was not the first time in history that conflict and women's political rights were linked, although not exactly in the same way. It appears that many of the same circumstances that led to higher rates of women's political representation after the 1990s were also evident after the 1905 and 1917 Russian revolutions and after World War I, leading up to the first wave of female suffrage in Europe and the United States. Following the initial Russian Revolution of 1905, Finnish women became the first in Europe to obtain the right to vote. Massive political upheaval and labor action led to the establishment of a constitutional monarchy and the creation of a State Duma in the Russian Empire and in the Grand Duchy of Finland, which was part of the Russian empire at the time. The 1905 revolution also led to the abolition of the Diet of Finland and the creation of a modern Finnish parliament in which women gained the right to vote and stand for election. Finland had the first elected female members of parliament in the world, who in 1907 comprised 19 (10 percent) of the parliamentarians. (Finland became independent during the Russian Revolution of 1917). The Russian Federation gained universal suffrage in 1918, also after the Russian Revolution.

After World War I, women obtained the right to vote in the United States and many European countries, notably Britain, Germany, and Austria, spurring other countries also to adopt suffrage for women. With interesting parallels to the trends described in this book after the 1990s, women in England began to take on new roles as nurses, munitions workers, soldiers, doctors, and drivers of buses and ambulances during the war. Sandra Gilbert describes this period as one where, "Even as wives and mothers, these formerly subservient creatures began to loom malevolently larger, until it was possible for a visitor to London to observe in 1918 that 'England was a world of women in uniforms' or in the words of a verse by Nina Macdonald, 'Girls are doing things/They've never done before.... All the word is topsy-turvy/Since the War began.'" Women who worked received levels of pay that only men had earned in the past. Gilbert argues that as women became more powerful, young men became increasingly alienated from their prewar selves. Traditional gender structures collapsed as did older hierarchies of status. Unlike male novelists of this period who rue the "grotesque sexual permission" the war gave women, women autobiographers of this time wrote about the exhilaration of mobility and "their feeling that the Great War was the first historical event to allow (indeed to require) them to use their abilities and to be of use, to escape the private 'staves' of houses as well as the patriarchal oppression of 'high towers' and to enter the public realm of roads, records, maps, machines" (Gilbert 1983, 440). Irene Rathbone, in her diary, compares 1915 with 1918 and discusses changes in gender relations, especially the effect of war on sexual taboos and prohibitions (Brassard 2003).

The changes in women's roles during the war necessitated changes in their rights as citizens. President Woodrow Wilson had not been keen on women's suffrage when he took office in 1913, but he was cognizant of women's contributions during the war, and by 1918 he had had a change of heart and finally came out publicly in support of women's right to vote. He made a speech in which he appealed to the Senate to grant women suffrage:

We have made partners of the women in this war.... . Shall we admit them only to a partnership of suffering and sacrifice and toil and not to a partnership of privilege and right? This war could not have been fought, either by the other nations engaged or by America, if it had not been for the services of the women, – services rendered in every sphere, – not merely in the fields of effort in which we have been accustomed to see them work, but wherever men have worked and upon the very skirts and edges of the battle itself. (Wilson 1918)

Switzerland stands out in stark contrast to these other countries affected by World War I. Because of its pursuit of neutrality, Switzerland has not experienced large-scale violent conflict since 1848 that might have shaken up its political status quo and dominant elite. Switzerland is notable in that it was the last country in Europe to grant women the right to vote, with federal approval coming only in 1971. The last canton approved female suffrage as late as 1990. Although one can point to its strong federal system and direct democracy, which relies heavily on referenda as influencing women's late suffrage, Switzerland's military neutrality and lack of engagement in war also maintained key political and elite structures in ways that made gender-related transformations more difficult. The fragmented women's movement also slowed change. Switzerland joined the United Nations only in 2002, which means that the normative changes that influenced other countries regarding women's rights, especially in the post-1995 period, became effective much later in Switzerland.

Thus, it appears that World War I had many of the same kinds of transformative effects and disruptions in gender relations that civil war had decades later in Africa. It sped up processes of change, however inadvertently, as an unintended by-product of conflict. For 70 years, women had been fighting for suffrage in the United States and Britain, yet immediately after the war, laws were changed, granting women the right to vote. As we see today in changing international norms regarding women's rights, after World War I there were changes in global thinking regarding female suffrage, as ideas spread from one country to the next regarding the viability of granting women the right to vote. Similar conditions were evident, including disruptions in gender relations during the war, pressures by women's movements, and international pressures for women's rights. Although generally I found that these women's rights reforms do not occur after international wars as mentioned earlier in the third corollary, one might argue that World War I did in fact have profound and similar transformative internal consequences for the societies involved, especially when it involved a change in elite structures.

Circumstances could not have been more different at the end of World War II, which famously did *not* bring about such changes in female citizenship. As in World War I, women had left the home to toil in factories and take on other formerly male occupations, but unlike after the World War I, they were basically told to return to their homes when the war effort was over. There weren't the same pressures from a women's movement at that time in Europe and the United States, whereas prior to and after World War I there had been active suffrage movements in many parts of the world.

RESEARCH DESIGN

Methodology

Because I am interested in explaining the causal mechanisms outlined in the previous section, I use *process tracing* to evaluate the mechanisms I have identified based on fieldwork, review of newspaper accounts, statistical and data analysis, and study of secondary sources. Process tracing helps us infer "the existence of an unobserved event or process" and to infer "a causal connection between one specific event or process and another" (Mahoney 2012, 586). In particular, I want to show how conflict is connected to women's rights reforms and that this path to reform speeds up changes in the gender regime.

Causal mechanisms are the factors that help explain outcomes. They allow us to look into the black box and explain more precisely what connects independent and dependent variables, and what links explanatory factors with outcomes. Some refer to them as intervening variables. As James Mahoney (2003) explains, a causal mechanism is "an unobserved entity, process, or structure that acts as an ultimate cause in generating outcomes. An 'ultimate cause' is a cause that itself does not require explanation but nevertheless can generate outcomes...." Thus, it is insufficient to say that there is a link between conflict and women's rights reforms. One has to show how and why that link exists and under what conditions. That is what this book sets out to do.

In Chapter 2, I elaborate on the causal mechanisms that connect the end of conflict with gender regime change, and I also challenge alternative explanations. The mechanisms include (1) gender disruptions in society; (2) women's movements, which emerged in the context of political liberalization, even if limited; and (3) changing international and domestic norms regarding women's rights, which influenced donor strategies. I carried out a *hoop test* of my claims that the aforementioned causal mechanisms are necessary conditions to explain the causal relationship between the end of major conflict and a new women's rights regime. A hoop test isolates the conditions or mechanisms that are necessary but not sufficient for a hypothesis to be true. If the mechanisms are not present, the hypothesis fails the test and can be eliminated. It helps evaluate unobserved events or processes to show that "there is a causal connection between two or more events or processes" (Mahoney 2012, 572, 576, 589).

I used this test in several ways to establish my argument (1) comparing postconflict with nonpostconflict countries through cross-national analysis (see Hughes and Tripp 2015, Chapters 6, 7, 8, and 9); (2) comparing the three postconflict countries to isolate the causal mechanisms through process tracing (Chapters 3, 4, and 5); and (3) comparing postconflict countries with countries that have experienced less conflict or ongoing conflict. I ask, following Mahoney (2012): (1) Did a change in gender regimes occur in the countries examined? (2) Are the hypothesized causal factors present? (3) Are the causes linked to the outcome (the hoop test)? The case studies in Chapters 3, 4, and 5 elaborate on the first three questions. I also ask (4) Are competing hypotheses eliminated? Competing hypotheses were eliminated in the process of comparing the more successful outcomes in Liberia and Uganda with the less-successful outcomes in Angola against the backdrop of cross-national comparisons in subsequent chapters.

Social movement theory offers important insights into understanding how *opportunity structures* may have allowed women's movements to assert their influence. Herbert Kitschelt has argued that opportunity structures are "specific configurations of resources, institutional arrangements and historical precedents for social mobilization," which facilitate and constrain social movements. According to Kitschelt, they depend on the (1) "coercive, normative, remunerative and informational resources that an incipient movement can extract from its setting and can employ in its protest." (2) They also depend on the institutional rules that govern relations between people and decision makers. (3) Openness depends on the appearance and disappearance of other movements (Kitschelt 1986, 58, 61–62).

Thus, building on Kitschelt's theory of social movement change, I would argue that women's movements, with the help of donors/foreign actors like the UN, were able to take advantage of new opportunity structures related to political liberalization and the end of conflict. These opportunity structures included peace agreements, constitutional reforms, electoral reforms, and truth and reconciliation tribunals, all of which reordered institutions and leadership configurations, thus allowing women activists to insert a women's rights agenda and press for increased representation in these newly reconstituted institutions. This book focuses only on two opportunity structures: peace agreements (Chapter 6) and constitutional reforms (Chapter 7). New electoral management arrangements are discussed in Chapter 8 on political representation. Other opportunity structures, like truth and reconciliation commissions, are not explored in this book, but are nevertheless part of these processes of transformation. Truth and reconciliation legislation, such as the 2005 Truth and Reconciliation Commission Act in Liberia, for example, called for the participation and inclusion of women in the TRC process. It stipulated that at least four of the nine commissioners be women, be sensitive to issues of gender and gender-based violence, and it called for special programs to enable women to provide testimony. In this way, the TRC created many of the same opportunities for women activists to press for inclusion in the peacemaking process. Such opportunity structures paved the way for later changes in legislative representation (Chapter 8) and legislative and policy reforms in women's rights (Chapter 9). Following Kitschelt's schema, new institutional rules for the inclusion of women were created, and past leaders, warlords, and militias were either removed as actors on the political scene or were constrained as a new leadership arrangement came into force.

Case selection

Uganda, Liberia, and Angola were selected to elaborate the causal mechanisms. Uganda was the first country in which the relationship between conflict and women's advancement became evident, whereas Angola and Liberia were among the more recent countries coming out of conflict. The timing of the end of conflict influences to some degree the extent to which changes took place and became institutionalized. I also drew on fieldwork in countries with ongoing conflict at the time of the study (Democratic Republic of Congo) and past limited conflict (Kenya).

Angola appears to have been less successful than some of the other postconflict countries in advancing a women's rights agenda, making it an especially useful case to compare with the others to better understand what it is about postconflict

TABLE 1.2 *Selected Measures of Women's Equality*

	Angola	Liberia	Uganda	Africa
Education				
Primary education, pupils (% female)	38	47	50	48
Ratio of female to male primary enrollment (%)	64	92	102	93
Ratio of female to male secondary enrollment (%)	65	82	87	82
Labor Force Participation				
Ratio of female to male labor force participation rate	82	90	96	83
Labor force, female (% of total labor force)	46	48	49	45
Politics				
Proportion of women in ministerial-level positions (%) 2010 figures	27.8	30.4	32	20
Percentage of women in legislature	37	11	35	23
Health				
Maternal mortality ratio (estimate, per 100,000 live births) 2010	450	770	310	500
Fertility rate, total (births per woman)	6.09	4.94	6.06	5.17
Life expectancy at birth, female (years)	53	61	59	57
Gender Gap Index (out of 136 countries)				
Overall rank (1 = highest)	92		46	
Overall score (1 = highest)	0.66		0.72	
Economic participation rank	92		37	
Economic participation score	0.61		0.73	
Educational attainment rank	127		123	
Educational attainment score	0.8		0.84	
Health and survival rank	1		1	
Health and survival score	0.98		0.98	
Political empowerment rank	34		28	
Political empowerment score	0.26		0.28	

Source: UN Data; World Economic Forum, Gender Gap Index, 2013, World Bank 2013.

countries that puts them on a different trajectory than nonpostconflict countries. In general, with some exceptions in measures of health and representation of women in the legislature, Angola does considerably worse than Uganda or Liberia and most of Africa on most measures of gender equality. This is despite the fact that it has a significantly higher GDP per capita rate than the other two countries and Africa overall as a result of its oil-based economy (Table 1.2).

All three countries experienced major conflicts that were long in duration. Angola's conflict lasted twenty-seven years. In fact, Angola had experienced thirty-seven years of almost continued war if one counts the previous conflict with Portugal. Liberia experienced two periods of conflict lasting roughly eleven to fourteen years. Even the brief three-year hiatus between the First Liberian Civil War (1989–96) and the Second Liberian Civil War (1999–2003) was hardly quiescent. The Ugandan Bush War (also known as the Luwero War) lasted five years (1980 to January 1986) and was followed by the war in northern Uganda, which concluded around 2006. The conflicts in the three countries are similar in that they were long and intense, and all three countries experienced gender disruptions. However, the similarities end there, and the differences between the countries serve to illustrate some of the causal dynamics at play.

First, I hypothesize that conflict changed women's roles and created disruptions at all levels of society. This allowed women to take advantage of changing elite and institutional configurations to push for further changes in women's status. At the national level these disruptions resulted in changes in gender policy and women's political leadership. Women were actively part of the armed conflict in all three countries. Women's organizations were also engaged in peacemaking in all three countries. However, unlike Angola, the women's movement was a major force for ending the conflict in Liberia. Building on nascent wartime mobilization, an autonomous women's movement emerged soon after the conflict to press for change. Comparing Uganda and Liberia, on the one hand, with Angola, on the other, allowed me to further look into the ways in which women's changing roles during the conflict influenced women's rights outcomes later. Ongoing conflict does not produce extensive changes, which is evident from the case of the DRC. Similarly, limited conflict, as in the case of Kenya's election violence in 2008, produced partial and incomplete reforms.

Second, I hypothesize that the existence of women's organizations autonomous from dominant political forces made a difference in charting a successful women's rights agenda and in building ties across parties and ethnicities. This proved to be an important difference between Angola and the other two countries, where independent movements emerged. Uganda and Liberia have active independent women's movements, whereas Angola has experienced minimal independent mobilization on the part of women, especially after the conflict. The main mobilization in Angola took place within the context of organizations linked to the ruling MPLA or the women's caucus within the parliament. This made it possible to examine the extent to which organizational autonomy mattered in bringing about change.

Associational autonomy and the expansion of an independent women's movement are tied to the level of democracy within a country, which, like the end of conflict, is a structural factor influencing gender regime change. Liberia emerged as the most democratic of the three countries, whereas Uganda struggled with political rights and civil liberties. However, even in Uganda, sufficient political space was created in the late 1980s and early 1990s to allow for the emergence of a women's movement. The women's movement was able to mobilize as long as it did not become "too political," and as such Uganda remained a classic semiauthoritarian regime. Angola was the most restrictive of all three regimes: It limited civil society mobilization and kept most women's rights mobilization tied to organizations that were linked to the ruling MPLA. This limited possibilities for influencing change in the postconflict period.

Third, I hypothesize that the change in international norms pertaining to women's rights and the role of donors, in particular, influenced gender regime change. This is borne out in the Ugandan and Liberian case studies, but not in the Angolan case. The UN agencies and foreign donors mostly pulled out of Angola after the war was over, but remained major players in Uganda and Liberia. The fact that Angola had other sources of revenue, namely oil, meant that after the end of conflict in 2002, most donors, who had been engaged in humanitarian efforts, left. Because of the way in which the conflict ended, there was no peacekeeping force to maintain peace, and the UN presence was relatively thin. Bilateral donors were similarly not as engaged in Angola, and therefore the traditional sources of international pressure simply were not evident. This contributed to the weak gender regime changes in the country. Thus, the Angolan case highlights the importance of external pressures on women's rights regime change.

I also test several corollaries (see earlier explanation). The first two corollaries were tested statistically in my article with Melanie Hughes (2015) in which we found that the relationship between the end of conflict and women's representation was confined to the post-1990 period. Similarly, we found that women's representation is tied to intense and long conflicts rather than conflicts shorter in duration and limited in their number of war-related deaths.

The third corollary hypothesizes that the patterns linking postconflict dynamics to women's representation are found primarily after civil wars or wars of national liberation, but not as much after international wars, localized wars, proxy wars, or coups d'état. The three case studies in this book include countries that experienced a variety of types of conflict, allowing us to examine these patterns closely. The conflicts include national liberation wars against colonialism (Angola, 1964–74), internal resource-based conflict (Liberia, 1989–96, 1999–2003; Angola, 1975–2002); warfare related to state collapse (Uganda, 1980–86); a localized and proxy war (northern Uganda, 1987–2006) and ethnic competition for control of the state (Uganda, 1980–86, First Liberian Civil War, 1989–1996, Second Liberian Civil War, 1999–2003; Angola, 1975–2002). Liberia and Uganda both experienced coups.

The fourth corollary suggests that for countries in which civil wars end in peace, negotiations have a better chance of implementing women's rights policies. The comparison of Liberia, which had peace negotiations through which women sought to influence policy, and Angola, which did not, illustrates some of the differences in outcome. The fifth corollary suggests that countries engaged in ongoing conflict are uninterested in women's rights policy reform. This is evident, for example, in their lack of interest in increasing women's legislative representation (see Chapter 7).

The sixth corollary observes that women's perceived noninvolvement in creating conflict afforded them greater legitimacy as leaders during and after the conflict. This is explored within the individual case studies as well as in Chapter 8.

In addition to testing the causal mechanisms and corollaries, I also selected cases that had been colonies of Britain (Uganda) and Portugal (Angola) and one country (Liberia) that had never been colonized. Although the British Commonwealth has been quite active in recent years in pressing for women's rights reforms, the main way former colonial powers might have influenced future gender policy occurred years prior to conflict in creating conditions for female leadership. The Belgian and Portuguese colonies did the least in this regard, whereas the British were more attentive to female education than the French. But even among countries with the same colonial legacy, there were differences. Pressure from colonial British women educators, from women's organizations, and from some of the African elite meant that Uganda, unlike its neighbors in East Africa, had a larger cohort of university-educated women at independence who were equipped to play leadership roles. Uganda also had a larger pool of secondary school-educated women. Liberia's lack of colonial influence meant that it could grant suffrage to the Americo-Liberian elite as early as 1946, making them the first black women in Africa to obtain suffrage. Early on in Liberia, as in Uganda, there emerged a cluster of elite educated women who were able to play political roles. These included women like Angie Brooks, who served as assistant secretary of state in 1958; in the 1960s as chairperson of the UN Committee of Trust and Non-Self-Governing Territories; and later as president of the UN Trusteeship Council. There was Ambassador-at-Large Ellen Mills Scarborough, who served as secretary of state for education between 1948 and 1952, and many others. These early impacts had ripple effects, which can still be felt today and are evident in the levels of education of girls in Uganda and Liberia (see Table 1.2). Thus, the colonial impacts are indirect, but they too had influences on the kinds of preexisting expectations there were for women within society.

Methods

In all three countries, my research strategy was much the same. I interviewed hundreds of leaders and members of national and local peace, human rights, and women's rights organizations; members of parliament; government representatives; women's ministry representatives; party leaders; policy makers; opinion leaders; academics; journalists; businesspeople; representatives of development agencies; representatives of peacekeeping forces (in Liberia); UN agencies (especially United Nations Development Programme, UN Development

Fund for Women (UNIFEM)/UN Women, United Nations High Commissioner for Refugees); bilateral and multilateral donors; religious and traditional leaders; and many others. I observed some of the proceedings of Uganda's Constituent Assembly in 1995 that culminated in the approval of a new constitution, which was a pivotal and historic moment for women. It helped me better appreciate the importance of women seizing this key opportunity to assert their interests. I drew heavily on a systematic review of newspaper articles from key newspapers in all three countries. I sought to interview individuals based on representativeness across ethnicity, religion, gender, age, region, and party affiliation.

I also drew on publications by women's organizations as well as online sources and unpublished reports by the Ugandan government and various international and domestic NGOs as well as an extensive secondary literature. I made concerted efforts to draw substantially on Ugandan, Angolan, and Liberian sources and perspectives.

I was fortunate to have been able to observe developments in Uganda since 1992, and have subsequently returned to the country almost every year. When I first went to Uganda, it had just come out of the Bush War in 1986. Traveling regularly to Uganda over the past fifteen years has allowed me to observe major changes over time with regard to the status of women. (To be more accurate, I first went to Uganda in 1969 when I was growing up in neighboring Tanzania, where I lived for fifteen years.) In Uganda I conducted fieldwork in Kampala, Gulu, Jinja, Mpigi, Luwero, Mbale, Kamuli, and Kabale. This involved a major survey in four parts of the country ($N = 1143$), in-depth interviews, use of secondary materials, as well as in-depth case studies of local gender-based conflicts over access to resources and power. In this book, I draw on roughly 210 interviews in Uganda carried out between 1992 and 1999, some of which became the basis of my first book on Uganda, *Women and Politics Uganda* (2000) as well as other publications (Tripp 2010; Tripp and Kwesiga 2002; Tripp et al. 2009). I also draw on several hundred subsequent interviews carried out primarily in Kampala, Mpigi, and Gulu in 2001, 2002, 2005, and 2011. In 2005, I conducted approximately sixty interviews related to the conflict in northern Uganda in Kampala, Gulu, and camps for the internally displaced outside Gulu (Pabbo, Unyama, and Palenga). These interviews took place while the war was going on, helping me better understand what women experienced during conflict and their scope of action. It also helped clarify for me that conflicts that are more localized and have an international dimension to them do not have the same postconflict impacts as conflicts that are national in scope and require a national reordering of the polity, as was the case after the Bush War, when Museveni came to power.

I conducted 120 interviews in Monrovia, Liberia, and surrounding areas in 2007 and another 110 interviews in 2012 (for a U.S. Agency for International Development study) in Monrovia, Nimba, Bong, and Bomi. This allowed me to observe changes over time in the postconflict context.

I carried out roughly sixty interviews in Angola in 2008 with the help of a translator. Erring on the side of caution because of security concerns, the interviewees in Angola are not identified by name, including high-ranking government and party officials, even when their comments appear innocuous. I also obtained, with the help of a highly capable Congolese assistant, about forty interviews with women leaders in Kinshasa, Democratic Republic of Congo (DRC). The interviews in DRC inform this study and alerted me to the negative impact of continuing conflict on gender regime change because the war had not ended in eastern Congo. In another study for USAID that is not referred to directly in this study, I conducted sixty interviews in Nairobi, Naivasha, and Kisumu in Kenya in 2014 and gained important insights into the impact of limited conflict on women's rights reform.

In addition to the interviews, I drew on Afrobarometer survey data of eighteen countries from 1999 to 2014 to determine gendered perceptions regarding conflict, peace, ethnicity, women's leadership, and political party affinities.

Throughout the fieldwork, I sought to identify which factors explained the pressures on governments to adopt women's rights policies during and after civil war. I tried to uncover why those pressures did not arise to the same degree in Angola. I was interested in what made it possible for women activists to take advantage of the window of opportunity after conflict to assert their demands.

The time frame of the study (1990–2014) allowed me to look at the key period of transition when the conflicts were ending in Africa, pressures for democratization were mounting in Africa, autonomous women's organizations were emerging along with civil society more generally, and international norms regarding women's rights and leadership were rapidly changing. Although women's mobilization in Uganda was clearly influenced by the Nairobi UN Conference on Women in 1985, it was the 1995 UN Conference on Women in Beijing that seemed to be pivotal for most countries coming out of conflict. Both conferences demonstrated the impact of changing international norms regarding women's rights and the donor agendas, which followed.

The study also allowed me to contrast multiple ends of conflict within each country: Uganda (1986 and 2006), Angola (1974 and 2002), and Liberia (1996 and 2003). This helped refine my hypothesis regarding the types of conflicts and their impact on women's representation and rights.

CONCLUSIONS

We have witnessed some important developments in women's rights with the decline of conflict in Africa after the 1990s, and especially after 2000, when the number of conflicts began to drop significantly. The increase of women in legislatures, the inclusion of significant woman-friendly constitutional clauses, and the passage of key land rights and gender-based violence legislation repre-sents a normative shift that has taken place regarding women's rights across the continent. In postconflict countries these changes have been relatively rapid compared to other nonpostconflict countries, suggesting that they are following a different trajectory. To be sure, from the point of view of women's rights activists, these same changes often seem painfully slow.

In a nutshell, the adoption of a new women's rights regime in the aftermath of conflict had to do with the fact that it converged temporally with political liberalization starting in the 1990s, which allowed for the emergence of women's movements. It also converged with changing international norms regarding women's rights, which translated into new United Nations and donor strategies. This explains why we saw these transformations after 1990 globally and in Africa and not after earlier conflicts. Similar conjunctures may produce similar outcomes for women's citizenship, as evident from the ways in which the gender disruptions of World War I and changing international gender norms were tied to the granting of suffrage to women shortly after the war.

However, the major difference that set postconflict countries apart from others was that conflict had already disrupted gender relations, especially at the local level. In some countries this had resulted in the emergence of peace movements, often led by women or involving extensive female participation. The goals of the international actors converged with and reinforced those of domestic women's movements. New elites and elite alliances emerged from conflicts, as did the impetus for institutional change. Thus, as conflicts came to an end, international donors and other international actors brought resources and political pressure to bear in the writing of peace agreements, new constitutions, and new electoral reforms, while women's rights activists seized on these opportunities to insert their demands. Local women's movements and international actors were the key drivers of change. Secondary drivers, which were influenced by these actors, included *in some cases* legislative women's caucuses, presidents, political parties, the media, peacekeeping operations, and women's policy agencies.

Women's movements initially sought to influence peace processes and were sometimes able to get women's rights language into peace agreements. Donors and international actors supported efforts to introduce women's rights within peacekeeping operations, which sometimes had positive impacts on women's mobilization. They also sought to influence constitution-writing processes. Later women's organizations, supported by donors, sought to impact government, party, women's policy agencies, and other leaders; and they sought to influence the media. This resulted in increased female representation in legislatures as well as legislative changes regarding women's rights.

These postconflict patterns of women's new political leadership are particularly visible in countries that have had especially bloody conflicts or conflicts long in duration. This is evident from the high correlation between women's political representation and the intensity and duration of conflict, as well as the change in sex ratio. All of these measures are indicative of the extent to which society was ruptured by war, making it easier to adopt new norms and institutions.

Civil wars that ended in peace negotiations had a greater chance of creating possibilities for negotiating women's rights rather than conflicts that ended in the decimation of an opposing side. With negotiations, there was a possibility of reordering society and creating opportunity structures like constitution-rewriting exercises and peace talks that allowed women activists to assert their agendas. The talks allowed women to signal their intent to become leaders in the newly constituted polity. This is because they required a major reordering of the polity that was not as likely after an interstate or proxy war and low-level conflict, local rebellions, or coups. Ongoing conflicts did not allow for sufficient stability to allow political actors to concern themselves with legislative reform; therefore one should not expect much legal change during conflict. The perception that women were outsiders to politics and had not been primary leaders of militia was also a contributing factor in opening up possibilities for female leadership that was perceived as a break with the status quo.

I reject an alternative hypothesis that argues that rather than experiencing advances in women's rights, women always experience backlash after conflict. Although there was backlash in earlier postconflict periods in Africa, the evidence squarely points to considerable change for women in most postconflict countries in Africa after the 1990s, at least in obtaining formal rights. Nowhere is this seen as clearly as in the adoption of gender quotas, which resulted in rapid changes in the numbers of women represented in African parliaments. I also reject an alternative hypothesis that suggests that a change in sex ratio and an absence of men allows women to claim leadership roles. The next chapter will show how war-related disruptions in gender relations lead to changes in women's status. This also challenges the claim that war changes gender roles but not gender relations. I argue that the transformations go beyond roles and lead to institutional and cultural changes, even if incomplete and flawed. It remains to be seen in many countries whether these more recent changes in political gender regimes, laws, norms, and institutions will result in continued changes in people's daily lives and whether they can be sustained.

2

Pathways to Change in Women's Rights

In moments of crisis, the wise build bridges and foolish build dams.
                                                          – Nigerian proverb

For women's rights activists, there may have been a silver lining to the relentlessly long and brutal conflicts that so many African countries experienced. Postconflict countries in Africa adopted distinct and more rapid trajectories of change in gender regimes after 1990 and especially after 2000. Gender regimes refer to gender-based systems of hierarchy and power within social systems or institutions. This chapter elaborates the causal mechanisms that explain the postconflict trajectories and processes of change, and the case studies in subsequent chapters go further in depth to trace the processes of change. I isolate the causal mechanisms by comparing the differences between the more successful outcomes in Uganda and Liberia with the less successful case of Angola in Chapters 3, 4, and 5, and they are considered against the broader backdrop of postconflict and nonconflict countries.

This chapter shows in broad strokes how the decline in conflict is linked to the emergence of a new gender regime (including positive women's rights and leadership changes) primarily through the following causal mechanisms: (1) gender disruptions, (2) women's movements, and (3) the spread of new international gender norms, resulting in interventions by international actors like the United Nations (UN) and foreign donors (see Figure 2.1). The conjuncture of these three conditions was necessary to explain the changes in Africa starting in the 1990s with respect to women's rights reform. If any of these factors was missing, considerably less change occurred. In Chapter 1 this was referred to as the hoop test, which identifies conditions that are necessary for a hypothesis to be true.

The precipitous decline in conflict in Africa was accompanied by political liberalization, which allowed women's movements and donors to press for the

33

Women and Power in Postconflict Africa

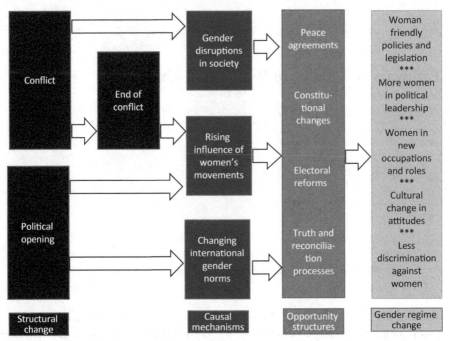

FIGURE 2.1 Model of Process of Postconflict Impacts on Gender Policy

increased adoption of women's rights in peace agreements, constitutions, and other changing opportunity structures (see Figure 2.1). The changes we have seen in postconflict African countries (and beyond) can be explained by a convergence of a series of developments that are global, but have a particular African dimension to them because so many countries in Africa had experienced conflict.

GENDER DISRUPTIONS IN WAR

Many countries in Africa, including nonconflict countries, were exposed to changes in international gender norms and new donor strategies, and many experienced the rise of women's movements starting in the 1990s. However, the critical causal mechanism linking the decline in conflict with women's improved legal status and higher rates of political representation was the *disruptions in gender relations and norms that occurred during conflict.* Women began to take on new roles and new forms of leadership in the household, community, and nation more generally, often in the absence of husbands and male community leaders. War inadvertently opened up new possibilities for women, creating new visions of what was possible. It also created incentives for women to demand greater political representation and more rights (Boyd 1989; Corrin 2002; Meintjes et al. 2002; Sambanis 2002; Tripp 2000; Turshen 2001).

This set postconflict countries onto a different and more rapid trajectory than other countries in Africa. During conflict, women assumed new roles in their homes, in their communities, and at the national level. Old elites were thrown out of power, opening up possibilities for new leaders like women. In countries where women became engaged in peace movements, one saw the greatest efforts by women to increase their influence through representation and legislation both during and after the conflict. These trends were also more pronounced in postconflict societies like Liberia and Uganda, where women already had enjoyed higher levels of education and had historically played leadership roles, however circumscribed.

To be sure, there is the example of Tanzania that did not experience conflict and has made similar reforms as the postconflict countries, but it started earlier because of the egalitarian ethos of its founding father, President Julius Nyerere, and change came incrementally (Meena 2003). Such examples are the exception, not the rule. These exceptions also experienced the rise of women's movements and the increased involvement of the UN and donors, but without the gender disruptions of war. However, if one looks at the top ten countries with the highest rates of female legislative representation in Africa, seven are countries that experienced major conflict.

Of the disruptions, the three types that were most important for changing women's status had to do, first, with women's new voice in the community. Their negotiations with the militia and demonstrations for peace created a new cadre of activists who had found their voice. In all the case studies, this newfound political voice was something women noted in my interviews. The second kind of disruption had to do with changes in women's economic status that forced women to become more important economic actors by diversifying or expanding their businesses and playing a larger, if not the dominant role, in the household economy and in their communities. These new economic resources gave women a basis for demanding greater political authority in the community and beyond. A third kind of disruption was symbolic. Women in all three case studies often explained that some of the biggest changes they had experienced were in what they began to envision. They could begin to imagine more control over their lives, taking on new roles in business; in governmental, educational, and religious institutions; as athletes, novelists, TV anchors; and in many other new roles.

All these changes had a cascading effect, where major historical events can trigger a series of consequences that transform structures and practices. These dislocations can disturb a social structure in such a way that it cannot be restructured, thus allowing for new understandings of what is imaginable and desirable (Sewell 2009). Thus, economic disruptions had consequences for women's status in the household, which in turn affected women's political standing in the community, and both of these types of changes had ideational and symbolic outcomes in terms of what became part of the realm of the possible for women in many other spheres. Of all the forms of disruption, however, the one that had the most immediate impact on future mobilization for women's rights and leadership was peace mobilization, especially at the local level.

Peace movements as precursors to gender regime change

Countries that experienced women's activism during the war tended to have more women's rights changes after the war. They were more likely to see gender regime transformations than countries where women simply participated as fighters, for example, Eritrea. This is because even though there were individual women fighters who became political leaders, women involved in peace and other forms of activism were more likely to continue pressing for women's rights changes after the war.

One form of disruption, and one of the most important new developments after the 1990s, was the emergence of national-level peace initiatives and peace movements, which were heavily subscribed to by women. These movements had important implications for demands for power in the postconflict polity and built on local-level peace mobilization, which certainly was not new.

Many of women's peacemaking activities arose from concerns driven by their household responsibilities and involvement in local communities. Conditions of conflict frequently forced women to become the sole provider for the family and to shoulder additional responsibilities in maintaining the household. Women were pushed into new economic roles with the absence of their menfolk. This also gave women the space that otherwise might not have been there to participate in civil society organizations and in peace initiatives.

For the first time in Africa, we saw this phenomenon in national-level mobilization in Uganda in 1985. The shift from localized peacemaking to national-level initiatives was a big change and one that has not been sufficiently acknowledged in the literature on women's mobilization. There had always been local-level mobilization for peace, but these movements now took on a national character, and the demands expanded to include women's need to be represented politically in peace talks and legislatures along with other concerns relating to violence against women, land, and other key issues. It was not, however, until the 1990s that we saw the rise of major national-level women's peace movements in DRC, Sierra Leone, Sudan, and the Horn of Africa, which had been learning from one another over time. Women adopted a wide range of strategies to build peace. Although their role has rarely been acknowledged or publicized, the Mali women's peace movement played an important role in initiating talks between the government and Tuareg rebels that had staged unsuccessful rebellions against the government in 1990 and 2007 and again in 2012. In 1990 they succeeded in bringing about reconciliation and restoring trust between conflicted communities. Women organized the first public ceremony that involved burning weapons, which became an annual celebration and protest of small arms and light weapons (Dirasse 2000; Kamau 1999).

The Association of Mozambican Women for Peace (MWFP) made sure that the 1994 elections were carried out peacefully in Mozambique, which had been embroiled in a seventeen-year war between the FRELIMO-led government and RENAMO-led rebellion. The women pleaded with the parties to stop threatening each other. They organized a major peace rally in Maputo and were successful in getting an ex-combatant organization to stop trying to disrupt elections. The meetings with the combatants were organized by the National Committee for Elections that included the MWFP and several Christian organizations (Snyder 2006). When conflict erupted in Kenya following the 2007 elections, human rights and women's organizations were at the forefront of monitoring the violence, speaking out against it, and taking measures to de-escalate tensions.

In Liberia, Mali, and Sierra Leone, women's groups walked into remote areas to persuade the militia to lay down their arms, in an effort to disarm child soldiers. In Uganda, an Italian deputy headmistress, Sister Rechelle Fassera, secured the release of the majority of 139 girls who were captured from St. Mary's College Aboke in 1996 by the Lord's Resistance Army and were taken to Sudan. Numerous newspaper accounts and books have subsequently detailed the activities of Angelina Atyam and other mothers of the Aboke girls, who formed Concerned Parents Association to raise international awareness of the abductions and continue to negotiate with the LRA for their release (Lacy 2003; Temmerman 2001). Similarly, when about 276 mostly Christian female students were kidnapped in April 2014 by the Al-Qaeda-linked Boko Haram in Nigeria's town of Chibok in Borno State, it was not until Muslim and Christian women rallied together to protest the action that the mass abduction received national and international attention. Boko Haram had been attacking schools and communities in northern Nigeria since 2010, killing thousands of people. Although there had been clashes between Muslims and Christians in northern Nigeria, Muslim and Christian women formed coalitions across religion and ethnicity and between secular and religious women to protest the Chibok kidnappings in the northern Borno, Kaduna, Jos, Kwara, Nasarawa, and Plateau states.

In postconflict countries like Angola, Chad, and Eritrea, however, few women were involved in peace movements or other forms of mobilization, and this contributed to the lack of change after the conflict in advancing women's rights. Similarly, the fact that women had been combatants in Angola and Eritrea had relatively little impact on women's future status.

WOMEN'S POSTCONFLICT MOBILIZATION

The second factor linking civil war and women's rights relates to women's continued mobilization after conflict. Out of civil conflict and political opening, came the emergence of new autonomous women's movements, especially after the 1990s. These new actors, some of whom had been involved in peace movements, created bottom-up pressures for change that were critical in ensuring that women's rights were brought into transitional institutions. The absence of such postconflict movements in countries like Angola, Eritrea, and Chad helps explain, in part, why change in key areas has been so slow in these countries. Because women's experiences during war – violence, loss of land, lack of education, and having to fend for one's family – gave them common cause, many activists mobilized around their gender concerns, building ties across so-called enemy lines. Conflict may have also diminished or temporarily disorganized the power of potential opposition forces or weakened their base, for example, political parties and conservative religious actors. The erosion of the formal judicial system also adversely affected women, making it all the more urgent to strengthen formal laws and legal processes protecting women.

Women activists who had fought for peace during the war continued to mobilize for power, drawing on the organizations, networks, and alliances that had built up during wartime. Women involved in peacemaking during the war, as in Liberia, realized very quickly that to influence peace processes and a transition to a more stable form of government and to influence policy outcomes for women, they would need to be in positions of power. Therefore, they began to increase their demands for greater representation during the war and during the transition. Thus, demands for power and peace went hand in hand. Their common agenda made women's movements one of the most organized sectors of society. The removal of old elites from power also opened up new possibilities for women.

One of the most important features of this mobilization was that it involved new organizations that were autonomous of political parties and the state in terms of funding, leadership, and agendas. This was a break from the past when key women's organizations, especially at the national level, were tied to patronage networks of the state and ruling party. They had been led by wives and daughters of the ruling elite, and they were depoliticized in terms of their agendas. At best they were involved in development-related work, but often the types of issues they concerned themselves with had to do with improving the household, handicrafts, monitoring the morality of their membership, and providing entertainment in the form of dancing, singing, and making food for visiting dignitaries (Cooper 1995; Geisler 1987; Gilman 2001; Ibrahim 2004).

In contrast, the new organizations were characterized by their heterogeneity and the extensive reach of their objectives, which had shifted from a narrow focus on developmental concerns to new issues of female political representation and advocacy on issues of the environment, women's status, land access, violence against women, access to loans and agricultural inputs, and many other such concerns. Women's organizations now openly broached topics that had been considered taboo in the past such as domestic violence, reproductive rights, sexual harassment, and female genital cutting.

Women's organizations often work in coalitions, generally formed in an ad hoc fashion around a particular goal such as legislative reform. Sometimes the coalitions are focused on women's rights concerns, but other times they deal with broader concerns having to do with debt, poverty, land, and other such issues. They often include an umbrella network of women's organizations; a multiparty caucus of parliamentarians; an organization of women leaders from different parties; a women's ministry; NGOs, including INGOs; and other such entities. They may be supported by various UN agencies and donors.

CHANGING INTERNATIONAL NORMS AND PRACTICES

The third factor that explains the aforementioned postconflict dynamics was international influences and new norms relating to gender equality, particularly those shaped by UN agencies. The timing of postconflict women's rights policy adoption relates to changing international norms regarding women's rights that have influenced the UN, but also donors and diplomats, as well as international nongovernmental organizations to expand women's rights and representation in postconflict countries, especially after the 1990s (Strickland and Duvvury 2003). New cross-national studies identify these pressures (Bush 2011).

However, as important as the international pressures were, they were not decisive. Uganda was able to advance considerably in the area of women's rights before it received substantial donor support in the 1990s, and most of the progress was fueled by a domestic women's movement. The stigma of being too closely associated with a foreign agenda also weighed on activists who, although they may have been inspired by international feminism, were still sometimes wary of adopting the term *feminist* along with its foreign connotations. By the 2000s, the apprehension of being labeled "feminist" had begun to fade as African women's rights activists began to redefine feminism in African terms (see, for example, Charter for Feminist Principles for African Feminists).[1]

Nevertheless, postconflict countries were generally more easily influenced by international norms relating to gender due to the prominent presence and influence of external actors. These norms permeated and spread through international institutions from the International Criminal Tribunals for Yugoslavia and Rwanda to the International Criminal Court, to the UN Beijing Platform of Action and the passage of UN Security Council Resolution 1325 (Anderlini 2011).

These new women's rights norms were mediated by regional bodies such as the African Union and subregional organizations, especially the Southern African Development Community (SADC), but also the Economic Community of West African States (ECOWAS) and the Economic Community of Central African States (ECCAS), which in turn pressured national governments for gender-related policy changes. They were also mediated by multilateral bodies like the UN agencies, most importantly, the World Bank, the

[1] www.africanfeministforum.com/the-charter-of-feminist-principles-for-african-feminists/

Commonwealth, and foreign donors, including bilateral agencies, international NGOs, foundations, and other such actors.

It should be pointed out that there is an interactive dimension to the relationship between global and local norms. Inasmuch as global norms have shaped local norms, they have also been heavily influenced by local women's movements. African women's movements have influenced global norms, especially in the areas of customary law, sexual violence during conflict, peacemaking, and microcredit, as well as gender budgeting and the introduction of quotas (Copelon 2000, 225; Snyder 2006; Tripp et al. 2009). Postconflict countries have been very much a part of this shaping of global norms, especially in debates around violence against women, land, and the treatment of refugees and internally displaced people.

An additional element to donor support has to do with the ways in which governments have themselves used women's rights to garner international support. Rwanda was able to buy considerable goodwill from the international community for being a world leader in women's female legislative representation, despite its dismal human rights record, partly because of its promotion of women in the political arena (Burnet 2008). Other governments and political parties have similarly used their advancement of women as leaders as an indicator that they are modernizing to gain international support and approval.

UN conferences

External influences were especially evident at the watershed UN conferences on women in Nairobi (1985) and Beijing (1995). These conferences, and the strategies and plans that came out of them, placed additional pressure on governments to respond to domestic and pan-African women's organizations. The 1995 Beijing Platform of Action, for example, heavily influenced quota adoption globally because it encouraged UN member states to find ways to promote women's leadership in all arenas (Krook 2006). Though most countries in Africa adopted quotas after 1995 as a result of such international encouragements, some postconflict countries had already adopted quotas prior to 1995, often for (left leaning/egalitarian) ideological reasons or in response to women's activism within the party. These countries included Uganda (1989), Eritrea (1994), Mozambique (1994), and South Africa (1994). In all these cases, quotas were promoted by the dominant political parties. Even nonconflict countries like Ghana had quotas in 1959, Tanzania in 1975, and Senegal in 1982 through the dominant party, Parti Socialiste. Thus, the international pressures were mediated by domestic and ideological considerations.

International treaties

International treaties are another mechanism through which international pressures and norms are expressed. Here the impact is uneven. The only countries in

Africa that have *not* signed the Convention on the Elimination of All Forms of Discrimination against Women (CEDAW) are two countries that have experienced major conflict, Sudan and Somalia, although the latter country is the process of ratifying it according to their 2014 country report to the UN Committee on the Status of Women. This will leave the Sudan, United States, and Iran along with two small Pacific Islands (Palau and Tonga) as the only holdouts in adopting this treaty. Somalia also plans to ratify the Convention on the Rights of the Child, which will make the United States the only country in the world not to have ratified this treaty, which has implications for the girl child.

One international commitment that ought to have had greater impact was the 2000 UN Security Council Resolution (UNSCR) 1325, which recognizes the specific consequences of armed conflict on women and requires the equal and full participation of women in conflict prevention and resolution, peacekeeping, and peacebuilding. Its impact has been mixed. On the one hand, it has yet to produce significant results in terms of incorporating women into structures of leadership within peacemaking and peacebuilding processes, and much of what women have accomplished has happened despite this resolution. Peacemaking involves activities aimed at stopping a conflict, whereas peacebuilding refers to activities that seek to prevent the start or resumption of conflict, often by addressing the deeper causes of violence.

Willett (2010) finds that ten years after its adoption, UNSCR 1325 remains more rhetoric than a real commitment. She argues that what is needed is greater funding, major restructuring of UN bodies, changes in the highly militarized culture of peacekeeping operations, and serious gender mainstreaming. Others also find that the resolution does not reference any accountability mechanisms to monitor its implementation and set benchmarks to measure progress (Otto 2009). Moreover, the resolution's actual impact has been hampered by the fact that UN Security Council resolutions are not binding and only apply to UN bodies (Tachou-Sipowo 2010). Some highlight the staff, funding, and enforcement deficiencies in the implementation of UNSCR in peacekeeping operations in countries like Liberia and Sierra Leone (Boehme 2011; Nduka-Agwua 2009).

At the same time, a number of authors are more optimistic about the impact of UNSCR 1325. Renee Black (2009), for example, found that prior to the adoption of UNSCR 1325, references to women in conflict in country-specific UN resolutions were sporadic and inconsistent and tended to refer to women primarily as victims. Since the passage of UNSCR 1325, there has been an increase in resolutions referring to women, and there are signs that gender mainstreaming is becoming more routinized within the Security Council. This can be attributed to efforts of NGOs like the NGO Working Group on Women, Peace, and Security and various agencies like UN Development Fund for Women (UNIFEM), UN Women, and the UN International Research and Training Institute for the Advancement of Women (INSTRAW), which have attempted to hold the Security Council accountable to its commitments in

UNSCR 1325. Donald Steinberg, former deputy administrator at the U.S. Agency for International Development (USAID), finds that the language of UNSCR 1325 could be stronger, but defends the resolution, saying that there has been noticeable change in UN structures since its adoption, more awareness of the issues, more gender advisers, more gender training of peacekeepers, and use of excellent guidelines for field action (2010a).

Chapter 5 shows that UNSCR 1325 did have an impact on the frequency of references to women's rights in peace agreements, particularly in comprehensive peace agreements. At the international level, "women, peace and security" concerns are now an accepted part of the normative peacebuilding efforts of institutions like the UN Peacebuilding Commission, but they still rely on key individuals who are committed to promoting women in strategic policy development (Tryggestad 2010). Senior women engaged in UN peace processes are ten times more likely to promote women in peace processes than their male colleagues (Conaway and Shoemaker 2008; Tinde 2009).

The UN Security Council has been forced to gender mainstream its operations and adopt a zero-tolerance policy toward sexual exploitation or abuse of civilians during peacekeeping operations. UNIFEM and its successor, UN Women, have been instrumental in trying to see that women are represented in peace talks. Miriam Anderson (2010) documents how Burundian and regional women activists rallied support from UNIFEM in New York to get them seats at the peace talks. They also gained considerable support from regional women's groups in Africa and, in particular, from South African activists. In December 1997, the regional organization Femmes Africa Solidarité (FAS) organized meetings with Burundian women's NGOs to help them gain awareness about the role they might play in peacemaking activities (Femmes Africa Solidarité 2003, 18).

Regional pressures for reform

Regional pressures for gender-based reform have been especially important in Africa. As a result of pressures from women's movements within Africa, subregional organizations like SADC, with fifteen member states,[2] ECOWAS, with sixteen member states,[3] and more recently ECCAS, with five member states,[4] have been encouraging gender equality in political representation. SADC has been especially successful in setting goals to increase female

---

[2] SADC member states include Angola, Botswana, Democratic Republic of Congo, Lesotho, Madagascar, Malawi, Mauritius, Mozambique, Namibia, Seychelles, South Africa, Swaziland, Tanzania, Zambia, and Zimbabwe.

[3] ECOWAS member states include Benin, Burkina Faso, Cape Verde, Côte d'Ivoire, Gambia, Ghana, Guinea, Guinea-Bissau, Liberia, Mali, Niger, Nigeria, Senegal, Sierra Leone, and Togo.

[4] ECCAS member states include the central African states of Burundi, Rwanda, DRC, São Tomé e Principe, and Angola.

representation in its member countries. In 1997, SADC set a goal in which female-held legislative seats of its member countries would reach 30 percent by 2005. In 2005, the goal of 50 percent was set for 2015. A SADC Regional Women's Parliamentary Caucus was formed in April 2002 in Luanda, Angola, to advocate and lobby for the increased representation of women in SADC parliaments. Regional NGOs like Gender Links, formed in 2001, have facilitated and publicized the work of SADC in this area.[5] Gender Links supports the Southern Africa Gender Protocol Alliance, formed in 2005, which is a network that campaigned for and is now pressing for the implementation of the SADC Protocol on Gender and Development. The protocol, which was adopted by heads of state at the 2008 summit, set twenty-eight targets for achieving gender equality by 2015. The only two countries that have not signed the protocol are Botswana and Mauritius, both nonpostconflict countries. As a result of SADC pressures, its member countries have 26 percent legislative seats held by women in the lower house; non-SADC African countries women have on average 19 percent of the legislative seats, although when other factors are taken into consideration the independent impact of SADC is lessened considerably (Hughes and Tripp 2015). ECOWAS also set targets to improve gender representation and pressured countries that were lagging. In 2004, ECCAS adopted a Declaration on Gender Equality (Déclaration sur l'égalité entre les hommes et les femmes),[6] which proposes steps to mitigate discrimination against women in its member states.

The African Union Charter on Human and People's Rights on the Rights of Women in Africa (Maputo Protocol) is the most important Africa-wide treaty regarding women's rights. Postconflict countries were among the first to sign the Protocol: in 2003–04, 88 percent of the postconflict countries had signed, whereas only 55 percent of the nonconflict countries had signed. By 2015, however, only 56 percent of the postconflict countries had ratified the treaty, while 76 percent of the nonpostconflict countries had ratified it.[7] Thus, compliance with some treaties in countries affected by war is more uneven than other indicators of women's rights reform. The Solidarity for African Women's Rights (SOAWR) is an umbrella organization of 44 NGOs that press for the adoption of the declaration. Because of the low rate of ratification in postconflict countries, it is perhaps no accident that a disproportionate number of the organizations in SOAWR that are not regional organizations are based in postconflict countries.

Some of the regional initiatives have targeted postconflict countries to address the particular issues facing women. A 2006 regional meeting sponsored by a joint secretariat of the African Union and the UN brought together leaders

---

[5] www.genderlinks.org.za.

[6] See document at http://pfbc-cbfp.org/docs/news/Nov2010-Jan2011/Atelier%20Genre%20decle galite.pdf.

[7] African Commission on Human and People's Rights www.achpr.org/instruments/women-protocol/ratification/.

of Burundi, the Democratic Republic of Congo, the Central African Republic, Rwanda, and Uganda to sign an agreement to guarantee property rights of internationally displaced people and returning refugees in their respective countries. Although the passage of national legislation rests with the individual countries, the agreement is an attempt to create a framework or model for them to address a mutual problem to protect internally displaced persons and refugees from losing their property to pillage, violence, military use, reprisal, and destruction. Individual countries may have ill-defined land rights for women, so this legislation is intended to help give women, in particular, a legal means to own and inherit land ("Officials Adopt Legislation ..." 2006).

Donor influences

Donor assistance is a major impetus for norm diffusion and may make some donor-dependent postconflict countries more likely to comply with these norms. However, not all gender-related norms are influenced by donors, and not all postconflict countries are heavily donor dependent. Sara Bush (2011) has argued that the presence of a UN peace operation supporting political liberalization, the amount of foreign aid, and whether a country has international election monitors are positively and significantly correlated with the adoption of gender quotas. This may not be the case in Africa, where Lindberg (2004), for example, found no correlation between foreign aid and female political representation. Similarly, Hughes and Tripp (2015) were also unable to find such a correlation in our Africa-based study of the impact of conflict on women's representation. Postconflict countries are generally *less* donor dependent than other countries in Africa. Overall the net ODA received per capita for postconflict countries averages around $72, whereas for nonpostconflict countries it averages around $97, which is considerably more. Based on field research, I suspect that the primary international influence that affects women's rights policy adoption is the UN and its various agencies.

Targeted aid similarly seems not to have clear impacts. Fragile states receiving the largest amount of aid addressing gender equality in Africa include Ethiopia, DRC, Nigeria, Kenya, Uganda, and Cameroon (OECD-DAC 2010). If one uses female political representation as a metric, neither DRC, Nigeria, Kenya, nor Cameroon (until recently) had large numbers of women in parliament. Moreover, targeted aid does not always address the specific needs of recipients. In a 2011 survey of 1,119 gender-based organizations around the world, including 37 percent from Africa, the Association for Women's Rights in Development found that the largest number (40 percent) in Africa had been formed between 2000 and 2005, and another 30 percent were formed between 2006 and 2011. In terms of issue areas, 55 percent of the respondents from Africa said their priority was women's economic empowerment followed by women's leadership and political empowerment (51 percent). Access to education and health and reproductive rights ranked third and fourth in importance. Nevertheless, donor funding was available at roughly the same amounts for each of the four categories (22–23 percent) and thus did not match the priorities identified by the recipients.

Although the overall patterns are inconclusive around specific indicators, one might argue that individual countries like Liberia may be more inclined to adopt women's rights policies because of their high donor influence, while Angola is less likely to do so because it receives very little assistance. In Liberia, for example, the demands of the women's movement regarding violence against women, education of girls and women, improving conditions for market women, recruiting women into the police and military, and ending sexual harassment are also promoted by the gender desk of the peacekeeping forces, the UN Mission in Liberia (UNMIL), UN Women, and the UN Development Programme (UNDP). In contrast, in Angola there is virtually no independent women's movement, yet women in this country have faced many of the same issues as women in Liberia in the aftermath of conflict. Moreover, the UN agencies in Angola have had relatively little impact in the area of women's rights compared with Liberia. However, the country's endowment of oil and diamonds, and possibly its close trade ties to China, have made it feel less beholden to the international community and to regional and subregional organizations within the continent. Women's rights activists told me this was one of the reasons Angola felt less obliged to comply with international women's rights norms.

Table 2.1 shows that countries like Angola, Chad, Eritrea, and Sudan have not received as much foreign aid as other countries, and these are countries that have also shown less compliance with international pressures except in the area

TABLE 2.1 *Net ODA Received per Capita, 2012 (US$)*

South Sudan	146
Liberia	136
Namibia	117
Somalia	98
Mozambique	83
Rwanda	77
Sierra Leone	74
Burundi	53
Uganda	46
Chad	38
DR Congo	36
Sudan	26
Eritrea	22
South Africa	20
Angola	12

Source: World Bank Databank, 2013.

of adopting quotas. Given the inconclusiveness of the donor impact on women's rights, the question then is, which way does the causal arrow point: Do countries adopt woman-friendly policies because they receive aid, or do they receive aid because they adopt woman-friendly and other related policies compatible with donor goals? It would seem that the latter statement is the likely scenario because the reasons for not complying are varied. For Angola, their natural resources and wealth make them less donor dependent, but it is more likely that the weaker UN influences in Angola along with the weakness of civil society have had more of an impact on their lack of gender policy. Some countries like Eritrea have isolated themselves from these international pressures as a result of their authoritarian rule. They do not, as a result, attract much international assistance. Sudan's authoritarian and Islamic state orientation similarly has made it less interested in complying with international norms, although some influences are evident. Like Angola, Chad and Eritrea have not had strong independent women's movements, and therefore they largely escaped pressures for gender reform. Thus, although donor influences are a factor in shaping postconflict gender policy reform, it may be that the international influences are felt more indirectly through UN normative pressures and through donor support of domestic actors. In other words, the cross-national statistical evidence suggests that we need to look beyond donors to domestic women's movements and coalitions to explain gender-related reforms. Of all the international influences, the UN presence in a country and its normative agenda had the most impact.

CONCLUSIONS

All the causal mechanisms outlined earlier are evident in nonpostconflict settings except for the first one, gender disruptions of war, which was necessary in explaining the link between conflict and women's rights reforms after the 1990s in Africa. These gender disruptions are often linked to changes in elite structures, which allow for new leaders to emerge, opening up new possibilities for women. Changes in international gender norms were also necessary but not sufficient developments that allowed for the changes to take place in postconflict settings. The emergence of women's movements and women's rights activists provided critical actors to push through the changes, and as such, their presence was also a necessary condition. There were other actors, such as political parties, women's policy agencies, women's ministries, and peacekeeping forces, but none had the impact of the domestic women's movements and UN pressures in consistently pushing contending sides in the conflict and governments into action around women's rights, as will become evident in the chapters ahead. They generally acted in coalitions with women's organizations and networks when they engaged in initiatives to change the status of women.

PART II

CASE STUDIES

3

Uganda: Forging a New Trajectory

I wish to make a heartfelt appeal to the women of Uganda ... let us move forward together to break through the gates of liberty. You see it is necessary to break through the gates, for no guard at the gates is prepared to open them for us. I know all too well that the remaining journey is long, and the road is narrow, steep and slippery. But along this rough road, women of Uganda shall have to walk ... until we achieve a triumphant entry in through the gates of liberty.
– Miria Matembe, *Gender, Politics and Constitution Making in Uganda*, 2002

BACKGROUND

Uganda was the first country in Africa where postconflict influences on women's status described in this book became evident. They became apparent with the takeover of Yoweri Museveni and his National Resistance Movement (NRM) in 1986 after a five-year guerrilla war. All three key factors described in Chapter 1 that help explain why postconflict countries have been quicker to promote women's rights and representation were present in Uganda. The patterns seen in Uganda became even clearer after the 1990s in other countries coming out of conflict.

To begin with, Uganda experienced the types of *gender disruptions* found in countries affected by civil war, resulting in what Raewyn Connell calls a change in gender regime. As in most countries, it was not a complete change, but a palpable shift occurred. As a result of these gender disruptions, women gained in political power, although not at the very heart of power within the military. Women began to take on new roles in business, government, academia, civil society, and other areas. These changes occurred at both the national and local levels. Attitudes toward women and women's leadership also changed. Chapter 9 discusses in greater depth some of the women's rights legislative reforms that were adopted.

TABLE 3.1 *Basic Political, Economic, and Social Data for Uganda, 2014*

Capital	Kampala
Type of government	Presidential republic
Independence	October 9, 1962 (from the UK)
GDP (current US$)	19,881,412,441 (2012)
GDP per capita (current US$)	547 (2012)
GDP growth	3.42%
Poverty level	Population below poverty line: 24.5% (2009 CIA) 37.7% of the population living on less than $1.25 a day (World Bank 2012).
Major sources of revenue	Agriculture: 23.1% Industry: 26.9% Services: 50% (2013 CIA)
Population	36,345,860 (2012)
Ethnicity	Baganda 16.9%, Banyakole 9.5%, Basoga 8.4%, Bakiga 6.9%, Iteso 6.4%, Langi 6.1%, Acholi 4.7%, Bagisu 4.6%, Lugbara 4.2%, Bunyoro 2.7%, other 29.6% (2002 census)
Religion	Roman Catholic 41.9%; Protestant 42% (Anglican 35.9%, Pentecostal 4.6%, Seventh Day Adventist 1.5%); Muslim 12.1%; other 3.1%; none 0.9% (2002 census)
Official languages	English (official), Ganda or Luganda, other Niger-Congo languages, Nilo-Saharan languages, Swahili, and Arabic
Head of government	President Lieutenant General Yoweri Museveni (came to power through armed takeover, elected by popular vote in 2006 and 2011 for five-year terms)
Cabinet	Appointed by the president from among elected members of the National Assembly, 28% women
Prime minister	Amama Mbabazi
Legislative branch	Unicameral National Assembly 375 seats total <ul><li>237 members elected to open seats by popular vote for five-year terms</li><li>137 members elected to reserved seats, nominated by legally established special interest groups, including Women: 112 seats Army: 10 seats Persons with disabilities: 5 seats Youth: 5 seats Labor: 5 seats</li><li>13 ex officio members</li></ul>
Women in the National Assembly	35 percent (includes women in both reserved and open seats)
Speaker of the House	Rebecca Kadaga

Judiciary	Chief Justice: Hon. Steven Kavuma
	Number of women justices on Supreme Court of Uganda: 3 out of 9
Electoral system	Candidate with simple majority of votes wins
Districts	West: Bulisa, Bundibugyo, Bushenyi, Hoima, Ibanda, Isingiro, Kabale, Kabarole, Kamwenge, Kanungu, Kasese, Kibale, Kiruhura, Kisoro, Kyenjojo, Masindi, Mbarara, Ntungamo, Rukungiri
	North: Abim, Adjumani, Amolatar, Amuru, Apac, Arua, Dokolo, Gulu, Kaabong, Kitgum, Koboko, Kotido, Lira, Maracha-Terego, Moroto, Moyo, Nakapiripirit, Nebbi, Oyam, Pader, Yumbe
	East: Amuria, Budaka, Bududa, Bugiri, Bukedea, Bukwa, Busia, Butaleja, Iganga, Jinja, Kaberamaido, Kaliro, Kamuli, Kapchorwa, Katakwi, Kumi, Manafwa, Mayuge, Mbale, Namutumba, Pallisa, Sironko, Soroti, Tororo
	Central: Kalangala, Kampala, Kayunga, Kiboga, Luwero, Lyantonde, Masaka, Mityana, Mpigi, Mubende, Mukono, Nakaseke, Nakasongola, Rakai, Sembabule, Wakiso
Parties represented in Parliament	National Resistance Movement (Yoweri Museveni) 263 seats
	Forum for Democratic Change (Mugisha Muntu) 34
	Democratic Party (Norbert Mao) 12
	Uganda People's Congress (Olara Otunnu stepped down in 2015) 10
	Conservative Party (Ken Lukyamuzi) 1
	Justice Forum (JEEMA) (Asuman Basalirwa) 1
	Independents 43

Second, an initial political opening in the late 1980s and early 1990s was important in allowing the emergence of an *active women's movement* that had sufficient autonomy to pressure the government to adopt key women's rights reforms. Women's mobilization was also facilitated by the new availability of the Internet, cell phones, and other forms of communications technology.

Third, Uganda was one of the first postconflict countries in Africa to begin to experience the effects of significant *changes in international gender norms* and interventions by international actors like the United Nations (UN) agencies and bilateral donors.

The Ugandan case highlights a number of dynamics that are important to our explanation of postconflict change. The Ugandan case brings into view the significance of women's peace mobilization as a jumping-off point for activism. In Uganda, a peace demonstration of 2,000 women in 1987 created a proto-template for later autonomous mobilization independent of the ruling party and state. The closing down of all formal women's organizations in 1978 under Idi Amin had left a vacuum in terms of women's mobilization, although it

UGANDA DISTRICTS

FIGURE 3.1 Administrative Map of Uganda. Credit: Eva Swantz

continued quietly at the grassroots level. Women's influence came from the fact that they represented a constituency that had begun to reconstitute itself during the war and had the potential to become a source of political support for the regime. They would have to be given positions of power and some policy concessions, and thus a quid pro quo lasted for some time between the women's movement and the Museveni government. But their independence also meant that they could and did withdraw some of their support as the Museveni government became less inclusive along ethnic lines and as the executive expanded its control.

A handful of women were able to leverage their involvement in guerrilla warfare into positions of power. These women joined the National Resistance

Army (NRA) during what was referred to as the "Bush War" that took place mainly in Luwero between the NRA and the government of President Milton Obote. Brig. Proscovia Nalweyiso, for example, became the highest-ranking army officer and led the women's wing of the NRA from the time of the Bush War in 1983 until 2001. Fighters like Gertrude Njuba, who gained political prominence after the war, did not associate themselves publicly with the women's movement, and even Janat Mukwaya, another fighter who became Minister of Gender, Labour and Social Development, distanced herself from some of the key demands of the women's movement such as the Domestic Relations Bill. The number of female fighters – around 100 – also may have been too small to have a major impact. Thus, in Uganda as elsewhere, female combatants generally were not the women who were at the forefront of the movement for pressing for women's rights changes (although there were some notable exceptions such as Winnie Byanyima). However, the women fighters did have an impact on changing gender roles in a way that was not evident after earlier wars in which women had participated as fighters (e.g., Angola, Mozambique, Zimbabwe). Many interviewees made remarks similar to that of Maxine Ankrah, who observed, "For the first time, women were seen visually in a role that was never anticipated; they were seen to be fighting in a uniform. They were seen to be in a men's role. Also in the formation of the NRA, women were made commanders over men ... that was a totally new thing."[1]

Although the new women's organizations that emerged had their roots in earlier associational experiences, they were different from the postindependence mobilization in that their agendas, finances, and leaders were independent of the ruling party and of the state. These changes were evident in other parts of Africa, but in the early 1990s, Uganda was a leader, as it was the first country to emerge from conflict where the new patterns of autonomous mobilization were clearly evident (Tripp 2000).

Peace negotiations provided an important venue for women asserting their demands, particularly for representation. Uganda did hold peace talks in 1986; however, the peace agreement that was concluded at that time was soon violated as fighting resumed. Nevertheless, this was the first time that women collectively pressed for political representation and leadership of women as a group, and it formed the basis for future demands of this kind. Women began to contemplate what their absence from power had meant during the years of war. Three NRM women were represented at the talks, but there were no independent women activists. Thus, this was a turning point in consciousness about the importance of political representation and of civil society having a seat at the table. This awareness emerged long before the passage of UNSCR 1325 and the manifestation of other international pressures.

---

[1] Interview with 1.34, Maxine Ankrah, Kampala June 19, 1992.

The war that ended in 1986 continued in the north until around 2006. Many of the same kinds of gender disruptions that occurred in the earlier war in central and southern Uganda were evident in northern Uganda as conflict continued unabated. Women were mobilized around peace-related activities and later sought representation in the Juba peace talks (2006–08). However, the decline of conflict in the north did not have the same repercussions as the decline of conflict in 1986. This localized conflict and proxy war did not result in a takeover in power as was the case after the 1981–86 conflict. There was no reordering of the entire polity as a result of the end of the conflict through the process of rewriting a constitution or reestablishing new electoral rules.

This chapter provides an overview of the three factors that characterize countries that experienced dramatic changes in the postconflict period. It then looks at the ways in which the gender regime changed in political, economic, education, cultural, and other institutions. It concludes by discussing the gender transformations that occurred in the conflict in the north but shows how and why this conflict did not result in the kind of transformative changes seen after the earlier civil war in Uganda that ended in 1986.

GENDER DISRUPTIONS

Gender disruptions emerged as the first factor that influenced gender regime transformations in Uganda. The Bush War left over 800,000 people dead, 200,000 exiled, and millions displaced within the country (Watson 1988, 14). The war-related disruptions in gender relations in Uganda were palpable, not only at the national level, but also at the grassroots as well, as I found in my study of local-level gender-based conflicts. Women were demanding more access to resources and economic opportunities and were pushing for a greater say in their communities. In my book *Women and Politics in Uganda* (2000), I examine a series of cases in which women were for the first time, for example, making demands to start a health clinic in Wakitaka, Jinja. They were demanding to control their market space in Kampala's Kiyembe market, fighting for the right to control the funds of an organization for traditional birth attendants in Kamuli, and fighting to control the terms of a World Bank infrastructure project in Kampala. It was evident that similar conflicts were brewing elsewhere in Uganda, and local residents observed that these were new kinds of struggles that had emerged as a result of women's newfound voice.

Even psychologist Helen Jane Liebling found in her study of war survivors of sexual violence from the 1981–86 war that women in Luwero took on male roles, and they increased in strength and resilience in response to the atrocities they faced. The war had changed their sense of what it meant to be a woman. They expressed themselves as autonomous and capable rather than as vulnerable and dependent. This shift, however, sometimes came at the cost of disempowering men, who lost their sense of identity because of the war, resulting in withdrawal, alcohol abuse, and domestic violence (Liebling-Kalifani 2004, 314–15).

The social supports that came to women from the Museveni government may have also contributed to women's positive adaptation. A later study in northern Uganda found a similar phenomenon: Unlike men, most women returning from armed groups were able to reintegrate socially and were more psychologically resilient (Annan et al. 2011). They exhibited little aggression and violence, even those who had been forcibly married and had borne children. While women's agency matters, it should be of concern that men have had a harder time adjusting to the new situation. The gender disruptions are not entirely positive insofar as men are having a harder time coping. This also has implications for women when it results in alcoholism, domestic abuse, and other behavior that harms the entire household.

The years of internal warfare in Uganda had a profound effect on women's self-perceptions and of men's perceptions of women (Walusimbe 2013). The conflict thrust women into new roles and situations that fundamentally transformed expectations about women (Ankrah 1987; Watson 1988). Women gained a new leadership presence in non-gender-based associations, religious institutions, businesses, the marketplace, and the workplace more generally. Women could be found in positions of decision making at the national level, but also in local associations like parent–teacher associations at the grassroots level. Women's presence became almost mandatory, suggesting that major changes in political culture had occurred. As one activist put it:

Last weekend we were forming a committee of an association for people from my village called the Rukungiri Development Association.... In electing the committee for the development association, somebody said ... "we must have women." That was the first thing he said. "Because if we don't have women things won't get done." Everywhere you go women are more and more visible. And also they have gained the courage and more confidence.[2]

WOMEN'S MOVEMENT

Women's mobilization before and after independence

The second factor that influenced gender regime change was the women's movement, which had its roots in earlier pre- and postcolonial mobilization. Despite the years of institutional decay and conflict, women in Uganda had a slight advantage over women in neighboring countries. They had been educated at the secondary and tertiary levels earlier, and they had enjoyed a longer history of female education, partly due to pressures from Baganda royalty and from women missionaries.

In Uganda, girls were already attending secondary schools in the 1920s, whereas it was not until the late 1940s that girls began to acquire secondary

[2] Interview with 1.3, Kampala, June 19, 2001.

education in Tanganyika and Kenya. Women's early access to secondary and tertiary education in Uganda meant that the country had larger numbers of career women before its neighboring countries. By 1964, women in Uganda were represented in a variety of professions: as members of parliament, doctors, teachers, social workers, as well as members of medical services such as nursing, midwifery, radiology, physiotherapy, and dietetics. Others were serving as civil servants and in private firms. Early on, Ugandan women possessed the experience and skills to lead national women's organizations. Moreover, Uganda had a larger pool of women with the skills to participate in politics, compared with Tanganyika and Kenya at the time. The university-educated women in the 1950s, some of whom had studied in England, provided elite European, Asian, and African women with shared cultural experiences on which they could draw in building friendships and working together.[3] These multiracial coalitions were important to bringing women into politics and advocacy through various women's organizations like the Uganda Council of Women. The UCW was also made up of women of various religions and denominations.[4]

Thus, these early efforts in girls' education had multiple benefits, pushing women and their daughters into new public roles. Far from simply locking women into lives of domesticity and being wives to professional men, as some of the literature on colonial women has implied, these early efforts at educating women expanded their roles in a variety of ways. One has only to compare the early education efforts in Uganda, Liberia, and South Africa with the slower initiatives in Kenya and Tanganyika to gain a sense of what a difference education made.

Female students were granted admission to Makerere in 1945, necessitating Makerere (then named Uganda Technical College) to change its 1922 motto "Let Us Be Men" to "We Build for the Future." In 1955, Eunice Lubega Posnansky became the first female graduate of Makerere University College. She founded the Uganda Association of Women, one of the first organizations advocating women's rights in that country. Sarah Ntiro was the first woman in East and Central Africa to graduate from Oxford in 1954. Sarah Ntiro went on to start the Teaching Service Commission in 1965, where she sought to standardize education in Uganda. She also served on the Uganda Legislative Council. Dr. Josephine Nambooze was the first African woman doctor to graduate from Makerere University College, and she became the first woman professor in Africa in 1959. She also became a medical doctor in 1959. Elizabeth Nyabongo, the Princess of Toro, graduated from Cambridge in 1962 and became the first East African woman admitted to the English Bar in 1965. She later gained notoriety when she served as Idi Amin's roving

---

[3] Interview 1.38, Hema Bhatia, Kampala, July 1995.
[4] Interview 1.39, Barbara Saben, Norfolk, January 1996.

ambassador and later as Minister of Foreign Affairs.[5] Victoria Mwaka, who started the Gender and Women's Studies Department at Makerere, was the first woman to be granted a PhD at the university in 1975 and later served as the deputy chairperson of the Constituent Assembly. She also became one of Makerere's six female professors in a university that had 55 male professors.

The early growth of educational opportunities, even if limited, helped allow for a larger number of female leaders. Already in 1958 women were represented in the Legislative Council. They were involved in organizations like the Mothers Union, Girl Scouts, Young Women's Christian Association (YWCA), and the Family Planning Association. Many of these organizations focused on girls' education and women's domestic roles as mothers and wives; however, many like the Uganda Council of Women (UCW) also sought to broaden women's interests into national and international political concerns, especially in anticipation of independence (Tripp 2000).[6]

The first postindependence government of Milton Obote and his Uganda People's Congress (UPC) party had little interest in advancing women's status in society, yet women were expected to show their support for the Obote government and UPC if they were to benefit in any way from the regime. After independence in 1962, women's associations like the UCW and later the Uganda Association of Women's organizations had their autonomy curtailed and were used by the UPC to expand its patronage networks (White 1973, 91–98). After 1966, when Uganda became a one-party state, the country became increasingly unstable. Like the rest of civil society, women's organizations operated within the context of suppression and intimidation, which involved the banning of large meetings. Women's associations found it increasingly difficult to press for their demands, while their members were reduced to the role of "social hostesses" at UPC functions (Tripp 2000; White 1973, 239).

The situation worsened when Obote's army chief of staff, Idi Amin Dada, staged a military coup on January 25, 1971, and overthrew the government. The Amin regime was marked by economic decay, institutional decline, massive human rights violations on the part of the state, and the expulsion of all Asians from the country in 1972. Women found Amin's various anti-immorality crusades particularly oppressive. He banned miniskirts shorter than 3" above the knee, skirts with long slits, wigs, and trousers as well as creams, perfumes, and deodorants. He also attempted to clear the streets of unmarried women, all of whom were considered prostitutes. Amin's militia attacked women who allegedly violated these bans on the pretext of maintaining law and order, and rape was a frequent terror tactic (Akello 1982).

---

[5] In 1975 Amin unceremoniously fired her and falsely accused her of misappropriating funds and threatening national security by making love to a European in a toilet at Orly Airport in Paris. She was tortured, placed under house arrest, and her reputation was tarnished by the publication of a "nude" photo of her on the front page of a Ugandan newspaper (Decker 2014).

[6] Interview with 1.40, Rebecca Mulira, Kampala, July 2, 1995.

Women wearing miniskirts were stripped in public and harassed. Some girls had their hair cut by crowds.

Amin also ordered the seizure of homes and properties of widows in 1975 on the grounds that their husbands were in exile. This was followed by a presidential declaration ordering the confiscation of all property of Ugandans in exile in 1976, which affected many women and children. In 1977 he decreed the formation of the National Council of Women (NCW), along with the stipulation that "no women's or girls' voluntary organisations shall continue to exist or be formed except in accordance with the provision of this decree." This was his effort to comply with the UN encouragement of the formation of women's policy agencies in 1975. The NCW was to exist under the auspices of the Ministry of Community Affairs. Women's organizations unsuccessfully resisted these efforts to eliminate their associations and protested the harassment of women by the security forces. As a result, many women's organizations ceased to exist, at least at the national level. In this period some worked quietly underground or at the local level (Tripp 2000).

After Amin imposed the ban on women's organizations, Joyce Mungherera, for example, continued her work as a YWCA leader. Amin then directly threatened her with execution if she did not close down the association, so she went into hiding, but continued her work from underground. In 1979, Amin was ousted from power, and women's organizations sought to use the NCW as a forum from which they could network (Katumba 1979). NCW's independence was short-lived. Milton Obote, who came back to power for a second time in 1980, sought to link the Council to his UPC party, although this too met with resistance from women (Guwatudde 1987, 11). The council remained a semiparastatal under the Ministry of Community Development during Obote's second government, while the Women's Wing of the UPC sought to control all women's organizations through the NCW, much to the dismay of women activists. As former president of NCW and former women's minister Joyce Mpanga explained: "Until 1986 when the NRM came into power, we were not allowed to choose our own office bearers ... mostly they choose people who would not articulate anything that was anti-governmental."[7]

Ugandan women leaders point to the 1985 Decade of Women conference in Nairobi as a catalyst for autonomous female mobilization in that country. Many women activists attended the conference on their own rather than as part of an official delegation. Women came back both cognizant of the fact that Uganda had fallen behind other countries with respect to women's status, but also inspired to reinvigorate women's mobilization in the context of the new NRM-led government that had taken over. Victoria Ssekitoleko, led the nongovernment organization of women to Nairobi. As she explained:

---

[7] Interview 1.10, Joyce Mpanga, Kampala, 1.7.1995.

First and foremost I discovered that Ugandan women were very far behind.... Because when I looked at the way others had prepared, most of us didn't know what to expect when we got there. The first and most important thing is actually to "conscientize" the women, because quite a number of women had expected the situation they were in as given. Anyway, it [Nairobi] did one thing for all of us: it whetted us, so when we got back here we managed to organize the real [International] Women's day, the first real Women's Day which was well organized...By then we knew exactly what was expected of us.[8]

Uganda also saw the beginnings of peace mobilization at this time. The Ugandan peace initiatives in the mid-1980s were among the first at the national level in Africa. There certainly had been efforts in all countries at the local level, but national level efforts were few and far between. Soon after Tito Okello came to power in a coup in September 1985, the NCW organized a protest in Kampala on September 6, 1985, of over 2,000 women to demand peace and an end to the mistreatment of women by soldiers (Ankrah 1987, 15; "Women in Uganda Stage ..." 1985). At that time insecurity was at its height in the capital: Schoolgirls were being kidnapped in Luwero and taken to the barracks, while women were being harassed at roadblocks. Kampala was divided and under the control of various fighting factions. The peace march ended at the parliament building, where the leader of the march, Florence Nekyon, handed a note to the chairman of the Military Council, Tito Okello, saying, "Ugandans are sick and tired of fighting, bloodshed, untold and unnecessary suffering." It urged the military and political leadership "and all those in the position to exert influence and all the fighting forces to put aside personal and parochial interests and ambitions and put the over-all interests of all Ugandans first" ("Women in Uganda ..." 1985).

The committee of women's NGOs that had planned the peace march also wrote to the Minister of Internal Affairs and to the Minister of Defense in October 1985, complaining of the treatment of women at the roadblocks. They condemned the fact that many women were being forced into marriages in Luwero District and were being raped. The memorandum called for the elimination of roadblocks, the medical treatment and compensation for women who had been brutalized, the punishment of soldiers who were guilty of these crimes, and the issuing of identity cards for all (Ankrah 1987, 14).[9] The Defense Ministry said it would investigate the charges (Tripp 2000).

The committee followed up with a second more hard-hitting memorandum in December 1985, linking the issues of peace and women's political power as we later saw in other movements. They demanded that women be consulted on key national issues and be given key ministerial posts and positions, arguing that the inability of women to penetrate power structures and have a say on

---

[8] Minister of Agriculture, Victoria Ssekitoleko, Entebbe Offices, Uganda, February 1990. Interview with Dee Aker.

[9] Interview with 1.1, Kampala, December 1992.

matters of war and peace stood in the way of peace (Ankrah 1987, 16). Even though the Okello regime was toppled before they were able to respond, the memorandum was significant because it was evidence of a shift taking place in women's mobilization, away from party- and state-affiliated mobilization to that of autonomous women's rights mobilization. This was a shift that was to take place through much of Africa after the 1990s.

The women's NGO committee also organized a peace seminar, which was attended by the minister of foreign affairs, Olara Otunnu, and the commander of the army, General Basilio Okello. At the seminar, the general told the women that they deserved to be raped. He said that it was the women who made his army steal: "You ask for handbags, watches, perfumes, nice shoes, nice dresses, so where do you think my men will get them? That is why they steal" (Tripp 2000, 58). The women were fearless in confronting the military officials.

Interestingly, Professor Kabwegyere, who has been a longtime supporter of the NRM and is presently in the Ugandan cabinet, gave a paper at the workshop advising the women that they should insist on having a woman at the peace talks that were held in Nairobi 1985 between the Ugandan government of Tito Okello and the National Resistance Army (NRA), which then was a rebel group led by Yoweri Museveni. The women's organizations demanded that they be represented, but they were not accommodated. The NRM had three women (Gertrude Njuba, Hope Kivengere, and Winnie Karagwa Byanyima) at the 1985 Nairobi negotiations. Kivengere was an observer, and Njuba was the only female signatory of the peace accords. The accords were signed in December 1985, but the cease-fire soon fell apart as the NRA took over the country in January 1986 (Kiplagat 2010; Nyanzi 2004).

Women's movement

The opening of political space in the late 1980s and early 1990s was accompanied by an increase in political will on the part of the Museveni government to be more inclusive of women and other groups that had been sidelined, mostly as a means of expanding political patronage (Muriaas and Wang 2012; Tripp 2000). Initially there was even openness to a broad-based government that encompassed all political parties that were represented in Museveni's first cabinet. Although this opening soon began to shrink, it was sufficient to energize the women's movement and allow for some initial gains. Early on Museveni won political support, especially from women, for adopting key policy measures that favored them and for bringing women into political leadership, even into top positions. Women were quite enthusiastic about the NRM and its antisectarian stance in the early honeymoon period of the early 1990s, and this, in turn, encouraged Museveni to continue backing women's rights and women leaders, even as he demonstrated less support for other forms of inclusiveness along ethnic lines. I have written elsewhere (Tripp 2010a) extensively about the limits of democratization in Uganda and the persistence of a semiauthoritarian hybrid regime in the country. While those same limits have been felt by women's rights activists, as this chapter shows, there was sufficient political opening to allow women to mobilize and press their demands.

About 30 women had attended the UN Conference on Women in Nairobi, many of whom had been dropped from the official government delegation, and they returned to Uganda determined to begin mobilizing women in order to have political impact. They returned on July 22, 1985, and on August 5, Action for Development (ACFODE) began to lobby the new government to place women in key decision-making positions.[10] The organizations that emerged in this period were quite unlike those that had been formed under Obote. They had autonomy in the selection of leaders, in their agendas, and in sources of funding. They were also more heterogeneous in the kinds of issues they took up. There were professional associations (women doctors, engineers, scientists, entrepreneurs) and advocacy groups (formed around reproductive rights, violence against women, disability, as well as concerns of refugees, widows, and second wives in polygamous relationships). Other groups formed to provide services to women, such as microcredit, legal aid, and education. Cultural organizations formed to promote women authors, musicians, and athletes. At the local level, a wide variety of multipurpose clubs engaged in savings, farming, income-generating projects, handicrafts, sports, cultural events, and other functions, depending on the needs and priorities of members.

National level networks formed while other organizations served as local chapters of Africa-wide networks such as the Forum for African Women's Educationalists (FAWE); Women in Law and Development (WILDAF); Akina Mama wa Africa, and many others. Others were regionally based, including Women and Law in East Africa and Southern Africa. Still others were part of international associations such as the International Federation of Women Lawyers (FIDA), YWCA, and Girl Guides.

Older organizations prior to 1986 had formed around nonpolitical concerns such as development, income generation, handicrafts, as well as advancing home economics skills. With the new political dispensation, an emphasis on political participation emerged in the late 1980s and early 1990s, especially with the introduction of quotas and the constitution-making process. New nonpartisan women's organizations formed to improve leadership skills, encourage women's political involvement, lobby for women's political leadership, press for legislative changes, and conduct civic education. Women's associations started mobilizing around issues like domestic violence, rape, reproductive rights, sex education in the school curriculum, the disparaging representation of women in the media, and corruption. They also took up other concerns that had rarely been addressed by the women's movements in the past

---

[10] Interview with 1.34, Maxine Ankrah, Kampala June 19, 1992.

and often were considered taboo by the government and society, such as female genital cutting and marital rape.

There is no one organization that claims to represent all women's associations in the way that the NCW did in the past, although there are umbrella and networking associations. Nevertheless, there has been greater cohesion among women's organizations than among any other societal sectors in Uganda despite the diversity of agendas and goals. For example, women's organizations wrote more memoranda to the Constitutional Commission than any other sector of society (Bainomugisha 1999, 93). They organized workshops nationwide to discuss the constitution and made concerted efforts to have an impact on its outcome at every step of the way and on many fronts. Women's impact on the Ugandan constitution-making process, which was a watershed moment for women's rights activists in this country, is explored in greater detail in Chapter 7. Uganda's women are highly organized even by world standards. To take one example, with 1.5 million dues-paying members and a staff of 1,000, the YWCA in Uganda is not only one of the largest nongovernmental organizations in Africa, but also Uganda has had for a long time the largest YWCA affiliate of in the world.

The number of networks, coalitions, and ad hoc issue-oriented alliances has multiplied in Uganda, and women's networks are among them. For example, the Gender and Growth Assessment Coalition has been active around issues of women's access to land and finance, the reform of labor laws, and commercial justice. There is also a Uganda Women's Coalition for Peace, Coalition Against Violence Against Women, Uganda Women's Network (UWONET), and many others. Women's organizations have also taken leadership of coalitions around issues that go well beyond more narrowly defined "women's issues," including land rights, hunger, debt, corruption, and poverty. Women are bringing their perspectives and concerns to bear on a wide range of social justice issues.

Because of historic divisions of labor, women may have a more hands-on pragmatic approach to problem solving, which is why they are so engaged in these organizations and why in a moment of transition they become so energized. As one activist explained:

> Of course when you look at the community level it is very obvious: Women always want to do something about a situation, they want to organize to do something. . . . Men talk about it but I think they are used to women doing it. . . . And even then you hear them saying "Ah, why haven't women done something about it? You women, what have you done about it?" Sometimes I think we have done more than our share of contributing to society.[11]

Although the changes in women's position in society have been significant, for activists they have seemed far too slow, and that too is an indication of changed expectations. It is important to recognize that there are multiple agendas at work here.

---

[11] Interview with 1.4, Kampala, June 9, 2001.

The women's movement has had its own goals, but so too has the country's leadership. As in many countries, the Museveni regime has done only as much as it has been pushed to do by the women's movement and by donors. In some cases Museveni adopted policies that favored women such as Universal Primary Education and Universal Secondary Education prior to elections in a bid to gain votes. In other instances, many of Uganda's gender-related policies were adopted to spread patronage to new constituencies and to gain political support from women. These motivations often placed important constraints on women's rights activists.

Women strongly supported Museveni in the 1996 presidential elections; however, this support subsequently diminished, especially among women leaders, after he withdrew support of an amendment to the 1998 Land Act that would have provided the right to spousal co-ownership of land. In 2006, the government also shelved a Domestic Relations bill, which had been proposed in various iterations for the past twenty years. As a result, some women leaders became disillusioned with the regime and started to align themselves more closely with opposition parties.

While the relatively large numbers of women in the parliament have been an indication of the success of women's lobbying for greater representation, some feel that women parliamentarians have been constrained and coopted. As former Ugandan parliamentarian and women's rights activist Miria Matembe explained at a 2012 United Nations Development Programme (UNDP) conference I attended in Nairobi: "Our voice has been hijacked at the highest organs, at parliament. Our voice there has been killed." Some argue that the affirmative action seats in parliament have created a group of legislators more beholden to the NRM in their loyalties than to the cause of women's emancipation (Tamale 1999). At the same time, not all women parliamentarians toe the NRM line, and with the increased disillusionment with the NRM, support among women has tapered off in parliament and within the movement.

INTERNATIONAL INFLUENCES

A third factor in explaining gender regime change – international influences – became increasingly evident in Uganda as the country emerged out of conflict in 1986. The Danish International Development Agency (DANIDA), SNV-Novib, and other donors were keen to support women's mobilization for change. Certainly the donors had been active elsewhere, even in postconflict contexts like Zimbabwe after 1980, supporting gender-related programming, but Uganda was the first country where major national shifts in policy and women's political leadership became apparent.

However, many of the gender policy innovations in Uganda also predated the expansion of UN and donor influences in that country, suggesting that internal dynamics were decisive. The 1985 UN Conference of Women in Nairobi had an impact on the nascent women's movement. But pressure as a result of changing international norms did not seriously mount until after the UN Beijing Conference on Women. The UN and donors played an important role in Uganda after the Ministry of Gender was established and with the emergence of women's NGOs, but their lack of influence at a critical moment when decisions regarding female political representation were made in the late 1980s shows the overriding importance of domestic actors. Even the creation of the Ministry of Women in 1988, which donors later supported, came about as a result of pressure from women activists in 1986 as did the creation of the Department of Women's Studies at Makerere University.[12]

GENDER REGIME CHANGE

The changes in gender regime that resulted from the gender disruptions, women's movement, and international influences were not just changes in gender policy – although that was an important aspect of the transformation – they were also reflective of normative and symbolic changes within society itself.

As we have seen, when it came to women's rights, the NRM was not consistently supportive of key demands of the women's movement, and this became even clearer later on around legislation pertaining to domestic relations and land inheritance. This is because the NRM did not have a clear program in women's rights and relied heavily on key women leaders to push various issues. The appointment of Specioza Kazibwe and Janat Mukwaya to head the ministry of gender – both of whom were known more for their commitment to the NRM than to women's causes – reveals the lack of appreciation of women's concerns in the Museveni government and how easily they were overridden by political considerations and loyalty. However, Uganda is no exception in this regard. One could say much the same of many other governments that adopted women's rights policies: that their commitment was largely utilitarian rather than based on a deep appreciation of the issues at stake. In the case of Uganda, these concerns had more to do with redistributing patronage to include new groups like women.

What form, then, did the gender regime take in Uganda? What was its scope, and what were its limits? Perhaps the most visible changes were at the level of government leadership.

Women and public leadership

Women made important gains in a variety of areas of leadership. However, this did not happen on its own, nor did it happen as a result of external pressures, as some have suggested. After the NRM took over, leaders of the NCW, Action

<hr>

[12] Interview with 1.34, Maxine Ankrah, Kampala, June 19, 1992.

for Development (ACFODE) and other women's NGOs met with President Museveni to demand more political representation of women. They sent him resumes and made recommendations of women qualified to fill key positions. The efforts of women were independent of any donor or UN pressures and illustrate the importance of domestic champions of women's representation.

The appointment of women was not a foregone conclusion, as there had not even been one woman appointed to the first cabinet. Only three members of the 38-member wartime National Resistance Council were women (Gertrude Njuba, Joy Mirembe, and Olivia Zizinga). Museveni had not included any mention of women in his Ten Point Programme during the Bush War and was highly suspicious of NGO activity right after the war (Tripp 2000). Like Angola, the pressure came primarily from activists associated with the ruling party. By 1999, the NRM's Ten Point Programme was updated to include fifteen points, one of which supported affirmative action as a means of encouraging political, social and economic participation of marginalized groups. It was included with the explicit intent of appealing to a female constituency (Goetz 2002, 570). It should be pointed out, however, that the adoption of the 30 percent quota for women in local government leadership was in part an extension of the NRM practice of setting aside seats for women in the resistance councils formed at the local level during the Bush War.

Women in parliament

Women were appointed to positions in the government and judiciary, and gender quotas were adopted in the legislature. There had been 1 woman in the National Assembly in 1980. By 1989, after quota was introduced, women held 18 percent of the seats, and by 2015 they held 35 percent. With each election, increasing numbers of women ran for the open constituency seats rather than the reserved quota seats. In 1989 only two women won constituency seats. This number increased to fifteen by 2006 and then dropped to eleven in 2011. The biggest change, however, was in the numbers of women running for office: this jumped from 135 in 1996 to 443 in 2011 (see Table 3.2, Inter-Parliamentary Union 1995).

Rebecca Kadaga claimed the position of first female speaker of the Ugandan Parliament in 2011, one of only a handful of female speakers in Africa. In Uganda's parliament, half of the standing (or permanent) committees are headed by women and half by men, but of the sessional committees (commencing with a new parliamentary session and lasting as long as necessary), only a quarter are headed by women. Because the speaker of the house is a woman, she also heads the Appointments Committee and the Parliament Business Committee. Women tend to head up committees like the HIV/AIDS, human rights, business, and equal opportunities standing committees rather than the heftier budget, national economy, public accounts, defense, internal affairs, and foreign affairs committees. Nevertheless, the current committee leadership

TABLE 3.2 *Women in Uganda's Parliaments (1962–2011)*

	1962	1967	1980	1989	1996	2001	2006	2011
Women contesting for parliament					135	203	226	443
Women running for constituency seats	NA	NA	NA		26	32	35	46
Women in reserved district seats	NA	NA	NA	34	39	56	79	112
Women in constituency seats	NA	NA	1	2	8	13	15	11
Women in reserved youth seats	NA	NA	NA			2	1	2
Women reserved disabled seats	NA	NA	NA			2	1	2
Women in reserved army seats	NA	NA	NA	0	0	0	2	2
Women in reserved labor seats	NA	NA	NA			1	2	2
Others	NA	NA	NA	1		1	1	4
Total MPs	90	82	126	238	276	304	305	386
Women MPs	2	0	1	42	52	75	101	135
% of women MPs	2	0	1	18	19	25	31	35

Source: Cabinet Library, Inter-Parliamentary Union 1995, Wang 2013a.

structure is an improvement over 2000, when women served as chairs of only two out of the twelve standing committees and two of the ten sessional committees.

Because the NRM dominates in the parliament, the majority of female MPs belong to the party. However, other parties have also promoted women's leaders. Alice Alaso is the secretary of the leading opposition party, Forum for Democratic Change. Beti Olive Kamya-Turwomwe became the first woman in Uganda to start a political party in 2010, the Uganda Federal Alliance. Miria Obote had been the president of the Uganda Peoples Congress (UPC) from 2005 until 2010 and ran for president in the 2006 election. Cecilia Ogwal served as UPC's Acting Secretary General between 1985 and 1992.

Women in the executive branch

The patterns evident in the legislature have been visible in the executive branch as well. Speciosa Kazibwe served as vice president for ten years from 1993–2013 and is to date the longest-serving female vice president in Africa. Most deputy presidents have served fairly short terms in Africa. In 1988 there was one woman in the cabinet (Victoria Ssekitoleko). A year later there were eight. By 2015 women held one-third of the cabinet positions. Although women are often placed in positions such as minister of Gender, Labour and Social Affairs, Education and Sports, Tourism and Wildlife and other "softer" ministries, they have also been appointed to positions such as minister of Defense, Internal Affairs, Trade and Industry, and Justice, and Constitutional Affairs.

Women in government bureaucracy

As in many countries, women are most visible in the second tier of top administrative positions. In Uganda, women constitute 37 percent of all permanent secretaries, 32 percent of ambassadors, 23 percent of public service directors, 20 percent of commissioners, and 82 percent of all undersecretaries (Rubimbwa 2010). Women have been appointed to key commissions like the Constitutional Commission, Education Review Commission, and Public Service Reorganisation Commission. It is notable that several key commissions have also been chaired by women who have made their mark, such as Margaret Sekaggya, who has led the Uganda Human Rights Commission (UHRC). Florence Mugasha was the first woman to head up the Public Service Commission and held this post from 1996–2002. During her tenure, women came to claim 44 percent of the positions on the Public Service Commission.

Women have also effectively served in other government leadership posts. Allen Kagina has been Commissioner General of the Uganda Revenue Authority. Her penchant for efficiency has allowed the Authority reach record collections, reduce corruption and bribery at the agency, and expand the taxpayer registry. As a result of her leadership, tax collections grew 317.5 percent between 2004 and 2013/14 (Sanya 2014b).

Other women leaders have also been influential. Maggie Kigozi has headed up the Uganda Investment Authority since 1999 and was extremely successful bringing in new investments, particularly from diasporic Ugandans. She has also helped advance women's investment and entrepreneurship ("UIA in New Push ..." 2001).

Kampala City Council Executive Director Jenifer Musisi Semakula has won a reputation of doing what previous EDs were unable to do. She is filling potholes, creating sidewalks, planting trees, and recovering green areas. She improved one of the largest markets and created a new taxi park. She got the motorcycle taxis (*boda boda*) drivers to register and presided over a highly successful City Carnival. Many other women have similarly made a difference in improving transparency and efficiency in government (Kafeero 2013).

Women in the judiciary

In the judiciary, a woman was appointed a High Court justice in 1986. By 1994 women made up 17 percent of judges and 23 percent of chief magistrates (Busharizi and Emasu 1995; Kakwenzire 1990; Matembe 1991). Today, of the eight Supreme Court justices, three are women and of the forty-six High Court judges, twenty are women. A 2012 study showed that about one-third of the justices on the court of appeal and one-third of the chief magistrates are women while 47 percent of the Magistrate Grade 1 are women (Global Network of Women Peacebuilders 2012).

The no-nonsense judge Julia Sebutinde became the first African woman to serve on the International Court of Justice in 2011. Prior to that appointment she had been seconded to the UN-backed Special Court for Sierra Leone and in 2007 was appointed the presiding judge in the trial of the former president of Liberia, Charles Taylor. She had served on the High Court in Uganda and directed three Judicial Commissions of Inquiry into Corruption in the Police Force, the Uganda People's Defence Force, and the Uganda Revenue Authority. In a relentless investigation, she uncovered serious cases of abuse, brutality, and corruption that reached all the way to the top. Her performance was so remarkable that minibus drivers pinned her picture on their windscreens to scare off policemen seeking bribes. As the hearings unfolded, her name became a household word: "to Sebutinde someone" became a popular way of talking about exposing lies (Kafeero 2013). As a result, Sebutinde has a reputation in Uganda of being an independent mind who is unafraid of speaking truth to power.

Outside the state sector, women leaders in the judiciary have also been strongly represented. Speaker of the House Rebecca Kadaga had been the first female Ugandan lawyer to open a law firm in Uganda in 1984. Salome Bossa (who later become a High Court judge) was the first woman elected to be head of the Uganda Law Society in 1993 and was followed by several other women, including Harriet Diana Musoke and Ruth Sebatindira. Laetitia Mukasa-Kikonyogo took over the presidency of the International Association of Women Judges in 2002, making her the first African president of the organization. In 1997, Mukasa-Kikonyogo was appointed the first woman justice of the Supreme Court of Uganda and later the first woman Deputy Chief Justice. In 2001 she became head of the Court of Appeal and president of the Constitutional Court of Uganda (Nsambu 2013). She has played a key role in defending the rights of opposition politicians who came under pressure from the executive as well as the independence of the judiciary.

Military and police

The locus of power in Uganda is with the president and the military, and in particular the high command of the military. Women have never been represented in this body, thus limiting their power. In the security sector, Lt. Col. Rebecca Mpagi became the first woman pilot in 1986, and in 2011 Proscovia Nalweyiso became the first woman to rise to the rank of brigadier in the history of the country. Similarly, military women make up only 1,566 of the soldiers in the Uganda People's Defense Forces (UPDF). While this is three times more than the number of female soldiers in 2000, it is only a fraction of the army. According to a 2010 CEWIGO report, there is a 1:99 ratio of women to men at the rank of colonel; 2:99 at the rank of lieutenant colonel; 3:97 at major; 6:94 at captain; 2:98 at lieutenant; and 11:89 at second lieutenant level. Until there are more rank-and-file women, it is unlikely there will be more changes within the higher echelons of the armed forces (Rubimbwa 2010).

Steps have been taken to make it easier for women to join and remain in the police force. Assistant Commissioner of Police Quartermaster Elizabeth Muwanga got an archaic rule overturned in the police force so that women police no longer would have to apply to the Inspector General for permission to get married. When police desks for women bringing complaints of domestic abuse and rape were introduced at stations in the early 1990s, this necessitated the hiring of more women police officers. Women still make up only 14 percent of police force and are situated mainly in lower positions. There are, however, a few exceptions. Elizabeth Kuteesa was the first woman to head up the Criminal Investigations Directorate (CID). In 2012, she was appointed an INTERPOL director, making her the first African to hold such a position in the world's largest international police organization (Candia 2012).

Women's economic activities

Women's entrepreneurial activity exploded after 1986, not just with small and medium-sized businesses and informal-sector activities but also larger-scale activities (Snyder, M. 2000). Women began talking about "touching money" in the 1990s in ways they had not done in the past. Access to an income improved their status within the household, although at times it added to tensions when women were seen as having greater access to resources than their husbands. Having greater economic clout has meant that women are listened to and are taken more seriously in community gatherings. Today there are women who have built up major businesses, have significant real estate holdings and large-scale investments, and are engaged in international trade. Many women are now demanding business management training, rather than simply cooking and handicraft skills.

One indication of women's changing role in business was the election of Olive Zaitun Kigongo as the first woman president of Uganda National Chamber of Commerce and Industry already in 2002. Women have also formed their own business associations such as Ugandan Women Entrepreneurs Association (UWEAL), which has promoted the purchasing of locally made products, created awareness of business and entrepreneurship among young women, established a mentoring program, helped women transition from the microenterprise to small and medium enterprise level by improving the performance of their businesses, and it has improved financial literacy,

Today there are businesswomen in Uganda operating in key niches and at a level that was not evident in the 1990s.[13] Maria Kiwanuka was the first Ugandan woman to own two radio stations. She later became finance minister. Alice Karugaba runs a successful and well-known furniture outlet, Nina Interiors. Benedicta Nanyonga makes bags, belts, and shoes from used drinking straws and sells them in international markets. Regina Mukiibi is the first female funeral director. These are just a few examples of the types of entrepreneurship women are engaging in.

Scottish Carol Cooke noted, when making a film about Ugandan businesswomen, that the country's "growing band of female entrepreneurs ... are defying the statistics, cultural stereotypes and credit restrictions and are taking the business world by storm. They are putting so-called hard working Western business women like me to shame on a daily basis."[14]

Today, 40 percent of businesses are owned by women, and yet just 7 percent of all credit is allocated to them. Although there have been a variety of traditional microfinance programs, new models of banking led by women are emerging as a result. The Uganda Women's Finance Trust was formed in 1984 by a group of women professionals to provide microcredit to women. In 2014 the Trust was transformed into the Uganda Finance Trust Bank, which is the first commercial bank wholly established by enterprising women to provide financial services to low- and medium-income people, especially women. It has a staff of 400 and a network of thirty-three branches, with 70 percent of branches in rural areas. It is owned by the Uganda Women's Finance Trust, Uganda Women Entrepreneurs, and Ugandan Sun Mutual Cooperative Saving, as well as by the Dutch Oikocredit and the French Investment & Partner (Sanya 2014a). This bank is a good example of the ways in which financial institutions are scaling up from microcredit to meet the needs of a new group of female entrepreneurs.

Women are not only helping other women by providing finance services. They are also engaged in top financial institutions. Edigold Monday is the only Ugandan woman to have risen to the position of a managing director of a top Africa-wide bank. In 2008 she had been appointed the first Ugandan female managing director of a commercial bank in 2008. Under her directorship, the Bank of Africa strengthened its financial position, growing its assets by 91 percent, deposits by 85 percent and loans and advances by 74 percent (Ladu 2014).

Women and education

The women's movement was especially active in the area of education policy and made major efforts to get girls educated at the primary level. We have seen

[13] Interview with 1.36, Mary Nannono, Coordinator, Council for Economic Empowerment for Women in Africa (CEEWA-UGANDA), Kampala, CEEWA, May 30, 2011.
[14] http://barefootinbusiness.com.

the ratio of girls to boys in primary schools jump from 79 percent in 1985 to 102 percent in 2011; from 53 percent at the secondary level in 1986 to 84 percent in 2009; and from 30 percent at the tertiary level to 80 percent in 2009, according to World Bank data.

Girls drop out from school at rates higher than boys because of early marriage, pregnancy, and family obligations that necessitate working. Girls also suffer sexual abuse, violence, and harassment in schools. Women activists have targeted female literacy. As a result of policy changes, by 2010, the gender gap between boys and girls in literacy was only 5 percent compared with 18 percent in 1991 (ages 15–24).[15] Overall the literacy rate for women (over age 15) increased from 45 percent in 1995 to 65 percent in 2012 (MGLSD 2014).

As a result of affirmative action policies promoted by women's organizations, the numbers of women in leading institutions of higher education have increased significantly. In addition to getting admissions policies changed, women activists established a scholarship program for disadvantaged women. Women also took the helm of universities such as Professor Mary Nakandha Okwakol, who was appointed the first Vice Chancellor of Busitema University in 2009. Professor Joy Kwesiga was appointed vice chancellor of Kabale University, after having served as dean of the Faculty of Social Sciences at Makerere University. She had been part of an initiative at Makerere University to increase female university scholarships for disadvantaged students. Maggie Kigozi was Chancellor of Nkumba University and now of Busoga University. It would have been unthinkable to have women in such positions even a decade earlier.

Women and health

Ugandan women have not only been leaders in the field of health in Uganda, they have gained international visibility because of their efforts. The AIDS activist Noerine Kaleeba, who started the first major AIDS activist group in Uganda, AIDS Support Organization (TASO), was promoted to UNAIDS Programme Development Advisor for Africa. Psychiatrist Margaret Mungherera became president of the World Medical Association in 2013 and also was the first African woman president of the association. Dr. Specioza Wandira Kazibwe was appointed UN Special Envoy on HIV/AIDS.

Women's organizations have also contributed to some of the positive results we see today in the area of health. Safe Motherhood, for example, has been very active in the field of women's maternal health. As a result of work by these types of organizations, fertility rates in Uganda, which are still high, nevertheless went down from 7.1 children to 6.0. Today, 93 percent of pregnant women

[15] http://databank.worldbank.org/.

receive prenatal care. Maternal mortality is also high, standing at 310 deaths per 100,000 live births in 2010, but it decreased from 505 in 2001. Illegal abortions account for many of these deaths. HIV rates for women are higher than for men: 4.0 percent for women compared with 2.3 percent for men in 2012 according to World Health Organization data. Women's organizations have been particularly active in promoting sex education in the school curriculum and have been founders and leaders of key organizations working in the area of HIV/AIDS education. Women activists have also been involved in associations improving traditional birth attendant skills and advancing reproductive rights more generally.

Nevertheless, reproductive health services and sex education are seriously inadequate, and activism continues to highlight these deficiencies. In March 2011, for example, the Centre for Health Human Rights and Development, together with a university lecturer at Makerere University, Ben Twinomugisha, took the attorney general to court, accusing the government of failing to provide basic maternal facilities in government health centers and tolerating imprudent and unethical behavior of health workers toward expectant mothers (Bath 2013).

Women and the media, culture, and sports

Women media workers, and especially the Uganda Media Women's Association (UMWA), actively sought to change the image of women in the media and to promote female media workers. UMWA executive director, Margaret Sentamu Masagazi, and three other women, launched the first and only radio station run and owned by women in Africa, Mama 101.7 FM, in 2001 to give greater voice to women's concerns and issues on air.

Agnes Konde Assimwe became the first Ugandan woman to be appointed managing director of NTV. With a strong track record as a brand and marketing expert, she has made the station highly competitive and has been able to prevent it from being outrivaled by upcoming competitors. Victoria Nalongo Namusisi was Uganda's first woman sports journalist. She later became a Resident District Commissioner of Mpigi and was elected the first woman in Africa to hold the position of Chief Scout Commissioner of Uganda's Scouts in 1999.

Prior to 1995 there were only a handful of published women writers. Since then there has been a flowering of women's literary creativity after the formation of the Uganda Women Writers Association that goes by the acronym FEMWRITE. It was established to promote a culture of reading and writing, help women authors improve their skills, publish their work, and network the community of writers. Subsequently there was an upsurge in women's literary output, which had an impact on the entire field of literature in Uganda (Ebila 2002). Today there are numerous women authors of fiction with national reputations, including Susan Kiguli, Mary Karooro Okurut, Regina Amolo,

Violet Barungi, Ayeta Ann Wangusa, the late Goretti Kyomuhendo, Lalobo Oryema, Jane Kaberuka, and many others.

Women have also made their mark in sports, which was previously dominated by men. For example, the Uganda Women Football Association successfully introduced women's soccer throughout the country. They sought corporate and government sponsorship for games, equipment, training, and uniforms (Zziwa 1996). Women's netball similarly became popular throughout the country. Two Ugandan women boxers, Betty Nalukwago and Irene Semakula, started competing in Africa-wide tournaments in 2001. There are now numerous women race car drivers in rallies, including sisters Eve and Betty Ntege, Irene "Leila" Blick (Mayanja), and Rose Lwakataka. In 2011, Ugandan motorsport driver Susan Muwonge became the first woman to win the National Rally Championship.

Women are breaking into other new fields as well. At 19, Phiona Mutesi earned the title of Woman Candidate Master in chess and made history when in 2010 she became the first Ugandan to play against a world champion.

THE IMPACT OF LOCALIZED WAR IN NORTHERN UGANDA

The aforementioned developments have forever changed the gendered landscape of the country's political, economic, social, and cultural institutions. The Bush War that ended in 1986 continued in northern Uganda's seventeen districts, as parts of the former national army fled to their home region in the north and into Southern Sudan. However, the conflict in the north, which lasted from 1987 to 2006, did not have the same widespread postconflict consequences as the 1980–86 war because it affected only one part of the country, albeit a large region, and did not result in changes at the helm of national power. Moreover, it was in part an interstate proxy war involving Sudan and Uganda, which also mitigated against gender regime change for reasons discussed in Chapter 1.

Nevertheless, similar patterns of gender disruption were evident after the conflict ended in northern Uganda. In many cases in northern and northeastern Uganda, women become the key decision makers and breadwinners in the family (Binder et al. 2008). Life was dire during the years of war between the Lord's Resistance Army (LRA) and the Ugandan government. For most Ugandans in other parts of the country, the war in the north seemed remote and was rarely covered in the media.

Because of a lack of information about the war, for a long time there was relatively little response to it by civil society in the rest of Uganda, although there were women's organizations like ISIS-WICCE that worked on peacemaking early on. The Uganda Women's Network (UWONET), which was based in the south, also criticized the government for not involving women in decisions about the war and for tribalizing the conflict. Northern Acholi women like Christine Lalobo similarly pressed for a peaceful settlement of the conflict ("Uganda Women to Form Lobby . . ." 1996). By the mid-2000s, more voices of women activists began to be heard.

The northern conflict resulted in the displacement of up to 2.5 million people in camps for the internally displaced peoples (IDPs), in the deaths of over 250,000 people, and in the abduction of tens of thousands of children and adults. As a result of the war, average incomes dropped from US$465 in 1999 to US$120 in 2003. Women did the bulk of the farming and 79 percent of household duties (Action Against Hunger 2003).

Women held their families together by engaging in small businesses and farming as best they could on limited plots of land surrounding the IDP camps within a 1 to 5 kilometer radius. In IDP camps near Gulu, some had brick-making businesses or engaged in the brewing of millet, which created its own set of alcohol-related problems. Others raised goats, cows, chickens, pigs, and turkeys. They grew and sold beans, millet, sesame, tomatoes, maize, cabbage, greens, eggplants, sorghum, and cassava. Local citizens could cultivate only between 9 A.M. and 4 P.M. five days a week because they had to observe a government-imposed curfew. They could not work Friday and Sunday because the LRA would attack them for working on these Christian and Muslim holy days, as the LRA adhered to both religions simultaneously. IDP women had to rent land or work as laborers to obtain a livelihood. Even then they often faced the risk of confronting rebels while farming. Moreover, both rebels and government forces stole their crops. This all took place under the threat of violence from both the rebels and the government troops. Soldiers regularly humiliated and intimidated people in the IDP camps, raped women, and exchanged sex for food with young women. They beat them if they violated the curfew or spoke at night in their huts.[16]

Women not only took on the role of provider in the household, they took on new leadership roles in the community. They engaged in rotating credit associations and developed new entrepreneurial skills. Sadly, many men gave in to the severe hardships of the time and resorted to drinking, which led them to take out their frustrations on women through abusive behavior.

Unlike the men, the women I interviewed in 2005 had self-help organizations. And while groups in the southern part of the country that had names that spoke of strength in togetherness and how much they could accomplish when united, the names of the organizations in Gulu reflected how extreme life had become. They included such names as: Poverty Follows Me, Where Should I Go? Poverty Does Not Leave Us, The Poor Do Not Sleep, Poverty Is Not a Relative, Fighting Follows Us, We Have No Hope, No Strength, and Digging Sand Is Hard. Some were involved in cultural groups and engaged in drama, dance, and singing, partly to forget their many problems.

---

[16] Interviews with women in Pabbo (1.18–1.25), Unyama (1.5–1.17), and Palenga (1.26–1.33) IDP camps 2005.

Peace activities

Organizations like the Teso Women Peace Activists, Kitgum Women's Peace Initiative, Gulu District Women's Development Committee, and Women Peace Initiatives played important roles in local dispute settlement, and as peace activists they provided services to victims of conflict, organized local peace groups and clubs, and set up detention centers for returnees who had been abducted by the Lord's Resistance Army (LRA). Women worked to appeal to fighters to come back home and sought various means to persuade their husbands, sons, and other male relatives from engaging in the war. The International Crisis Group found that women's organizations in Uganda were better connected and more active than comparable organizations in the Democratic Republic of Congo and Sudan. This may have been a function of the fact that women's mobilization was more extensive in Uganda and was more connected to networks in Africa and globally.

Women's organizations protested the armed conflict between northern rebel forces of the Lord's Resistance Army and the government forces that intensified after 1989. The Gulu District Women's Development Committee organized a peace march of more than 1,500 women in April 1989 to protest the "bitterness of the war." Some fighters returned home, and a period of calm followed the protests. The women-led Concerned Parents Association raised international awareness of child abductions and continued to negotiate with the LRA for the release of girls who had been kidnapped from St. Mary's College Aboke (Lacy 2003). Women worked with demobilized ex-combatants in reintegration, reconciliation, and regeneration projects. Yet leaders of such organizations were systematically left out of talks between the Ugandan government and the LRA despite their many efforts at peace building.

These strategies took on a national character when women peace activists from around Uganda organized a Women's Peace Caravan in November 2006 that crossed the country from Kampala to Kitgum and then on to Juba, Sudan, where peace talks were being held between representatives of both the LRA and the Ugandan government. A peace agreement was never signed because the leader of the LRA, Joseph Kony, did not trust the government's motives and feared he would be captured if he appeared. The LRA then fled to DRC and continued to operate within the region, including the Central African Republic and Sudan.

After the war, groups like the Teso Women Peace Activists (TEWPA), Lira Women Peace Initiatives (LIWEPI), Kitgum Women Peace Initiative (KIWEPI) and Kasese War Widows Association (KWAWA) continued to mobilize women to deal with life problems (Global Network of Women Peacebuilders 2012). Women like Sister Rosemary Nyirumbe created shelters for ex-LRA women to help them rebuild their lives and deal with some of the ostracism they faced within their communities. In 2009, a UNSCR 1325 civil society task force made up of thirty-five organizations was formed to monitor the implementation of the National Action Plan on UNSCR 1325 and 1820 as well as the regional 2009 Goma Declaration, all of which were designed to address the impact of war on women and their involvement in peace-making activities during and after armed conflict (Rubimbwa 2010).

Despite this activism and these gender disruptions, the localized nature of the conflict did not create conditions that were conducive to reordering society more generally in Uganda. Moreover, even though the peace agreement included gender-related provisions, the accord itself was never signed. The Ugandan constitution was not rewritten as it had been in 1995. In other words, there were no changes in opportunity structures that would have allowed for women to have an impact of the kind that occurred after the 1986 war. Nevertheless, women's new leverage within households and communities may have allowed for other types of transformations. The peace movement may have also had repercussions for women's mobilization after the war. While on the one hand certain types of change did not occur, on the other hand, the experiences in northern Uganda illustrate the importance of gendered disruptions of conflict, resulting in more localized impacts.

CONCLUSIONS

Uganda was the first country in Africa representing the trends described in this book, linking conflict with women's rights. The profound gender transformations that occurred within Ugandan society as a result of the Bush War contributed to changes in the gender regime at the national level after 1986. The continuing war in northern Uganda after 1987 resulted in similar gender disruptions, but because of the localized nature of the conflict, the gender impacts after the war ended in 2006 were not felt in the same way in national policy change as had been the case with the end of the Bush War. Changing opportunity structures gave women activists key openings to press their demands, particularly for positions of power. This occurred in the constitution-making process leading to the 1995 constitution, which allowed women to advance their demands for greater representation and rights.

Although Uganda remained a semiauthoritarian hybrid regime, there nevertheless was sufficient political opening in the late 1980s and the 1990s to allow for the emergence of an active women's movement. Although the lack of democracy remained a major constraint on government responsiveness to women's demands and it fed into tendencies of patronage, which kept some women activists more beholden to the NRM than to women's rights, there was enough space for women to push forward with the passage of significant women's rights legislation, which is discussed in Chapter 9, and increase the rates of women's political representation and leadership. Overlapping and sometimes conflicting agendas of the women's movement and the government coexisted when it came to women's rights.

Women's rights activists drew inspiration from the UN conferences on women in Nairobi (1985) and Beijing (1995) as well as regional meetings of women activists from East Africa and elsewhere in Africa. Moreover, shifting donor strategies gave greater emphasis to nongovernmental organizations in the 1990s, and women's organizations were among the main beneficiaries of the new funding orientations. The fact that the momentum to increase representation of women began before significant donor funds were available and before 1995, when UN pressures for increased female representation strengthened, suggests that domestic considerations were more important than international pressures in this regard.

Thus, the Ugandan case is one of the clearest in illustrating the patterns described in this book. All the elements linking the end of conflict with the expansion of women's rights are evident, from the presence of key opportunity structures, particularly the constitution-making process, to the causal mechanisms (gender disruptions, women's movement advocacy, and international normative pressures regarding women's rights).

4

Liberia: The Power in Fighting for Peace

You can tell people of the need to struggle, but when the powerless start to see that they really can make a difference, nothing can quench the fire.

– Leymah Gbowee, *Mighty Be Our Powers*

A single straw of a broom can be broken easily, but the straws together are not easily broken.

– Liberian proverb

One small but visible sign of change can be seen on the walls of the Supreme Court building in Monrovia, Liberia, where President Ellen Johnson Sirleaf made a small but telling edit, indicative of the gender regime change that has occurred in this country. In the past it had the motto emblazoned on the outside: "Let justice be done for all men." Today, it reads, "Let justice be done for all."

Liberia was the first country to elect a woman president in 2005. In many ways, this came as no surprise given its history of civil war, but also its long history of women in national leadership. Just as Uganda was the first country where we see the pattern linking the decline of conflict with the emergence of a new women's rights regime, Liberia is one of the more recent cases of this phenomenon. The case illustrates how the decline of conflict led to the introduction of women's rights provisions in the peace agreement, women's heightened engagement in electoral politics, and their increased involvement in legislative reform affecting women. Although not all the patterns evident in Uganda have completely unfolded in Liberia, if one looks at the kinds of debates over the constitution and over the legislative representation of women, they are all moving in the same direction.

This chapter first provides an overview of the conflict and factors that gave rise to it. It traces the three causal mechanisms mentioned in Chapters 1 and 2, starting with the gender disruptions that occurred during the war.

TABLE 4.1 *Basic Political, Economic, and Social Data for Liberia, 2014*

Capital	Monrovia
Type of government	Republic
Independence	July 26, 1847
GDP (current US$)	1.767 billion (2012 IMF)
GDP per capita (current US$)	$700 (2013 CIA)
Poverty level	80% of population below the poverty line (2000 CIA).
Major sources of revenue	Agriculture: 76.9% Industry: 5.4% Services: 17.7% (2012 World Bank)
Population	4,128,572 (2011 World Bank)
Ethnicity	Kpelle 20.3%, Bassa 13.4%, Grebo 10%, Gio 8%, Mano 7.9%, Kru 6%, Lorma 5.1%, Kissi 4.8%, Gola 4.4%, other 20.1% (2008 Census, CIA)
Religion	Christian 85.6%, Muslim 12.2%, Traditional 0.6%, other 0.2%, none 1.4% (2008 Census)
Official languages	English 20% (official), some 20 ethnic group languages few of which can be written or used in correspondence
Head of government	President Ellen Johnson Sirleaf (since January 16, 2006); Vice President Joseph Boakai (since January 16, 2006)
Cabinet	Cabinet appointed by the president and confirmed by the Senate
Legislative branch	Bicameral National Assembly consists of the Senate (30 seats; members elected by popular vote to serve nine-year terms) and the House of Representatives (73 seats; members elected by popular vote to serve six-year terms)
Women in Congress	11% (2013 World Bank).
Speaker of the House	Alex J. Tyler
Electoral system	President elected by popular vote for a six-year term (eligible for a second term); elections last held on October 11 and November 8, 2011 (next to be held in 2017)
Judiciary	Chief Justice: Hon. Francis S. Korkpor Number of women justices on Liberian Supreme Court: two out of five
Counties	Bomi, Bong, Cbarpolu, Grand Bassa, Grand Cape Mount, Grand Gedeh, Grand Kru, Lofa, Margibi, Maryland, Monstserrado, Nimba, River Cess, River Gee, Sinoe
Parties and leaders	Alliance for Peace and Democracy or APD (Marcus S. G. Dahn) Alternative National Congress or ANC (Orishil Gould) Congress for Democratic Change or CDC (George Weah) Liberia Destiny Party or LDP (Nathaniel Barnes) Liberty Party or LP (J. Fonati Koffa) Liberia Transformation Party or LTP (Julius Suku) Movement for Progressive Change or MPC (Simeon Freeman)

(continued)

Table 4.1 *(continued)*

National Democratic Coalition or NDC (Dew Mayson)
National Democratic Party of Liberia or NDPL (D. Nyandeh Sieh)
National Patriotic Party or NPP (Theophilus C. Gould)
National Reformist Party or NRP (Maximillian T. W. Diabe)
National Union for Democratic Progress or NUDP (Victor Barney)
Unity Party or UP (Varney Sherman)

FIGURE 4.1 Administrative Map of Liberia. Credit: Eva Swantz

It then traces the rise of the peace movement and women's movement in the context of advocating for peace. The chapter discusses the role of the international actors in pushing for a women's rights agenda and concludes with a description of some of the changes that have occurred as a result of these factors.

BACKGROUND

Freed slaves from the United States and the West Indies founded Liberia in 1816, and it became an independent republic in 1847. Much of the country's history has been plagued by tensions between Americo-Liberians and the local population, who did not support the creation of the republic and resisted the American Colonization Society, which had sponsored the repatriation of former U.S. slaves to Liberia. Americo-Liberians came to dominate the country politically and economically, even though they made up only 2.5 percent of the population. Their party, the true Whig Party, dominated the country until the coup d'état of Samuel Doe, who was of African Krahn descent. Doe's forces executed President William R. Tolbert and thirteen of his top officials, who were mostly Americo-Liberians. The current president, Ellen Johnson Sirleaf, was one of the few who were spared.

Doe's takeover as president plunged the country into years of rampant corruption, economic turmoil, and violence as the Gio, Grebo, Mano, and other groups felt sidelined. This period saw the ascendance of the Mandingo, who were seen as outsiders from Guinea. Doe held elections in 1985, which were widely regarded as rigged. Soon after, Army Commanding General Thomas Quiwonkpa attempted a coup d'état, which was foiled, and he was executed. This was followed by retribution against his Gio and Mano supporters in Nimba County, which fed into the unrest that followed.

In 1989, the Americo-Liberian warlord Charles Taylor and his National Patriotic Front of Liberia (NPFL) launched an invasion of the country with backing from Côte d'Ivoire and Burkina Faso. This sent the country spiraling into conflict that continued until 1996. The war contained multiple conflicts: the historic dominance of the Americo-Liberian people over the indigenous people, the politicization of ethnicity, the entrenchment of corruption and patronage, and unresolved conflicting land claims. Taylor was able to build on the anger among the Gio and Mano for the killing of Quiwonkpa to strengthen support against the Krahn and Mandingo. This period was characterized by extreme violence that affected almost the entire population. It involved the kidnapping of children, rape and violence against women, holding people hostage, torture, and the destruction of the state. Women and family members were forced to take part in and witness the torture, rape, and murder of their family members. While it is impossible to know exactly how many were killed, United Nations estimates indicate that at least 250,000 were killed, a half million were forced into exile, and about half the country's people were internally displaced out of a population of 3.3 million. For long periods, the capital city of Monrovia was without food. Large-scale massacres occurred at different times. In one instance, over 600 civilians, mainly women and children, were killed at St. Peter's Lutheran Church. In another incident, 200 women and children were burned in Sinkor Supermarket (AWPSG 2004).

For much of the conflict, the NPFL was based in Gbarnga, which was strategically situated to allow Taylor's forces to cut off much of the traffic throughout the interior of the country. Militia manned checkpoints, where they demanded goods or money, and could easily kill someone if they did not comply or if they spoke the "wrong language."

Various external efforts sought to bring an end to the fighting. The peacekeeping force, Economic Community of West African States Monitoring Group (ECOMOG), which was mainly made up of Nigerians and Ghanaians, arrived in 1990. Meanwhile Prince Yormie Johnson's Independent National Patriotic Front of Liberia (INPFL) broke away from Taylor's NPFL and killed President Doe on September 9, 1990. An Interim Government of National Unity (IGNU) was formed in October 1990 with the help of Economic Community of West African States (ECOWAS). Dr. Amos Sawyer became interim President. Taylor refused to accept the Interim Government of National Unity (IGNU) government and continued fighting.

Seeking revenge for the killing of Doe, Alhaji Kromah formed the United Liberation Movement of Liberia for Democracy (ULIMO). ULIMO eventually split into the Mandingo-led ULIMO-K led by Kromah and the Krahn-dominated ULIMO-J led by Roosevelt Johnson. Other militia groups included the Nimba Defense Council, the Movement for the Redemption of Liberian Moslems, the Krahn-based Liberian Peace Council, and the Lofa Defense Force. During the war, people were killed on a variety of pretexts: on suspicion of being or looking like Krahn, Gio, Mano, Mandingo, or some other group; for not being able to speak a particular language; or for some other inexplicable reason.

Over forty-six peace talks were held between 1989 and 1997, often under ECOWAS auspices. Over a dozen peace agreements were signed; however, they rarely lasted very long as conflict resumed. Taylor eventually agreed to a five-person transitional government in negotiations between the United States, the United Nations (UN), the Organization of African Unity, and ECOWAS. The Abuja peace agreement of 1996 set the stage for disarmament and elections. Taylor and his National Patriotic Party (NPP) won the elections, capturing 75.3 percent of vote against Ellen Johnson Sirleaf's Unity Party, which won only 9.6 percent of the votes. Taylor won much of the popular vote because many feared he would return the country to war if he did not win. Although the elections were seriously flawed, many international observers regarded them as Liberia's best hope for peace. The war nevertheless resumed in 1999 as Sekou Conneh's Liberians United for Reconciliation and Democracy (LURD) mounted an incursion from Guinea. Later Thomas Nimely-Yaya's Movement for Democracy in Liberia (MODEL) launched an attack on Liberia from Côte d'Ivoire.

In June 2003, peace talks were held in Akosombo, Ghana. No sooner had the talks got underway, than the chief prosecutor of the UN-mandated Special Court for Sierra Leone issued a warrant for the arrest of Charles Taylor.

Yet another round of peace negotiations took place in Accra, Ghana, to negotiate a comprehensive peace agreement (CPA). Meanwhile, the war escalated, and the negotiators came under intense pressure from thousands of women peace activists both inside Liberia and at the talks in Accra to conclude the agreement. Taylor was forced to flee into exile in Nigeria. As a result of pressures from the peace activists, the CPA was signed in August 2003. This allowed for the formation of a transitional government, which was led by the late Gyude Bryant, and the eventual holding of elections in October 2005, bringing Ellen Johnson Sirleaf into office. Johnson Sirleaf was reelected in 2011.

The years of war had destroyed the country's political, economic, and social institutions. Liberia's infrastructure was decimated, and the lives of individuals, families, and communities were shattered. The violence profoundly disrupted societal norms: Children were forced to kill; large numbers of people were raped; the traditionally revered Zoe elders were targeted; churches became sites of mass atrocities; combatants killed people, dismembered their body parts, and some even ate their hearts in the hopes of gaining added strength.

Today, almost half the country's population of 4 million lives in urban areas, with 882,000 living in Monrovia alone. This is largely a consequence of the war, which forced Liberians to flee to urban areas for protection. Young people face high rates of unemployment. The median age is eighteen years, and 44 percent of the population is under fourteen years of age, so the problem of unemployment is a growing one. The Ebola crisis of 2014 exacerbated these problems.

While the Americo-Liberian/indigenous division is a key one, there are multiple cleavages that create forms of exclusion. The country is made up of over twenty ethnic groups, none of which constitute a majority. Although English is the official language, there are twenty other indigenous languages. One division that persists to this day has to do with the treatment of the Mandingos, who are often pitted against the Gio, Mano, and other groups. Even though the Mandingo migrated to Liberia from neighboring Ghana over the past four hundred years, to this day they are often classified locally as foreigners. The majority of Mandingo were exiled during the civil war. After 2004, many Mandingos returned but were often prevented from reclaiming their property and denied access to marketplaces and farmland (Fuest 2010). The Gio and Mano of Nimba, and Kpelle and Loma of Bong and Lofa counties had taken over much of the commercial activity of the Mandingos. Some conflate Mandingos with Muslims; however, Muslims, who make up 12 percent of the population, can be found in a variety of ethnic groups in Liberia. Many Muslims also feel marginalized, largely due to their sense of a lack of opportunities and overall lower levels of formal education.

The first of the three causal mechanisms at play in Liberia – the women's movement – had emerged prior to the war but took an entirely different form after the First Liberian War. During the Liberian civil wars, women organized marches, petitions, and prayer meetings held weekly in Christian and Muslim religious institutions throughout the country. They conducted peacemaking workshops with the militia and adopted initiatives to get them to disarm.

GENDER DISRUPTIONS

Some of the most palpable changes for women in Liberia were evident at the local level during the war. Women who lost their husbands in the war were forced into running their households and finding food for their children. Married women often had to hide their men from danger, from being killed or abducted into fighting. Thus many Liberian women became the primary breadwinners in the family for the first time. Some women opened up their homes to orphans and other homeless victims of the war. Women described to me how during the war they mapped their communities and took down the names of households and distributed food to them when food shortages ensued. Thus they became more active in their communities than in the past. Veronika Fuest (2008) writes about how women took on traditional male tasks of brick making, building and roofing houses, and clearing farmland. As a result of such changes, today there are more women in business than men. Women's organizations proliferated after the war.

Market women were often singled out as being especially brave and as having kept the food supplies coming into Monrovia at great personal risk. For months there were shortages of food in Monrovia but also as far as Maryland, Sino, Grand Kru, and Grand Bassa. Food was also going bad in the hinterland as normal trade channels had been cut off. Women traders took it upon themselves to transport food from the hinterland to the city and other parts of the country. They negotiated safe passage with NPFL forces in Gbarnga and then through the ULIMO checkpoints. At checkpoints the market women faced intimidation, demands for bribery, sometimes even rape or death at the hands of the soldiers and militia. Sometimes they had to bribe soldiers while negotiating as many as fifty checkpoints (AWSPG 2004, 9, 11).[1] They filled in as traders, often because the male Lebanese and Mandingo traders had fled the violence. As women, they found it easier to cross into "enemy" territory and negotiate the checkpoints in order to exchange goods with other women traders who had aligned themselves with local factions. They engaged in barter, trading rice for salt and oil for example (Fuest 2010). Some women even maintained communication across enemy lines.

Annie Yeneah was head of the Marketing Association between 1990 and 1997. She also served in the House of Representatives after that time. During the war she negotiated with Taylor and ECOMOG to allow the market women to go into the interior to bring food to the urban areas. They were able to move through all thirteen counties and had relationships with the superintendents in

[1] Interview with 2.18, Monrovia, October 7, 2007.

all counties. They also continued their trade with Guinea and Côte d'Ivoire, bringing food, salt, and soap. At one point Yeneah was imprisoned by Taylor because of her connections to another politician who had been killed. They beat her ears and eyes, trying to get information out of her and permanently damaged her hearing. Later she was freed.[2]

The gender regime changes are perhaps best illustrated through women's own descriptions of what transpired during the years of war and how their experiences were different from those of men. I quote them at length to give a sense of how profound the changes were and also how similar the perceptions.

Conflict forced people to reflect on the gender status quo in new ways and to question why they had lived the way they had when reality no longer matched their beliefs. As the president of the Association of Female Lawyers of Liberia (AFELL) explained to me:

Most of the time for human beings, something has to happen as an eye opener. War opened our eyes to see what was hidden. We asked: "Why are these things happening? Why do we do things this way?" Society had been male dominated and we just followed what the man says. War and crisis had its own advantages on the minds of people. We [women] realized we could rise up and do things for ourselves. We got women to come forward and start talking. We learned that when we saw injustice we could rise up and say certain things. When women saw others coming out and talking, they too felt they could discuss freely and would not risk reprisal by male family members.[3]

Mary Brownell, the founder of the Liberian Women's Initiative (LWI), similarly offered her perspective on the gender disruptions of war:

Men were affected by war, but they had to be hiding. If they were captured, they were killed. They suffered too a great deal and were humiliated. Women became the bread-winners because they could go out. Women became more independent. But they too could be raped and killed. Women had to go out of their way to do anything to keep their families going. During the war, Monrovia was divided into sections controlled by various warlords. The market women were especially brave and took a lot of risks, they traveled across the divisions in the city. We would have starved to death without the market women.[4]

Women were the ones who generally risked life and limb to get food for the household. They generally worked collaboratively with other women, and that emboldened them. As one peace activist put it:

Women were braver. It was easier for them to go out. They said, "God will protect us and we need to arrest this situation [of war]." We had to stand by each other, support each other, regardless of whether we were illiterate, market traders or educated women, and regardless of our religion, tribe or anything else. We were all in the same situation.[5]

[2] Interview with 2.18, Monrovia, October 7, 2007.
[3] Interview with 2.12, Monrovia, September 17, 2007.
[4] Interview with 2.13, Monrovia, September 12, 2007.
[5] Interview with 2.14, Monrovia, September 17, 2007.

The sense of gender transformation was shared by people in many walks of life. Professor Tarnue Sherman from the University of Liberia described the changes to me in similar ways:

Women were tired and fed up with warlords saying, "We are going to liberate you." Women were more involved than men in the peace movement. As mothers, they were tired of seeing young children killed. Men were perpetrators of violence. Other men never ventured out. Men were hunted or in hiding. Women brought news to men. Women were so brave. We survived because of them.[6]

Liberian journalist Davidetta Brown described to me the changes that took place in this way:

The culture of male domination made it hard for women to have their voices heard. Women felt disadvantaged during war. Women during the war became heads of household. They became decision makers in their home. Men were sought to enlist in the fighting or they were killed, or hid under their beds or in the ceilings for security.[7]

One women's rights activist described the change that happened in gender roles quite succinctly:

The woman became the man and the man became the woman when there was war. Most men just sat there and women did everything.[8]

Men's roles also changed as a result of the war and they began to take on more of the roles women had traditionally assumed. As Yeahnee King of the nongovernmental organization (NGO) Foundation for International Dignity (FIND) explained:

Before the war, men thought they were all knowledgeable and all powerful. But during the years of conflict, men were in the house, hiding, and could not move freely. Women had to go from one village to the next to search for food. After the war, men had a greater appreciation for women. If women were given the opportunity to excel, the family would do better than if women were kept down. With war, the burden was shared more between the husband and wife. Some men do cook and take care of the home now, but don't admit it to others because most men still feel certain things in the house should be done purely by women. Also, some of our sisters were part of the fighting forces, and that also taught the men that women could do the same as men and they started to rethink things.[9]

King's comment about the women fighters was borne out in the experiences of women combatants. It is estimated that 20 to 30 percent of the fighters were women. One of the most famous and fiercest of the female fighters was a young woman who went by the *nom de guerre* Black Diamond. She joined the rebel

---

[6] Interview with 2.15, Monrovia, September 11, 2007.
[7] Interview with 2.16, Monrovia, September 15, 2007.
[8] Interview with 2.4, Monrovia, October 5, 2007.
[9] Interview with 2.17, Monrovia, October 4, 2007.

group Liberians United For Reconciliation and Democracy (LURD) after being gang-raped by the army forces of Taylor in Lofa county in 1999 (Carroll 2003). Her parents were killed during the war. Her story is similar to that of others, many of whom were recruited from refugee camps in Guinea and Sierra Leone. At twenty-one she became pregnant and fought on the front lines until she was eight months pregnant. In her pocket she kept a photo of her daughter, who remained in a refugee camp in Guinea. Roy Carroll described her as sporting mirror sunglasses, a frizzy wig beneath a red beret, silver earrings, denim bell-bottoms, a silky red blouse, red painted nails, and a Colt .38. She served as head of the women's auxiliary corps (WAC). She was known for handcuffing and relentlessly beating people who had "misbehaved" with a long rubber pipe. One senior LURD official said of the combatant women, "They [the women] take a bit longer to train but become better fighters than the men. Black Diamond is one of our best."

"Men are stronger than women, but we shoot straighter and are more disciplined," said Teah, who kept a loaded .38-caliber colt in her jeans and an AK-47 nearby. "The same thing the men do here, the women do" (Itano 2003). Teah, a lieutenant-colonel in LURD, had a scorpion and a cobra tattooed on each bicep. "They bite, and I bite. I'll bite any man," she told Carroll. "Growing up I prayed to be stronger than the men. They made me a commander because of my hardiness. We wanted to fight so we formed our own lady unit. We shoot better than the men. Last week I shot a government soldier in the head, here," she recounted to journalists during the time of the war. According to civilians who lived near the women's auxiliary, the women rarely drank, smoked, or used drugs. Some women fighters also ended up serving as concubines or partners to other soldiers and as cooks. While many women were fighters, these experiences rarely translated into positions of power after the conflict.

In many ways women had slightly more options than men, especially young men, during the war. Basically, young men could join one of the rebel armies, flee into exile, hide in their homes, adopt a life on the run from forced conscription, or be killed if suspected of belonging to an enemy militia. Not only was men's mobility restricted, but there were few job opportunities. Some men joined the peace movement, but the bulk of the movement involved women. It is possible that because women were heavily involved with religious institutions that this also helped propel them into peacemaking activities because many of the religious institutions had become active in the peace movement and in fostering interfaith work.

The changes in gender relations today are palpable. As one Monrovia-based male finance officer explained to me: "Before [the conflict] men were breadwinners, now women are main breadwinners. Before women were not doing much except income generation. Today women are generating income and playing an equal role. They are deciding on how to use money in the household. My wife provides funds, finances children in school, and uses money to build a house. I put a door in our house and my wife puts chairs and furniture [they divide expenses]. In the past, we did not decide together, today the father and mother decide things together. In the past, the father controlled most of the property. There is some jealousy between husbands and wives, especially if the wife works and the husband does not. The husband feels insecure and makes noise."[10]

Yves-Renee Jennings (2012) studied the impact of these changes on men in Liberia and found that men's responses to these changes were not always so positive because they felt they were losing control over women, their homes, and even their lives. She also found negative sociopsychological impacts. As one man explained to her:

The impact of the increased focus on women in leadership positions on men is simple. Men are losing power. Power is authority. With authority comes economic benefit which men are also losing. And lastly, men are losing prestige. (Cited in Jennings 2012, 213)

Nevertheless, while Jennings's 2010 survey showed that men were less supportive than women of the changes in gender relations and had reservations about women in leadership (Question 1), they still were overwhelmingly supportive of women in public leadership positions (Questions 3, 12) and of gender equality (Question 2; see Table 4.2). As Hon. Gloria Scott, former Chief Justice of the Supreme Court explained to me:

Because of the new strength of women [as a result of the war], women made gains. It was easy for the population to accept that a woman did not have to be in the background any longer, she could step up and carry the family. It was also easy to accept women in leadership. Men accepted it as well. There were still some diehards who had their egos, but even they had to accept the fact that things had changed.[11]

WOMEN'S MOVEMENT

Women's early leadership

Like Uganda, it is important to note that historically Liberia had a relatively large number of educated women in leadership, even earlier than most African countries. Some have attributed this to the fact that the Americo-Liberian male elite preferred having their women in political positions rather than placing educated indigenous men in these positions (Fuest 2008). However, Mary Moran (2012) persuasively argues that most of the women leaders like Ellen Johnson Sirleaf and Ruth Sando Perry were indigenous women who had benefited from elite education. As she explained to me, there had been a "long pre-war history of prominent Liberian women in public life both in the state

---

[10] Interview with 2.19, Monrovia, September 17, 2007.
[11] Interview with 2.20, Monrovia, July 11, 2008.

TABLE 4.2 *Male and Female Perceptions of Women's Leadership Gains*

		Agree with Statement %	
		Men	Women
1	Liberian men are ambivalent about the postwar agenda of increasing women in leadership positions.	70	72
2	Liberian men understand the importance of gender equality.	68	48
3	Liberian men do not believe women should be in public leadership positions.*	24	54
4	Liberian men are threatened about the increased numbers of women in leadership positions.*	40	72
5	Liberian men believe that the increased numbers of women in leadership will have a negative impact on Liberia's cultural values.	48	50
6	Liberian men are opposed to women in leadership in various public sectors.	38	62
7	Liberian men fear that women will take over.*	34	70
8	Liberian men are domineering.	64	70
9	Liberian men believe that women leaders cannot be as competent as men.*	56	62
10	Liberian men relate to women leaders differently than they do to men leaders.	68	54
11	Whenever possible, Liberian men will undermine women in public leadership positions.	36	62
12	Having women in leadership positions could provide a constructive space for both men's and women's personal development.	86	86

N = 100, 50 men, 50 women *Statistically significant gender difference
Source: Jennings 2012.

and in more private, rural settings, where women, especially as elders in kin groups, have a great deal of recognized authority, just as elsewhere in West Africa"[12] (see also Tables 4.3–4.6).

From the 1950s almost one-quarter of the students in Liberia's two universities were women (Fuest 2008). Liberia was the first country in Africa to grant suffrage to all Americo-Liberian women in 1946 and indigenous women in 1951. Women held ministerial positions as early as 1948, when Ellen Mills Scarborough was appointed Secretary of the State of Education for four years. Angie Brooks – who received a BA in my own department of political science at the University of Wisconsin–Madison – had served as Assistant Attorney

---

[12] Communication with Mary Moran, January 2, 2015.

TABLE 4.3 *Liberian Women Leaders*

Year	Leader	Position
1948–52	Ellen Mills Scarborough	Secretary of State of Education
c. 1946–1956	Etta Wright	Assistant Secretary of Minister of Defense
1958	Angie Elizabeth Brooks-Randolph	Chief Executive when the President and Secretary of State were abroad (as Assistant Secretary of State)
1961	Angie Elizabeth Brooks-Randolph	Chairperson of the UN Committee of Trust and Non-Self-Governing Territories
1966	Angie Elizabeth Brooks-Randolph	President of the UN Trusteeship Council, Ambassador-at-Large
1972–73	Ellen Johnson Sirleaf	Secretary of State of Finance
1972–78	Bertha Baker Azango	Assistant Minister of Education for Planning and Research
1978–80	Bertha Baker Azango	Deputy Minister of Education for Planning and Research
1972–76	(Edith) Mai Wiles Padmore	Minister of Health and Social Security
1973–77	Dr. Kate Bryant	Minister of Health and Welfare
1975–77	Angie Brooks-Randolph	Ambassador to the United Nations
1975–78	Hanna Abedou Bowen Jones	Minister of Post
1975–79	Florence Chenoweth	Minister of Agriculture
1977–78	Hanna Abedou Bowen Jones	Minister of Communication
1977–79	Ellen Johnson Sirleaf	Secretary of State of Finance
1978–81	Hanna Abedou Bowen Jones	Minister of Health and Social Security
1979–80	Ellen Johnson Sirleaf	Minister of Finance
1981	Dr. Kate Bryant	Minister of Health and Welfare
1981–85	Hanna Abedou Bowen Jones	Ambassador to the United Nations
1981–87	Major Martha Sandolo Belleh	Minister of Health and Social Security
1983–84	Hanna Abedou Bowen Jones	Vice-President of the General Assembly of the United Nations
1985–87	McLeod Darpoh	Minister of Commerce, Industry and Transport
1987–90	McLeod Darpoh	Minister of Post and Telecommunication
1989	Dorothy Musuleng-Cooper	Vice-Chairperson of the National Patriotic Front of Liberia (the guerilla movement of Charles Taylor

Year	Leader	Position
1991–95	Amelia Ward	Minister of Planning and Economy
1994–95	Dorothy Musuleng-Cooper	Minister of Foreign Affairs
1995–96	Victoria Refell	Minister of Information, Culture & Tourism
1996–97	Victoria Refell	Member of the Council of State
1996–97	Ruth Perry	Acting President, Leader of Government
1996–97	Ruth Perry	Chairperson of the Council of State
1997–98	Sandra Howard	Minister of Planning and Economy
1998–01	Amelia Ward	Minister of Planning and Economy
1998–03	Evelyn White-Kandakai	Minister of Education
1999–01	Amelia Ward	Minister of Commerce and Industry
2001–02	Amelia Ward	Minister of Planning and Economy
2001–03	Dorothy Musuleng-Cooper	Minister of Gender Development
2001–03	Cora Peabody	Minister of Commerce and Industry
2001–03	Emma Wuor	Minister of Post and Telecommunication
2002–03	Grace Minor	President Pro Tempore of the Senate
2003–06	Vabah Kazaku Gayflor	Minister of Gender and Development
2003–06	Wheatonia Dixon-Barnes	Minister of Youth and Sports
2003–10	Vabah Kazaku Gayflor	Minister of Gender and Development
2003–05	Frances Johnson-Morris	Chairperson of the Electoral Commission
2004	Una Kumba Thompson	Acting Foreign Minister
2006 September; 2007 February	Frances Johnson-Morris	Acting President during absence of President and Vice-President
2006–07	Olubanke King-Akerele	Minister of Commerce and Industry
2006–07	Frances Johnson-Morris	Minister of Justice and Attorney General
2006–08	Antoinette Monsio Sayeh	Minister of Finance
2006–10	Vabah Kazaku Gayflor	Acting Minister of Commerce
2006–	Ellen Johnson Sirleaf	President of Liberia
2007–08	Frances Johnson-Morris	Minister of Commerce and Industry
2007–10	Olubanke King-Akerele	Minister of Foreign Affairs

(continued)

Table 4.3 *(continued)*

Year	Leader	Position
2007–10	Etmonia Davis Tarpeh	Minister of Youth and Sports
2008–10	Frances Johnson-Morris	President, Anti-Corruption Commission
2008–10	Miata Beysolow	Minister of Commerce
2009–	Christiana Tah	Minister of Justice and Attorney General
2010	Christiana Tah	Acting Minister of Finance
2010	Vivian J. Cherue	Acting Minister of Health & Social Welfare
2010	Elfreda Tamba	Acting Minister of Finance
2011–	Julia Duncan-Cassell	Minister of Gender and Development
2011–	Vabah Kazaku Gayflor	Minister of Labour
2012–	Miata Beysolow	Minister of Commerce
2012–	Etmonia Davis Tarpeh	Minister of Education
2012–	Aletha Brown	Minister of Commerce and Industry
2012–	Antoinette Weeks	Minister of Public Works
2012–	Dr. Florence Chenoweth	Minister of Agriculture

Source: www.guide2womenleaders.com/Liberia.htm.

TABLE 4.4 *Women in Liberian Supreme Court*

1977–	Angie Brooks-Randolph	Supreme Court justice
1996–97	Frances Johnson-Morris	Chief Justice, Supreme Court
1997–03	Gloria Musu Scott	Chief Justice, Supreme Court
2007–	Jamesetta Howard Wolokollie	Supreme Court justice
	Felicia Coleman	Supreme Court Justice
2010–11	Gladys Johnson	Supreme Court Justice
2012–	Sie-A-Nyene Yough	Supreme Court justice

TABLE 4.5 *Women Mayors of Monrovia*

1970–73	Ellen A. Sandimanie
2001–09	Ophelia Hoff Saytumah
2009–13	Mary Broh
2013–	Clara Doe Mvogo

Source: www.guide2womenleaders.com/Liberia.htm.

TABLE 4.6 *Liberian Women Superintendents* *

2004–06	Haja Washington	Bomi
2011–12	Lucia F. Herbert	Bong
2012–	Selena Polson Mappy	Bong
2006–12	Gertrude T. Weah Lamine	Gbarpolu
2006–12	Julia Duncan-Cassell	Grand Bassa
2012–	Etweda Gbenyon Cooper	Grand Bassa
1987–	Irene Jaleiba Paasewe	Grand Cape Mount
2006–12	Catherine Watson-Khasu	Grand Cape Mount
1997–05	Ruth Milton	Grand Gedeh
2006–12	Rosalind T. Sneh	Grand Kru
2011–	Elizabeth Dempster	Grand Kru
2012–	Nazarene Brewer Tubman	Maryland
2005–06	Josephine George-Francis	Montserrado
2006–10	Nyenekon Beauty Snoh-Barcon	Montserrado
2010–	Grace Tee-Kpaan	Montserrado
2001–13	Rachel M. Yeaney	Nimba
2009–11	Edith Gongloe-Weh	Nimba
2011–	Christina Duo Dagadu	Nimba
1999–02	Wilhemina Davis	Sinoe

*Only Lofa, Margibi, Rivercess, and River Gee counties have had no women superintendents.

General (1953–58). She eventually became ambassador to the UN (1975–77) and a justice in the Supreme Court after 1977. While women led in government as ministers, senators, mayors, superintendents, and Supreme Court justices (see Tables 4.3–4.6), others were leaders in other spheres as well. Early on, Tete Gayfor was a market leader, Marie Washington led the Liberian Marketing Association, Madam Korpo Howard led the Liberian Rural Women's Organization, Senator Collins of Bong County founded the Federation of Liberian Women in 1952, and Mary Antoinette Brown Sherman had been president of the University of Liberia from 1978 to 1984 (Steady 2011). This earlier generation of women leaders inspired later women leaders. Amelia Ward, who herself became Minister of Planning and Economy and Commerce and Industry in the government of Charles Taylor in the early 1990s and ran for vice president in the 2005 elections against Ellen Johnson Sirleaf, explained:

Angie Brooks, Etta Wright,[13] Mai Padmore,[14] Bertha Baker Azango[15]: these are women I admire so much. I thought if they could get to these places, I could reach what they

---

[13] Assistant Secretary of Minister of Defense (c. 1946–1956).
[14] Minister of Health and Social Security (1972–76).
[15] Assistant Minister (1972–78) and Deputy Minister (1978–80) of Education for Planning and Research.

reached. They were my role models. When I was in high school, Ellen Johnson Sirleaf[16] spoke at a graduation class before men. She was the first woman I saw who stood up to make a speech with so much strength. I wanted to be like her. People clapped because her delivery was so powerful. I was really mesmerized. She was very charismatic. I have never forgotten that image of her. It was the first time seeing a woman performing in that role, and I said I want to be able to do that.[17]

Early expansion of the women's movement and the first Liberian war (1989–96)

The earliest formal women's organizations, established from the 1950s to 1970s, were membership organizations (Massaquoi 2007). Formed in 1952, the Federation of Liberian Women was made up of female relatives of the ruling elite and was largely tied to the patronage network of President Tubman (Williams 2008). It was typical of other such organizations in Africa in this period, concerning itself primarily with adult literacy, income generation, hygiene, and running homes for girls who became pregnant out of wedlock. In the 1980s, President Doe banned the Federation, along with other organizations, for being "too political" because of its association with former leaders of the Tubman government. According to Filomina Steady (2011), women's organizations were among those that put pressure on the Doe government to end human rights abuses. The lack of associational life during this period explains why it took until 1994 for women to begin to mobilize to deal with the conflict. Thelma Sawyer and Evelyn Diggs-Townsend revived the organization in the early 1990s and changed its name to the National Women Commission of Liberia (Kindervater 2013).

During the first 1989–96 war, the Liberian Women's Initiative (LWI), Concerned Women of Liberia, Women in Action for Goodwill, the Muslim Women's Federation, Women's Development Association of Liberia, and the National Women's Commission of Liberia worked together to support communities through food distribution, caring for internally displaced peoples, providing trauma counseling, organizing basic literacy programs, and running healing and reconciliation workshops. These groups were explicitly formed to forge a common agenda across party and ethnic lines around women's rights concerns. Women's organizations also networked with Liberians in the diaspora and kept the international community informed about their goals.

Religious leaders like Catholic Archbishop Michael Francis were also heavily involved in peacemaking activities, as were key human rights and religious associations such as Catholic Justice and Peace Commission (JPC) and the Center for Law and Human Rights. Methodist Bishop Arthur Kulah and

---

[16] Secretary of State of Finance (1972–73) and President of Liberia (2005–present).
[17] Interview with 2.1, Monrovia, September 16, 2007.

Sheikh Kafumba Konneh, chairman of the National Muslim Council of Liberia, collaborated in interfaith activities that led to the establishment of the Interfaith Mediation Committee in 1990, which later became the Interfaith Council of Liberia, and in 2001 the present-day Inter-Religious Council of Liberia. During the civil war, such organizations played important roles in promoting peace. The Interfaith Council of Liberia was one of the first organizations to mediate between warring factions because of the religious dimensions of the conflict and because of their local authority and connections.

At the Cotonou meeting in 1993, the warring factions (NPFL, ULIMO, and the Armed Forces of Liberia [AFL]) had agreed to disarm to ECOMOG under the supervision of the UN Observer Mission in Liberia (UNOMIL). The main concern of women's organizations was to ensure that elections be held only *after* disarmament was completed, as they feared a return to fighting if this process was not completed properly. Women activists also demanded that the four key positions in the transitional government (secretaries of Defense, Finance, Justice, and Foreign Affairs) go to civilians who had no ties to the fighting militia.

The women activists did everything they could think of to prevent the formation of a government without full disarmament. They collected and confiscated small arms. They petitioned various authorities. Women's associations acted as monitors to see that promises were kept. The LWI mobilizers attended regional peace talks and engaged in letter-writing campaigns with the Economic Community of West African States (ECOWAS), the United Nations, and the Organisation of African Unity (OAU). They sent delegations to the U.S. and Nigerian ambassadors, the OAU representative, the UN Special Representative, and the Field Commander of ECOMOG as well as to President Rawlings of Ghana (Massaquoi 2007). Women also started seeking participation in peace talks in 1994 (see Chapter 9).

Their warnings were not heeded, and Interim President Amos Sawyer took power. That same day, women held demonstrations in the streets of Monrovia denouncing the creation of a transitional government without full disarmament. Even Sawyer himself admitted,

If disarmament had taken place back in 1994, as indeed it should have, we probably wouldn't have had April 6, 1996 [when the war came to Monrovia]. The advice of women had been "Stick to your agreements. Implement your agreements." (AWPSG 2004, 20)

Women continued to press for peace throughout this period up through the election of Taylor in 1997. In the middle of the war, after the UN Conference on Women in Beijing in 1995, it became apparent that Liberia had to establish some kind of national machinery. As a result, gender focal points were established in the fourteen line ministries and agencies. In 1995, a Women and Children Coordination (WACC) Unit was established in the Ministry of Planning and Economic Affairs, which despite its lack of funding became an important focal point for women's mobilization. From its inception there was the view that the ministry should partner with NGOs and should not be competing. Its purpose was to see that women's concerns were met and oversee women-related programming in the country.

Women NGOs and the Ministry of Planning worked well together at this time, and there wasn't the kind of acrimony one often finds between women's organizations and ministries. Part of this can be attributed to the conflict, which forced women to pull together.[18]

The selection of Ruth Sando Perry to head the Liberian National Transitional Government III in 1996 was an early victory for women activists. A Muslim of Vai origin who came out of the women's movement, Perry oversaw the legislative and presidential elections, which were held in 1997. Perry was outgoing and, above all, was perceived as someone who could clean up a mess. Being a woman gave her greater credibility, especially because there was a widespread perception, according to women's rights activist Esther Page, that "men had messed up the peace process."[19]

A National Gender Forum was established in 1998 and was made up of all stakeholders involved in women-related programs. It was to serve as the policy advisory board to ensure that women's rights policy was mainstreamed in all ministries and was incorporated into national policy. It was chaired by President Taylor and was made up of ministers and heads of government agencies, local and International NGOs, institutions of higher learning, and UN agencies (GOL 2008). It was organized around the twelve critical areas of the Beijing Platform of Action. Even to this day its mandate is to advise and monitor the government in developing national policy on gender equality issues.

Donors had been conflicted about where to channel resources because they did not want to direct them through the government in this period. The NGO Women's Secretariat was formed in 1998 by the Ministry of Planning with United Nations Development Programme (UNDP) support to coordinate the activities of women's organizations and to serve as an independent watchdog of government, to see that the government implemented programs affecting women. The secretariat was to present their independent views to government, lobby the government for legislation, and design collaborative programs. It worked closely not only with the UNDP but also the broader international community, including the United Nations Development Fund for Women (UNIFEM), United Nations Children's Fund (UNICEF), United States Agency for International Development (USAID), and United Nations Mission in Liberia (UNMIL), which were major sources of funding for women's concerns. These donors and other agencies channeled their funds to women through this mechanism during the war years and after.

---

[18] Interview with 2.2, Monrovia, September 18, 2007.
[19] Interview with 2.3, Monrovia, September 12, 2007.

Expansion of Women's Movement: Second Liberian War (1999–2003)

Liberian women continued to mobilize across religious and ethnic differences when fighting again flared in the 1999–2003 war, particularly with the creation of the broad-based Women of Liberian Mass Action for Peace. They held sit-ins at Sinkor airfield, where they prayed, sang, danced, and cried for peace. At one point they organized a sex strike and emphasized the religious aspect of it, saying that they would not have sex with their men until they saw God's face for peace. This gave the strike added potency and persuaded many men to support the women activists, although it was perhaps more useful as a means of gaining media attention than as an actual tactic for ending conflict. They received most of their funding from the churches and ordinary people, but also from businessmen and politicians. They also raised international funds from the Global Fund for Women, the American Jewish World Service, and the African Women's Development Fund (Gbowee 2011). Women put pressure on the peace talks in Accra in 2003 that sped up the conclusion of the talks (see Chapter 6).

Abibatu Kromah, a leader of United Muslim Women and Liberian Muslim Women for Peace, told me that at this time

We put the factions behind us. People fought for different reasons, some were forced to fight and some fought because of greed because at the time, Taylor had a lot of money. We blamed one another. This is why we fought the war for fourteen years, all because of blame. So we women [of all ethnicities] looked at this situation and said we have to put this behind us, God forbid we have another war: we will suffer, children will be killed, husbands will be killed, women will be raped. We need to put aside our differences and move ahead. We said "why don't we embrace our Christian sisters and work together." They got support from their religious leaders and we went ahead to work closely with Christian women in 2002–03 to bring an end to the conflict.[20]

Women had traditionally been mediators, interceders, and negotiators in Liberian society (AWPSG 2004, 7). A community leader, Esther Page also, described how women played this role in the Liberian civil wars:

The women decided to get the rebels to put down their guns. We had fasted and prayed throughout the war. Women played a major role in bringing the war to an end. We were the cause for peace to enter into this country. We talked to men to be calm for elections. We were more involved than men in making peace. We talked to our brothers and sons who were fighting. We carried food to the rebels and convinced them to stop fighting. If you did not go with food they would kill you. We brought palm oil, sugar cane, and rice. We told them, "Put your arms so we can have an election...."[21]

---

[20] Interview, 2.4, Monrovia, October 5, 2007.
[21] Interview, 2.3, Monrovia, September 13, 2007.

A market woman from Nimba explained

Personally I talked to over 50 men to persuade them to disarm. I made a difference. I went to a soldier I was trying to disarm and I would talk in a polite way.[22]

Another described the rhetoric they used to persuade the fighters:

We took white chickens, kola nuts, and palm necklace in hand and said to the boys, "We bore you, nursed you, and raised you. Put down your arms." About 100 women went at a time. We used many strategies with the young boys. Women went and spoke with the boys in their own languages. Bassa talked Bassa language, Mano talked with Mano boys, Gio, Kpelle, Mandingo with their own boys in dialects.[23]

White chickens were used in lieu of white doves and served as symbols of peace. Kola nuts were reminders that women that gave life, and palm branches symbolized Jericho welcoming Jesus, or a welcome home.

For much of the conflict, Taylor's NPFL was based in Gbarnga, which was strategically situated to allow his forces to cut off much of the traffic throughout the interior of the country. Militia manned checkpoints, where they demanded goods or money, and could easily kill someone if they did not comply or if they spoke the "wrong language." Nevertheless, women traders kept the lines of communication with the interior open by bringing in food to the urban areas at their own peril.

Even as fighting mounted, the House Speaker Nyudueh Morkonmana sought passage of a women's bill that addressed issues of gender equality, and in particular the status of customary law, which often discriminated against women ("Speaker Wants Women Bill Passed ..." 2003). In 2001, the WACC unit was upgraded to a Ministry of Gender and Development through an act of parliament. It became the lead agency to "coordinate the Government wide gender mainstreaming efforts, focusing on gender equality, women's empowerment and the development of children." Charles Taylor named former Foreign Minister Dorothy Musuleng-Cooper its first minister, and interim president Gyude Bryant replaced her with Vabah Gayflor in 2005.

Women activists' energies, however, were focused at this time on ending the war. According to activist Etweda "Sugars" Cooper, the Muslim Women for Peace Network had met with her three weeks earlier and "they decided that they must do something about peace in this country."[24] They sold this idea to the Christian women during a meeting, adding that at their second meeting, they invited other women to participate in the presentation of a position

---

[22] Interview with 2.5, Nimba, October 7, 2007.

[23] Interview with 2.6, Monrovia, September 28, 2007.

[24] Interview with 2.7, Monrovia, October 5, 2007. This chronology, which was confirmed by many others, contradicts the one depicted in the popular documentary, *Pray the Devil Back to Hell*, which brings the Muslim women into the picture after the Christian women had started mobilizing.

statement to the President of Liberia, any representative of LURD in Liberia, the international contact group on Liberia, and the new armed group, the Movement for Democracy in Liberia (Jarkloh 2003).

Women had marched to the executive mansion to meet President Taylor and demanded that he come and speak to them. They did not receive a reply, so they sat on an airfield near where the president lived from five in the morning to six in the evening, singing, praying, and displaying placards with messages about ending the war.[25]

On April 11, 2003, in an emotion-laden demonstration, about 1,000 women showed up at Monrovia's City Hall dressed in white *lapa* wraparound skirts, T-shirts, and headpieces to protest the war. They shouted: "We are fed up, we are fed up," protesting the destruction of their homes, the killings, and the drugging and abduction of their children into the fighting forces of the factions. Cecelia Danuweli from Gbarnga talked about her father dying of hunger. She said: "We are tired, the women of Liberia say they are tired. Women are sick of seeing our children dying," adding that, "it doesn't matter what it will take us, the women of Liberia say they want peace, and now. Should we sit on ... the fence behind and wait for a man to say that they want to fight for peace? We cannot any longer sit to see the future of Liberia ruined by arms-toters" (Jarkloh 2003). The women demanded an immediate and unconditional cease-fire and appealed to the international community to monitor it once it was concluded. They also called for a fruitful dialogue between the warring parties for the restoration of peace in Liberia. Government representatives, who had been invited, were absent from both rallies.

Radio Veritas, the Catholic radio station, helped connect the women to the international media, and in this way they were able to get coverage of their activities on CNN, BBC, and Reuters. Once their story became international, they felt that the warlords could not touch them, especially because they were women. International and local media workers started connecting with them.[26]

On April 16, hundreds of women went to the parliament and were chided by the speaker of the house, who yelled at them for their alleged failure to book an appointment with his office before going to the Capitol Building to present a statement to the National Legislature. Women in Peacebuilding Network (WIPNET) leader Leymah Gbowee interrupted him, saying, "With all due respect, when the bullets were flying, no one told these people to pack their loads to displaced camps. But because we are after peace, that's why we came." She said the women had written and asked the Senate President to attend their peace rally earlier that week, "but we did not see anyone. We also sat at the Airfield to get a response from Government and we again didn't see anyone." So they marched on the legislature ("Women, Speaker, Fuss ..." 2003).

---

[25] Interview with 2.8, Monrovia, September 14, 2007.
[26] Interview with 2.8, Monrovia, September 14, 2007.

Finally the women were able to get a hearing with the president at the height of the fighting. Over 2,500 women showed up dressed in their white T-shirts, wraps, and headscarves. Taylor said he would only meet with ten of them. So Leymah Gbowee, who by now was very angry, said, "Hell, no, he will see all of us." Taylor finally agreed to meet with all of them. The women held hands and prayed for Gbowee as she started her speech to him: "The women of Liberia, including the IDPs [internally displaced persons], we are tired of begging for bulgur wheat. We are tired of our children being raped. We are now taking this stand, to secure the future of our children. Because we believe, as custodians of society, tomorrow our children will ask us, 'Mama, what was your role during the crisis?'" After she finished, Taylor stood up and relented: "No group of people could make me get out of bed but the women of Liberia, who I consider to be my mothers." He then agreed to attend the peace talks. (Gbowee 2011, 141). He said the same should be asked of the rebel groups. The talks that he attended, which finally brought the conflict to an end, were held in Ghana starting in June up through August 2003 (detailed in Chapter 6).

One of the most important aspects of the peace movement was that it critiqued the view that peace could be achieved through the barrel of the gun. The Liberian Women Initiative (LWI) issued a statement April 3, 2003, saying that they did not understand why there was the need to rely on the fighters to liberate and reconcile through fighting: "We have experienced enough of the wave of redeemers, freedom fighters, liberators, defenders, peacemakers, reconcilers, democrats, angels and saviors amongst others." The women then called on the international community to redouble their efforts in supporting the subregional initiatives toward peace and security ("Women Want International Force Deployed ..." 2003).

Women's organizations also networked with Liberians in the diaspora and kept international women's organizations and international human rights organizations as well as United Nations agencies informed about what was going on. They publicized their struggles and built links with women peacemakers around Africa and the world.

Tensions within the movement

One of the most remarkable aspects of the movement was its unity, especially considering all the pressures and divisions that had the potential to tear them apart. There were, nevertheless, tensions within the movement, particularly between the leadership of the newer Women in Peacebuilding Network (WIPNET) and the older and more elite-based LWI as well as Mano River Women Peace Network (MARWOPNET). Partly, the tensions were based on class and education, but some divisions were also political and even personal. When it came to the peace talks, WIPNET fully supported and worked with MARWOPNET, which was representing women in the peace talks. The MARWOPNET women inside the talks fed information to those on the outside, and WIPNET then agitated on the same issues from the outside and to the media (Gbowee 2011).

But the movement did confront challenges, and there were a few who compromised their goal of peace. There were women, including the current president, Ellen Johnson Sirleaf, who helped start the war by providing resources to Charles Taylor when he began his effort to oust President Doe. By her own admission, she was a leader in an organization that had a hand in funding Charles Taylor's invasion into Liberia (Johnson Sirleaf 2009). At one point in the 1990s she had infamously declared, "Level Monrovia and we will rebuild it." She was also a major supporter of Quiwonkpa's failed coup against Doe in 1985, and as a result, her main opponent in 2005 won most of the Krahn vote. Johnson Sirleaf later abandoned Taylor after his erstwhile associate Prince Johnson killed President Doe and when it became clear Taylor had a personal agenda that was at odds with the original purpose of the struggle. Later she became one of Taylor's fiercest opponents and assisted with the women's peace movement. Moreover, she ran against him in the 1996 elections. To her credit, she appointed an ethnically balanced cabinet when she took power in 2006, which helped smooth over some of the problems of the past (Massaquoi 2007).

Other women facilitated Taylor's contacts throughout the region (Badmus 2009; Johnson Sirleaf 2009). Even though Taylor was one of the worst abusers of children as soldiers, a senator and one of his fellow female party members, Myrtle Gibson, lobbied for and succeeded in getting child rights legislation passed.[27] According to UN estimates, about 15,000 Liberian children were recruited into various rebel armies, including Taylor's own Small Boys Unit (SBU), which was associated with unimaginable atrocities. Myrtle Gibson also was involved in a fundraising effort for a children's village that ended up in the loss of $1.4 million in funds raised by Luciano Pavarotti along with Stevie Wonder, Spike Lee, Celine Dion, Jon Bon Jovi, Vanessa Williams, and other singers and entertainers (Smith 1998).

Some women in Taylor's government played divisive roles, exacerbating differences between the Americo-Liberians and indigenes in his government (Aning 1998). There were also some women peace activists who rejected all the factions, but there were others who supported particular political faction leaders and were involved in the peace movement on that basis. This, however, made them vulnerable to accusations of partiality, even if they sincerely believed they were pursuing peace. Some had been fighters. Others were leaders of women's organizations. Some were ministers in the Taylor government, who used their positions to help women through enabling humanitarian assistance and other such supportive programs. Some were informants. Mary Brownell described how they had to feed some of the women information "with a long

---

[27] Interview with 2.9, Monrovia, September 21, 2007.

spoon" because they discovered that plans they made in private would be broadcast on the radio the next day. In one case, one of the women activists had helped set up an ambush that almost got a large swath of the leadership of the peace movement killed. Factional differences sometimes stood in the way of strategic coalitions so that at the Liberian National Conference in 1994 women failed to unite to nominate a woman for the position of civilian representative on the Council of State for the transitional government. As a result, a man was selected. They eventually came together and were able to get Ruth Perry elected in 1996 as head of the ruling council, according to Conman Wesseah (AWPSG 2004, 33).

Other leaders within Taylor's government played more complicated roles. One peace activist, Victoria Refell, a journalist who became an NPFL representative to the Second Liberian National Transitional Government (LNTG), was promoted to Minister of Information under Taylor and participated in many peace talks on behalf of the Taylor government. Peace activist Amelia Ward was minister of planning in Taylor's government and played an important role in facilitating the provision of humanitarian relief during the war. She was also a MARWOPNET delegate in the peace talks. Another peace activist, Evelyn Kandakai, was a minister of education in the Taylor government. Grace Minor, a close associate of Taylor, was a major funder of WIPNET (Gbowee 2011) and was also on the UN Travel Ban list. Minor handled Taylor's investments as late as 2005. According to the Coalition for International Justice (2005), she helped "recruit couriers, coordinate their movements, and handle the money coming and going from Calabar," where Taylor was in exile from 2003 to 2006. Because of their close association with Taylor, some of these activists like Myrtle Gibson, Grace Minor, Victoria Refell, and Amelia Ward, were placed on a 2001 UN Security Council list of 120 people who were banned from travel outside Liberia.

A few women who worked for peace and continued to maintain political and factional alliances sometimes caused tensions among women peace activists, making some of them vulnerable to accusations of partiality. Thus, the women's peace movement included not only women who played positive roles in ending conflict, but there were also a handful who played ambiguous roles, while a few were implicated in fomenting conflict and in assisting Taylor and the warlords.

Women's movement in demobilization and transition

The women's movement continued its peace-building activities as the country demobilized. They were very critical of the way in which demobilization was carried out, partly because they were not fully engaged even though they understood the conditions in their communities and could have been brought in to advise.

Even without an official role, WIPNET, Crusaders for Peace, and other women's and religious organizations nevertheless intervened in the demobilization process. In December 2003 UNMIL began to disarm soldiers, trading weapons for cash. At one point a fight broke out among those being demobilized, and they started shooting at one another. Liberian women activists intervened to encourage the combatants to remain calm. WIPNET carried out sensitization sessions with the Public Affairs unit of UNMIL. They laid the groundwork for actions of UNMIL. WIPNET told UNMIL that the demobilization that had been planned for five days was too quick for the communities, who had to absorb the soldiers. UNMIL nevertheless ended up taking fighters to the cantonment and demobilizing them without training in the short time period allotted. They gave them supplies and carpentry packets, but because they had no training, the fighters simply sold the packets and did not use them to start businesses.[28]

Another key problem was the treatment of female combatants. An Action Plan of October 2003 was developed by the National Commission for Disarmament, Demobilisation, Rehabilitation and Reintegration (DDRR), UN agencies, donors, and NGOs. The plan targeted only 2,000 women, even though the number of women was considerably more as women made up 20 to 30 percent of the fighting forces (Ollek 2007). Although funds were set aside for allocations for child combatants and disabled ex-combatants, they were lacking overall, and the program was underfunded by 63 percent of what was required.

By the end of 2004, a total of 22,000 women and 2,740 girls out of 103,000 combatants had been disarmed and demobilized. According to Campbell-Nelson (2008), few efforts had been made to involve women's groups in the process of disarmament of women, and the women's organizations confirmed this. Women combatants in general had little information about the disarmament program; they reported being harassed in the process and found the cantonment sites too crowded. There was little effort to pay attention to their special needs, which had to do with reproductive issues, psychological concerns due to sexual abuse, problems associated with having borne children as a result of rape, and problems reintegrating because of having been female fighters. Where women ex-fighters were given training, they often were more likely to take advantage of it than men. Part of the problem was that those who were demobilized had to be over 18 and have "serviceable weapons." Not all women had weapons because of the support roles they played, and therefore they were not eligible for DDRR support. Similarly, child soldiers were left out of the demobilization programs because they did not meet the age requirements, although there were other programs for them.

There were efforts to recruit women into the army and police once the war was over, but these were challenging. The all-women police unit from India, which patrolled the Foreign Ministry and Office of the President, were

---

[28] Interview with 2.11, Monrovia, September 17, 2007.

extraordinary role models for the local police force. But it was still very hard to recruit more women into the police force because so few had high school certificates. UN Police set up a program with the Ministry of Gender and Minister of Education for an educational program and examination.[29]

Political liberalization and impacts on women's mobilization

Liberia has made important improvements in its civil liberties and political rights since 2005, which have facilitated women's mobilization. Today the country enjoys considerable freedom of expression and association and a significantly improved human rights environment despite lapses, as one human rights activist Afril Quijamdr explained. During the years of war from 1989 to 2003 there were grave and widespread human rights abuses, humanitarian violations, and flouting of the law. There were massacres, disappearances of opposition leaders and of ordinary people, brutal harassment, and intimidation across the country. After 2003, the human rights violations were primarily related to structural violence, involving the violation of economic and social rights: People do not have adequate access to school and health services, and they often do not have employment opportunities.

The presidential elections in 2005 and 2011 were seen as free and fair. The very high turnover in the 2011 legislative elections suggests that the elections are generally competitive. WIPNET also registered female voters in the 2005 election and helped set up polling stations in an election that brought Ellen Johnson Sirleaf to power.[30]

There are no political prisoners, and political rights and civil liberties are generally protected. The country jumped from a Freedom House ranking of 6 to 3.5 between 2003, when the war ended, and 2006. This moved the country from a "not free" category to "party free." Overall, Liberia has experienced greater stability and security. At the same time, it continues to be plagued by problems of executive dominance, corruption and a lack of accountability. The legislature and judiciary do not generally act as a check on the executive. To the extent that there are efforts to curb corruption, they have come primarily from civil society, the media, and donors. Watchdog organizations have sought accountability and transparency; civil society representatives increasingly sit on oversight boards and are involved in writing regulatory legislation. The media has been engaged in exposing corrupt practices but in general civil society remains weak.

The country enjoys freedom of the press, although there have been lapses, especially at times of elections. Freedom House scores for Liberia signaled an improvement in media freedom from a rating of 65 in 2007 to 56 in 2013. The 2010 Freedom of Information Act guarantees access to public information and

---

[29] Interview with 2.10, Monrovia, September 24, 2007.
[30] http://nvdatabase.swarthmore.edu/content/liberian-women-act-end-civil-war-2003.

is considered a model piece of legislation of its kind, although in reality access to information remains a problem. Journalists I interviewed were generally positive about the freedom of press. Ownership of the media is open to all and represents a mix of journalist-owned papers (e.g., the *Inquirer*), to papers and radio stations owned by politicians, religious organizations, and business-people. The media still suffers from problems of quality of reporting and vulnerability to the influence of money, which is used both to suppress stories and to have them written.

Despite anticorruption legislation, the creation of an Anti-Corruption Commission, and the reorganization of the General Auditing Commission, governance and transparency remain serious problems. The Comprehensive Peace Agreement provided for the creation of a Truth and Reconciliation Commission, which made its recommendations in 2009. They were to be implemented by the Independent National Human Rights Commission, which was created in 2010, but they were never implemented because of the controversial nature of some of their recommendations, including the banning of Ellen Johnson Sirleaf from holding public office. No war crimes tribunal was established, and no prosecutions were pursued. Instead, the president has focused on implementing the Palava Hut program, which uses customary reconciliation processes to promote forgiveness.

While there is much room for improvement in democratization, nevertheless, the extent of political opening since the war has been significant and has had positive impacts on civil society in general, including women's mobilization.

INTERNATIONAL INFLUENCES

The third causal mechanism linking the end of conflict to gender regime change pertains to external influences, which have taken many forms from donor aid to UNMIL and United Nations programs that emphasize women's empowerment. They have also included travel to international conferences on women's rights, participation in regional and international women's organizations, media and Internet influences, as well as goals set by regional and international organizations of which Liberia is a member.

Donors have contributed significantly to the women's rights agenda in Liberia, and Liberia remains one of the most heavily donor-dependent countries in Africa. Most recently, various UN agencies,[31] the Government of Liberia, and the Danish government funded and implemented a Gender Equality and Women's Economic Empowerment Joint Programme from November 2009 to April 2013. UN Women was the lead agency. The program had three main goals: to establish gender-sensitive policies and coordination mechanisms; capacity building for the Ministry of Gender and Development, line ministries,

---

[31] International Labor Organization, UNDP, UNESCO, UNIFEM, UN Office for Project Services

and civil society; and to support the Implementation of Priority Initiatives to Empower Women, particularly in the areas of income generation and education.

Over the years there have been many externally funded programs regarding women's rights. President Johnson Sirleaf has done a lot to raise foreign funds, and women's rights is an area that has attracted a lot of international interest. The Swedish Kvinna till Kvinna Foundation, for example, has been an important support in debates regarding the 30 percent legislative quota for women. The Nike Foundation, World Bank, and the Danish government have implemented economic empowerment programs for adolescent girls. The Spanish Fund for African Women and the New Economic Partnership for Africa's Development (NEPAD) implemented a two-year project to improve women's well-being, building safe houses in targeted counties, and providing microcredit to 3,000 vulnerable women and victims of gender-based violence. The Italian government donated $1.5 million to Liberia through the UNIFEM to support its implementation of UNSCR 1325. Many other such initiatives have been launched since 2005.

I asked activists at every opportunity in both 2007 and 2012 whether they found the international agendas an imposition, and the answer was uniformly, no. They felt that the agendas being supported by UN Women, UNMIL, and others were in accordance with their own priorities having to do with women's education, health, violence against women, and representation. I suspect these claims will require closer scrutiny over time.

Although external funds may have contributed to influencing some of the women's movement activities, women activists I interviewed were more directly influenced by their contacts with other activists in other parts of Africa and the world, including the UN Conference on Women in Beijing and other regional conferences in Africa. They were also strongly influenced by other peace organizations elsewhere in Africa, such as Femmes Africa Solidarité, which helped form MARWOPNET.

GENDER REGIME CHANGES

After the war, women's roles expanded, particularly as a result of increased educational and economic opportunities. Some women started new businesses to support themselves. Women learned new skills such as carpentry and masonry from UN programs. As Esther Page, who was on the NGO Women's Steering Committee, explained, "What changed during the war was that there is now the idea that you cannot succeed without education. Education is the key to success and getting ahead."[32]

---

[32] Interview with 2.3, Monrovia, September 12, 2007.

Women also contributed to their communities in new ways as a result of the breakdown in public services. Korpoh Sheriff, chair of the Bong County Women's Initiative, recounted how she and forty-five other women volunteer to sweep the streets in her hometown. Two times a week they get together from 8 A.M. to 12:30 P.M. to clean the city streets and police station because Gbarnga township does not do it. They pull grass and plant flowers. They also attend an evening, adult literacy class, where they discuss the next day's volunteer activities. They work in four different groups. A foundation gave them a loan, and they have a tailoring business in which they also make tie-and-dye cloth and beads and sell cloth in bulk. Sheriff noticed that the biggest difference between the period of the war and today was that women were now working together across different ethnic groups and across the Christian–Muslim divide. They had less problems because they were able to put their resources together and keep Gbarnga clean.[33]

The leader of a Bomi women's organization explained in a 2012 interview how life had changed for women in her community:

During the war we got to know our value because we were forced to find food for the children; men could not go out. Sometimes the husband was under the bed hiding [from being abducted or killed]. When Ellen [Johnson Sirleaf] took over, things changed for women. We praise God for the leaders God gave us. There is no way women could speak in the past. If we did, nothing would happen. Women can speak anywhere [in public] now. In the past, women were in the back and were silent. Now we speak well at meetings. We say what we want. I can speak well in front of men and women. Women stayed at the back too long, and now we have decided to speak for ourselves. The voice of women should be heard. When Ellen took over, no more women at the back, men in the front, now men and women 50–50 side by side. In the past women did not read and write. There are now more girls going to school in Bomi. Adult women can write their names. We have had a "climate change." Now more women carry money, more women are in business. Women are now trading and doing business as far as Nigeria and Guinea. In the past they only did business in Liberia.[34]

Salome Swa of the Women and Children Development Association of Liberia also explained the symbolic impact of having women leaders:

Before, women were like trash, we did not have a voice in the home. We did not want to send our children to school. We were married early. Now with a woman being president, we know education is very important. She is a great example for women. We now know, don't sit in the back. You can be like Ellen.[35]

The changes in the household took on a broader societal dimension. As former Supreme Court justice Hon. Felicia Coleman explained:

---

[33] Interview with 2.21, Gbarnga, October 7, 2007.
[34] Interview with 2.22, Bomi, June 12, 2012.
[35] Interview with 2.23, Monrovia, October 10, 2007.

After war, women continued in these new roles. Women realized they had experienced a major role change. Women began to play more of a role in politics and society is better for it. Women gained more confidence because of their role during war. These changes took place across classes. The women's movement said that women need an active role in the legislature to make changes.[36]

After the end of the war, there was a shift in civil society activities from a focus on humanitarian aid and peace to an emphasis on issues relating to development, advocacy, and interest representation. A wide array of women's organizations became activated, including organizations focusing on women's rights as well as poverty, debt reduction, land rights, the environment and other such concerns. According to Lene Cummings of WIPNET, the main issues women's organizations mobilized around had to do with violence against women, discrimination in hiring, the need for jobs, and participation in politics.[37] There are advocacy organizations like Women Won't Wait Coalition, the Association of Female Lawyers of Liberia (AFELL), and Forum for African Women Educationalists (FAWE). Women NGOs Secretariat of Liberia (WONGOSOL), formed in 1998, coordinates fifty-one women's NGOs. Some focus on women's political power, like the Women Legislative Caucus, and the Coalition of Political Parties Women in Liberia (COPPWIL). At the local level there are development associations focusing on women's economic empowerment like the Bassa Women Development Association, Margibi Women Development Association, and the Lofa Business Women Association while at the national level there are organizations such as Women Development Association of Liberia (WODAL), Women In Sustainable Development (WISD), Liberia Rural Women Association, and Community Empowerment Programme that work with chapters around the country. There are organizations that focus on specific issues like the Association of Disabled Females International (ADFI) and Liberia Women Empowerment Network, an association of women living with HIV. There remain a good number of peace-related organizations from the earlier period that focus on conflict prevention. These include WIPNET, MAR-WOPNET, ECOWAS Women, West Africa Network for Peacebuilding (WANEP), and Women of Liberia Peace Network (WOLPNET).

The United Muslim Women and the Federation of Muslim Women's Organizations (umbrella organization of twenty groups) have worked to provide Muslim women access to education, adult literacy, leadership training, microfinance, and other opportunities. Muslim women have been advocating around legislation for women including the Gender Parity Bill. They have also successfully fought to gain access to key positions within the National Muslim Council that has been male dominated in terms of leadership. And some like United Muslim Women president Marietta Williams have been

---

[36] Interview with 2.24, Monrovia, September 18, 2007.
[37] Interview with 2.25, Monrovia, September 18, 2007.

conducting dialogue with fellow Muslims to reinterpret the Quran to show that women have rights and can work together side by side with men on a basis of equality.[38]

In addition to the local women's organizations and coalitions, there are hundreds of international NGOs that work on a wide variety of concerns that have to do with providing services to communities, including shelters for abused women; training about GBV issues in communities, in the police, and military; providing rape kits to clinics; and counselors to victims of rape and domestic abuse (Abramowitz and Moran 2012).

Unlike Angola, there was a proliferation of NGOs with the end of the war. The Liberian NGOs Network (LINNK) was formed to coordinate civil society organization activities. It worked together with the National Civil Society Council of Liberia (NARDA) and the Ministry of Planning and Economic Policy. Civil society is still constrained by problems of capacity. This has been exacerbated by the trend of top personnel leaving to work in better-paying jobs with the government, international NGOs, or donors, thus depleting civil society of its best talent. As a result, donors often fund internationally run NGOs at the expense of local NGOs, creating a new set of tensions.

In contrast with the Taylor years when in 1998 civil society organizations were suppressed, today civil society organizations work fairly well with the government and feel they are able to influence policy. One finds in many African countries that women's movements have experienced tensions with the ministry of gender because it tried to control them. In Liberia the women's movement has been quite autonomous. They may have disagreed with the ministry over their perception that it was attempting to usurp the NGO role and act as an implementer of programs rather than a facilitator of policy. They may have also objected to what they felt was competition for funds, but for the most part the ministry has worked well with the organizations and has not curtailed their activities.

The most dramatic change for women in Liberia was the election of a female president, Ellen Johnson Sirleaf. Women activists played a major role in getting her elected in 2005 by launching an aggressive registration campaign across the country and registering large numbers of women prior to the second round of the election. In the first round of the presidential election, few women voted, based on data obtained from the Electoral Commission. With the second round, the number of women registered was equal to that of men. However, the overall numbers of voters declined by 186,857, suggesting that women voters accounted for most of the increase in support for Johnson Sirleaf. Based on a review of the Liberian media, Jacqui Bauer (2009) found that the activities of women's groups remained stable while activities by other groups dropped after the first round of elections. Thus, there is little question that women activists had a hand in getting Johnson Sirleaf elected. As former

---

[38] Interview with 2.26, Monrovia, June 2012.

Gender Minister Vabah Gayflor, who was one of the leaders the registration effort, explained to me:

Women were grossly marginalized in the National Transitional Assembly, 4 women and 19 men. Women saw this as indicative of discrimination. Men were presumed to be the main actors. Women's advocacy was ignored and undervalued. This left women with little option but to seek political equality and that is why they backed Ellen so forcefully.[39]

Women are better represented in the Liberian government than most. One-third of the cabinet ministers and one-third of county superintendents are women. Women account for 36 percent of all top ministerial positions. Monrovia already had a woman mayor in 2000 (and 1970) and has continued to have an uninterrupted stream of women mayors since that time. Women are also found in other key positions in the judiciary, even in the Supreme Court, police, and elsewhere (see Chapter 8). Women are well represented on key transitional commissions with half the positions on the National Elections Commission and Constitutional Commission and four out of nine positions on the Truth and Reconciliation Commission.

Women, however, remain poorly represented in the national legislature. The Liberian Women's National Political Forum made up of politically active women, party representatives, and some NGOs sought to implement a gender quota. They developed a Liberian Women's Manifesto, outlining a political framework for change in ten critical areas of concern, including demands for a 30 percent female legislative quota. Thus, before the 2005 elections the National Elections Commission had introduced a 30 percent quota, and some political parties tried to adhere to it. The Senate passed a 30 percent Gender Participation Bill in 2014, but the bill failed to pass the House of Representatives. Efforts to introduce quotas are ongoing at this writing. It is now being taken up by the Constitution Review Committee and will need to be taken to a referendum. The committee is also considering a provision that no gender would exceed 50 percent representation in elected, selected, or appointed positions in government. In 2014, women made up 11 percent of the seats in the House and 13 percent in the Senate (Karmo 2014).

The Constitutional Review process is considering numerous other provisions, including giving women rights to pass their citizenship to their children, as well as rights regarding personal security and freedom from cruel and degrading treatment, sexual and gender-based violence provisions, marriage and property rights, and other such provisions (Karmo 2014).

Femocrats, or women's rights advocates in government, pushed for change from above, supported by a president who has been strongly committed to gender equality and has ties to the women's movement. As a result of pressure from women's groups as well as international actors, the government developed

[39] Interview with 2.27, Monrovia, October 7, 2014.

a National Gender Policy in 2009 and created a National Gender Forum to lead its policy in this area. It established Rural Women Structures to give rural women a mechanism through which to express their concerns and take steps to address them. The Girls' Education Policy of 2006 and Education Reform Act of 2011 tackled girls' education, while the 2011 Children's Law also addressed concerns of girls. The Domestic Violence Act was passed in 2014 along with a new rape law.

Right from the outset, there were a number of policies in place, including a national gender-based violence plan of action, which was to be implemented by a gender-based violence secretariat within the Ministry of Gender and Development.

Efforts have also gone into legislative reform. The 2003 inheritance law gives women the right to a third of their husbands' property without interference from the husband's family, and the remainder is divided between the children. It ensures that women married traditionally or formally are all entitled to the same rights in their marriages. A married woman may retain any property she brought into the marriage. Nevertheless, community norms and practices continue to restrict women's access to land. Male elders who grant communal land to villagers for cultivation prefer men. Of the women I spoke to, not surprisingly it was the widows who were most bitter about their difficulty of accessing land. Hon. Gloria Scott, the former Supreme Court chief justice, explained how the reality of having so many widows forced changes in inheritance laws:

AFELL [Association of Female Lawyers of Liberia] began to discuss the opportunity to correct the situation for women in inheritance. Our first project was on inheritance rights of women. There were so many widows after the war and under the traditional system women could not inherit property. In fact, she was the inheritable item. It was difficult for men to give up that power, even the educated men. There was resistance when AFELL tried to organize. Even men lawyers asked why we needed female lawyers when they should be sufficient. They did not understand that women's issues needed special attention. We set up a committee under the bar. We did eventually get the cooperation of the male lawyers. But it took us from 1995 to 2003 to pass the [inheritance] bill. It also became clear women did not even know the power that had come to them and with this power, the whole landscape of this country could be transformed.[40]

Members of AFELL also worked on rape legislation passed in 2005, which strengthens penalties for rape, making it a nonbailable offense, carrying a sentence of ten years for rape of a woman and life imprisonment for rape of a minor. It raises the age limit for statutory rape to seventeen and recognizes that rape was perpetrated not only against females. It defined rape beyond penile penetration to account for the use of gun butts and other horrific forms of terror. AFELL organized radio programs and held public fora to publicize the bill.

[40] Interview with 2.20, Monrovia, July 11, 2008.

The government has also worked with the UNMIL to review national laws for bias or discrimination against women. The president made women's rights a signature area of policy reform within her efforts to rebuild the country. An act had been passed to create a Land Reform Commission that would remove existing barriers to women's land ownership. Efforts were made to educate people about women's rights. Education campaigns were launched around CEDAW. These involved "mini dramas" that explained the Convention in simple language and were aired on local radio stations nationwide and performed on street corners in Monrovia.

A new policy of free primary school education allowed for an increase in the enrollment of girls by 40 percent. Thus, the gap between girls and boys has largely closed in education, with enrollments of 38 percent male to 37 percent female at the primary level and 16 percent male to 14 percent female at the secondary level. However, adult literacy rates outside Monrovia reveal that only about one-third of women can read, compared to about 60 percent of men (GOL 2008). Numerous initiatives have been made to improve education for girls. The Ministry of Education set up "girl-friendly" schools in targeted areas and community-managed childcare centers. To ensure pregnant girls received an education, evening classes were set up where they could continue their studies free from teasing and shaming of their peers. After giving birth, they were encouraged to return to their regular school. Teachers who sexually harassed girls in schools were suspended without pay for five years, or indefinitely, depending on the seriousness of the offence.

Under the leadership of Liberian President Ellen Johnson Sirleaf, the Ministry of Gender and Development launched a campaign against rape with the slogan "No sex for help. No help for sex. Sex is not a requirement for jobs, grades, medical treatment or other services." Some older wealthier men have sexually exploited poorer women and girls with the promise of payment, jobs, and other benefits. This practice reached epidemic proportions, causing the president in December 2006 to warn perpetrators of this practice "not to use your wealth and power to sexually exploit children and women. It is an unacceptable behavior, and a major challenge currently facing all of us" ("Government, Women's Groups …" 2007). No other country in Africa has had such aggressive leadership at this level in an effort to end violence against women and address other issues affecting women.

The Ebola crisis, which started in 2014, was particularly harsh on women because of their caregiving roles and responsibilities in preparing the dead for burial. Their ability to access health care services was also seriously affected by the crisis. Much of the progress that had been made in healthcare for women was undermined by this crisis. However, prior to the crisis, maternal mortality rates were down to 770 per 100,000 live births from a high of 994. This remains one of the biggest problems in Liberia and is a result of poor prenatal care, large numbers of teenage pregnancies, and few trained medical personnel. Fertility rates have also gone down, but women still experience high rates of fertility at 5.2 children per woman and 6.2 children per woman in rural areas.

Women, especially in the rural areas, are limited in their access to credit and inputs. Various schemes have been implemented by the government and NGOs to help women in this area. For example, Cross Border Trade Association had increased financial services to thousands of rural businesswomen through the Joint Program on Gender Equity and Women Empowerment, supported the establishment of fifteen Villages Saving Loans Associations, and helped market women gain literacy and business training. Other programs have included the Empowerment Program for Adolescent Girls (EPAG), which provides girls with life skills. The National Transit Authority runs a "Girls Behind Wheels Program" to train women as drivers of large vehicles for a living.

The national police force under the Ministry of Justice installed Women and Children Protection Units in all of Liberia's fifteen counties, and each of the Ministry's political subdivisions now had a county attorney to prosecute cases. Sexual and gender-based violence crimes units provided prosecutorial and support services to victims, while local citizens lent support through community policing forums. Support to rape victims was also being strengthened, along with efforts to properly collect evidence, and awareness was being built so that women felt more confident to report incidences of the crime.

CONCLUSION

Even though the Liberian conflict ended much later than the Ugandan conflict, the patterns evident after 1986 in Uganda were present in Liberia as well. All three causal factors were evident in the Liberian case: the role of the women's movement, the gender disruptions of war, and the international influences. While in Uganda the women's movement became more visible after the conflict, in Liberia, a strong peace movement was a precursor to later mobilization around women's rights and political power. International diffusion effects may account, in part, for the stronger women's engagement in the peace movement; however, the primary momentum for this movement, as in Uganda, came from within the country.

5

Angola: The Limits of Postconflict Gender Policy Reform

Céu ja clareá	The sky has cleared
Consciença ja desanuviá	Consciousness has brightened
Ja tchiga hora, pa enfrentá realidade	The time has come to face reality
Um povo sofredor	A suffering people
Ja calmá sê dor	Have soothed their pain
Pa'l bem vivê, na paz e na progresso	To live in peace and progress
Si nô tiver fê	If we have faith
Na nôs capacidade	In our capabilities
Mâe Africa, ta ser feliz um dia	Mother Africa will one day be happy

– Lyrics to *Nossa Africa*, written and sung by Cesária Evora

The case of Angola is contrasted with the Ugandan and Liberian cases as well as cross-national data to show how the absence of key causal mechanisms made it less likely that Angola would adopt woman-friendly policies. The country did increase female political representation; they adopted a few woman-friendly policies; and they did make some constitutional changes, but not at the same pace or extent as found in other postconflict countries. They share many of the same characteristics as other postconflict countries where we did not see much significant change, for example, Chad and Eritrea.

The length and intensity of the conflict may have resulted in even more extensive gender disruptions in Angola than in the other cases (e.g., men taking on female roles in the household). But these ruptures did not translate into the same positive changes for women overall. The extent to which gender regime change occurred was dampened by the lack of democratization, of a peace movement, and of the emergence of an independent women's movement both during and after the war. It was also hampered by the withdrawal of most donors after the war and the redirecting of remaining donor funds to the state. This is not to say that there were no pressures for gender regime change. There were efforts for political reform initiated by the existing women's

TABLE 5.1 *Basic Political, Economic, and Social Data for Angola, 2014*

Capital	Luanda
Type of government	Republic, multiparty presidential regime
Independence	November 11, 1975 (from Portugal)
GDP (current US$)	$114 billion (2012 CIA)
GDP per capita (current US$)	$5,484 (2012 CIA)
GDP growth	9.7% a year
Poverty level	Two-thirds living on less than $2 a day, and an unemployment rate of 26%
	40.5% of population below the poverty line (2006 CIA)
Inflation	8.9% (2013 CIA)
Major sources of revenue	Agriculture 10.2%, industry 61.4%, services 28.4% (2011 CIA)
Population	20.82 million (2012 World Bank)
Ethnicity	37% Ovimbundu, 25% Kimbundu, 13% Bakongo, 2% mestico (mixed European and native African), 1% European, 22% other
Religion	Indigenous beliefs 47%, Roman Catholic 38%, Protestant 15% (1998 CIA).
Official languages	Portuguese (official), Bantu, and other African languages
Head of government	President Jose Eduardo Dos Santos (since September 21, 1979); Vice President Manuel Domingos Vicente (since September 26, 2012)
Cabinet	Council of Ministers appointed by the president
Prime minister	The post was abolished due to the 2010 Constitution, which integrates the functions of the prime minister into the office of the president, who is not subjected to the confidence of the parliamentary majority, contrarily to the prime minister
Legislative branch	Unicameral National Assembly or Assembleia Nacional (220 seats; members elected by proportional vote to serve five-year terms
Women in National Assembly	34% women (Quota Project 2012)
Speaker of the House	Valentina Matvienko
Judiciary	Constitutional Court (Tribunal Constitucional) President: Juíz Conselheiro Presidente Number of women justices on Constitutional Court: 4 out of 11
Electoral system	Executive branch: president indirectly elected by National Assembly for a five-year term (eligible for a second consecutive or discontinuous term) under the 2010 constitution; note – according to the 2010 constitution, ballots are cast for parties rather than candidates, the leader of the party with the most votes becomes

(continued)

Table 5.1 (*continued*)

	president; following the results of the 2012 legislative elections DOS SANTOS became president (eligible for a second term)
Districts	Zaire, Ufge, Lunda Norte, Lunda Sul, Luanda, Bengo, Kuanza Norte, Kianza Sul, Huambo, Benguela, Malanje, Moxico, Bie, Kuando-Bubango, Cunene, Huila, and Namibe
Parties and leaders	Broad Convergence for the Salvation of Angola Electoral Coalition or CASA-CE (Abel Chivukuvuku)
	National Front for the Liberation of Angola or FNLA (Lucas Ngonda)
	National Union for the Total Independence of Angola or UNITA (Isaias Samakuva) (largest opposition party)
	Popular Movement for the Liberation of Angola or MPLA (Jose Eduardo Dos Santos) (ruling party in power since 1975)
	Social Renewal Party or PRS (Eduardo Kuangana)

FIGURE 5.1 Administrative Map of Angola. Credit: Eva Swantz

organizations, most of which were tied to the ruling party directly or indirectly, by women within the ruling party, and by women within the parliamentary women's caucus. A few of the external foundations and donors did attempt to influence debates over increasing the representation of women in parliament. However, these efforts were muted compared to what was seen in other post-conflict countries.

BACKGROUND

Angola's recent history has been defined by several wars, the first being the war of independence against Portugal, which lasted from 1961 to 1974, with Angola gaining independence in November 1975. Peace, however, was short-lived, as the country plunged into a civil war that lasted from 1975 to 2002. This war could be divided into three major periods of recurring conflict: 1975–1991, 1992–1994, and 1998–2002. The wars ravaged the country, leaving 1.5 million dead, 2–4 million displaced, and over 330,000 refugees in a country with a population of 11 million. The social and physical infrastructure of the country was shattered. For example, 58 percent of adults were illiterate, and whole cities like Huambo were leveled.

With independence, MPLA leader Agostinho Neto became the first president. He died in 1979 and was succeeded as president by José Eduardo dos Santos, who was also elected head of the ruling People's Movement for the Liberation of Angola (MPLA). He holds the presidency to this day. Major civil conflict broke out between groups that had fought the Portuguese during the war of independence, primarily between the Afro-Marxist party MPLA, which controlled the government, and the National Union for the Total Independence of Angola (UNITA). A third group, National Liberation Front of Angola (FNLA), that had fought with UNITA was also embroiled in the civil war until 1992, when it became a political party. The Front for the Liberation of the Enclave of Cabinda (FLEC) has been fighting for the independence of this small oil-rich province of Angola, first against the Portuguese and then against the MPLA after 1975. Cabinda is a small piece of territory geographically separated from Angola and sandwiched between Congo Brazzaville and the Democratic Republic of Congo. In 2006, Angola captured the major FLEC-Renovada faction, and a cease-fire was signed.

The Angolan civil war that followed independence is regarded as the longest Cold War proxy conflict. The MPLA was supported by the Soviet Union and Cuba, while the United States and South Africa backed UNITA. FNLA also received some support from the United States as well as from the People's Republic of China, Zaire, and a variety of other sources. The civil war continued long after the Cold War dimensions of the conflict dissipated. The conflict, however, took on a stronger ethnic dimension, with the Kimbundu people being associated with the MPLA, which primarily had an urban base and a leadership that had its origins with an educated mixed-race *mestico* and *assimilado* group trained in Luanda and Lisbon. *Assimilados* were nonwhite Angolans who were said to have adopted Portuguese culture, language, and at least theoretically had met the qualifications to become Portuguese citizens. UNITA's base was in central Angola among the Ovimbundu people, and the FNLA was based in the Bakongo region of the north.

A series of efforts to reconcile the contending parties resulted in the signing of numerous peace agreements, beginning with the 1988 New York Accords, the 1991 Bicesse Accords, followed by the 1994 Lusaka Protocol. However, it was really the death of UNITA leader Jonas Savimbi at the hands of the MPLA government troops in 2002 that led to a cease-fire that held. With the death of Savimbi, a cease-fire was signed between UNITA and the Armed Forces of Angola (Forcas Armadas de Angola [FAA]) on April 4, 2002, after MPLA unilaterally ceased hostilities. The cease-fire was the outcome of a total FAA military victory over UNITA troops (Grobbelaar and Sidiropoulos 2002). The way in which the conflict ended, without a real peace negotiation, but rather with the complete defeat of UNITA, had an impact on gender policy. It affected the extent to which the MPLA was willing to reconfigure the polity. There were no new opportunity structures that allowed for women to press their demands for electoral or legislative change. The continuity in the domination of the same group of elites did not allow for new actors to enter the political stage.

The MPLA dominated the political scene in Angola throughout the conflicts. The 1992 elections and their failure left an indelible mark on Angolans. José Eduardo Dos Santos received 49.57 percent of the vote, and Jonas Savimbi received 40.6 percent in the first round. In the parliamentary vote, MPLA won 54 percent of the votes and UNITA 34 percent. Allegations were made that the elections were rigged; that 500,000 UNITA voters had not been allowed to vote; and that there were secret polling stations. Fighting broke out in Luanda and spread throughout the country as thousands if not tens of thousands of UNITA members were killed by the MPLA. It took 16 years before the country was ready once again for elections. In 2008 dos Santos won the presidential election, while the MPLA claimed 82 percent of the parliamentary seats, with UNITA winning 10 percent. In 2012 MPLA lost some support, winning 72 percent of the seats, while UNITA claimed 19 percent. A new party, Broad Convergence for the Salvation of Angola – Electoral Coalition (CASA-CE) won 6 percent of the seats. The 2010 constitution introduced a provision that the majority party head would automatically become president, thus Dos Santos was confirmed as president after the 2012 elections.

Although the 2008 and 2012 elections experienced irregularities, opposition parties accepted the results, knowing that to object would be futile. The voter turnout, however, declined precipitously with the 2012 elections. It had reached a high of 87.36 percent in 2008 compared to 62.75 percent in 2012. The other political parties do not play the role of an opposition nor do they present themselves as a viable alternative to the MPLA, although they gained ground with the 2012 elections. The MPLA is more of a front than a party. Most of the major elite rifts can be found within the MPLA, and they are over priorities, but they are not visible and cannot be expressed publicly (Messiant 2001). One reason the prodemocracy forces have been so weak in Angola has to do with the splits within the elite, which are too weak to align themselves with civil society to adopt a more prodemocracy stance (Chatham House 2005).

The MPLA dominates political life in Angola today and has been remarkably successful in coopting elements within civil society that might press for more radical changes. There are about 350 registered domestic nongovernmental organizations (NGOs). There was a peace movement, but it was very small, and women played virtually no public role in it, although they carried out informal actions at the local level. The women's wing of the MPLA, Organização da Mulher de Angola (Organization of Angolan Women; OMA), dominates women's mobilization, but it has lost in strength over the years. Besides OMA there are only two other major women's organizations involved with supporting economic, social, and political rights of women: Rede Mulher (Women's Network; RM) and Movimento Angolano Mulheres Paz e Desenvolvimento (Angolan Movement for Women, Peace and Development; MPD). Both are extremely weak, although Rede Mulher has had some impact on policy in recent years.

GENDER DISRUPTIONS

As in Uganda and Liberia and other postconflict countries, major gender disruptions occurred in Angola. Women often became the main breadwinners in the family. Perhaps because of the lengthy duration of the conflict, men began to carry out domestic activities along with women as desperation forced women to seek an income and the pressures of conflict wore on (Ducados 2000). El-Bushra found in a study of Viana settlement of internally displaced persons (IDPs) on the outskirts of Luanda that women had revived traditional forms of savings known as *kixiki* and that they bore the main financial burden of the household, while men were taking on responsibility for children and domestic work. However, she found that men felt this role reversal was borne out of failure, resulting in frustration. The men accepted their dependence on women "passively, acknowledging that women's resourcefulness and industry have pulled them through crises" (2003, 257). A 2008 study by the Rural Development Institute found that 25 percent of the households were headed by women as a result of death and displacement (SIGI 2014). Many of these themes are reminiscent of the experiences of men and women in the previous case studies of Liberia and Uganda. These trends continued after the war and even became worse. As a leader of MPD and the Democratic Front Party explained, after the war was over, women continued to provide food and support the household because their husbands had died in the war or came back amputated. Other men were jobless.[1]

One activist talked about how women traders were responsible for the survival of the country during the war. They traveled to Zimbabwe and Namibia during the war for foodstuffs and later even to Ponta Negra in Brazil, Hong Kong, Dubai, South Africa, China, and Thailand to buy goods to sell in Angola. They would pool funds and have two or three women travel to make purchases for a group of about twenty women.

Some of these gender disruptions resulted in transformations at the individual level. Because of women's involvement as fighters in UNITA, they learned Portuguese, which helped them advance later on. One women's rights activist talked about how parents today are more concerned about putting girls through school while in the 1970s they would only think about educating their sons. She said every educated young woman wants to go to university these days and wants to find a way to support herself.

While such gender disruptions occurred in Angola, they were not reinforced by other factors that we saw in Uganda and Liberia, including the mobilization of independent women's movements and United Nations (UN) along with donor influences. Moreover, even though the war had ended, political liberalization was mostly absent, making it especially difficult for civil society and potential donors to operate. This constrained women activists' overall impact, especially in national politics.

PEACE MOVEMENT

The most important role of civil society organizations, including women's groups, came at a crucial moment at the end of the civil war in 2002, when they prevented an escalation of conflict at a time when the government threatened to decimate the vanquished rebel movement of UNITA after the death of its leader, Jonas Savimbi. Societal peace mediators sought to bring contending parties together through behind-the-scenes negotiations (Campbell 2001; Comerford 2005). A top UNITA leader explained to me that if it had not been for civil society, the government would have wiped UNITA out. Because of civil society, the government had to take the initiative to dialogue and sign the Luena peace agreement. Civil society played an important role in providing a middle ground to keep the process of integration as inclusive as possible, while isolating extreme elements. However, the MPLA ultimately dictated the terms of the peace and how fast reconciliation would occur (Grobbelaar and Sidiropoulos 2002). Apart from this, civil society in general has been fairly muted in Angola's recent history.

---

[1] Interview with 3.2, Luanda, June 12, 2008.

First wave of peace mobilization (1990–1993)

At the end of the 1980s, the only national Angolan organizations that were allowed to operate were Caritas Angola and the Council of Evangelical Organizations of Angola. The Committee of Non-governmental Organisations in Angola (CONGA) had also operated since 1988 as a platform for international NGOs, which worked closely with the UN Coordinating Office (formed in 1993).

Although there had been some peace mobilization in the 1990s, the level of repression and volatility in the country made it difficult to operate. There was a sense that peace could only be achieved by aligning with one party or another, which was very different from most other peace movements in Africa. The whole notion of civil society was new to Angola. It was only the churches that had any ability to maneuver in this early period. Between 1974 and 1998, sixty-four pastoral communications were released at a time when no other independent voices were permitted.

Civil society is a relatively recent phenomenon in Angola. In 1991, a law was passed that allowed associations to register independent of the ruling party. It also allowed for political parties to organize. It provided for freedom of assembly, of speech and of movement, the right of political parties to organize, and the right to strike. However the criteria for belonging to this status was not clarified until 2000, and so people were reluctant to test the limits of the law. Proximity to the MPLA was assumed to be the most important criteria.

The passage of the law was followed by an expansion of NGOs. International NGOs emerged to deal with the humanitarian crisis during the 1992–94 war following the elections. The number of these organizations was still quite small. By 1996 there were only twenty-six national and international NGOs registered in Angola, which gives some sense of how constrained civil society was relative to other countries in Africa (Chatham House 2005).

The beginning of civil society dates back to 1989 with the formation of two NGOs, Acçao Angolana para o Desenvolvimento (Angolan Action for Development [AAD]) and Acçao para o Desenvolvimento Rural e Ambiente (Action for Rural Development and the Environment [ADRA]). Even these NGOs initially had close ties to the MPLA. ADRA later become more independent and became one of the leading NGOs. It focused on land rights, the environment, and democratic participation. A third NGO, which emerged also at this time in 1990, Sociedade Civil Angolana (Angolan Civic Association [SCA]), was related to the Catholic Church. MPLA at the time opposed its formation, claiming that it would become a political party. Police surrounded its first meeting, and the MPLA wanted to select its leaders. Conveniently, SCA and MPLA had the same individual in mind, thus averting a potential crisis. Also, the former MPLA chairman and prime minister intervened on behalf of SCA (Comerford 2005). However, this gives a picture of how limited the political space for mobilization was at the time. Forum of the Angolan

Non-Governmental Organizations (FONGA), a network of NGOs, was formed in 1991 and was focused on victims of war. Four commercial private radio stations started broadcasting in 1992, but they too were closely tied to the MPLA.

Second wave of peace mobilization (1994–1998)

A second generation of mobilization emerged after the Lusaka Protocol around human rights, more commonly referred to as "civic education." This included organizations like Mãos Livres (Free Hands), which focused on building human rights awareness; the Catholic-based Mosaico, which trained human rights activists throughout Angola; and Paz, Justicia y Democracia (Association for Justice, Peace and Democracy), which focused on prison detentions.

The second wave of civil society organizations was formed after the 1994 Lusaka Protocol. Private media expanded, although not all were given permits, including the UN radio. Some journalists were intimidated, and some even lost their lives under questionable circumstances. By 2001 there were 95 international NGOs and 365 national NGOs registered.

In this period, the only other pocket of independent civil society mobilization was a few Angolan trade unions, including the Central Geral de Sindicatos Independentes e Livres de Angola (Center of Independent and Free Labor Unions of Angola) of 50,000 members and a small Sindicato Independente dos Marítimos de Angola (Independent Union of Maritime and Related Workers). The larger 400,000-member national union was tied to MPLA (Tvedten 2001).

Third wave of peace mobilization (1999–2002)

In December 1998 there was a famous speech by the president, who said he would seek peace through war. He rejected the Lusaka Protocol and asked the UN peacekeeping forces to leave the country. A massive offensive called Operation Restore against UNITA followed in 1999. The president aimed at decimating UNITA rather than talking to them. This prompted the churches to intensify their peace efforts. As one leader of the peace movement explained to me: "This was a key moment for us, we said there must be alternative."[2]

The real beginning of the peace movement took place in 1999, with the formation of a series of peace and religious organizations. However, the return to fighting in 1999 represented another setback in the capacity of civil society to operate freely. New women's organizations were also founded in this period. Mulheres Paz e Desenvolvimento (Women, Peace and Development [MPD]) was formed in 1999. It had sought in 2001 to meet with Savimbi

---

[2] Interview with 3.1, June 27, 2008.

and had requested UN facilitation. However, Savimbi was killed before they could pursue this further.

The Catholics bishops formed the Movimento Pro Paz (Pro-Peace Movement) in 1999, and an ecumenical Comite Intereclesial para a Paz em Angola (Inter-Ecclesial Committee for Peace [COEIPA]) was formed in 2000. Both organizations called for both the MPLA and UNITA to stop fighting and hold elections, which had last been held in 1992. Movimento Pro Pace was aimed at drawing in civil society and other churches to demand peace. COIEPA brought the Conferência Episcopal de Angola e São Tomé (Episcopal Conference of Angola and São Tomé [CEAST]), which is the Catholic Bishop's Conference, together with the Anglican Evangelical Alliance (AEA) and the Council of Christian Churches in Angola (CICA). The organization challenged the view that an armed solution was the route to peace and made the claim that a peaceful resolution to the conflict was the way forward. COIEPA brought together various civic associations, NGOs, and other leaders in the Rede da Paz peace network.

COIEPA organized a major peace congress in 2000 that brought together NGOs, twenty-two churches, Angolan government representatives, and foreign ambassadors. The churches sought to arrange a peace between UNITA and the government, but the government rejected the olive branch. A major peace demonstration was organized in 2000 by COEIPA, which drew several denominations together. Comeford argues that the formation of COEIPA was especially important because it broke the polarized discussion of peace in Angola that had focused only on pro-MPLA or pro-UNITA solutions and sought a path that transcended factions. It also argued that war had no support among the Angolan population. The churches led the peace movement, but it also included the private media, civic organizations, some NGOs, some women's organizations, and a coalition of fourteen opposition parties.

An important rallying call for peace at this time came from a Group Angola Reflexo de Paix (Angolan Group Reflective of Peace [GARP]) in April 1999. GARP was made up of influential activists including Rev. Daniel Ntoni Nzinga, who headed COEIPA; Rafael Marquês de Morais, a journalist and well-known human rights activist; and other opinion leaders. They published a memo to the nation, calling for alternative ways of dealing with conflict. Two similar memos followed, one from the women's organization MPD. All three called, among other things, for an immediate cease-fire, the establishment of formal communication between warring sides with the use of civil society mediation, and the elaboration of a peace agenda (Comerford 2005).

However, for much of the time, the peace movement's impact was slow in coming and limited because it was divided and was not united around an ecumenical vision (Messiant 2000). The Methodists, Baptists, and Congregationalists were divided because they each had supported the various factions MPLA, FNLA, and UNITA, respectively. Some single out the Methodist church, in particular, because of its close affiliation to MPLA and criticize it for not playing more of a leadership role in lobbying for peace both with respect to other religious organizations and the MPLA. Even then, the reach of COEIPA was not fully acknowledged because individual churches used their own names rather than COEIPA to promote their activities, giving the impression of a fractured movement.

Thus, while the churches spoke out against the war especially after 1990s, ultimately they failed to prevent the government from pursuing its "peace through war" strategy, which aimed at destroying UNITA rather than talking to them. Moreover, international actors (most Western countries, Brazil, Russia, and most African countries) thwarted their efforts by supporting the government's "peace through war strategy" (Chatham House 2005).

PEACE MOVEMENT AND WOMEN'S MOBILIZATION

Many of the constraints on the broader peace mobilization plagued the women's peace movement as well. However, the most striking difference between Angola, on the one hand, and Liberia and Uganda, on the other, is the virtual absence of a national peace and or women's movement. As in Uganda and Liberia, much of the peace mobilization was informal and undocumented. Angolan women tried to get into the peace process, but were completely shut out of the peace negotiations as were other groups within civil society. There wasn't the same mobilization across political and ethnic differences that one saw in other countries. This may partly be attributed to physical separation of the factions, which meant that opportunities for such cross-ethnic mobilization were difficult to organize, especially given the fact that the bases of MPLA and UNITA were located in different parts of the country.

During the war many women became active in the churches because the church replaced the government in many rural areas, and the churches often helped feed the poor, educated people, and preached tolerance and peace. They created vocational training for jobless youth. The Kimbanguist and Tokoist independent churches and other Pentecostal and messianic churches also flourished, and women, like Mama Mwilu and Mama Rosa to name a few, found more possibilities for leadership roles in these churches than was possible in the more formal religious institutions.[3]

Comerford (2005) provides an account of how groups of women would take food and other forms of assistance to prisoners and hospital patients. He describes how in Benguela in 1999, women belonging to Promaica peace organization challenged the military and police personnel who were stealing goods and money from women returning from the market or from their fields. Promaica women would go to the army barracks and police stations in groups and meet with the soldiers and police. They found out where they were from,

---

[3] Interview with 3.3, Luanda, June 27, 2008.

asked them how the war was affecting their families, whether their families had been displaced, and whether they had access to food and land. The Promaica women referred to them using familial names (brother, son) to build a relationship with them, even though they had no blood ties with them. They then asked how they would feel if someone were to steal from their mothers and fathers and harass them if they did not comply. The soldiers and police agreed that these things should not happen. The women then asked them why these things were happening to the women of Benguela. The men ended up apologizing and some wrote letters to thank the women for the visit, indicating the regret they felt for their actions. Promaica women saw these activities as part of their duty as Christians. It is interesting that the women developed their own model of peacemaking that sought to frame the problem as based on familial and experiential commonality rather than pitting the armed soldiers and police in opposition to the community.

This approach followed the emphasis of MPD on dialogue. In contrast to the government and international community's strategy of "peace through war," MPD advocated "peace through dialogue and reconciliation." As a former MPD leader argued:

Within the African societies we belong to, [which are] based on orality, dialogue presents itself as the socializing element between men and women, and the most effective mechanism for the resolution of conflict. Therefore, for peace to be achieved in Angola, the only means to do so is through inclusive and encompassing dialogue.... (Comerford 2005, 149)

In 1995 the Lutheran World Federation sponsored a meeting of the South African Council of Churches (SACC) in Rustenburg, South Africa, for party women who had seats in parliament to talk about what role they could play in Angola, which had just reverted into war. The goal was to strategize to find ways to end the conflict. The Ministry of Women's Affairs did not support the meeting. After the conference, the women met with the president and UNITA's Savimbi, but there was no action taken on their resolutions (Ducados 2000). Nevertheless, it is interesting that even given the divisions between the women based on party allegiances, there were moments during the conference when one saw the same kind of cross-party alliances that have been evident in conflicts in other parts of Africa. MPLA, UNITA, and FNLA were all represented. Initially when the meeting started on the day of arrival, the various factions kept to themselves. They feared that if their leaders were made aware that they were talking to "the enemy," they might be threatened, and in fact, participants told me the parties had instructed them not to cooperate. The four UNITA women did not even come to the dining room the first day. After the second day at lunch, the women started sitting with and talking to others. They began to acknowledge that they had similar experiences and could share information and perspectives. However, the General Secretary of the SACC, Brigelia Bam, in an effort to discredit Savimbi, compared him to Zimbabwe's Bishop Abel Muzorewa (who briefly presided over an interim government in Zimbabwe in 1979) and Mangosuthu Buthelezi (president of the Inkatha Freedom Party based in South Africa's Natal province, who clashed with the African National Congress during the apartheid era). In a remarkable show of unity, the Angolan women across the board stood up and said to her that this was nonsense. They were ready to leave the conference. They said: "We came here to talk peace, and you as outsider should not be saying such things. We will not accept what you are saying."[4]

There were pockets of antiwar activity elsewhere. In 1999 women in Cabinda protested the conscription of their sons into the war. The government finally stopped recruiting the men because of pressure from the women. In another protest, women throughout Cabinda protested in solidarity with the mothers who had lost their sons in the war.

Some of the NGOs like SCA and MPD were run by women. By 2001 MPD had about 1,000 members. It advocated on behalf of the wives and mothers who had lost children in the war and mobilized women to become conscientious objectors and not allow their children to join the fighting. They made their appeals explicitly as a consequence of their gender. They organized a first women's peace conference in Luanda June 14–16, 2001, entitled *"Pelo Direito à Vida, Busquemos a Paz com Amor"* ("For the Right to Life, Let Us Seek Peace with Love"). They focused on displaced women, building a culture of peace, and on the impact of war on women.

One femocrat in a key ministry explained some of the limitations of women's mobilization:

On the one hand, Angolan women have been excluded from peace negotiation processes and seem to have been relegated to passive agents and victims of the process, as if the war was an "all-men's business." It seems that Angolan men have declared that the war is their preserve. Indeed, the male dominated urban, Angolan elite is devoid of purpose beyond the illegitimate rape of the country's natural and human resources. They have no legitimate political constituency and they have presented no visible manifesto or viable strategy. Their reality is a short-term situation. They live at the periphery of Angolan society – separated from ordinary Angolans by language, security guards, air conditioning, and dual nationality (Ducados 2000, 21).

The main constraint on all mobilization of women is the same as the general constraints on autonomous organizations by the state. Some of the peace movement women leaders found that the government was very partisan. People feared that if they became very engaged, the ruling party would target them. They could be denied jobs, housing, admission to university, loans, a business license, a passport, and other opportunities. Today the system is a little more

---

[4] Interview with 3.4, Luanda, July 8, 2008.

open, but during the war it was very difficult to function without being part of the ruling party. One could not survive.

Therefore to stay safe, women and others stayed away from the peace movement.[5] And as many NGO leaders told me, organizations themselves found it difficult to function without ties to the MPLA. There was simply no space for autonomous action.

When I asked one of the leaders of UNITA, who was one of the founding members of MPD, why it was so difficult for women to come together across political differences, she said it was because most MPLA women seemed to agree with the war. She said that at that time, the ruling party and government had an exaggerated view. "Whenever there was an NGO fighting for peace, the government thought that those ones fighting for peace and dialogue were politically linked to UNITA because society at that time was too politicized and if you were not with MPLA you had to be with UNITA" irrespective of the reality.[6] However, other peace activists found that UNITA women themselves were reluctant to participate in the peace movement because they were too heavily engaged in the war as guerrillas.[7] Thus, it seems that women in general were not interested in building ties across political differences because the party system was much more deeply entrenched, and party women had too much to lose from asserting themselves in this way. The extreme lack of autonomy by women's organizations from the ruling party sets Angola apart from countries like Uganda and Liberia, where autonomous women's mobilization was possible.

WOMEN'S MOVEMENT TODAY

Although women made enormous contributions to the struggle for independence, much to their dismay, this did not translate into political or other gains for women in the postindependence period. The postconflict outcomes in Angola were equally disappointing after the 2002 conflict.

After the war, the Luena Memorandum provided for demobilization, disarmament, and reintegration; however, noncombatant women were left out of being beneficiaries of the program despite pressures from the World Bank and UN agencies. Widows were not provided for. Women who had been abducted by UNITA had a hard time knowing whether they should return to their homes or stay with their UNITA husbands, fearing stigma and rejection in their homes.

I spoke with one woman who had been a major with UNITA and had fought on the front line. She told me that Savimbi had established women's units to

---

[5] Interview with 3.5, Luanda, July 10, 2008.   [6] Interview with 3.6, Luanda, July 20, 2008.
[7] Interview with 3.7, Luanda, June 12, 2008.

incentivize the men to fight because they did not want to be seen to be not as courageous as the women. At the end of the war, UNITA's 50,000 to 55,000 troops were demobilized, and about 5,000 UNITA fighters were integrated into the FAA. Male fighters received job training and other forms of support, whereas the women were not considered for these benefits even though these women had fought on the front lines as well. Most of the women fighters had lost their husbands in the war and therefore could not rely on their husbands. The major estimated the number of women combatants to be around 20,000. Some women had received benefits in Kwanza-Sul and Huambo, but the benefits were not spread throughout the country.[8]

Much of women's mobilization today is limited to OMA, which was established in 1962 as the women's wing of the MPLA. It played an important role in supporting the guerrilla fighters, making food for them, providing healthcare, running literacy programs, carrying out political education, and serving as porters over long distances (Akesson 1992, 20). The OMA leaders were well-educated wives and relatives of the MPLA leaders. They constituted 10 percent of the party leaders. By 1983 OMA had 1.8 million registered members (Ducados 2000). The organization played an important role in the 1980s, shepherding through the introduction of the Family Code and introducing a free family planning program for women. The Family Code recognized common-law marriage, introduced protections for children born out of wedlock, and encouraged an equal division of labor within the home. It also encouraged debate on customary marriage, abortion, and other controversial topics.

Comité Nacional da Liga da Mulher Angolana (The Independent League for Angolan Women; LIMA) was formed in 1972 as the women's wing of the National Union for the Total Independence of Angola (UNITA). However, unlike the MPLA, the leaders did not have personal family ties to the UNITA leadership.[9] The National Front for the Liberation of Angola (FNLA) also had a women's wing. During the war they provided social assistance to orphans and amputees and carried out literacy programs.

Today, however, OMA is fairly irrelevant. It does not have any concrete programs except for a program for women suffering domestic abuse and some projects for children. Its leadership is detached from rural women because the leaders are based in urban areas. One woman in LIMA, the women's wing of UNITA felt that OMA leaders live far from rural women, and when they go to them, "they offer things just to show off that they are in a better position, that they are in a political party." But neither OMA nor LIMA have a real strategy that addresses women's concerns. OMA is not very interested in working with smaller organizations around particular issues. It is fairly self-contained, which speaks to the limitations of party women's wings more generally and their

[8] Interview with 3.8, Luanda, July 17, 2008.   [9] Interview with 3.9, Luanda, June 23, 2008.

difficulties in serving as forces for more fundamental change. Thus, the organization has diminished considerably in importance. In the single-party era this type of arrangement was commonplace throughout Africa. Today the role of OMA seems more like a throwback to a distant past.

Not surprisingly, like much of civil society, the women's movement is weak. It is not coordinated and lacks capacity. It is largely in the hands of elite women, many of whom are tied to the political parties, primarily the MPLA. It does not have independent and external sources of funding, and therefore, unlike the women's movements in Uganda and Liberia, it is largely dependent on the government.

OMA lobbied for a women's ministry and was instrumental in getting the State Secretariat for Women's Affairs, which was later transformed into the Ministry for Family and Women (Pehrsson et al. 2000). This had the effect of removing women's issues from being central to other ministries, and as a result women's concerns have not been treated as very important in other ministries. The women's ministry has been allocated one of the lowest budgets of all ministries. OMA has had a difficult time tapping into donor funds because it is regarded as a party organization, and donors have restrictions on the extent to which they can fund such organizations. Moreover, MPLA has discouraged OMA from seeking independence.

Not surprisingly, virtually all women's organizations, even the "independent" ones, are tied to MPLA. RM, which was the main independent network of women, was active in the late 1990s. But it has declined in importance, partly because it was supposed to be a network, but then started competing with other organizations for funds, thus alienating them. After the war in 2002, RM became even more closely tied with the state and lost whatever independent edge it had. When I was doing field research in Angola the president of RM was an OMA member and a top MPLA functionary. Many join MPLA because they want a top position, and they can only go so far in government without being an MPLA member.

INTERNATIONAL INFLUENCES

There are two claims in the cross-national literature regarding women's representation and international influences. One argues that the presence of peacekeeping troops correlates with female representation in parliament (Bush 2011). Neither the cases of Uganda nor Angola support this claim because neither had peacekeeping troops, yet both have relatively high rates of female legislative representation. Liberia, which has had peacekeeping troops, has low rates of female legislative representation and so it too does not support the claim. However, these cases alone don't refute the proposition either.

The other claim has to do with the role of donor aid and its impact on women's representation (Bush 2011). Once again, there is no direct correlation between aid and female representation in the Angolan case because as aid decreased, quotas were adopted and female legislative representation increased. The forces pushing for these changes have been almost entirely internal, with a nod to the Southern African Development Community (SADC) and the influences of the UN Fourth Conference on Women held in Beijing in 1995. Because of its oil and diamond wealth, Angola's per capita Overseas Development Assistance (ODA) stands at $13 compared to $329 in Liberia and $55 for Uganda (2008 figures). ODA as a percentage of GDP is 0.32 for Angola, not even a third of a percentage point, while for Uganda it is 11.13 percent and Liberia 57 percent (Aid Data).[10] Yet with minimal donor influence Angola adopted quotas and increased female representation. While three cases do not prove or disprove a proposition, they do reflect some of the broader patterns identified in this study.

Thus, in the cases explored in this book, it is likely that we must look elsewhere for the operative international factors that are at play. It is still likely that Angola's lack of dependence on donors is one contributing factor in explaining why it is not pursuing women's rights policies as aggressively as the other postconflict countries.

The UN presence has been weaker in Angola than in other countries. Because of the way the war ended, there was no continued UN peacekeeping presence that might have pushed women's rights policies nor were there opportunities for women's organizations to press for women's rights language in a peace agreement. Moreover, UN agencies have not been as active in Angola around gender issues as they have been in other countries, according to United Nations Development Programme (UNDP) sources. Partly because of the government's own lack of prioritization, there has been little emphasis on women in the Millennium Development Goals and Poverty Alleviation Strategy. There has not been much awareness about UNSCR 1325 and how it might be used. Unlike Liberia and Uganda, Angola has yet to adopt a National Action Plan on United Nations Security Council Resolution 1325 (UNSCR 1325). Donors, many of whom have traditionally been active in promoting a women's rights agenda, pulled out or decreased their involvement in Angola after the war ended.[11]

What money came in after the war either dried up or was diverted away from civil society to the state programs, thus adding to the difficulties the women's organizations faced in establishing an independent agenda. The donors that had historically been active in supporting women's rights included the European Union, United States Agency for International Development (USAID), Norwegian Agency for International Cooperation (NORAD), Department for International Cooperation (DFID), Netherlands Organisation for International Development Cooperation (NOVIB), Swedish International Development Cooperation Agency (SIDA), Canadian International Development Agency (CIDA), UNDP, United Nations Development Fund for

---

[10] http://aiddata.org.   [11] Interview with 3.11, Luanda, June 9, 2008.

TABLE 5.2 *External Funding to Angola, 2003–2009*

	2003	2004	2005	2006	2007	2008	2009
Net ODA received (% of GDP)	3.54	5.78	1.35	0.36	0.42	0.43	0.32
Net ODA received per capita (current US$)	32	71	25	10	14	20	13

Source: Aid Data. http://aiddata.org.

Women (UNIFEM), United Nations Children's Fund (UNICEF), Norwegian Peoples Aid, German Agency for Technical Cooperation (GTZ), and Friedrich Ebert Foundation. NORAD and DFID funded an anti-poverty program in Luanda with Save the Children, which ended in 2007. The traditional funders of women's rights and human rights concerns pulled out: SNV closed offices in 2007. Ibis closed in 2011, and DFID also closed its offices. Key international nongovernmental organizations (INGOs) also left. Friedrich Ebert Foundation, which had been one of the most active supporters of civil society advocacy efforts, moved its Angola office to Namibia. Thus, women's organizations like RM saw their funding reduced after 2002. The drop in funding is evident from Table 5.2 with a major decline occurring after 2005.

Angola signed key international conventions regarding women's rights, for example, the Convention on the Elimination of All Forms of Discrimination against Women (CEDAW) in 1986, and it ratified the Protocol to the African Charter on Human and Peoples' Rights on the Rights of Women in Africa (The Maputo Protocol) in 2007. It also sought to comply with SADC's representation targets.

However, compared with other countries, Angola has received less general donor aid and less aid targeted at women's rights. Because of the weakness of the women's movement there have been less engagements globally and within the region around women's rights, thus lessening norm diffusion into the country. The insularity of the country has sometimes added to its lack of international engagement around women's rights, but this seems not to have been as much of a consideration in Portuguese-speaking Mozambique. In general, Angola's natural wealth may have contributed to its sense of independence, thus making it less susceptible and interested in international norms regarding women's rights. These influences are not entirely absent as evident in the adoption of legislative quotas and the passage of key legislation; however, they are more muted than what one finds in other countries.

GENDER REGIME CHANGES

In terms of outcomes, the Angolan government, despite its enormous wealth, has done very little for women. Although there are a group of elite women who are gaining access to education and to leadership, the majority of Angolan women have little support from the government. Angola has one of the highest maternal death rates in the world. There is no social safety net. The health budget, which is one of the lowest in the world, was cut from 5 percent in 2010 to 2 percent in 2011, while military and public security spending was increased to 7 percent of the budget. Most people have no public provision for healthcare. They have no pension plans nor insurance for illness or unemployment. Infant mortality rates are among the highest in the world, with 180 deaths per 1,000 children under the age of one in 2011. Only 50 percent of the population has access to clean drinking water. Two-thirds of the population lives on under $2 a day (SIGI 2014). Women have a 57 percent literacy rate compared to men at 82.8 percent. Women are the major breadwinners in the family and are based in the informal sector.

Civil society organizations are concerned about the prevalence of early marriage, the slowness of implementing the domestic violence law, the lack of protective mechanisms for women's inheritance rights, and other such concerns.

The quota law was adopted in 2005 as a result of pressure from RM and the Women's Parliamentary Group (WPG). The WPG has been fairly active, and there has been considerable cooperation across party lines. The WPG was influenced by SADC targets to increase representation and got ideas from them on how to do it.[12] In the subsequent election, the number of women in parliament jumped from 15 percent to 39 percent in 2008 and then back down to 34.5 percent in 2012. The efforts to introduce the quota started in earnest after RM returned from the UN Conference of Women in Beijing in 1995, where it became convinced of the importance of women's political power. UNITA had also adopted an internal 30 percent quota from all provinces attending the First Congress in 2003 and the second in 2007. They also implemented a 30 percent female representation quota within UNITA leadership.

In other areas, women make up 21 percent of the cabinet and 29 percent of ministers, 21 percent of secretaries of state, 34.4 percent of lawyers, and 31 percent of judicial magistrates. Women hold three out of eighteen (17%) governorships ("UN Informed ..." 2014). There are a few very powerful women like Albina Assis Pereira Africano, currently special adviser to President Jose Eduardo dos Santos; however, women do not hold key positions within the MPLA, even though there are more women in the MPLA than men.

Although the legal age of marriage is 18 for both boys and girls, the law allows girls to marry at fifteen, and the Committee of the Rights of the Child has found that girls are being married at even younger ages. One indication of

---

[12] Interview with 3.10, Luanda, June 2008.

this is the high adolescent (15–19) fertility rate, which is 175 in Angola, one of the highest in the world, exceeded only by Niger. The Family Code does not allow for polygamy but the practice is widespread in rural areas. The Family Code states that men and women are equal in the family and have the same rights, duties, and parental responsibilities. The Family Code provides for the inheritance rights of women but customary law prevails, leaving the inheritance rights of widows and divorced women especially precarious. The Rural Development Institute found that only 23 percent of widows were able to use the land left by their husband (SIGI 2014).

There have been a handful of gender-related policy changes and legislative gains since the civil war ended. The government created the Ministry of Women's Affairs, which is responsible for family and women's issues. Its rhetoric often focuses on projects having to do with the "transmission and retrieval of moral values and promotion of family education," which is reminiscent of the rhetoric of the one-party era. A law was established in 2011 that criminalizes domestic violence. This law was championed by the Women's Parliamentary Group, RM, and OMA, although generally there is not much contact between women's NGOs and the parliament. A National Plan to implement the policy has been announced that involves the creation of 109 counseling rooms, eight women's professional training centers, and eight shelter homes.

Women's organizations have slowly expanded in number in Angola since the 1990s, but few are engaged in advocacy. Overall most women's organizations, like civil society more generally, are tied in one way or another to the MPLA and do not adopt policies that in any way challenge the government's goals. This forces them to focus more on developmental objectives. For example, Promaica, a Catholic women's association, has been active for some time in literacy programs and mutual assistance. Women's Network – Angola is another older organization formed in 1999 that exchanges information regarding experiences in gender and development. It lobbies the government around gender-related issues; seeks to empower women to advance gender equality, and provides training to member organizations. There are active professional associations of women, including entrepreneurs, judges, and journalists. The Forum das Mulheres Jornalistas (FMJ) is an organization of female journalists in both state and private media that works to increase women's visibility in the media. They also focus on issues like violence against women, especially after the law was passed in June 2011.

Finally, there are groups pressing for greater political representation for women. Plataforma Mulheres em Acçao (Women in Action Platform) was established in 2006 to get more women into politics and promote gender justice in Angola. Groupo de Liderança e Feminina is a similar group based in Sumbe and Kwanza Sul provinces that is seeking to encourage more female participation in politics and to implement the government's strategy of 50 percent women in decision-making bodies.

DISCUSSION OF ANGOLA'S DIVERGENT PATH

There are a number of factors that set Angola apart from many other post-conflict countries and help explain why it has not enjoyed the same level of gender regime change as Uganda, Liberia, or even a fellow Lusophone country, Mozambique. The explanations primarily have to do with Angola's extensive oil wealth, which helps keep a ruling elite in power and allows them to rule by limiting political freedom and suppressing autonomous civil society, including women's mobilization. They are not donor dependent and maintain extensive trade with countries like China that don't put pressures on them for gender reform; therefore they feel less restrained by international norms than more donor-dependent countries.

Impact of resources

Angola, which has substantial oil and diamond wealth, has major constraints on democratization, which keeps power ensconced in the executive, who is head of state, head of government, commander of armed forces, and president of the ruling party. Resources have also influenced other aspects of Angola's sociopolitical life. If one can generalize, Angola is a proud country, and the abundance of oil reinforces the sense that Angola is different from other African countries and it does not depend on donors. Since 1990, Angola has increased its oil production. As of 2012, the oil sector accounted for nearly 46 percent of GDP and 96 percent of exports. Angola is the second-largest oil exporter in Africa after Nigeria. Angola is China's largest trading partner, and it is the country's second-largest oil supplier after Saudi Arabia. Angola is also the fourth-largest diamond producer in the world (Pasquali 2014).

The years of war, reinforced by language, created a sense of being separated from the rest of Africa. Tens of the thousands of Portuguese are now migrating to Angola in search of jobs, as wealthy Angolans buy up Portuguese companies. Hence Angola is less beholden to outside donor pressures, not only when it comes to women's rights as mentioned in the previous section, but also in terms of democratization. While this gives the government autonomy, it also makes them less dependent on international opinion and changing global norms.

Oil and diamonds account for 99.3 percent of the economy, resulting in a heavy dependence on a few products. This suppresses competition in the local economy because the real exchange rate is kept elevated, making agriculture less competitive. Price volatility similarly creates considerable uncertainty in government planning (Amundsen and Abreu 2006, 5). Because of the enormous wealth, taxes are kept low, and therefore the citizenry has little motivation to play a watchdog role and make demands on their government to become efficient, put resources to good use, and fight corruption.

High oil and diamond rents also fuel a system of patronage and favorites, which keeps NGOs coopted and potential political rivals bought off. Angola is one of most unequal countries in Africa, yet there is little done to address problems of poverty and inequality. Angola is run by a political elite made up of ministers, deputies, army, police chiefs, and members of the judiciary, who have appropriated oil revenues, thus leading to a system of clientelism.

Constraints on civil society

After 1977, civil society became even more constrained than it had been. The events of May 27, 1977, cast a shadow on protest for years to come, and to this day people still speak with veiled references to these events, often lowering their voices. There is still no definitive understanding of the events, but the Angolan government claims there was an attempted coup by factions seeking to destroy the MPLA led by Nito Alves (a nom de guerre), a former Minister of Interior, and José Z. Van Dunem, a former political prisoner. Both had served on the MPLA Central Committee, but opposed the pro-Cuban orientation of the government. It is estimated that the government, with the help of Cuban troops, killed 28,000–40,000 civilians and jailed and tortured thousands in the two years that followed. About 3,000 disappeared. Some of the killing had to do with localized disputes and vendettas that had nothing to do with the alleged coup. Its impact was felt for years to come and ended all debate within the MPLA (Heywood 2011; Pawson 2007). To this day people are fearful of demonstrations, and these events contributed to the self-censorship that still exists within Angola. Some religious organizations like Mosaico linked to the Catholic Church have quietly raised issues of human rights abuse in a "soft way." They feel they are unable to directly criticize the government but they have been able to shine a light on various situations.[13]

It was not until 1991 that one saw civil society reemerging after the 1977 events. It was also at this time that the parliament passed a 1991 NGO law explicitly prohibiting NGOs from advocacy and from participating in "all activities of state organs; electoral processes; and from influencing national policy through the government or parliament." The 2004 NGO law placed further restrictions that required NGOs to submit detailed reports to the government.

At the end of the 1990s, civil society organizations began to talk more about human rights, and they were able to get the government to postpone the passage of a draconian media law in 2000. Even though freedom of association and expression is guaranteed in the constitution, there is little toleration of the expression of views that diverge from those of the government. Restrictions on the media and harassment of opponents of the regime have made it difficult for civil society to operate freely.

---

[13] 3.16 Interview, Luanda, June 19, 2008.

Activists are routinely intimidated and receive anonymous death threats because of their involvement in demonstrations. They are harassed and threatened with violence if they do not cease their protest activities. More than 292 people were detained ahead of protests in 2012 according to press reports (U.S. Department of State 2013). Moreover, the government maintained extensive internal security networks that left the NGOs intimidated. NGOs find their activities arbitrarily restricted depending on how threatening the state finds their agenda. Because of harassment of journalists and media houses, they engage in self-censorship. They also face cumbersome registration processes. The Angolan government jailed journalist and human rights activist Rafael Marques de Morais in 1999 because of his articles critical of the regime. Then they brought new charges against him over his 2011 book, *Blood Diamonds: Corruption and Torture in Angola,* documenting 500 cases of torture and 100 killings carried out in the diamond-producing province of Lunda Norte in northeast Angola. His 2015 trial ended with Marques being handed a six-month suspended jail term.

Gradually, civil society organizations have become more emboldened.[14] Around the mid-2000s people started calling in to radio stations and airing their grievances. However, there was generally a price to be extracted. On May 27, 2012, demonstrations were held in Luanda to remember the victims of May 27. Police brutally beat the protestors and took some into custody. There have been mounting antigovernment protests, and they have increasingly come under attack, often by undercover thugs. The governor of Luanda, Bento Joaquim Bento, warned in 2013: "Whoever tries to demonstrate will be neutralised because Angola has laws and institutions and a good citizen understands the laws, respects the country and is a patriot." The secretary general of the party, Dino Matross, was equally blunt: "Anyone who demonstrates: we're going to get you."

Women have been among the bravest of protestors. In June 2013, 15,000 mostly women took to the streets to protest the brutal murders of female peasants in Lunda-Norte Province. While the authorities had done nothing to address the murders, the government soldiers opened fire on the demonstrators and arrested protestors.

There are other reasons for the weakness of civil society in addition to repression and legal constraints. The population was deeply traumatized by the war. Most organizations during the war were based in Luanda and had a weak grassroots base. Communication throughout the country was limited because of the collapse of the infrastructure. Many NGOs remained coopted by the government. The state needed to control civil society to prevent it from challenging the blatant kleptocratic practices of the dos Santos family. The family's businesses include the president's daughter Isabel dos Santos's

---

[14] 3.16 Interview, Luanda, June 19, 2008.

massive holdings in various diamond, oil, cement, media, retail, finance, and telecommunication companies in a country where 70 percent of Angolans live on less than $2 a day. At 40, she is the wealthiest woman in Africa, who according to *Forbes* (Dolan 2013), allegedly was able to acquire her wealth through kickbacks diverted by her father from companies seeking to do business in Angola.

Another reason for the weakness of civil society has to do with the fact that many of the most prominent members of civil society are former leaders of the MPLA and have not shed their old ways of thinking. Many of the practices within the state are replicated within civil society, including the lack of accountability. Younger citizens grew up during the war, which was extremely long and don't have other models for ways of thinking. Physical insecurity often led people to gravitate toward a governing party that asserted control and worked through a command structure (Chatham House 2005). But it is much more than a way of thinking. Many people are simply bought off or the costs of challenging the system are personally too high, as mentioned earlier.

Thus, political opening has not taken place in Angola even though there has been a lessening of repression since the time of conflict. As one activist told me:

Since the time of colonialism we have not had free access to public space. To create a transformation towards democratization, we need to have a theoretical life, we need to have a civil society, a public space, and the capacity to exercise rights, and mainly the capacity to be a citizen. Instead we have a culture of fear, from the old legacy of a Marxist past, we have a fear of advocacy. We are told "You are not here to talk, you are here to divide 100 kgs of rice."

By the end of the 1990s, many of the coopted civil society organizations simply served as "chains of transmission" of paternalistic patronage to society and as conduits of pro-MPLA messages. Only those civil society organizations (CSOs) that supported the ruling party survived and had access to funding. With the end of the 1990s and early 2000s more NGOs began to see themselves in opposition to the state, and the state, in turn, saw them as enemies (Fernando 2009). The government still regards advocacy as opposition to the government and holds the view that if one advocates for something, one must be anti-government. When an NGO gets registered, all it can say is that it will help the poor and reduce poverty. It cannot mention advocacy. Even many Angolan NGOs themselves don't realize that CSOs in other countries can carry out advocacy to improve or change public policies without being antigovernment. The MPLA vision of civil society is primarily that of service provider and not advocate, watchdog, partner in making policy, or any of the other of the functions normally associated with civil society.

This influences women's organizations. As one women's rights activist told me, the selection of leaders of OMA and LIMA are controlled by their political parties, not by members of their associations. Many learned this the hard way during party congresses in which they tried to put forward their own leaders. Women have little freedom of speech within the MPLA, and if they speak freely they can lose their party card.[15]

Weak donor and UN role

Yet another reason for the decline of civil society has to do with the aforementioned drying up of donor funds after the war as they started working more closely with the government. Humanitarian funds disappeared, which put many local NGOs at risk. Donor support was directed at decentralization and capacity building in local administration through collaborations between government and NGOs like ADRA. CARE International, Save the Children UK, and other such international NGOs continued their work, primarily focusing on development type activities. The government stepped up efforts to control national and international NGOs through a new NGO law in 2002. External funding to NGOs is closely monitored and controlled by the government, while their capacity to operate is controlled through licensing (Soares de Oliveira 2015). Some organizations like FONGA collapsed, in part due to internal problems. Other NGOs collapsed as a result of efforts by the government to infiltrate and destroy them. Even though civil society has been weak in Angola and was often unfairly portrayed in the media as squandering public funds from donors, it has been one of the more dynamic sectors of society (Chatham House 2005).

In 1996, the president formed the Eduardo dos Santos Foundation (FESA), and as its patron he is the leading supporter of civil society in Angola. FESA asks the main foreign companies doing business in Angola as well as banks and construction companies for startup fees and other contributions. Even Angolan public companies contribute to this Foundation, which is run by the president in his personal capacity. At the same time, the state has virtually abandoned public welfare, allowing the Foundation, and by implication dos Santos, to present themselves as generous benefactors concerned with the needs of the people, the poor, the disabled, and schoolchildren. FESA often does so in collaboration with the government or with the oil company Sonagol. This has been a way that clientelistic support is distributed to civil society and women's organizations. For example, the Association of Aid to Rural Women, whose patron is the wife of the president, is supported by FESA. FESA, however, was created to separate the image of president and his wife from the inefficiency of government. The president's daughter, Ana Paula dos Santos, founded Lwini Foundation, which serves much the same purpose as FESA (Messiant 2001).

---

[15] Interview with 3.12, Luanda, June 12, 2008.

Comparison with Mozambique

Angola could be usefully compared with Mozambique, which shares a common history. Both countries share a common colonial past; they both had Afro-Marxist governments; they gained independence at the same time; and then both plunged into lengthy civil wars. Women's organizations in both countries were cut off from the influences of the rest of the world for much of the 1970s, 1980s, and 1990s (in Angola) and were tied to the ruling party. They both had a similar linguistic tradition of Portuguese, which made engagements on the continent and beyond sometimes more challenging than they were for other countries that had English, French, Arabic, or Swahili as a lingua franca. These similarities provide important controls that allow one to look for variance that might explain what accounts for the changes in so many postconflict countries with respect to women's rights.

For example, an independent women's movement emerged in Mozambique in the 1990s but not in Angola. This might be a function of time, but even Uganda, a country that had been conflict ridden for over a decade, saw the emergence of an independent women's movement almost immediately after it came out of conflict in 1986. In Liberia, the independent women's movement emerged during the conflict. Thus, Angola's lack of an independent women's movement points to some key elements that explain what has happened in many postconflict contexts.

Unlike Angola, which was insulated by its oil and mineral wealth, Mozambique was much more oriented toward the broader international community and influences regarding women's rights. As many activists told me in Angola, the nexus between oil and the lack of democracy kept the women's movement divided, and women leaders felt they had more to lose in terms of positions and wealth if they sought to work too independently of the ruling party and if they collaborated too closely with women outside the party. Mozambique democratized much more than Angola, and this allowed for a vibrant women's movement to emerge in Mozambique, which pressed for important legislative and other policy changes.

Because there have been changes in legislative representation and some legal reforms, Angola follows the other postconflict countries up to a point. But in other respects it has fallen behind the other postconflict countries. Thus, the comparison between Angola and other postconflict countries like Uganda and Liberia (as well as Mozambique) point to possible theoretical explanations of the causal mechanisms at work linking postconflict dynamics to gender regime change.

CULTURAL RENAISSANCE

While there may be aspects of civil society and politics that became fossilized because of the war, oil, and an elite class that is trying to maintain power, one also finds Angola to be highly modern and dynamic in other respects. A discussion of cultural renaissance may seem as though it is a bit of a tangent, but it is the product of having other channels for political expression closed off. In fact, some of the bravest expressions of defiance of the system have come from the cultural scene by men and women artists who have addressed some of the deepest sorrows, silences, and divisions within society. Women have very much been part of this movement.

Luaty Beirão, a popular Angolan rapper also known as Ikonoklasta, has been speaking out and getting involved in protest actions. In many ways his protest has targeted not only the MPLA party and elite, but also the weakness of civil society and opposition parties as well as attitudes of ordinary people. He said in an interview:

This country is being run by a mob and a mafia. By being silent people are being complicit and they are contributing to the injustices. Everyone knows things aren't right, but the people are too scared for their own jobs and families to stand up to what is happening. It's like a spider's web of fear and patronage, and it's so thick that people are trapped. We need to cut those strings so we can renew this country and start again.

Ikonoklasta belongs to a wider transformation in the cultural scene. Hip-hop more generally has been the most important art form openly critical of the regime. Banned from the airwaves, protest rappers have become enormously popular as their CDs are produced in makeshift studios, copied, and circulated throughout Angola's cities on USB sticks and MP3 players via the *candongueiro* taxi network and the marketplaces.

But there is a broader cultural renaissance taking place in Angola. António Ole is perhaps the best-known artist. Fernando Alvim is creating the first museum of contemporary art in Luanda. Angola is exporting its dances like the *kuduro, kizomba, tarrachinha*, and *samba* to clubs in Europe. Women are very much a part of this scene, including singers and songwriters like Margareth do Rosário, Ana de Oliveira "Nani," and Sonia Ferreira; architects like Paula Nascimento; and artists like Marcela Costa, who works with plastic. The influences are African and Brazilian, and they are optimistic, creative, and cheerful. It is something of a paradox that amid repression and the incivility of poverty, one finds a thriving cultural scene. As one Angolan put it. "After the civil war, it's not simply a matter of the physical reconstruction of our country, but of mental reconstruction," explains Tekasala Ma'at Nzinga. "We want to overcome the *confusão*," or the confusion of having lived for five hundred years of foreign rule and thirty years of war (Grill 2002).

Another Angolan actress and activist summed up the cultural undercurrents to me in this way:

Arts play a very important role in political reform. Theater is something that speaks about life. We have a lot of theater companies that are raising the most critical social problems that we have. One group composed mainly of young actors performed a play recently talking about crime in this society and the reasons the level of crime

is increasing. The interesting thing for me was that the clear argum
that all the criminal people that were in prison were not guilty. I ca.
through social movements. During the Marxist regime, people in theater ι.
expose in an open way the social problems as they do today. The main difference ι.
that when I see now a critical play, I can clearly say that they are raising this and that
issue, speaking in direct language. In the past we criticized but we did it in a subtle
hidden way.[16]

CONCLUSION

This chapter has contrasted Angola with Liberia and Uganda as well as
Mozambique to show that while these countries share the gendered disruptions of war, they differ along key dimensions, which help explain why
Angola has not been as aggressive in adopting a women's rights agenda
compared with these other countries. The key factors have to do with the lack
of democracy in Angola, which did not allow sufficient space for an autonomous civil society and women's movement to emerge. Civil society is plagued
by cooptation and intimidation. Angola's economic reliance on oil and
diamonds lessened its need to please the UN and other international donors
and to respond to international and regional pressures regarding women's
rights norms. This is not to say there were no external influences, but they
were muted. The way the war ended abruptly in 2002, with one side over-
powering the opposition, did not provide women activists with an opportunity
to insert themselves into peace negotiations or a constitution-making process.
Thus the lack of democracy, weak civil society and women's movement,
30 years of war with little institutional growth, and weak international pressures along with poor opportunity structures for influencing peace talks and
constitution-making processes, all contributed to a weak impetus on government to make major changes in women's rights.

[16] 3.16 Interview, Luanda, June 19, 2008.

PART III

NEW OPENINGS FOR WOMEN'S RIGHTS

6

Women's Rights in Peace Agreements

There are opportunities even in the most difficult moments.

— Wangari Maathai, *Unbowed*

Like war, peacemaking is gendered and gendering. Like violence, peacemaking itself creates and reifies existing gendered power relationships. At the negotiating table, male warlords and leaders have divided up the spoils of war in new arrangements, that is, who gets which positions of power and the trappings of power that go along with them. Men negotiate at formal peace talks and come up with formal peace agreements, while women tend to be relegated to the informal, invisible, and localized peacemaking strategies. If this sounds too crude and simplistic, this is mostly how it has been in the conflicts discussed in this book, and there is little evidence to suggest otherwise.

However, women activists in many conflict countries in Africa in recent years have attempted to disrupt the gendered nature of this process by demanding seats at the peace table and by insisting that their demands be incorporated into the peace agreements. Their visions of what a peace agreement should look like have differed radically from what has been the norm. They realized they had to demand power if they were going to have any influence. Many were forced to think strategically.

The reality is that women have been largely excluded from peace negotiations, even after the passage of UNSCR 1325 in 2000 that was intended to remedy this by calling "on all actors involved, when negotiating and implementing peace agreements, to adopt a gender perspective." Nevertheless, peace agreements have begun to incorporate women's rights language as a result of domestic and international pressures. This is evident in Africa to a greater extent than other parts of the world, as references to women between 2000 and 2012 tripled in all peace agreements (12% to 34%) and more than doubled in all comprehensive peace agreements (33% to 78%) from the

TABLE 6.1 *African Peace Agreements, 1989–2011*

Women's rights mentioned in all peace treaties 1989–2000	Women's rights mentioned in all peace treaties 2000–2011	Women's rights in comprehensive peace agreements 1989–2000	Women's rights in comprehensive peace agreements 2000–2011
12%	34%	33%	78%

N = 89
Source: African Peace Agreement Database.

previous decade (see Table 6.1). This helped set the stage for the later incorporation of women's rights into constitutions and into legislation as well as for women's presence in key governmental, legislative, and transitional institutions (see Chapters 7, 8, and 9; DPA 2004).

This chapter looks at women's rights provisions in peace agreements in comparative perspective. It then focuses on the case of Liberia to show how women's rights activists pursued their agenda in the peace agreements, both on issues affecting the entire nation, but also for women's rights. It looks briefly at the Burundi, Somali, and DRC negotiations to show how women in all these cases, and many more, were involved in building cross-ethnic and cross-clan ties around a common agenda. This common agenda was quite distinct from that of other negotiating parties that focused on differences from the outset rather than on points of unity. The chapter also shows how in the DRC and Liberian cases, women played a crucial role in preventing the talks from derailing. Thus, not only were peace negotiations and peace agreements gendered, but they also became sites of contestation over the nature of the gender regime.

As has been mentioned earlier, civil wars that ended in peace negotiations had a greater chance of creating possibilities for women activists to negotiate women's rights as part of the peace agreement. This was especially true when women were included in the negotiations. Countries like Angola that did not end their conflicts with a CPA faced much steeper hurdles in including women's rights later in the process compared with countries like Liberia that did sign a CPA.

WOMEN'S REPRESENTATION IN PEACE NEGOTIATIONS

Only a handful of women have ever led peace negotiations. Mary Robinson, former president of Ireland, became the first female United Nations (UN) Special Envoy when she was appointed by the UN Secretary General in 2013 to lead a peacekeeping delegation to the Great Lakes Region. Since 1992, women have been represented on only 9 percent of the negotiating delegations and have constituted 4 percent of the signatories. While women have not made gains as chief mediators, negotiators, or signatories, there have been more consultations between mediation teams and women's organizations. Between 2008 and 2012, mediation teams consulted regularly with women's organizations in seven out of eleven processes. In the few cases where women were included in the talks, this often came about as a result of interventions by United Nations Development Fund for Women (UNIFEM) and later UN Women. For example, in the case of northern Uganda, UNIFEM funding and advocacy helped women participate in the Juba talks, although women's rights activists in Uganda also put pressure on the government to include women when they discovered that the government delegation had no women at the negotiating table. As a result, two women were included, and the Lord's Resistance Army had one woman (O'Connell 2011).[1] Women experts were consulted in twelve out of fourteen mediation efforts supported by the United Nations in 2011 (UN Women 2012).

Because of these types of exclusions, women sometimes took it upon themselves to serve as mediators anyway, working behind the scenes. Betty Bigombe had been appointed as Ugandan minister of state for the pacification of the North in 1988 and had served as chief negotiator for the Ugandan government in 1993–94 and 2004–05 in the northern Uganda conflict. She continued to play a behind-the-scenes role prior to and during the Juba peace talks in 2006–07 and expended her personal resources in some of these activities.[2]

UN agencies were critical in ensuring a role for women's rights activists at the peace talks and in seeing that women's rights language made it into peace agreements. Key UN agencies were involved in promoting women's political and other forms of empowerment, particularly after the passage of UNSCR 1325 in 2000. These included UNIFEM (later UN Women), Department of Political Affairs, Department of Peacekeeping Operations (DPKO), Office of the Special Adviser on Gender Issues and Advancement of Women (OSAGI), the gender advisor or focal point in a UN Peacekeeping mission, and other assorted UN agencies like the United Nations Development Programme and UN Population Fund. Other international women's rights political entrepreneurs who supported these efforts included the International Foundation for Electoral Systems (U.S.), National Democratic Institute (U.S.), International Republican Institute (U.S.), Friedrich Ebert Foundation (Germany), Kondrad Adenauer Foundation (Germany), and various other such international NGOs, many of which are funded by bilateral donors. And although there is no clear correlation between bilateral donor support for women's political leadership and women's representation, it is probably more useful to think of this funding as part of a nexus of activity that sustains local level movements in their efforts to advance women's political empowerment.

---

[1] Interview with 1.37, Caroline Bunga Idembe, March 7, 2008.
[2] Interview with 1.38, Betty Bigombe, April 2, 2008.

New scholarship now argues that civil society, including women's organizations, can make a difference in enhancing peace outcomes (Barnes 2002; Bell and O'Rourke 2007; Belloni 2001; McKeon 2005). According to Nilsson (2012), civil society is often seen as bringing added legitimacy to the process. They may be consulted, brought into the talks, and used to intervene at the grassroots level to engage local populations. Barnes (2002), for example, showed how in Mali, the engagement of civil society at the grassroots level had important consequences for bringing about peace.

Civil society involvement in peace negotiations also has implications for preventing a return to conflict. Nilsson's new quantitative research has suggested that civil society can also play a major role in influencing the outcomes for peace. This has important consequences for work on women in peace talks. Out of eighty-three peace agreements since the end of the Cold War, twenty-eight, or 34 percent, have included at least one civil society actor. Nilsson (2012) finds that if civil society actors are included in peace agreements, the risk of peace failing is reduced by 64 percent. These findings held across regime type.

These cross-national studies are reinforced by accounts of women peace activists themselves, who describe the ways in which they influenced peace talks in countries like Burundi and Liberia, as constrained as they were. They had to be persistent and forceful, and they needed to work as a unified movement to impact the talks (AWPSG 2004; Gbowee 2011; UNIFEM 2001). Women lobbied both national and regional, as well as international actors in almost all cases.

WOMEN'S RIGHTS IN PEACE AGREEMENTS

Even given women's marginalization from the formal peace process, women often made a difference in those instances when they were given a seat at the table, not only to advance a women's rights agenda, but also to the overall peace process itself. This, in turn, had impacts on constitutional and legislative reform.

The figures for women's rights incorporation into peace agreements vary depending on the time frame and database consulted. I found, using the African Peace Agreement Database of the University of Antwerp,[3] that women were mentioned in 34 percent of all African peace treaties between 2000 and 2011 compared with 12 percent in the previous decade. More important, women were mentioned in 78 percent of the comprehensive peace agreements between 2000 and 2011 compared with 33 percent in the previous decade (Table 6.1). This suggests that the UNSCR 1325 has had an impact on the attentiveness

---

[3] https://www.uantwerpen.be/en/rg/law-and-development/research-topics/power-sharing-and-human-rights/african-peace-agreement-database/.

of the agreements to women's concerns, even though the substance of these references may leave much to be desired.

The global data on the incorporation of women's rights in global agreements is less impressive. Using the Uppsala Conflict Data Program (UCDP) database, Miriam Anderson (2010) found that of the 148 peace agreements signed between 1989 and 2005, at least 38 (30%) contain explicit references to women. She found too that African peace agreements had proportionately the greatest percentage of such references. Christine Bell and Catherine O'Rourke (2011) developed a Transitional Justice Peace Agreements Database of 585 peace agreements in 102 peace processes from 1990 to 2010 and found that the number of agreements that mentioned women increased overall from 11 percent to 27 percent with the introduction of UNSCR 1325.

I used peace agreement data from the United Nations that had a longer timeline than the aforementioned studies. I found a big jump in the adoption of a variety of peace agreements after 2000 when comparing the 1949–2000 period with the 2000–2012 period. While women's rights language was incorporated into some peacekeeping and peace negotiations after the passage of UN Security Council resolution 1325 in 2000, its impact was far greater in civil conflicts than in interstate conflicts, as evident from the references to gender in interstate peace agreements.

African peace agreements had proportionately the greatest percentage of references to women's rights in all time periods, which speaks to the greater importance of international pressures in this region. Sub-Saharan Africa has experienced not only more conflicts than any other region numerically, but also some of the most devastating wars. African peace agreements mentioned women's rights 5 percent more often than other world regions for intrastate war, and between 2000 and 2012, this gap increased to 11 percent. The gap is even larger when contrasting Africa's interstate and regional wars with those of other world regions (Tables 6.2 and 6.3). In comprehensive peace agreements there was more mention in general of women's rights across the board, particularly after 2000, and once again the African peace agreements did slightly better than other world regions.

GENDER-RELATED PROVISIONS

The provisions take a number of different forms. In the African Peace Agreement Database, which has an N of 89, one of the most important types of provisions has to do with legislative and other forms of public representation of women and, in particular, quotas for women (DRC, Somalia, Liberia).[4]

---

[4] Inter-Congolese Political Negotiations – The Final Act, 4/2/03; Somali Roadmap Signatories, 2012 Protocol Establishing the Technical Selection Committee, 6/22/12; Peace Agreement between the Government of Liberia, the Liberians United for Reconciliation and Democracy, the Movement for Democracy in Liberia and the political parties, 8/18/03.

TABLE 6.2 *African Peace Treaties*

Types of conflicts	Women's rights mentioned in all peace treaties 1949–2000	Women's rights mentioned in all peace treaties 2000–2005	Women's rights in comprehensive peace agreements 1949–2000	Women's rights in comprehensive peace agreements 2000–2012
Intrastate	8%	28%	15%	61%
Interstate	1	27	5	20
Regional	7	56	11	100

Source: UN peacemaker: http://peacemaker.unlb.org/index1.php.

TABLE 6.3 *Global and African Peace Treaties*

Types of conflicts	Women's rights in all peace treaties (1949–2012)	Women's rights mentioned in all peace treaties (2000–2012)	Women's rights in comprehensive peace agreements up to 2012	Women's rights in comprehensive peace agreements (2000–2012)
Intrastate				
Africa	32/140 (23%)	28/92 (30%)	10/25 (40%)	8/13 (62%)
All other regions	27/155 (17%)	6/31 (19%)	9/28 (32%)	3/5 (60%)
Total	59/295 (20%)	34/123 (28%)	19/53 (36%)	11/18 (61%)
Interstate				
Africa	3/22 (14%)	3/11 (27%)	2/5 (40%)	2/3 (66%)
All other regions	1/56 (2%)	0 (0%)	1/16 (6%)	0/7 (0%)
Total	4/78 (5%)	3/11 (27%)	3/21 (14%)	2/10 (20%)
Regional				
Africa	6/13 (46%)	5/9 (56%)	4/6 (66%)	4/4 (100%)
All other regions	2/31 (6%)	0 (0%)	1/3 (33%)	0 (0%)
Total	8/44 (18%)	5/9 (56%)	5/9 (56%)	4/4 (100%)

Source: UN Peacemaker: http://peacemaker.unlb.org/index1.php.

Some specify an electoral arrangement that will guarantee women representation (Burundi), while others refer to gender balance in a more vague way.[5] The most common gender-related provision has to do with gender equality,

---

[5] Article 20: Elections: 8. The electoral system for the National Assembly shall be the system of blocked lists with proportional representation. The revised electoral code shall prescribe that lists be multi-ethnic in character and reflect gender representation. For each three names in sequence on a list, only two may belong to the same ethnic group, and for each five names at least one shall be a woman. Arusha Peace and Reconciliation Agreement for Burundi (PA11) 8/28/00

equity, or discrimination against women, which is mentioned twenty-six times. This is followed by human rights in relation to women's rights, which is mentioned sixteen times. Only six agreements mention violence against women or sexual violence. Seven make mention of the international Convention on the Elimination of Discrimination Against Women (CEDAW), while two mention the Universal Declaration of Human Rights. Three mention land and property rights of women. Burundi has the most extensive provisions, which were won by women participants in the peace talks.

WOMEN'S EXCLUSION FROM TALKS: THE CASE OF ANGOLA

The difference women can make in peace negotiations is evident in comparing the Angolan and Liberian peace processes. There had been negotiations in Angola in 1994 with the signing of the Lusaka Protocol. Women activists told me they had tried to participate in these negotiations to no avail. One of the U.S. negotiators, Donald Steinberg (2007), boasted at the time that "the agreement was gender neutral" because there was not a single provision that discriminated against women in the document. He bitterly regretted the comment once President Clinton appointed him U.S. ambassador to Angola and a member of the Luanda-based Joint Commission in charge of implementing the accords. Donald Steinberg reflected on this years later, saying, "I have no doubt that the exclusion of one-half of the population from the Angolan peace process – and from institutions of governance and the formal economy – meant that inadequate attention was paid to areas essential to consolidate peace and reconstruct the country. This contributed to the return to another three years of fighting that ended only with Savimbi's death in 2002" (Steinberg 2007). He later realized that the exclusion of women and gender became a key factor in the Commission's inability to implement the Lusaka Protocol. Angola eventually fell back into conflict in 1999. There were no women on the Joint Commission and not one woman on delegations from the Angolan government, National Union for the Total Independence of Angola (UNITA), the UN, Portugal, Russia or the United States. This meant that women's concerns were completely absent from the discussions, including problems of internal displacement, sexual violence, and abuses by rebel security forces. Moreover, the reintroduction of social services involving maternal health and girls' education were not even broached. The agreement only addressed the needs of male combatants in the disarmament, demobilization, and reintegration programs, excluding the thousands of women who had been kidnapped by rebel forces and forced to fight and support the rebels. Many women served as cooks, messengers and sex slaves, but because they were not defined as combatants they remained ignored. Male ex-combatants received some funds and tools and were returned to their communities; however, they did not have marketable skills. This also meant that women now had to cope with their husbands' alcoholism, drug abuse, domestic violence, and other new problems created by the war (Steinberg 2010).

It was not only women who were left out of the peace process. Comerford (2005) argues that there was no mechanism established to guarantee the inclusion of civil society and that this exclusion contributed to the failure of the many peace settlements in Angola. By the time the Joint Commission started addressing these concerns, it was too little too late. There was insufficient commitment for the peace process on the part of the government and UNITA, and civil society was too weak to prevent a return to conflict in 1999.

When the conflict finally ended in 2002 there was no comprehensive peace agreement signed at that time, and this once again created a situation where women were deprived of an opportunity to assert their demands. Peace agreements serve as an important opportunity structure for women's rights activist to influence broader constitutional and legislative outcomes regarding gender and other key policies. As a result, one activist explained to me, "UNSCR 1325 had no impact in Angola. Moreover, oil insulated us from the international community and those in power know how to manipulate and stay in power."[6]

SEEKING A SEAT AT THE TABLE: THE CASE OF LIBERIA

In Liberia, women had fought long and hard to be included in the peace talks. They made modest gains, but not nearly what they had hoped for. It is a story mostly of injustice: Not only of the horrific violence perpetrated against civilians by the Liberian warlords, but also of the injustice of the international community in failing to recognize the voices and demands of those who were fighting for peace at the grassroots and in refusing to give them a seat and a vote in official negotiations until the very end. The women's demands were consistent and clear: They did not want the negotiations to reward the warlords for their mass violence and looting by giving them government positions. They wanted disarmament before elections, an international peacekeeping force in place, and seats at the negotiating table.

The Liberian women's peace movement's efforts to obtain seats at the peace negotiations started long before international pressures mounted to increase women's visibility in the peace talks. This same story is one that can be told in countless conflicts from Somalia and Sudan to Sierra Leone. While UNSCR 1325 changed UN practices, it is clear that in Liberia and elsewhere it came long after women were already pressing for recognition.

Without pressure from below and from women themselves, who were the driving force for gender regime change, the transformations in international norms and practices would not have had much impact. Tragically, the very people who had fomented conflict were seen by the international community as the ones to lead the nation out of war, while those who had most consistently fought for peace were ignored or pushed to the sidelines despite their insistent

---

[6] Interview with 3.14, Luanda, June 12, 2008.

pleas to be given a voice and a say in their future. And while women did important work at the grassroots through informal initiatives (see Chapter 4), their impact was circumscribed by their inability to be integrally incorporated into the negotiations. Thus, it was not until 2003 during the Accra talks that the broader international community and regional leaders began to pay attention to women's demands in Liberia, but even then, they allowed them only minimal input.

What makes the international community's response even more egregious is that in Liberia and so many other contexts, from the outset, women activists worked collaboratively across religious, ethnic, and class differences. They, along with some of the religious organizations, were among the true leaders in fighting for peace, yet they were mostly denied key roles in the endless peace talks that ensued. To be sure, there were differences between the women, and they were contentious, sometimes resulting in betrayals (see Chapter 4). They were based on the divisions that ravaged the country. Yet the women's peace movement was able to overcome these differences by focusing on their common agenda forged through years of conflict that had bonded them around demands for political representation, an end to violence against women, and peace. As hard as they fought and as much as they insisted on being included, their gender and their civil society status kept them sidelined. And even this did not deter them.

It is clear that from the outset, the demands for peace and power, or peace and representation were intertwined. As far back as 1994, women's organizations had demanded (1) representation in peace talks but also (2) representation in government and parliament. Women realized very quickly that their demands for peace required their presence and full involvement to ensure that conflict would not resume. As Davidetta Brown, a journalist, explained: "Women wanted first to participate and then they wanted representation.... The women's agenda and peace agenda emerged at the same time and they were interwoven, not separated. The war reawakened women's interest in politics and decision making. It had been advancing all along but it was speeded up because of the war."[7]

In the end, women did gain observer status at many of the talks. Some were delegates at the final Accra Meeting, and some were signatories to the Comprehensive Peace Agreement in 2003. Most of their key demands were met, and the Comprehensive Peace Agreement did acknowledge the need for female representation.

Women activists had made other important gains along the way. In 1996, one of the peace activists, Ruth Perry, became head of the interim National Council and de facto president of the country. One of the participants in the Accra talks, Ellen Johnson Sirleaf, was eventually elected president in 2005.

---

[7] Interview with 2.15, Monrovia, September 11, 2007.

Three women, including the chair, were included on the Electoral Commission in 2005. Johnson Sirleaf and peace activist Leymah Gbowee were recognized internationally through their Nobel Peace Prize awards in 2011. In 2003 Mano River Women Peace Network (MARWOPNET) was awarded the United Nations Prize for Human Rights by the UN General Assembly in recognition of its outstanding achievement in the promotion of human and women's rights.

But given how hard they had to struggle even for this much and how many years it took to bring an end to the fighting, it is impossible to justify the exclusion of women, especially when there was no question about including the warlords, who had fomented war. Even though women's organizations were essential to the peace that was eventually brokered, they were not given a formal role in the peace talks until 2003 in Accra. Hon. Vabah Gayflor, former Minister of Gender in Liberia, explained that women

were not considered as peacemakers at any time. Yet Liberian women drew attention to the horrible political situation and how the war adversely affected women. They took it upon themselves to serve as go-betweens. Women shuttled between international and national actors through their women's organizations. Women's organizations like the Liberian Women's Initiative (LWI), Federation of African Women's Peace Networks (FERFAP) and the Mano River Women Peace Network (MARWOPNET) were very active. (Gayflor 2005)

For years the warring factions kept going to conferences and signing agreements (Table 6.4). The agreements would fall apart, and they would continue fighting and make excuses for not honoring the agreements. As feminist peace activist Etweda "Sugars" Cooper, also known as the godmother of the women's movement in Liberia, explained to me:

We started with the NPLF (Charles Taylor's National Patriotic Front of Liberia) and the government and ended up with 5–6 warring factions. Frankly it seemed to me that all of these men were looking for jobs and ways to steal. It had nothing to do with ideology, nothing to do with good governance. These were a bunch of men who would not have ascended to power without arms, and so they were using small arms and child soldiers to get jobs. They were not concerned with peace, they just wanted to divide up the government positions. One warring faction wanted foreign affairs, another forestry development, or the port authority. These were lucrative positions. Because of this, women were tired of these men going after these jobs. We said to ourselves, we can put an end to this. We all have husbands, fathers and sons. We have influence over these people. We need to strategize about how to reach them and how to push them into agreeing to what we want.[8]

The following section details how difficult it was for women activists to gain access to the peace talks.

---

[8] Interview with 2.28, Monrovia, October 5, 2007.

TABLE 6.4 *Peace Agreements Relating to Liberia*

Banjul III Agreement	October 24, 1990
Bamako Ceasefire Agreement	November 11, 1990
Banjul IV Agreement	December 21, 1990
Lomé Agreement	February 13, 1991
Yamoussoukro I	June 30, 1991
Yamoussoukro II	July 29, 1991
Yamoussoukro III	September 17, 1991
Yamoussoukro IV Peace Agreement	October 30, 1991
Geneva Agreement	April 7, 1992
Final Communiqué of the ECOWAS Committee of Five on Liberia	July 4, 1992
Cotonou Peace Agreement	July 25, 1993
Akosombo Peace Agreement	September 12, 1994
Accra Agreements/Akosombo clarification agreement	December 21, 1994
Abuja I Peace Agreement	August 19, 1995
Abuja II Peace Agreement	July 1996
Supplement to the Abuja Accord	August 17, 1996
Agreement on the Ceasefire and Cessation of Hostilities between the Government of Liberia and Liberians United for Reconciliation and Democracy and the Movement for Democracy in Liberia	June 17, 2003
Comprehensive Peace Agreement between the Government of Liberia and Liberians United for Reconciliation and Democracy (LURD), the Movement for Democracy in Liberia (MODEL) and the Political Parties	August 8, 2003

WOMEN AND PEACEMAKING DURING THE FIRST LIBERIAN CIVIL WAR (1989–1996)

In 1989, with the support of then-Libyan President Muammar Gaddafi, Charles Taylor launched an armed attack on Liberia from neighboring Côte d'Ivoire with the intent of overthrowing the government of Samuel Doe. This led to the First Liberian Civil War. Various external efforts were made to bring an end to the fighting. Dozens of peace talks were held between 1989 and 1997, often under Economic Community of West African States (ECOWAS) auspices. Over a dozen peace agreements were signed in this period; however, peace rarely lasted very long as the conflict reignited. An ECOWAS-sponsored peacekeeping force, Economic Community of West African States Monitoring Group (ECOMOG), which was mainly made up of Nigerians and Ghanaians, arrived in 1990. ECOMOG put in place the Interim Government of National Unity (IGNU) led by Amos Sawyer. The first talks that women activists attended were in Banjul in August 1990, where the interim government was formed. Although women's organizations sought neutrality, some of the women attendees belonged to various factions, creating tensions among the women.

Charles Taylor and his National Patriotic Front of Liberia (NPFL) then launched his Operation Octopus, leading to his assault on Monrovia in October 1992 that resulted in a siege lasting over two months. ECOMOG intervened and by the end of the year was able to push back his troops. Peace talks were held in Cotonou, Benin, in July 1993, resulting in a treaty between NPFL, IGNU, and another faction of Doe's supporters known as the United Liberation Movement of Liberia for Democracy (ULIMO). This resulted in the formation of a new Liberian national transition government as a coalition between the factions. Women's organizations had been unable to gain recognition from the UN or ECOWAS either as observers or participants in the 1993 peace negotiations in Cotonou.

The UN Observer Mission in Liberia (UNOMIL) started its operations in Liberia in September 1993. Women peace activists, however, felt that UN Special Representative of the Secretary General who headed up UNOMIL, Trevor Gordon-Somers, was not neutral and was siding with Taylor. They contacted UN Headquarters in New York to inform them that he was not neutral. They marched to the UN offices in Monrovia and demanded that "Gordon-Somers must go!"[9] In November 1994 he was recalled from his position and was replaced by a Tanzanian, Anthony B. Nyakyi.

The initial focus of women's mobilization was disarmament, and they opposed the holding of elections without disarmament. They formed the core of the Civic Disarmament Campaign, chaired by an Interfaith Mediation Council that sought to stop the sale of guns to Liberia and promote disarmament. The Liberian Women's Initiative (LWI) met with various parties involved in setting up the government, including the U.S. and Nigerian ambassadors to Liberia, the Organization of African Unity representative to Liberia, and various UN representatives to express their opposition to the installation of a new government before a disarmament agreement had been signed. They then organized a public demonstration March 4, 1994, to press for disarmament. They also opposed the September 1994 Akosombo Agreement to replace the coalition and hold elections before disarmament had taken place.

The women's peace movement included from the outset Christian, Muslim, rural, and urban women, as well as women of different ethnicities and classes. Women organized marches, petitions, and prayer meetings, which were held weekly in Christian and Muslim religious institutions throughout the country. Women's organizations wrote to President Clinton, to the British parliament, the European Union, the Organization of African Unity (OAU), and ECOWAS

---

[9] Interview with 2.13, Monrovia, September 12, 2007.

to press their demands.[10] They also held individual meetings with some heads of states, ECOWAS, and other representatives.

Women's organizations made their first concerted effort to attend peace talks in December 1994 when they tried to participate in the Accra Clarification Conference. They were initially kept out of the conference, but as a result of wide coverage of this exclusion in the Ghanaian media, women's organizations were allowed to participate as official observers on the second day, and by the third day they had official participant status. Encouraged by this initial victory, hundreds of women came together and drafted a position statement on the impact of the Liberian war on women and their communities. Women leaders used this statement as a mandate to gain access to peace negotiations organized by ECOWAS, the OAU, and the UN. They raised funds and sent a delegation to the ECOWAS Heads of State Mediation Committee in Abuja, Nigeria, in May 1995 even though they had not been invited. Theresa Leigh Sherman, Evelyn Townsend, and Clara d'Almeida went on behalf of the women's organizations.

President Jerry Rawlings of Ghana allowed the women to speak even though they were not officially on the program. Some women feared they may have been invited just to humor the delegates, but if this was the case, the delegates soon realized that they were dead serious. Exhausted and shaking from nerves, the women were pleased to have finally been given a platform. The women clasped each other's hands as Theresa Leigh Sherman began to speak. Sherman said she quietly thanked God and then boldly demanded representation of women in the peace negotiations: "Our lack of representation in the ongoing peace process is equivalent to the denial of one of our fundamental rights: the right to be seen, be heard, and be counted. This [denial] also deprives the country [of] access to the opinion of 51% of its human resources in solving the problems, which affect our lives as a people." She not only called for women's participation in the talks, but also for "no elections without disarmament" and for a government of inclusion (AWPSG 2004, 27).

The women leaders' recognition at the Abuja conference was a major achievement and inspired the women to continue mobilizing for recognition. A key moment of reconciliation took place in July of 1995 when ECOWAS encouraged the women to get the warlords to talk to one another. Women met individually with the various faction leaders to gain their trust to bring them all together. This was based on traditional Liberian peacemaking strategies of treating everyone equally without bias and thereby building confidence in the process. Elizabeth Mulbah, who was director of the Christian Health Association of Liberia, and Marian Subah organized the session. There were two other mediation efforts planned for the same day, but the faction leaders came to this one because, as one faction leader put it, "When your mother calls you, you must show up," signaling the authority the women had achieved but also

---

[10] Interview with 2.28, Monrovia, October 5, 2007.

a recognition of the power of women in society. The participants all observed a day of fasting and prayer before the meeting and started the session with prayers. They engaged in various mutual confidence-building exercises and games that helped break the ice. Even though the participants had arrived ready for a fight, they ended up softening their positions. The event was an opening at a moment when it seemed there was no possibility of talking (AWPSG 2004, 27).[11]

Women activists were still not given a seat at the Abuja meeting in July 1995, even though they would have been in a good position to build off the successes of their peacemaking workshops. The Abuja peace agreement was followed by fighting in April of 1996, leading to the evacuation and destruction of much of Monrovia. The key warlords included Charles Taylor (of the National Patriotic Front of Liberia), George Boley of the Liberia Peace Council, and Alhaji Kromah of ULIMO-K faction. In the meantime, Ruth Perry headed up the National Council. She had been the only opposition figure in the Doe parliament and remained an advocate of peace throughout. Women, however, were invited to the August 1996 Abuja meeting, and it was at this meeting that Ruth Perry, a founding member of LWI and numerous other peace and women's organizations,[12] was selected as Head of the Council of State, or de facto president of the third transitional government. This was a testament to the achievements of the Liberian women peace activists. She saw her appointment not only as a personal challenge, but as a challenge "for the women of Liberia and African women as a whole" (AWPSG 2004, 30). There had been two Councils of State prior to this one, and the members had fought bitterly among themselves. In contrast, Perry was able to keep the process going and accomplish its mission. Perry oversaw the disarmament of some of the warring factions, the repatriation and resettlement of refugees and IDPs, and the holding of elections.

An Abuja Accord, signed in 1996, paved the way for the elections. However, the country was not completely disarmed, and this frustrated the women peace activists, who felt that disarmament was a precondition to holding free and fair elections. The LWI opposed the Carter Center, which was helping organize and monitor the elections, because they felt they had sided with Taylor during the elections. They told former U.S. President Jimmy Carter that it was impossible to hold elections when people were armed, but he did not heed their warnings.[13] Thus, under circumstances of widespread intimidation and insecurity, Charles Taylor won the 1997 elections, and his National Patriotic Party (NPP) party came to dominate Congress. According to Ellen Johnson Sirleaf (2009),

---

[11] Interview with 2.29, Monrovia, September 19, 2007.
[12] Perry had also helped found Peace Now, Peace for Liberia Movement, and was also a founding member of the Women's Development Association of Liberia, the Liberian Women's Initiative, and Women for Action and Goodwill.
[13] Interview with 2.13, Monrovia, September 12, 2007.

he won the election because he had an endless supply of funds illegally obtained from looting the country. He was able to hand out free T-shirts and rice in a society living in abject poverty; he controlled much of the media; and he was able to play on people's fears. Thus one of his famous campaign slogans was "Better the devil you know than the angel you do not."

It is therefore no mystery why Taylor won the 1997 elections, but even assuming the elections were rigged, he did nevertheless have a following and was regarded by many at the time as someone who could bring peace to the country, given that he had the largest militia. Rumors of his exploits abounded, which added to his mystique. He sometimes dressed head to toe in white robes to suggest supernatural powers; he was said to eat human hearts and drink blood; and he acquired a bevy of young girlfriends referred to as "Charlie's Angels." During the elections he gained notoriety through a popular song with the lyrics "You kill my ma, you kill my pa. I will vote for you." This sent the clear message that if one did not vote for him they would come to regret it (Johnson Sirleaf 2009).

I heard from supporters and detractors alike that Taylor was enigmatic and had a charm that was irresistible. Rumors abounded about his ability to make almost anyone believe anything he said. As one woman peace activist put it: "Taylor was very charismatic and a superb actor. Taylor could make you take your clothes off and walk down the street naked and you would think you had your clothes on. He had ardent supporters."[14] Another minister who served in his government explained to me: "He would put you under a spell. If you don't want to like Charles Taylor, don't meet him and look into his eyes because once you have met him, you will like him."[15] He had garnered the support of Rev. Jesse Jackson, Pat Robertson, and Congressman Donald Payne prior to the 1997 elections. When President Carter visited Liberia in his capacity as an election observer with the Carter Center, Taylor is said to have trotted out his mistress and led Carter to believe she was his wife. Taylor persuaded Carter that he was a devout Baptist and told him that God had given Liberia to him, saying, "Yes my son, well done." He shared with Carter his vision of democracy. By all accounts, Carter was completely fooled by Taylor and ended up supporting and legitimizing the warlord, portraying him as a reasonable man who was simply misunderstood. Taylor won 75 percent of the vote, and amazingly even the NPP won exactly the same 75 percent of the vote in parliamentary elections.

The Carter Center issued a Preliminary Statement about the Liberian Special Elections on July 21, 1997, saying: "Overall, the election represents a very important step forward for Liberia, and its long-term prospects for lasting peace and democracy. Although we have noted several problems about the

[14] Interview with 2.28, Monrovia, October 5, 2007.
[15] Interview with 2.30, Monrovia, October 7, 2007.

process, we feel that none were serious enough to have altered the peoples opportunity to select their leaders freely and fairly." This lent international credibility to Taylor at the time, although it was short-lived. Carter even asked Ellen Johnson Sirleaf, who was running for the presidency at the same time, to join Taylor in his new government. This angered her because she believed Taylor had engaged in fraudulent elections, and she said there was no way she was going to support him after all the death and destruction he had caused. She told Carter he should have spoken out against the fraud instead of trying to cajole her into joining the Taylor government (Johnson Sirleaf 2009). As journalist Tom Kamara wrote of Carter years later: "President Carter should have heeded the African adage that a stranger visiting a village must listen to its children regarding roads to take, or whom to deal with, etc. A caring and careful stranger, however knowledgeable and good intentioned, who disobeys soon finds trouble" (Kamara 2000). ECOMOG troops pulled out after the 1997 elections, leaving the country unstable and facing sporadic outbursts of fighting between government forces and various factions.

WOMEN AND PEACEMAKING DURING THE SECOND LIBERIAN WAR (1999–2003)

Liberian women continued to mobilize across ethnic and religious differences when fighting again flared in the Second Liberian War (1999–2003). Since 1990, there had been continued conflict in the Mano River Basin between Sierra Leone, Liberia, Côte d'Ivoire, and Guinea. The conflict was revived when a rebel group, backed by the Liberians United for Reconciliation and Democracy (LURD), became active in the north after 1999, while the Movement for Democracy in Liberia (MODEL) emerged in the south in 2003. Monrovia was once again besieged by fighting, and thousands were displaced.

As a result of women's mobilization at the Accra and Abuja meetings, they had garnered significant credibility as a result of their peacemaking efforts. Because of the regional dimensions of the conflict, new forms of mobilization emerged. For example, the Mano River Women Peace Network (MARWOP-NET) was formed in November 1999, when 56 women activists from Sierra Leone, Liberia, and Guinea met in Abuja, Nigeria, to talk about restoring peace in the region. They built on the earlier experiences of LWI and were spurred on by the efforts of Femmes Afrique Solidarité (FAS), an NGO of thirty umbrella organizations. They launched their first mediation effort in 2001 when Sierra Leone and Liberia were in conflict and Guinea was similarly experiencing instability. They met individually with President Charles Taylor of Liberia, President Lansana Conté of Guinea, and Sierra Leonean President Ahmed Kabbah and persuaded them all to engage in peace talks in Morocco in May 2002. Despite minimal resources and being excluded from the formal peace process, they were able to get the feuding heads of state to a regional peace summit. At one point Conté had been adamant about not meeting with Taylor of Liberia. Mary Brownell, the LWI founder, was on the MARWOPNET delegation that met with Conté in Conakry, As Brownell recounted to me:

At the end of his political talk, I put up my hand and when he recognized me, I told him like I was talking to a little boy: "The fate of millions of people is in your hands. Women are delivering babies in the bushes. You men just gamble with our lives. You must meet with Taylor. When you meet, I am going to be there. If you don't talk, I will take the keys to your room and lock you up and sit on them until you talk." He was shocked. No one had ever spoken to him like that before. When I spoke, my voice trembled, I thought about how he was after power and greed and was not thinking about the ordinary citizen. I was so surprised that I did this. Why? I believe it was God's direction. Like Esther, God sent me at this time for this purpose. Afterward Conté arranged for a meeting with Taylor in Morocco.

Taylor heard about the incident, and when he met with the women later, he teased Brownell, saying: "You are ready to lock us up? Mother, only you could do something like that."[16] The women activists also got Taylor to agree to recall the ambassadors he had expelled from Sierra Leone and Guinea.

The fighting between LURD and MODEL intensified in March of 2003, and the Muslim Women of Peace network reached out to the Christian women to seek a solution to the fighting. A new organization, Liberian Women in Peacebuilding Network (WIPNET), was formed by Leymah Gbowee in 2002. WIPNET launched the Women of Liberia Mass Action for Peace movement (2002–05) that demanded peace and that Taylor and the rebels negotiate. They had done peacemaking trainings prior to this mass action. The Catholic Radio Veritas helped them connect to the international media, including CNN and BBC. They distributed fliers in schools, mosques, churches, checkpoints, guard posts, and elsewhere. Their slogans were "We want peace, no more war" and "Never again war." The mass action included hundreds of women from IDP camps near Monrovia. Over 1,000 strong and dressed in white, they marched to City Hall on April 11, 2002, to express their frustration with the war and demand an immediate cease-fire, dialogue among opposing parties, and an international peacekeeping force to monitor a cease-fire. They organized thousands of women to sit, dance, sing, pray, and protest at the airfield in Sinkor opposite the fish market. Others started sitting protests in towns throughout the country. Dressed in white T-shirts and headscarves to symbolize peace, they demanded a neutral peacekeeping force that would allow refugees to return home and called for free and fair elections. They also called for the strengthening of Monrovia's infrastructure because it was unable to accommodate the thousands of refugees who were returning home.

On April 23, 2002, over 1,000 women met with Taylor. Leymah Gbowee (who was depicted in Abigail Disney's documentary *Pray the Devil Back to Hell* and later became a Nobel Peace Prize laureate) presented Taylor with a

[16] Interview with 2.13, Monrovia, September 16, 2007.

statement as the women held hands and prayed. The women demanded an unconditional cease-fire, peace talks, and the presence of international peace-keeping forces. Taylor agreed to attend the peace talks in Accra, Ghana. The women persuaded the LURD and MODEL leaders also to attend the Accra peace talks.

The Mano River Women Peace Network (MARWOPNET) organized a conference in May 2003 to build consensus on how to end the conflict. The Coalition of Women of Political Parties in Liberia (COWPPIL) did the same. There had been no plan to include women leaders in the 2003 Accra Peace negotiations nor was there any consideration of the concerns articulated by the women's movement at the time.

Gbowee then led a WIPNET delegation to the Accra talks, and they remained there for three weeks. Over 150 to 200 Liberian women refugees from the Buduburam camp in Accra joined the mass action protests daily as women became the major civil society actors pushing for an accord. They held candlelight vigils and spontaneous protests and talked to the delegates one-on-one.

ECOWAS accredited the regional women's organization MARWOPNET to attend the Accra talks, which took place from July through August 2003. The four MARWOPNET delegates, who were part of the official delegation, included Mary Brownell, Ruth Perry, Theresa Sherman, and Amelia Ward, and Sherman became a signatory to the final accord. In the evening, MARWOPNET delegates to the talks briefed the women about developments in the talks and solicited their views.[17]

Although they went as delegates, the MARWOPNET leaders regarded themselves as representatives of all interested women's groups, including WIPNET, which was formed in 2002 and saw itself as a grassroots movement. In the talks, MARWOPNET demanded greater civil society participation in the talks and 50 percent representation of women in the talks. They were firm in insisting that no warring party lead the government. They called for an immediate cease-fire because violence had been escalating in Monrovia.[18] MARWOPNET called on the UN Security Council to provide for a peacekeeping force and the establishment of a transition government that would "disarm, demobilize, reintegrate and resettle troops, prepare the way for elections, provide humanitarian relief, or for reconciliation and restructure the army and security forces" (AWPSG 2004, 49).

Other women's groups attended the talks as observers, including the Association of Female Lawyers, WIPNET, and Refugee Women. Ellen Johnson Sirleaf was also there as her party's representative and was one of the most forceful negotiators. Although she was not a civil society representative, she

[17] Interview with 2.1, Monrovia, September 16, 2007.
[18] Interview with 2.1, Monrovia, September 16, 2007.

collaborated with the women's organizations and kept them informed. One constraint the women's organizations faced was that many of the women leaders had limited knowledge of the Heads of State's initiative of ECOWAS, of the goals of the UN facilitators, and of how best to insert themselves into the process, especially as observers (Bruthus 2003). All the warlords were using the talks as a means of lobbying for positions, but the women's organizations, which obviously did not constitute an armed group, did not have this objective nor did they have this as a personal goal, although they did demand legislative representation for women as a group.

In July, the fighting between the government forces and those of LURD and MODEL intensified, as LURD attempted to take Monrovia. The women activists in Monrovia, in turn, stepped up their protests, as did the women protestors at the Accra talks. The women activists were firm that they did not want any of the warring factions to end up holding power. As Amelia Ward explained, "Because of this, the warring parties intensified the fighting in Monrovia so that things would get so bad that we would give up.... We did not want warlords to share power. We stuck to our position, they are fighting to get us to give in. People suffered. We said we don't buy that. We could not make headway on that."[19]

Even as the war intensified in Liberia, the warlords appeared to be in no hurry to conclude the talks. As Gbowee described it, they were enjoying their ocean view hotel rooms, leisurely breakfasts, crisply ironed shirts, lounging around at the pool, and having drinks, all the expense of the international community. The protestors accused ECOWAS of pampering the negotiators and said the talks should have been held instead in Buduburam refugee camp on the Accra-Winneba road to help the negotiators understand the urgency for peace ("Paper Hails Liberian Women ..." 2003). The talks were going nowhere. The warlord participants were not serious; moreover, they were mocking the women by making threats to kill everyone in Monrovia. The women were furious. The refugee women held up placards saying "Butchers and murderers of the Liberian People: Stop!" Drawing on funereal symbolism that has deep roots in West African history of women's protest, the women wept to protest the ongoing violations of a cease-fire on all sides. They block-aded the door where the talks were being held and did not let the delegates out for several hours (even to use the toilet) until they came to a comprehensive peace agreement. Everyone was locked inside, including the European Union representatives, U.S. representatives, MARWOPNET, and the warlords. The only way out was to accept holding elections.

In the midst of the commotion, one warlord started trying to make an escape. Two of the leaders, Leymah Gbowee and Etweda Cooper started to undress, thus threatening to engage in one of the most powerful forms of

---

[19] Interview with 2.1, Monrovia, September 16, 2007.

protests used by women in West Africa. For a group of men to see older or married women naked is the strongest curse that can be meted to anyone. The Nigerian General Abubakar, who was running the talks, told the women to stop. He forced the warlord to halt and said to him, "If you were a real man you would not be killing your people. But because you are not a real man, that is why these women will treat you like boys. I dare you to leave this hall until we have negotiated a peace with these women." The man returned to the room. Eventually the "hostages" were freed, and the women had made their point. Charles Taylor resigned August 11, 2003. The CPA was concluded, an interim president was selected, and elections were agreed upon. Meanwhile ECOWAS troops intervened in Liberia on August 4, and by August 15 the rebels had lifted their siege of Monrovia. U.S. troops provided logistical support to the peacekeepers (Gbowee 2011).

The United States pressured Taylor into leaving Liberia, and Nigeria offered him exile in Calabar in the eastern part of Nigeria. Vice President Moses Blah took over temporarily until he was replaced by Gyude Bryant's transitional government in October 2006. Taylor eventually was extradited by Liberia's President Ellen Johnson Sirleaf to stand trial in the Special Court for Sierra Leone. After an attempted escape and capture, he was finally sent to The Hague, where he was convicted on all eleven counts of "aiding and abetting" war crimes and crimes against humanity and sentenced to fifty years in prison.

The women activists highlighted the importance of emotion and passion in moving the talks along, two traits that are generally not associated with such talks. Yet the women embodied the urgency of the sentiments of the Liberians suffering back home amid the fighting and the urgency of the need to bring the talks to a conclusion and not to take hard lines that would delay the process.[20]

Over forty-five women's groups that were attending the peace talks hammered out a charter at the Golden Tulip Hotel in Accra on August 15, 2003, three days before the CPA was signed. They insisted that women be included in all proposed institutions within the transitional government, within peacekeeping missions as well as disarmament, demobilization, and reintegration processes, and that women comprise 50 percent representation in transitional institutions (executive, legislative, judiciary). They also drew on the UN Security Council Resolution 1325.

Inside the negotiating hall, multiple shenanigans were underway. Ellen Johnson Sirleaf received the most votes in a competition between three finalists for interim president, and she had the overwhelming support of civil society and political party delegates. However, the warring factions did not approve of her because they feared she would attempt to bring the perpetrators of human rights violations to account and felt this would lead to

---

[20] Interview with 2.31, Monrovia, October 4, 2007.

further conflict.[21] Gyude Bryant was agreed on as a compromise interim president. Moreover, only 7 out of 100 women who participated in the talks were allowed to vote for the chair and vice-chair of the Transitional Government (Bruthus 2003). According to MARWOPNET delegate Amelia Ward, "The men quietly divided the ministries among themselves and did not include the women. They ... informed us the next day."[22] Thus, only three women claimed executive positions in the Education, Gender Development, and Youth and Sports ministries.

Based on discussions with numerous participants in the peace talks, it is evident that the women's protests speeded up the conclusion of the talks. As a result of their pressure, the talks were concluded in seventy-five days. They also got many of their key demands met, including the demand that none of the warring factions head the government, which should be a civilian government, and that disarmament take place before elections were held. They were not able to keep the warlords from running for office or for legislative positions.[23]

Because of the important mediation role MARWOPNET had played between the various factions involved in the peace talks, the network (specifically Theresa Leigh Sherman) became one of the signatories as witness to the August 18, 2003, peace agreement between the Government of Liberia, Liberians United for Democracy (LURD), Movement for Democracy in Liberia (MODEL) and all the eighteen political parties. The talks resulted in the setting up of a transitional government that was installed October 15, 2003, and for the establishment of the UN Mission in Liberia (UNMIL), which arrived two weeks before the transitional government of Gyude Bryant took over.

One key outcome of the Peace Agreement for women was the stipulation that women be included in the Governance Reform Commission (Article XVI.3), National Election Commission (Article XVII.2), the National Transitional Legislative Assembly (Article XXIV.3) and in all elective and nonelective appointments (Article XXVII). However, no mention was made of percentages of female representatives, nor of the mechanism by which a quota might be implemented. Moreover, there were no sanctions for noncompliance. As a result, only three women were elected to the 76-member transitional legislature. The Association of Female Lawyers of Liberia (AFELL), however, was able to participate in the nomination of judicial appointments. Significantly, women's groups succeeded in getting Frances Johnson-Morris to chair the National Election Committee (NEC), and they got Mary Brownell and Elizabeth Boyenneh onto the NEC as well (Bruthus 2003). Women also chaired the Constitutional Review Committee later on. Thus, there were some important gains for women, but many setbacks as well, which could

---

[21] www.ictj.org/sites/default/files/ICTJ-Liberia-Negotiating-Peace-2007-English_0.pdf, p. 13.

[22] Interview with 2.1, Monrovia, September 16, 2007.

[23] Interview with 2.1, Monrovia, September 16, 2007; Interview with 2.31, Monrovia, October 4, 2007.

be directly attributed to their weak voting capacity and inability to participate in backroom deals.

The peace agreement was problematic in other respects as well. It recognizes women as a "vulnerable group": "The NTGL shall accord particular attention to the issue of the rehabilitation of vulnerable groups or war victims (children, women, the elderly and the disabled) within Liberia, who have been severely affected by the conflict in Liberia." Some have criticized this reference to sex as a sociological variable thus "undermining the potential of women as independent actors with rights." Women are thus defined by who they are rather than what they do. By defining women solely "in need of special protections," they become further marginalized in the peace process, leaving the work of war and peacemaking in the male domain (Puechguirbal 2005, 3).

COMPARATIVE PERSPECTIVES

If one looks comparatively, some interesting patterns emerge. Women activists' engagement with peace negotiations in most African conflict countries generally started from a position of unity across political divisions, whereas for male warlord and faction negotiators, the differences were what defined them. The Liberian women activists from different parties worked together from the outset. This was also the case in the Burundian, Somali, and DRC negotiations. In the Burundi peace negotiations, in which women only had observer status, women from nineteen parties came together at an historic All-Party Women's Peace Conference and drafted a joint document to be incorporated into the peace accord. It included provisions for punishing war crimes against women, including rape and sexual violence; guarantees for women's rights to property, land, and inheritance; and measures for education for both boys and girls. Twenty-three of the provisions were included in the final peace accord (FAS). But what was notable about the women activists involved in the talks was that from the outset they sat and worked together. Peacemaking and unity for them was a starting point, and forging a common agenda was a process, not an endpoint.

Women had sought to participate in the Somali peace talks since the 1990s. Women were excluded from the March 1993 National Reconciliation Conference in Addis Ababa, although they had asked to participate. When the men failed to come to a consensus, the women fasted until an agreement was reached. Twenty-four hours later, the men had a peace plan that outlined provisions for a transitional government, elections, disarmament, and a UN-supervised cease-fire. Between 1991 and 1999, women had been left out of thirteen reconciliation conferences, along with all other civil society groups. Only the warring factions were included. In 2000 they began in earnest to press for representation at the talks. At the 2000 Somali peace negotiations in Arta, Djibouti, women were told that they could not participate because only the leaders of five Somali clans were allowed to participate. So the women formed a sixth "clan of women" (a "rainbow coalition" or Sixth Clan Coalition) that cut across all clans. Finally they were included in the negotiations on this basis. After considerable struggle and dealing with clan manipulations, the women were able to gain 12 percent seats for women in the constituent assembly, which ultimately translated into key gains for women in the constitution and close to 14 percent seats in the new parliament.

One of the major obstacles to women's political representation has been clan politics because the clan is the key mechanism through which one can access political power in Somalia. Power sharing, according to the new constitution, is divided between the clans in a 4.5 formula that divides power between the four clans (Darood, Hawiye, Dir, and Digil and Mirifle, who constitute one clan) and 0.5 for other minority groups. This means that women cannot claim leadership because men represent the clans. Dr. Shukria Dini found it ironic that this system, which is at the root of so much of the conflict in Somalia, is being used as a basis for reconstructing the polity (Dini 2012). I imagine that if women leaders had been given more say in the talks, they might have come up with a different basis for power sharing.

As in these other cases, women had difficulty trying to participate in the DRC peace talks. According to Doris Mpoumou (2004), the Congolese government, as well as the warring factions, strongly opposed the participation of women in the talks. Many participants felt that because women had not fought, they should not be represented in political institutions and that they had no role in the peace negotiations. In the Kivus, a women's organization was threatened by the Rassemblement Congolais pour la Démocratie (RCD) because it was sending delegates to the Sun City peace talks. The organization's offices were ransacked, and their peace marches were disrupted. Six female delegates out of seventy-three were eventually selected to participate in a 2001 preparatory meeting in Gabarone, but they were explicitly told not to advocate around women's issues. In response, women delegates wrote a joint letter to the delegates to demand 30 percent participation in the talks as stipulated by SADC, CEDAW, and UNSCR 1325. Forty women (out of 340 delegates) participated in the March–April 2002 Inter-Congolese Dialogue (ICD) in Sun City, making up 9 percent of the participants or 25 percent of the civil society participants. A meeting organized by Femmes Africa Solidarité (FAS) and Women as Partners for Peace in Africa (WOPPA) prior to the Sun City meeting came up with a plan of action for women. UNIFEM worked with the women throughout the Sun City meeting to help them strategize (Whitman 2005). UNDP and UNIFEM got another forty expert women involved.

All the women attendees came to the March 8, 2002, ICD plenary session wearing the same style dress and print. They represented government, armed groups, parties, and civil society and made up 30 percent of the plenary. They performed a short play expressing what women had suffered due to the war and read a declaration demanding political representation and that their concerns be incorporated into the final accord. They advocated for a unified Congo, transcending ethnic, regional, and political divisions. Their demands consistently had to do with mainstreaming women's concerns, including women in the transitional government, taking steps to end violence against women, disarming and reintegrating child soldiers, and supporting traumatized civilians. They also demanded that Congo remain as a united territory and called for the removal of external forces (FAS 2003).[24] Many of the male negotiators were moved to tears as a result of the performance and said they had not fully appreciated what the exclusion of women had meant.

An ICD humanitarian Social and Cultural Commission, which was chaired by Ellen Johnson Sirleaf, who had been just been elected president of Liberia, called for the formation of rehabilitation centers for traumatized women and girls in DRC, the application of a 30 percent quota for participation of women in decision making at all levels, doing away with laws and customs that discriminate against women or violate international treaties, and setting the age of marriage at eighteen (Whitman 2005).

When the Sun City talks were flagging, the women used back channels to get them going again. They contacted the president of South Africa, Thabo Mbeki, and his wife, Zanele Mbeki, to intervene.[25] On the evening of the ICD signing ceremony, when at midnight it looked like some participants were going to back out of the agreement on technical grounds, the women delegates formed a human chain and blocked the exits, not allowing the men to leave until they had signed (Whitman 2005). As one of the women activists at the Sun City talks put it: "We are the ones who have secured peace through the Sun City agreement, we had put end to conflict."[26]

A women's caucus was formed during the process with support from FAS, UNIFEM, and UNDP to mediate with various parties and the negotiating team. They also kept the national and international media informed. At the same time, they reached out to the public via the international, national, and local media by issuing regular media advisories and convening several press conferences (FAS 2003). Although women were united at Sun City, after the talks some of this unity dissipated, and they were unable to realize their demands, particularly around representation of women.[27] They had been encouraged by external experts to set up a quota system that depended on party cooperation rather than a reserved seat system. Party quotas had worked in the context of parties like South Africa's African National Congress, Mozambique's FRELIMO, or Namibia's SWAPO that were committed to women's representation. But it was not suitable in a context where parties had emerged as private fiefdoms of warlords. One positive development, however, that came out of the

---

[24] Interview with 4.2, Pretoria, August 29, 2007.
[25] Interview with 4.1, Kinshasa, October 28, 2009.
[26] Interview with 4.3, Kinshasa 16, June 2009.   [27] Interview with 4.4, Kinshasa, June 20, 2009.

Pretoria Agreement, the Final Act, in April 2003 was the creation of a Ministry of Women and Family Affairs.

In all three cases described and in many more instances, women played extraordinary roles as peace brokers, coming to the talks united across their ethnic and party differences and united around a common gender agenda. It is incomprehensible to me why those actors in society most willing to advocate for peace across differences and work toward concrete solutions were not fully included in peace negotiations.

CONCLUSIONS

This chapter has focused on the impact of peace negotiations and peace agreements on setting the stage for constitutional and legislative gender reforms as well as for women claiming public leadership roles. Peace negotiations and peace agreements were not only sites of recreating gendered power relations, they also became sites where the gender transcript was rewritten and sites of contestation over gender norms and practices. Historically, women in Liberia and other postconflict countries had been seen as the mediators and peace-makers within the family and community. But in the context of contemporary state and international politics, women's organizations had to fight every step of the way to be included in national peace negotiations and other formal peace processes. Studies have shown that the participation of civil society actors like women is crucial in guaranteeing that the country does not revert back to conflict.

Focusing on the case of Liberia, the chapter showed how women activists used the negotiations to advocate for women's rights and for more general societal demands. From the outset, women activists built important alliances across political, ethnic, religious, and other differences. In many instances, they helped keep the talks on track through societal pressure. The chapter outlined key differences between women activists and male warlord participants in peace negotiations in Liberia and beyond. Formal peace negotiations were almost exclusively the domain of men, while women were relegated to the important yet often hidden localized peacemaking initiatives. Women peace advocates had to struggle painfully hard to gain the little recognition they could claim. They often did this with the help of UN agencies and sympathetic peace negotiation leaders.

Women activists' engagement with peace negotiations generally started from a position of unity across political divisions, whereas for male negotiators, the differences were what defined them from the outset. Civil war reified gendered differences of these kinds, and the framework for peace negotiations perpetu-ated these gendered divisions. As Laura Shepherd has argued, war and violence is not only gendered, violence itself creates gender. Violence in war is one of the sites where culturally and historically specific understandings of gender as a power relationship are reproduced (Shepherd 2008, 50). Women and men engaged in peace negotiations differently, also reproducing gendered power relations. But as this book has shown, war itself can also lead to disruptions of these same norms and expectations. Similarly, peace processes and peace agreements became sites of contestation of these so-called traditional norms and expectations. The peace negotiations not only reified and recreated gender, but women also began to shatter the status quo and redefine gender relations.

7

Women's Rights in Postconflict Constitutions

The most important thing is to lay the foundation of peace.

– Ethiopian proverb

Several changes in opportunity structures during and after conflict created new openings, particularly for women in countries where conflicts were ending. Peace agreements, which were discussed in the previous chapter, paved the way for later constitutional, legislative, and electoral reforms. As numerous conflicts came to an end in Africa after 1995, women's movements sought to influence constitutional reform processes, particularly in areas of equality, customary law, antidiscrimination provisions, violence against women, quotas, and citizenship rights. Countries that came out of major civil conflict and violent upheaval in Africa after the mid-1990s, but especially after 2000, have made more constitutional changes with respect to women's rights than other African countries.

While these constitutional reforms were most evident in countries that had experienced civil war, even countries like Kenya, which experienced massive election-related violence in 2008, subsequently saw the conclusion of what had been a protracted and acrimonious constitutional process in which women activists were able to insert key provisions.

Since the mid-1990s we have seen an increase in constitutional provisions addressing gender concerns in Africa. Most of these changes, especially the most far-reaching ones, are found in postconflict countries. The decline of conflict after 1995 led to political opening, even if limited. Nevertheless it was often sufficient to allow for the autonomous women's organizations to press for constitutional changes.

Virtually all African countries have rewritten their constitutions since 1990. Many of these changes were precipitated by the shift to multipartyism. Since 1995, forty-four constitutions have been rewritten in sub-Saharan Africa (or are in the process of being rewritten), and of those, nineteen have been countries embroiled in conflict and fourteen in countries where conflicts were high in intensity and or long in duration. The only postconflict constitution that has not been rewritten since 1990 is Liberia's, which is in the process of being rewritten. The remaining five are nonmajor postconflict countries (Botswana, Guinea Bissau, Mauritius, São Tomé e Príncipe, and Tanzania, which has yet to ratify its revised constitution).

One might argue that the introduction of women's rights language is a function of the newness of the constitutions. While newness is one factor in these developments, it is not sufficient as an explanation. Since 1990, almost all African constitutions have been rewritten or amended, and the differences between the two groups are striking. Thus, I contrast the language in the postconflict and conflict constitutions within a context that created opportunity structures for women in almost all contexts.

Similarly, although a small number of women were present in some of the early postindependence constitution-writing exercises, these constitutions did not result in the kind of language and provisions we are seeing today. Interestingly, women had been involved in constitution-making efforts in several African countries such as Ghana, Mali, Nigeria, and Sierra Leone at the time of independence (Turrittin 1993, 63). In fact, the Sierra Leone Women's Movement petitioned to be included in the constitution-writing exercise when women were left out of the process at the time of independence. They expressed their outrage at the fact the government had purposefully ignored them and their demands to incorporate women's rights in the new constitution (Denzer 1987, 450). Two women were eventually included and ended up playing an important role in reconciling differences between the delegates (Tripp et al. 2009).

The connection between the end of conflict and constitutional reform regarding women's rights is also not as evident in countries where the conflict was localized or where it ended without a peace agreement, that is, in contexts where there was no necessity to reconstruct the polity in a new and more inclusive way. In Angola, the civil war ended when the People's Movement for the Liberation of Angola (MPLA) won the war against the National Union for the Total Independence of Angola (UNITA) in 2002. No peace talks were held to establish a process for political reconstruction, and the subsequent postconflict constitution did not reflect an impetus to build an inclusive polity or one that incorporated extensive rights for women. While the 1992 constitution had opened up the country to multiparty elections and the direct election of the president, the 2010 postconflict constitution expanded the powers of the president and abolished presidential elections so that the head of state would be the leader of the party with the parliamentary majority, while the position of prime minister was abolished. This concentrated all power in the president and blurred the executive and legislative branches. In terms of women's rights, there was little impetus to make the kinds of changes we see in other postconflict countries. There was little consultation with independent women's organizations. Angola, because of its heavy dependence on oil and weak United Nations (UN) influence, was somewhat insulated from international pressures and norms around women's rights. Thus, while the 2010 constitution introduced some improvements over the 1992 constitution, it did not go as far as the other postconflict constitutions in Africa, particularly in the area of customary law. It provided for state promotion of equal rights regardless of sex and state promotion of equality between men and women. It also had an antidiscrimination clause regarding sex, but these are fairly standard fare in most African constitutions.

In contrast, in the Ugandan process – which is detailed in this chapter – women's organizations were extensively consulted during the process, and they also participated of their own accord by sending memos to the constitutional commission. Women's rights activists actively participated in the writing process and in the Constituent Assembly (CA) that voted on the 1995 constitution. International organizations supported efforts to encourage the inclusion of women's rights in the new constitution. And even though the Ugandan civil war from 1980–86 did not end in a peace agreement, the constitution was an effort, at least ostensibly, to create a more inclusive polity. Whether it accomplished that with respect to the political opposition is debatable.

Finally, some have argued that these postconflict constitutional changes addressing women's rights are primarily a product of international donor pressures. There is no doubt that international actors, like the United Nations agencies and various foreign technical advisors and constitutional experts, have influenced these constitution-writing processes, and it is very clear that the diffusion of norms and practices in constitution writing are taking place. The UN even has a mandate to ensure that "A country's constitution should explicitly guarantee equal human rights for women."[1] However, there are different levels of international involvement in constitution-making processes, such as providing a procedural framework based on UN law, as was the case in East Timor. Another model for external actors involves them not only in the process, but they may also seek to impose substantive outcomes as was the case in Iraq. Finally, a third model is the Sudanese one where external influence through a regional organization and a group of interested states moderated and financed the negotiations, but did not influence them otherwise. In Sudan, the constitution-making process was hosted by the East African Intergovernmental Authority on Development (IGAD) led by a Kenyan national, who was assisted by envoys from Eritrea, Ethiopia, and Uganda. International experts in international law came from South Africa, Switzerland, Italy, and Norway while the United States and UK helped fund the process. The UN was represented, while the German Max Planck Institute for Comparative Public Law and

[1] www.un.org/womenwatch/osagi/wps/publication/WomenAndElections.pdf.

International Law provided constitutional expertise. The international actors' roles were simply to moderate, mediate, and assist in finding a solution (Dann and Al-Ali 2006).

Thus, one cannot solely attribute the constitutional outcomes in women's rights provisions to foreign actors. If one looks closely at the actors, as is evident in the Ugandan case, the donors played a role, but the primary driving forces were women's movements, women's rights lawyers, and their domestic allies (Kabira 2012). Were this simply a matter of implementing an international blueprint, there would be less variance between the postconflict constitutions and between all the new constitutions in general. Moreover, there would be less contention over gender-related provisions if it were simply a matter of complying with donors. Even countries like Sudan and Angola, which experienced weak external influences in their constitution-writing processes, adopted some women's rights–friendly provisions. The fact that there are women's rights provisions next to ones that are quite hostile to human rights suggests that whatever international influences are evident, they are unevenly incorporated. Sudan's constitution has provisions for quotas for women and an important provision that commits the state to combating harmful customs and traditions that undermine the dignity and status of women. Yet it also has a provision of the death penalty that stipulates that "(3) No death penalty shall be executed upon pregnant or lactating women, save after two years of lactation" (Art. 36).

One small but important indicator of the spirit of the gender-related reforms we are seeing relates to the use of pronouns, especially in postconflict constitutions. Postconflict constitutions are proportionately more likely to use gendered pronouns. In the case of Ethiopia, the pronouns are not gendered, but there is a recognition of the issue: "In this Constitution, provisions enacted in the masculine gender shall be deemed to include the feminine gender" (Art. 7). Sometimes women activists had to be creative in how they got this language included. Somali women activists, for example, lobbied the Charter Drafting Committee and got them to insert gender-sensitive language into the constitution ("he and she"). By getting the technical committee to make this change, they were able to avoid a major uproar had it been raised at the conference for debate. This language is reflected in the final 2012 constitution (Abdullahi 2009).

CONSTITUTIONAL CHANGES

The postconflict constitutions were generally the first to adopt the new generation of women's rights–related provisions. The least challenging constitutional reforms from a women's rights perspective in Africa relate to equal citizenship and nondiscrimination provisions, terms and conditions of employment, and legislative quotas. These provisions make demands on the state or employers, but do not touch the more controversial matters that pertain to the family,

TABLE 7.1 *African Countries with Constitutional Provisions Relating to Women's Rights, 2015 (%)*

	Postconflict	No major conflict
Equality clause	100	91
Antidiscrimination	94	78
Labor	94	56
Quotas/representation	75	25
Status of customary law	56	28
Positive measures	39	15
Violence against women	38	13
Land and property	38	16
Citizenship of children	30	8
Average	63	37

Note: This table refers only to sub-Saharan African countries.

clan, and custom. Also the labor-related clauses make numerous references to maternity provisions, which tend to align easily with women's maternal roles and the protection of the family, thus they too are less controversial (Table 7.1). Most countries in Africa provide for maternity leave. These types of provisions were much easier to include than reforms that promoted women's rights and equality within the closer relationships of family, clan, and religion (Hassim 2005).

EQUALITY AND ANTIDISCRIMINATION PROVISIONS

Historically, equality and nondiscrimination provisions were evident in the postcolonial constitutions, although they did not usually mention women. Even one of the most gender-conscious countries such as Tanzania did not mention women explicitly in its 1977 constitution. It is typical of these earlier constitutions. It states that "All persons are equal before the law and are entitled, without any discrimination, to protection and equality before the law" (Article 13.1).

Starting in the 1990s, the postconflict constitutions led the way in the trend that specified equality of men and women and specifically mentioned women's protection from discrimination, often along with other groups. South Sudan's 2011 constitution is typical of the newest constitutions in this regard: "All persons are equal before the law and are entitled to the equal protection of the law without discrimination as to race, ethnic origin, colour, sex, language, religious creed, political opinion, birth, locality or social status" (Art. 14). Thus today almost all of sub-Saharan Africa's constitutions incorporate some clause specifically mentioning equality between men and women, and all the postconflict countries have such a provision. It is only the nonpostconflict Mauritius, Seychelles, and Nigeria that do not include such a provision.

Along the lines of older constitutions, Nigeria's constitution mentions equality of all citizens but not specifically gender equality.

Similarly, over two-thirds of all constitutions have an antidiscrimination clause specifically referring to women. However, 94 percent of postconflict countries have such a provision (Liberia's constitution has yet to be revised), while only 78 percent of the nonpostconflict countries have such a provision (Table 7.1).[2] Several have general antidiscrimination provisions, but they don't specifically mention women. Seven postconflict countries refer to positive measures the state needs to take to address the status of women or past discrimination, whereas four nonpostconflict countries do so. It is with these relatively uncontroversial provisions of gender equality and nondiscrimination that postconflict countries depart the least from nonconflict countries.

LABOR

There has also been relatively little controversy over constitutional provisions regarding labor. Many of the countries adopting such provisions have not necessarily had active women's movements nor have they incorporated these provisions as a result of pressure from women's rights activists, suggesting that these are not highly controversial provisions. Nevertheless, only 56 percent of nonpostconflict countries mention gender in relation to employment issues, whereas 94 percent of the postconflict countries do so (Table 7.1). Some of the references in this category are to maternity leave, and quite a few are to equality in employment in general, while in some cases the references are to equality in the state sector and judiciary. Somalia's constitution even refers to gender equality employment in the armed forces. Some prohibit sexual harassment, gender segregation, and discrimination based on gender at the workplace. Others call for equal pay and benefits for women, equal opportunity for promotion and training, protection of working conditions of women during and after pregnancy, the provision of childcare facilities for children under school-going age, medical care for pregnant and lactating women, and paid maternity leave. Some references mention freedom from slavery and forced labor, as well as the right to work and freely choose one's employment.

QUOTAS

The biggest gap between postconflict and nonconflict countries is in the adoption of quotas. In general, the rates of representation for women in parliament in postconflict countries are double those of nonpostconflict countries in Africa. While most of these changes are the result of the adoption of electoral quotas,

---

[2] Comoros, Côte d'Ivoire, Djibouti, Guinea Bissau, Liberia, Mauritania, Seychelles, and Togo do not have antidiscrimination clauses.

either as a result of legislation or voluntary party quota adoption, some countries also have constitutional provisions regarding quotas. Globally only twenty-five countries mention quotas in their constitutions, and ten are in Africa. Over 75 percent of postconflict countries in Africa mention specific quotas or women's legislative or political representation in their constitutions, while only 25 percent nonpostconflict countries do so. Not all constitutions explicitly offer a mechanism or indicate a precise number of seats that need to be set aside.

Gaining political power is seen as a major way for women to take control of their lives and exert control over other arenas as well. The 2005 Ethiopian Constitution is fairly explicit about taking action to increase women's representation as an affirmative action measure: "Considering that women have traditionally been viewed with inferiority and are discriminated against, they have the right to the benefit of affirmative action undertaken for the purpose of introducing corrective changes to such heritage. The aim of such measures is to ensure that special attention is given to enabling women to participate and compete equally with men in the political, economic, and social fields both within public and private organisations" (Art. 34.3). As a result of this provision, Ethiopia almost quadrupled its women representatives in parliament to 28 percent of seats in the House and more than doubled female representation in the Senate, primarily through the introduction of party quotas.

African women's movements are leading many of the efforts to promote political representation of women. Organizations have also formed to support women running for office and to engage in civic education, provide leadership skills training, and other such activities that strengthen women as political actors and leaders. As a result, half the countries in Africa have adopted quotas to increase the numbers of women in legislatures with the result that Africa has some of the highest representation of women in parliaments in the world, particularly in postconflict countries (see Chapter 8).

Africa's quota systems are evenly divided between countries that have quotas adopted voluntarily by political parties; legislated quotas that require parties to comply with a quota for women; and reserved seat systems, which are generally mandated by constitutions. Reserved seat systems guarantee that a minimum number of women will be represented in the parliament. In general, these reserved seat systems have equally high rates of female representation as legislatively mandated candidate list quota systems or voluntary party systems (see Table 8.5).

CUSTOMARY LAW

Many contemporary struggles in Africa regarding women's rights have focused around customary law. These struggles are part of the ongoing contestation over the nature of the legal system in Africa. They have their origins in the legal systems established during colonial times. Independence reinforced colonial legal systems and practices. African legal systems are the product of a mix of legal traditions. These systems built on colonial common law traditions (e.g., in former British colonies) and civil law traditions (e.g., in former French, Portuguese, Belgian, German, Italian, and Spanish colonies). Both legal traditions have coexisted at different levels of comfort with customary law (Tripp 2009).

After independence, countries dealt with customary laws in different ways. Some sought to integrate civil and customary law. Some of the former French colonies like Senegal sought to combine civil and customary laws into more comprehensive family codes; however, the result has been a mixture of measures that both protect and discriminate against women. Nevertheless there is often a considerable gap between the law on the books and what is practiced on the ground (Boye et al. 1991). Similarly, the former Portuguese colonies absorbed customary law into general law (Banda 2005). Other countries abolished customary law altogether to create their own civil code. Côte d'Ivoire similarly abandoned customary law entirely to adopt a civil code that resembled the French one. Ethiopia, which was not colonized, eliminated customary law to create the Ethiopian Civil Code because it was felt that there was too much variance in customary law from region to region and that it was too unstable to codify (Bennett and Vermeulen 1980). Thus, there was considerable variance in how customary and common/civil law was treated in different parts of Africa, although in general the legal systems remained plural. These legal legacies have had important implications for the efforts of contemporary women's rights movements and are among the most significant changes seen in the constitutions drafted after major civil war or violent upheaval (Tripp 2009).

Since the 1990s, women's rights organizations in Africa sought the introduction of clauses that allow the constitutional guarantees of equality to prevail should there be a clash between women's rights and customary laws and practices that violate women's rights, discriminate against women, or infringe on bill of rights provisions regarding gender equality. These are extremely profound challenges. They are, in principle, attempts to legitimize new legal-based sources of authority for rights governing relations between men and women, family ties, and relationships between women and traditional, clan, and religious leaders. In the past, even when laws existed to regulate marriage, inheritance, custody, and other such practices, customary laws and practices coexisted and generally took precedence when it came to family and clan concerns. Even though, in practice, these customary norms may still prevail today, even with the constitutional reforms, women's movements now have the means to challenge these practices through constitutional and legislative changes. But challenges to customary law have been particularly difficult because there can be strong feelings of support for customary practices, even among women themselves (Logan 2009). Therefore, it has been much harder to pass legislation affecting these institutions, such as laws ensuring women's rights to property through land and inheritance. Much of the active and organized resistance to improving women's legal status, particularly in the area of family law, has come from religious leaders, chiefs, elders, clan leaders, and individuals who are wedded to older norms and cultural practices. Many of these people also stand to benefit politically and even economically from older practices and beliefs (Tripp 2009).

In practice, however, the constitutional legitimization of customary rights and traditional authorities, often within the context of promoting cultural rights, sometimes results in conflicts with the constitutional provisions protecting women's rights and gender equality. These constitutional protections for customary law, and perhaps more critically, activism on the part of customary law advocates, often pose obstacles to enacting legislative reforms that protect women's bodily integrity (reforms having to do with reproductive rights, age of and consent to marriage, domestic violence, and female genital cutting), women's access to property (land rights, inheritance, polygamy), and the related unequal treatment of women as property (bride wealth, levirate). By recognizing the authority of traditional leaders and by allowing the constitution to trump their authority when it comes to women's rights, advocates of both sources of law are emboldened in ways that sets them on a collision course, particularly because customary law is legally recognized in most African countries and because it prevails within communities (Tripp 2009).

While most African constitutions protect traditional authorities, at least 56 percent of the postconflict countries have a provision that allows the constitution or statutory law to override customary law, while only 28 percent of the nonpostconflict countries have such a clause (Table 7.1). The clauses ensure that constitutional or statutory law prevails over customary law, particularly where there is a divergence between women's rights and customary practice, that is, where customary practices violate women's rights or discriminate against them in some form. Some charge the state with eliminating such practices. For example, Ethiopia's constitution states: "The state shall enforce the right of women to eliminate the influences of harmful customs. Laws, customs and practices that oppress or cause bodily or mental harm to women are prohibited" (Art. 35). At least four constitutions – all postconflict – allude to female genital cutting, and some are explicit about it [Somalia: "Circumcision of girls is a cruel and degrading customary practice, and is tantamount to torture. The circumcision of girls is prohibited" (Art. 15)]. While it is understood that such practices are not abolished by constitutional or legal decree, the recognition of the harm they perpetrate establishes a new norm and understanding of what is acceptable in a given society. It gives women a legal basis for challenging such practices.

Only a handful of constitutions refer specifically to gender with respect to these provisions regarding customary law, and most of these are postconflict/ conflict constitutions (Ethiopia, Somalia, South Sudan, and Uganda). Generally it is understood that family law pertaining to women is an area of customary law that might conflict with the constitution. Uganda's constitution refers to women in this regard. Article 33 of the 1995 Ugandan constitution states that "Laws, cultures, customs and traditions which are against the dignity, welfare or interest of women or any other marginalised group ... or which undermine their status, are prohibited by this Constitution."

Even countries that have tried to harmonize these contradictory impulses by directly addressing the tension within the constitution have run into problems in practice. For example, Uganda's 1995 Constitution states: "Cultural and customary values which are consistent with fundamental rights and freedoms, human dignity, democracy and with the Constitution may be developed and incorporated in aspects of Ugandan life." And "[l]aws, cultures, customs and traditions which are against the dignity, welfare or interest of women or any other marginalised group ... or which undermine their status, are prohibited by this Constitution." Moreover, women have the right "to affirmative action for the purpose of redressing the imbalances created by history, tradition or custom."

The limits to these contradictory provisions in Uganda emerged with the debate over the amendments to the 1998 Land Act. When the women's movement started to demand a co-ownership (common property) clause so that women could inherit land or keep their share of land if they were divorced or thrown out by their husbands, there was immediate pushback in defense of the clan and customary practices, suggesting that the practice of customary law is more powerful than any written law or constitution.

PROPERTY RIGHTS

As indicated earlier, closely related to the issue of customary law is the protection of property rights[3] of women. Only 38 percent of postconflict countries in sub-Saharan Africa have provisions referring to the elimination of discrimination of women in the acquisition and inheritance of property. Such provisions compared with 16 percent of countries that did not experience major violence (Table 7.1). Thus, the Ethiopian constitution states: "Women shall have the right to acquire, administer, control, enjoy and dispose of property. They shall, in particular, have equal rights with men regarding the use, transfer, administration and control of land. They shall enjoy the same rights with men with respect to inheritance (35.7)."

Constitutional changes and laws that challenge customary authority and resources in the area of land rights have been particularly contentious, especially in postconflict contexts, where property rights were disrupted by conflict and by dislocation as refugees and internally displaced peoples. The bases of customary ownership have been eroded since the time of colonialism, making women's access to land significantly more precarious as the protections

---

[3] The following section on property rights draws heavily from Tripp (2009).

traditionally ensured by the clan system have been peeled away. This became all the more true after conflict. When people moved back from the internally displaced person (IDP) camps in northern Uganda, having been placed in these camps for up to a decade, it was primarily widowed women who remained behind without adequate protections from their communities to reclaim land. Over 1.8 million people had been moved to IDP camps from 1996 until 2006, when hostilities diminished. The affected Acholi and Langi areas in the North are patrilineal, which means that women who are widowed, separated, or divorced are disadvantaged by the fact that their families and clans do not allow them to inherit or own land.

With increased commercialization of land and with problems of land scarcity, local leaders have felt mounting pressures to protect the clan system and in so doing have placed even greater constraints on women's access to land (Gray and Kevane 1999). However, the clan system they are seeking to preserve is no longer one that affords women the supports it is once said to have guaranteed.

Land is of critical importance to women because they depend on it for cultivation and therefore their livelihoods. Unequal access to land is one of the most important forms of economic inequality between men and women and has consequences for women as social and political actors. Women provide a large percentage of all agricultural labor, especially labor involving food production, yet they own only a fraction of the land in most African countries. Women are often responsible for providing for the household; therefore their access to land for food production is critical to the welfare of the entire household. Even women who want to get into business need land as collateral to obtain bank loans. Because women are almost completely dependent on men to access land in patrilineal societies, women who are childless, single, widowed, disabled, separated/divorced, or with only female children often have little or no recourse because they may have no access to land through a male relative (Tripp 2009).

In patrilineal societies, women generally do not inherit land from either their fathers or their husbands. Their fathers may not bequeath land to their daughters because daughters marry outside the clan and will therefore take the land with them to another clan. Husbands often do not bequeath land to their wives for the same reason: They need to ensure that the land remains in the clan because they worry that the widow might sell the land to nonclan members. Unlike men, women generally marry outside their clan or family, so the widow is considered an "outsider" in her husband's clan or family and may be suspected of being less loyal to clan or family interests. In some societies, if the husband dies, the wife and children are inherited by the husband's brother or another family member so that he may provide for them. This practice is dying out in many parts of Africa, raising fears that if a widow remarries outside the clan, the clan land she has acquired is lost. Thus, under customary law in many countries, a woman may have jointly acquired land with her husband and may have spent her entire adult life cultivating the land, but she cannot claim ownership of the property. If the husband dies, the land may go to the sons, and even to the daughters. Nevertheless, he may still leave the wife with no land and therefore no source of livelihood (Tripp 2009).

Because of women's increased vulnerability due to disruptions in property ownership during conflict, constitutional reforms in this area have been especially important for postconflict countries.

VIOLENCE AGAINST WOMEN

Gender-based violence has become one of the most important areas of new legislation and of constitutional provisions: 26 percent of postconflict constitutions mention violence against women, whereas only 8 percent of nonpostconflict constitutions do so (Table 7.1). Although many constitutions mention violence in general, we are seeing more specific references to violence against women in the postconflict/conflict constitutions. The 2006 Democratic Republic of Congo Constitution mentions all forms of violence against women, including domestic violence: "*Les pouvoires publics ... Ils prennent de mesures pour lutter contre toute forme de violences faites a la femme dans la vie publique et dans la vie privée.*" ["The public authorities ... will take measures against all forms of violence against women in public and private life."]

POSITIVE RIGHTS

One of the most striking elements in the African constitutions that are responsive to women's movements is the extent to which they seek to guarantee positive rights for women, which are proactive measures taken by the state. The most extensive such provisions are in postconflict constitutions. Nevertheless, these are the most elusive of rights to guarantee in resource-poor countries, regardless of whether or not there is political will. Thus the Mozambican constitution states: "1. The State shall promote, support and value the development of women, and shall encourage their growing role in society, in all spheres of political, economic, social and cultural life of the country. 2. The State shall recognize and hold in high esteem the participation of women in the national liberation struggle and in the defense of sovereignty and democracy" (Art. 122).

CITIZENSHIP OF CHILDREN

All but one of the countries specifically mentioning that the citizenship of the children can follow that of the mother are postconflict countries. Of the postconflict countries, 30 percent have such a provision, while only 8 percent of nonpostconflict countries do (Table 7.1). Today only a handful of African constitutions specify that citizenship is determined by the nationality of the father only (e.g., Nigeria, Zambian, Ghana, and Swaziland), and some countries, like Tanzania, have legislation to this effect. A few, for example, Mozambique and Eritrea, explicitly mention that citizenship can be passed to children by either the mother or father; the Malawian constitution mentions the acquisition and retention of citizenship and nationality in the context of women's rights. But it is mainly the postconflict constitutions like the Namibian constitution that do not permit gender discrimination with respect to the right to pass citizenship to one's children (Tripp 2009).

WOMEN'S RIGHTS IN UGANDA'S CONSTITUTION-MAKING PROCESS

The making of the 1995 constitution in Uganda illustrates many of the key elements of constitution-making in postconflict countries. The efforts of women activists and organizations to amend the Ugandan Constitution had a profound impact on the substance of the constitution that was adopted in 1995. The previous 1967 Constitution prohibited discrimination based on race, religion, and tribe and other grounds but not sex. There were no gender equality provisions. Customary law prevailed in family law. Women were not allowed to inherit the property of their fathers or husbands, nor were they allowed to own land. In effect, women were treated as minors and not as full citizens.

The 1995 constitution changed all this. The innovations in gender provisions came about largely as a result of the efforts of women activists and women's movement pressures both in the constitutional commission and in the CA (Kanyeihamba 2002; Matembe 2002; Odoki 2005; Waliggo 2002). At the same time, the ruling party, the National Resistance Movement, was also supportive of these changes and had sought to promote women leaders.

Mary Maitum and Miria Matembe played key roles in this process while serving on the constitutional commission, although, in general, the commission itself was receptive to women's rights. According to the secretary of the commission, Fr. John Mary Waliggo: "Miria Matembe and Mary Maitum, the two women members, were both active in the national women's movement. They articulated the interests of women and found all other commissioners fully supportive of women's liberation and empowerment. They did not need to convince the rest, they needed only to remind them occasionally of additional points which may have been forgotten" (Waliggo 2002). Justice George Kanyeihamba, another commissioner, who also had served on the Uganda Supreme Court, as Minister of Justice, and Minister of Commerce, as well as attorney general, concurred with Waliggo that the dozens of men who advised the legal and drafting committee were keen to see that women's rights were protected (Kanyeihamba 2002, 198; Matembe 2002, 199).

Both Maitum and Matembe were lawyers, and Maitum was particularly knowledgeable about international legal conventions on human rights and women, which she brought to bear on the process. They got all the gender provisions into the draft that they wanted except for provisions regarding the representation of women, which was to be based on regional rather than district representation. The representation of women at the local level was also not mentioned in the draft. They had wanted gender-inclusive language, but the technical drafter claimed he found it cumbersome to make the changes. Also, the provision to create an Equal Opportunities Commission was not developed in the draft. Because of these omissions, Matembe decided to run for CA and vowed to get these provisions in at a later stage. Indeed, she was elected to the CA. She worked closely with the CA Women's Caucus and succeeded in addressing all these concerns in the final draft of the constitution.

Popular participation

One of the characteristics of Uganda's constitution-making process was the extent to which it engaged the public. In fact, Father Waliggo argued that the constitution-making exercise served a larger purpose than simply crafting a new constitution and that it provided a nationwide program of civic education. The Commission held seminars throughout the country to collect opinions and to hold civic education workshops on a series of topics, including "Women and the Constitution." Organizations like the Women Lawyer's Association (FIDA), Action for Development (ACFODE), Muslim Women's Association, the Catholic Women's Guild, the Mothers Union, and many other groups held seminars and invited the commissioners to speak.

Waliggo felt that the topic of women's rights evoked some of the most animated discussions in these seminars. Women were provided with the opportunity to speak in public meetings, and for some this was the first time in their lives they had done so. As Waliggo explained: "The women of Uganda talked. They articulated their interests and needs with insight and intelligence. As a matter of fact, the women constituted a force that really embraced the Constitution making exercise. I came to believe that women viewed this exercise as a main hope for liberation. Gauging from the questions they were asking, their contributions to the debate and the level of mobilization, one could argue that women believed that the Constitution was going to be the Savior, a panacea for the many problems they face" (Waliggo 2002, 130–131). When the fiery feminist Miria Matembe spoke at these gatherings, Waliggo noted,

Participants would laugh, ululate, shout and clap as she challenged the old fashioned male domination and oppression! In some places you would find people who were a little bit conservative who would say: "Oh my goodness, she's saying things which are not usually said."

The Constitutional Commission invited any group or section of the population to submit memoranda. Almost half of the 26,000 memoranda sent from civil society organizations came from women and women's organizations, and most focused on issues of discrimination against girls and women and the need for gender equality (Matembe 2002, 138). According to Waliggo, they conveyed a unity of purpose that cut across class lines. This was reflected in the Report of the Commission in aspirational terms. It stated that "Both men and women want to see an end to the discrimination and marginalization of women in every sector and aspect of life" (Uganda Constitutional Commission 1993, 150). One of the memoranda came from the Ministry of Women in Development, which had worked with women's organizations in 1991 to coordinate a nationwide discussion of the constitution as it was being drafted. The Ministry's memorandum addressed questions of national concern, for example, national language, but also issues of particular concern to women, including the elimination of discrimination on the basis of sex, which would involve the repeal of marriage, divorce, inheritance, and property laws that discriminated against women.

Matembe found that one by-product of these seminars around the Constitution was that they inspired more women to run for local council seats, and gender issues became important in every election manifesto. Local courts were also empowered to enforce women's rights and together with the legal aid clinics provided an important informal mechanism to help settle disputes.

Constituent Assembly

Women were active in the CA that debated the Commission's draft of the constitution. Out of a total of 286 delegates to the Assembly, 52 (18%) were women. Most women delegates to the Assembly participated in a Women's Caucus, a nonpartisan organization aimed at building consensus among women delegates on issues that related particularly to women's rights. It was by all accounts one of the most cohesive and effective caucuses in the Assembly. It lobbied the CA and worked with sympathetic male CA members. The main leaders of the caucus included Winnie Bynamima, Specioza Kazibwe, Miria Matembe, Beatrice Lagada, and Faith Mwondha. The caucus had an alliance with other CA groups like the youth, workers, and people with disabilities. CA delegate George Kanyeihamba observed that: "Women played such a key role in the Constituent Assembly that men were afraid to oppose amendments that were moved by women" (Matembe 2002, 196).

Their main accomplishment, as mentioned earlier, was to increase the number of women in parliament, provide for the representation of women in the local government, strengthen language around the Gender Equality Commission, and ensure gender-inclusive language in the constitution. The main debate around gender concerns related to the provision for reserved parliamentary seats for women. Non-NRM (ruling party) groups resisted the special seats given to women, youth, the disabled, and the Army. They felt that there was an alliance between these groups and the NRM and that this was another way to ensure NRM dominance (Waliggo 2002).

Women CA members had complained about the way some men spoke to them during the proceedings. There was eventually a turning point in the assembly after which the ways in which men and women communicated with one another was transformed. This happened when a male delegate compared women to diplomats: "When a lady says 'no,' she means 'perhaps' (laughter), and when she says 'perhaps' she means 'yes,' and when she says 'yes,' she means 'no' (laughter)." The women politicians asked the speaker to discipline the delegate, and so he asked the delegate to withdraw his offensive remarks. Not only did the delegate refuse to do so, but he continued: "If somebody has not got a wide scope in life, I am not going to apologize for her ignorance. There is a Russian saying (laughter) that a frog in a pot can only see the size of the sky which is equal to the mouth of the pot ... some of us have lived in a pot with a larger mouth; therefore we are able to see a large part of the sky" (Matembe 2002). This was simply too much for the women delegates, and they walked out of the assembly, refusing to return until the male delegate in question apologized. No such incident occurred after that point.

The Friedrich Ebert Foundation helped fund public dialogues in which they brought key politicians to talk about issues affecting women. They held these dialogues at the Sheraton Hotel. The Women's Caucus would arrange for one of the male members of the CA to present an amendment that they wanted to move and then have the audience discuss it. They tried to identify men who spoke with eloquence and who were respected and listened to.

The National Association of Women's Organisations in Uganda (NAWOU), with support from the Friedrich Ebert Foundation, formed a Gender Information Center at the conference center where the CA meetings were being held. The center provided caucus members with educational materials, monitored debates, offered legal consultancy services to women delegates, and provided facilities for meetings (Friedrich Ebert Foundation 1995). The Center also produced a weekly radio program that allowed women delegates to share their views with the public.

In 1994, with support from the Ford Foundation, groups like Action for Development (ACFODE) and National Association of Women's Organisations in Uganda (NAWOU) along with the Foundation for Human Rights Initiative, Human Rights and Peace Centre, Department of Political Science at Makerere University, Radio Uganda, and Uganda Television launched a program called "Link" that involved seminars, discussions and radio programs, television programs, a news bulletin, and newspaper articles aimed providing information and civic education to the public in the constitution making process. ACFODE itself published a regular bulletin as part of this program called *The Link Bulletin* that included articles about the CA proceedings, debates among influential figures with varying viewpoints, and in depth articles on the issues being discussed in the CA. Part of the impetus for this program was to broaden its work to include men as well. They worked in twenty districts and at schools and institutions of higher education.

During the CA proceedings, the Ministry of Gender also launched a program of skills development training programs funded by the Danish International Development Agency (DANIDA) with the help of the Uganda Gender Resource

Center, which had support from Austria's North-South Institute for Development. They organized regular workshops and seminars for the Women's Caucus members that educated them on the substance of the proposed constitution, procedural questions, negotiating techniques, coalition building, debating skills, utilizing the media, and how to lobby (Matembe 2002, 186–7).

Constitutional provisions regarding women

Almost all of these activities paid off as they resulted in the incorporation of multiple provisions regarding women's rights into the constitution. The only reference to women in the 1960 constitution had to do with establishing maximum working hours for minors and women (26.5). Some of the most important provisions for women in the 1995 constitution included the following:

- The Constitution provides for equal protection for all people under the law regardless of sex, race, color, ethnic origin, tribe, religion, social or economic position, political opinion, or disability.
- The Constitution ensures women's right to equal opportunities in political, economic, and social activities. It guarantees reserved seats for groups marginalized on the basis of gender or other reasons for "the purpose of redressing the imbalance which has existed against them." Moreover, it calls for the creation of an Equal Opportunities Commission that would ensure that this principle is applied. This preferential treatment provision can be applied to education, politics, economics, and other areas. It allows for one woman to run for parliament as a women's representative in each district. Women may also run for openly contested seats. Women can claim one-third of the local government council seats.
- The Constitution allows for women to be eligible for the same jobs as men, and they should be paid the same as men for the same work. Women are given job protection before and after pregnancy.
- The Constitution recognizes the "significant role women play in society." This permits recognition of the heavy responsibilities women shoulder in contributing to the income and welfare of the family and to society. It allows for the protection of the family, thereby paving the way for the enactment of a law that addresses domestic violence. There is recognition of women's unique contributions to society and to be recognized through laws that facilitate women in bearing children through a maternity leave.
- The Constitution supports customary values insofar as they promote human rights, freedom, human dignity and democracy, but prohibits "laws, cultures, customs and traditions which are against the dignity, welfare or interest of women or which undermine their status...."
- The Constitution requires the state to register all births, marriages, and deaths, which gives protection to women who have customarily not

registered their marriages, making them especially vulnerable in terms of their rights in the event that their husband were to die. It protects widows, allowing them to keep their deceased husband's property; to decide on a burial place for their husband; to choose where they themselves want to be buried; and it gives them the right to reject being married to their husband's brother. Widows have the right to act as guardians of their children upon the death of their husbands.

- The Constitution sets a minimum age of marriage at eighteen. It also provides for equal rights in marriage and equal rights to acquire and use property, and equal rights to share family property on the dissolution of the marriage. Married women have the freedom to attend and participate in meetings. Women have the right to choose whom to marry because forced marriages are forbidden.
- The Constitution allows foreign men who marry Ugandan wives to claim Ugandan citizenship. In previous constitutions, citizenship was only granted to foreign women who married Ugandan husbands.
- Finally, the Constitution protects children and vulnerable persons against abuse, harassment, and ill-treatment. This refers to women in specific occupations, including maids, cocktail waitresses, secretaries, and women who travel at night, for example, nurses and midwives (Friedrich Ebert Foundation 1995, 27–43; Tripp 2000; Waliggo 1996).

At the time, women were very pleased with the extensive constitutional recognition of women's rights and gave the NRM considerable electoral support in subsequent elections. Over the years, the constitution allowed for a steady stream of women's rights legislation to be passed, especially in the eighth parliament. Yet legislation which challenged customary law and authorities, such as key amendments to the 1998 Land Act that would allow women to inherit land and the Marriage and Divorce Bill, did not garner government support, revealing the tenacity of customary law even among leaders who appear to support women's rights. This, along with other measures, led to diminished support of the Museveni by many women's rights activists.

CONCLUSIONS

Since the 1990s, new constitutions throughout Africa have often included nondiscrimination or equality provisions, while prohibiting customary practices if they undermined the dignity, welfare, or status of women. These are marked changes in constitution making, most evident in postconflict constitutions. These are new developments in African constitution making and can be contrasted with constitutions passed prior to 1990, in which customary law generally was not subject to any gender-related restrictions. Women's movements played an important role in ensuring that these clauses were included.

The fact that women's movements in the 1990s started tackling some of the most intransigent and difficult societal issues within constitutional reform is an indication of how far norms have changed. Some of the issues being taken up could not even be mentioned in public and were considered taboo well into the 1990s (e.g., domestic violence and female genital cutting).

Nevertheless, the tensions between customary law and women's rights remain an important constraint on advancing women's status in postconflict societies. Even in countries where customary law is subordinate to a constitution that bans gender discrimination, the reality generally is far from the ideal. The issue of customary law and the arbitrariness of rulings by traditional authorities remain a major source of concern for women's rights activists.

At the same time, the very fact that there is resistance to many efforts at constitutional and legislative reform regarding women's rights suggests that laws matter, and that laws are not merely passed to satisfy changing international norms. Their passage is a mark of changing societal norms, expectations, and sensibilities regarding the rights of women and girls, particularly in postconflict countries. These legal changes are evidence that culture is not static and is evolving in ways that require changes in the laws. The fact that postconflict countries were motivated to go the furthest in making these changes is not simply a reflection of the newness of their revised constitutions because even more nonpostconflict constitutions were revised in this same period without the same outcomes. It suggests that gender disruptions during the conflict, especially those affecting women relating to their access to power, violence, and property rights, were among the most important changes that took place in these countries.

PART IV

GENDERED OUTCOMES

8

Women and Leadership in Postconflict Countries

The voice of women is the voice of the nation, let them be heard.
– Sign in Sierra Leone village[1]

Since the early 1990s we have witnessed many important changes in Africa with respect to women's political engagement, especially in postconflict countries. These trends have been identified globally as well (Hughes 2009; Luciak 2006, 6; Zuckerman and Greenberg 2004, 71). Rwanda claimed the world's highest ratio of women in parliament in 2003, and in the subsequent election, Rwandan women became the first in the world to hold a majority of a country's national legislative seats (56%). By 2012, the figure jumped to 64 percent. The countries with the highest levels of legislative representation in Africa are almost entirely postconflict countries and they were among the first to adopt higher rates of representation. Moreover, it is no accident that postwar Liberia was the first African country to elect a woman president, Ellen Johnson Sirleaf, in 2005. Postconflict Uganda already had a woman vice president for a decade between 1993 and 2003. Five members of Sudan's postwar cabinet are women, a significant increase from the previous cabinet. Similar postwar patterns that catapulted women into leadership roles were evident in local government, in the judiciary, and in regional bodies throughout Africa.

This chapter connects the end of conflict to women's political representation, which is one of the more dramatic changes in postconflict countries. It looks not only at women's legislative representation, where the changes have been most striking, but also at other areas of leadership in the executive, at the local level and elsewhere. It shows how these patterns are related to the causal mechanisms described earlier in the book: disruptions in gender

---

[1] www.womankind.org.uk/policy-and-resources/women-peace-and-security/.

ations, rise of women's movements fueled by a modicum of political liberalization, and the changes in international norms and pressures. It also discusses some of the other factors that have been used to explain women's political representation.

LEGISLATIVE REPRESENTATION

The changes in women's political representation in Africa have been most dramatic in legislatures, where female representation tripled between 1990 and 2010 (Figure 8.1). This changing sex ratio is most visible in postconflict countries in Africa, where women claim considerably more seats (29%) on average compared with other countries (16%). In 2010 postconflict countries in Africa had over twice as many seats as other countries, indicating the trend-setting role the postconflict countries played on the continent (see Table 8.1; Figure 8.1). The patterns in sub-Saharan Africa were also evident in North Africa in Algeria, which went through a bloody civil war between 1991 and

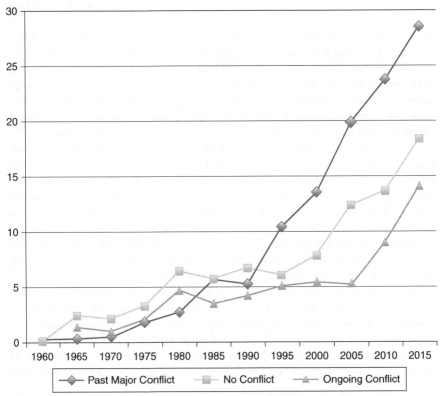

FIGURE 8.1 Levels of Conflict and Female Legislative Representation in Africa (%), 1960–2015

TABLE 8.1 *Rates of Female Representation in Postconflict Legislatures, 2015*

World region	Postconflict female legislative representation %	No conflict female legislative representation %
Africa	29	16
South Asia	22	13
Southeast Asia	32*	18.5

*This represents only Timor-Leste.
Source: Inter-Parliamentary Union. Countries with ongoing conflict are not included in this table.

2002, and now has the highest rate of female representation in the Middle East, with women claiming 32 percent of the parliamentary seats. Although we are seeing these changes in a few countries where there have been lower levels of violence, the outcomes are not that different from nonconflict countries.

Even more important than the rates of representation are the changes that occurred in individual countries. In Uganda female legislation representation jumped from 0.8 percent in 1980 to 35 percent in 2015; in Mozambique from 12 percent in 1977 to 40 percent in 2015; and Algeria from 2.4 percent in 1987 to 32 percent in 2015. During the same period we have seen declines in female representation in nonpostconflict countries like Ghana, Benin, Botswana, and Mauritius, coinciding with a rise in interparty competition and party system volatility (Shella 2013). Similarly, women are disproportionately represented as speakers of the house in postconflict countries, with women in postconflict countries having held seven out twelve such positions in sub-Saharan Africa: South Africa (1994), Ethiopia (1995), Liberia (2003), Burundi (2005), Rwanda (2008), Mozambique (2010), and Uganda (2011).[2]

Most explanations for the leap in female representation in Africa have been related to the adoption of quotas, electoral systems based on proportional representation, international pressures, democratization, and other such factors. However, a longitudinal study I carried out with Melanie Hughes (Hughes and Tripp 2015) found that while some of these other factors are important, *the end of conflict has powerful independent effects* in explaining the tripling of female legislative representation over time between 1990 and 2010. Most cross-national studies of women's legislative representation to date have been static and cross-sectional. In our longitudinal statistical study using Latent Growth Curve modeling, we examined all independent countries in sub-Saharan Africa at five-year intervals from 1980 to 2010. The article forms

---

[2] www.ipu.org/wmn-e/speakers.htm; Botswana: 2009; Equatorial Guinea: 2013; Gabon: 2009; Gambia: 2006; Ghana: 2009; Lesotho: 2000; Madagascar: 2013; Nigeria: 2007; Sao Tome and Principe: 1980; Swaziland: 2006; United Republic of Tanzania: 2010; Zimbabwe: 2005.

TABLE. 8.2 *African Countries with Highest Percentage of Legislative Seats Held by Women*

Country	Seats held by women in 2015 (%)
Rwanda	64
Seychelles	44
Senegal	43
South Africa	42
Namibia	41
Mozambique	40
Angola	37
Tanzania	36
Uganda	35
Algeria	32

the statistical basis for the arguments made in this chapter. In addition to finding that the end of long-standing conflict has had large impacts on women's political representation, we also found that incremental changes in civil liberties may also influence long-term growth in women's legislative numbers. The following findings build on this quantitative study and explain further how postconflict effects influence women's political empowerment.

TEMPORAL DIMENSION OF INCREASED REPRESENTATION

The relationship between major conflict and women's representation is temporally defined. Such increases in female representation did not occur after the end of wars of independence prior to 1986 (e.g., Kenya in 1956, Guinea Bissau 1974, Mozambique 1974, Cape Verde 1974, Angola 1974, Rhodesia/ Zimbabwe 1979). Even though women sought greater representation at the end of these earlier conflicts, often having played important roles in many of the wars of liberation, they were told to put their demands on the back burner and wait until development reached levels that could accommodate women's political emancipation (Staunton 1990; Sylvester 1989).

This changed roughly around the time of the takeover of the National Resistance Movement (NRM) led by Yoweri Museveni in Uganda in 1986. Uganda was the first of a new generation of postconflict countries in Africa that introduced quotas and adopted measures to increase the political representation of women. Many more countries followed suit, especially after the 1995 UN Fourth Conference on Women held in Beijing that encouraged countries to adopt measures to increase female legislative representation and other forms of leadership. The difference between the Ugandan women's experiences after 1986 and the earlier postconflict situations had to do with the emerging international norms that gave women new impetus to demand a political presence. This, combined with the emergence of an autonomous women's movement and Museveni's own efforts to build a patronage system on a new footing and create new bases of support that drew heavily on women, resulted in a new political configuration. Thus, one has to look at a confluence of strategies of both internal and external women's movements as well as of the state or dominant parties.

ADOPTION OF QUOTAS

It has been well established that quotas are a key mechanism that have allowed for women to be better represented politically in Africa (Bauer 2014; Britton 2005; Geisler 2004; Goetz and Hassim 2003; Tamale 1999; Tripp 2000; Tripp et al. 2009) and beyond (Dahlerup 2006; Krook 2009). In this book I am treating the adoption of gender quotas primarily as a consequence of the end of conflict, rather than simply as a causal factor explaining female representation, although it does also have this impact. The higher rates of female legislative representation in postconflict countries are, in large part, due to the introduction of quotas aimed at increasing the representation of women. The question, then, is why are postconflict countries adopting quotas at higher rates than non-postconflict countries?

Of the postconflict countries adopting quotas today, 76 percent have quotas compared with 58 percent of the remaining countries. Only Chad, Liberia, and Sierra Leone of the postconflict countries do not have quotas (Table 8.3). On average, in African postconflict countries with quotas, women claimed 32 percent of the parliamentary seats, whereas in nonconflict countries with quotas they claimed on average only 21 percent of the seats (Table 8.4). Thus quotas appear to have a much stronger impact in postconflict countries because of the independent effects of conflict on women's representation, which the Hughes and Tripp (2015) study demonstrates longitudinally. The gap between conflict and nonpostconflict countries is slowly beginning to close as quotas are diffusing throughout sub-Saharan Africa, but the trend is still quite clear, and the earliest adopters since 1985 were postconflict countries, thus setting them on a faster trajectory.

TABLE 8.3 *Adoption of Quotas in African Countries, 2015*

	Postconflict	No major conflict	Ongoing conflict	Total
Quotas	13 (81%)	19 (59%)	3 (50%)	35 (65%)
No quotas	3 (19%)	13 (41%)	3 (50%)	19 (35%)
Total	16 (100%)	32 (100%)	5 (100%)	54 (100%)

Source of data: Freedom House, https://www.freedomhouse.org; Global Database of Quotas for Women www.quotaproject.org.

TABLE 8.4 *Average Levels of Female Legislative Representation in Africa, 2015*

	Postconflict	No major conflict	Ongoing conflict	Total
Quotas	32%	21%	19%	25%
No quotas	13%	15%	9%	14%
All countries	29%	18%	14%	21%

Source of data: Freedom House, https://www.freedomhouse.org; Global Database of Quotas for Women www.quotaproject.org.

TABLE 8.5 *Quota Type and Level of Conflict in African Countries, 2015**

Level of conflict	Party quotas # countries	Legislated quotas # countries	Reserved seats, # countries
Major conflict	4	5	4
No conflict	5	9	5
Ongoing conflict	0	2	2

*There is some overlap in categories because some countries have multiple types of quotas.
Source of data: Freedom House, https://www.freedomhouse.org; Global Database of Quotas for Women www.quotaproject.org.

There have been three types of quotas introduced to influence the candidacy of women running in elections and thus the representation of women: The first involves *reserved seats* or *women's lists*, mandated by constitutions or legislation or both. These are seats that only women can compete for. Generally a percentage of seats, for example, 30 percent, are set aside for which only women candidates can compete. Increasingly these goals have been set at 50 percent. A second arrangement of *compulsory legislated quotas* requires that all parties include a certain percentage of women on their candidate lists. Some arrangements mandate where or how they should be placed on the list, which is crucial to the success of such a provision. Finally, parties themselves may have *voluntarily adopted a quota*, regardless of whether there was a constitutional or legal mandate. The party quotas may exist alongside reserved seat or compulsory arrangements.

The patterns of quota adoption after conflict differ markedly from countries that have not experienced conflict. Countries that have not experienced conflict are most likely to have legislated quotas that affect all parties, whereas postconflict quotas tend to be evenly divided between party, legislated, and reserved seat quota systems (Table 8.5). The postconflict countries that had left-leaning parties in power with long-standing commitments to gender equality have tended to adopt party quota systems (e.g., Mozambique, Namibia, and South Africa). Reserved seats were favored by more authoritarian regimes, where the ruling party wanted to ensure that women were represented and had the hope that they could control the women in those seats. Often after conflict, the surest way women could increase their representation was through a reserved seat system that set aside seats for which only women could contest. Reserved seats circumvented relying on parties that had little interest in women's political advancement. Indeed, one of the reasons that quotas were not adopted in DR Congo had to do with the fact that the women activists were ill-advised by external experts to push for party quotas and not the reserved seat system. Similarly, in Liberia, a soft quota with no teeth was introduced in 2005 that relied on parties to voluntarily adopt a 30 percent quota. Only one out of twenty-two parties adhered to this recommendation despite vigorous lobbying by women's organizations and activists.

While the importance of quotas increased particularly after the 1995 UN Conference on Women in Beijing, these efforts were bolstered by regional pressures in Africa from Southern African Development Community (SADC) in southern Africa and Economic Community of West African States (ECOWAS) in West Africa, which set a series of targets for the adoption of quotas. This was an especially popular strategy after the end of conflict as a result of pressure from women's movements (Tripp et al. 2009) and international actors (Anderson and Swiss 2014; Bush 2011).

Generally countries that had reserved seats adopted quotas as a result of decisions within the ruling party leadership, often as a result of pressure from women within the party leadership or women's party wings. Party quotas were adopted as a result of similar pressures from within the party and women party activists. However, legislated quotas were generally a result of mobilization by women's organizations, which worked in coalitions to press for such legislative and constitutional reforms. They included coalitions of women's organizations and – depending on the country – a multiparty caucus of parliamentarians, an organization of women leaders from different parties, the women's ministry, and other human rights organizations and nongovernmental organizations (NGOs). They were generally supported by a United Nations (UN) agency like UN Women and or United Nations Development Programme (UNDP) or United Nations Population Fund (UNFPA), which received funds from foreign donors. They also were often supported by international nongovernmental organizations (INGOs), like National Democratic Institute, International Foundation for Electoral Systems, Oxfam, Kvinna till Kvinna Foundation, Friedrich Ebert Foundation, and other such groups.

EXECUTIVE WOMEN

Of the few women who have been head of state or head of government, a disproportionate number claimed their positions at the end of civil war or even during times of instability and political uncertainty. These patterns are evident globally, although generally the circumstances are characterized more as moments of flux and transition (Jalalzai 2008). It was not an accident that it was in a postconflict context that Ellen Johnson Sirleaf of Liberia became the first elected woman president in Africa in 2005. In the 2005 elections, two women ran for the presidency in Liberia and one for the vice presidency. Liberia already had a woman interim head of state in 1996 during another period of turmoil, when Ruth Perry led the National State Council of Liberia that governed the country after the ouster of President Samuel Doe. More recently Catherine Samba-Panza was elected as interim president in Central African Republic in the midst of civil strife in 2014. Sylvie Kinigi served briefly as president in Burundi following the murder of President Melchior Ndadaye in October 1993. When women have held the position of head of state in Africa, it has often been in an interim capacity or for a very brief period.

Women have been running in presidential elections in increasing numbers throughout Africa, but noticeably in postconflict countries. Prior to 2000, only nine women ran for presidential office. From 2000 through 2013, seventy-one women ran for the presidency throughout sub-Saharan Africa. Specioza Kazibwe served as vice president for ten years right after Uganda came out of major conflict. While there were internal political calculations that went into her appointment based on ethnicity and religion, her appointment as a woman added to her appeal.

Women prime ministers have similarly held positions in postconflict contexts and periods of turmoil. The late Agathe Uwilingiyimana served as prime minister of Rwanda from 1993 until her death on April 7, 1994, during the Rwandan genocide. According to the UN commander Roméo Dallaire's book, *Shake Hands with the Devil* (2004), she and her husband surrendered to the presidential guard to save the lives of their children, who eventually escaped to Switzerland. In less dramatic circumstances, Luísa Días Diogo served as postconflict Mozambique's prime minister between 2004 and 2010. Other prime ministers also served during periods of turmoil and violence in their countries: Sylvie Kinigi (1993–94) in Burundi, Cécile Manorohanta (2009) in Madagascar, Cissé Mariam Kaïdama Sidibé (2011–12) in Mali, and (Acting) Adiatu Djaló Nandigna (2012) in Guinea Bissau.

One reason for the increase in women within executive positions in the government has, in part, to do with the perception – regardless of the reality – that women represent a new style of leadership, especially in dealing with corruption, conflict, and the ills of the past. Women leaders often represent themselves as being outsiders to politics and as being untainted by the problems of the past. They also are often *perceived* as not being culpable of the problems that led to conflict, for example, corruption, militarism of society, warlordism, regardless of the reality as we saw in the case of Ellen Johnson Sirleaf in Chapter 4. Rather than experiencing backlash, women's perceived noninvolvement in creating conflict sometimes afforded them greater legitimacy as leaders after a conflict. The rhetoric is often uncomfortably gendered and essentialist. A campaign T-shirt for Ellen Johnson Sirleaf when she first ran for president read: "All the men have failed Liberia – Let's try a woman"

(Dukulé 2005). Women voters, in particular, felt moved to mobilize in her support, and they rallied in large numbers to support and campaign for her. As Liberian femocrat Harris Parleh explained:

Women are perceived as less corrupted. As a mother you can't be associated with corruption. Character for men is just to be hard and strong. It does not matter so much what people think. But women tend not to be as corrupt, not at the level of a man. There is a stigma that goes with corruption for women.[3]

Most recently when Catherine Samba-Panza (who is a women's rights activist and human rights lawyer and is nicknamed "mother courage") took over as interim president of Central African Republic in 2014, the news reports reflected similar raw sentiments in this country, which had been undergoing massive violence between Muslims and Christians: "Everything we have been through has been the fault of men," said Marie-Louise Yakemba, who heads a civil-society organization that brings together people of different faiths and who cheered loudly when the speaker announced Ms. Samba-Panza's victory. "We think that with a woman, there is at least a ray of hope," she said. "As a woman, she can understand the sufferings of the people, and as a mother, she will not tolerate all of this bloodletting," observed Annette Ouango, a member of a women's organizations. "The men have done nothing but fight," noted Judicaelle Mabongo, a student in Bangui. "The men, they are fighting. But they are only destroying the country. This woman, she might be able to change things" (Nossiter 2014).

In postconflict countries women are heading up key ministries and are no longer relegated only to the ministries of women, education, health, youth, and community development as they were in the past. Today they are taking up ministerial portfolios in foreign affairs, defense, finance and planning, trade and industries, and other such key ministries. While in 2015 African countries had on average as many women in legislatures (22.6%) as the world average (22.4%), they had proportionately more women in the cabinet (20%) than other parts of the world (18%). As with parliamentary representation, postconflict countries have higher rates of female ministerial representation (23%) compared with nonpostconflict countries (19%; Interparliamentary Union 2015).

WOMEN IN LOCAL GOVERNMENT

While some of the most dramatic changes have been at the national level, changes have also taken place in local government. According to Gender Links, over 45 percent of village councils are headed by women in Namibia, and over one-third of local government seats in postconflict Uganda and

---

[3] Interview with 3.2, Monrovia, September 19, 2007.

Mozambique are held by women. In Liberia, one-third of all superintendents are women, and plans to hold elections for local government positions, including chiefs, will no doubt allow for even more women to gain access to these historically patriarchal structures.

In the first postwar elections in 2004 in Sierra Leone, women won only 10 percent of the local level seats. After the elections, a system of Ward Development Committees (WDC) was established, and considerable public awareness was raised by national and international NGOs regarding their purpose. These organizations carried out leadership training workshops for women. The Local Government Act of 2004 provided for a minimum of 50 percent representation of women on Ward Committees (Abduallah and Fofana-Ibrahim 2010). Despite aggressive intimidation of female candidates, the number of elected women in the WDCs nearly doubled to eighty-six (19%). Civil society groups are now advocating that elections be held for Paramount Chiefs, who are almost all men, to bring the country into compliance with the constitution (Kellow 2010). Nevertheless, in Sierra Leone, according to Castillejo (2008), women politicians reported that they often had to take out large loans to pay to be selected by the political party and then to bribe customary leaders and to gift their constituents. It remains to be investigated whether the postconflict impacts found in the formal arena spill over into representation of women among traditional authorities, although there is new evidence of this in Liberia.

WOMEN IN THE SECURITY SECTOR

Even in appointments in the security sector, where women are the most poorly represented, some changes are evident. For example, there are more women police commissioners in Africa than elsewhere in the world, and most are in postconflict countries. Of the four female police commissioners, three are in postconflict countries: Beatrice Munah Sieh in Liberia since 2006, 2008–09, Acting Commissioner General of the National Police Mary Gahonzire in Rwanda, who later become Commissioner General of Prisons, and since 2012 National Police Commissioner Mangwashi Victoria Phiyega in South Africa. In Latin America female directors of the police are found in two postconflict countries, Nicaragua and Guatemala. The other two were found in Nordic countries.[4]

Perhaps the most interesting development is the appointment of three new female army generals in postconflict Algeria in 2014, bringing the number up to four, thus making Algeria the Arab country with the most high-ranking female army commanders.

---

[4] www.guide2womenleaders.com/Police-Chiefs.htm.

EXPLAINING FEMALE POLITICAL REPRESENTATION

Gender disruptions

As mentioned in Chapter 1, Melanie Hughes and I (Hughes and Tripp 2015) found that conflicts that had the most casualties or were longest in duration correlated strongly with higher rates of female representation. We also discovered that a change in the sex ratio as a result of civil war was only weakly correlated with female representation. This suggests to us that although the absence of men had an impact, it was primarily the social disruptions that accompanied longer and more deadly wars that were driving changes in gender relations and roles. This set in motion a series of developments that eventually manifested themselves in an increased female presence in national and local legislatures as well as in other spheres of governance in the executive and judiciary.

To recall, when I refer to "postconflict" countries, I am referring to countries that have exited "major conflict." "Major conflict," for the purposes of this study and for the sake of parsimony, is sustained civil war involving over 1,000 deaths (per Peace Research Institute Oslo [PRIO] categorization). Countries outside these categories are treated as countries with "no conflict" and "ongoing conflict," with the understanding that there may be low-grade conflict or intermittent election-related violence in a "no-conflict" situation as well as other forms of violence (e.g., domestic violence).

Countries with limited conflict experience on average rates of female legislative representation that are similar to countries that had no conflict in this period. As I have suggested in the first chapter: (1) they do not result in a change in elites that would open space for new types of leaders, but also (2) the conflicts in many of these countries may be localized in one region of the country or they may be limited in duration or in impact and therefore do not compel societal actors to push for a major reordering of society in ways that longer, widespread, and more deadly conflicts do.

Countries experiencing "ongoing conflict" have lower rates of female legislative representation than countries with no conflict (see Table 8.6). This suggests that ongoing disruptions to society do not allow actors enough political space to mobilize to change the status quo, and leaders and militia are too preoccupied with conflict to be interested in appeasing various constituencies at the ballot box or in polishing their international image. One cannot put too much weight on these figures for ongoing conflict because the N is so small (6), and the percentages can shift dramatically with the inclusion or exclusion of even one country in the category, but the existing pattern certainly makes sense.

Women's collective mobilization

Another factor that influences women's representation are women's coalitions. The adoption of quotas became a global phenomenon especially after the UN

TABLE 8.6 *Conflict Intensity and Female Legislative Representation in Africa, 2015*

	Average levels of female representation %
Postconflict	29
Ongoing conflict	14
No conflict	18

Conference on Women in Beijing in 1995. At the same time, the fact that so many countries had adopted quotas before 1995 suggests that internal women's movement and coalitional pressures were critical in ensuring the implementation of these policies.

Uganda is a case in point. After the conflict, the new government did not have any particular program addressing women's concerns. Human rights activist Joan Kakwenzire recalled that one of Museveni's first speeches in 1986 was disappointing because he called on women to participate in societal change but told them not to make too many demands for women's rights.[5] Gradually, as a result of women's lobbying efforts, which had been, in part, inspired by the 1985 UN Conference in Nairobi, Museveni changed his orientation regarding women's organizations. He also began to see possibilities of tapping into women's organizational capacity to promote his own goals and build his own base of support among women on a quid pro quo basis. Seeing the endorsement of women leaders as critical to the regime's success, Museveni encouraged women's leadership at all levels of the government. This began to result in changes in women's representation in the legislature, judiciary, and executive branches, as detailed in Chapter 3.

UN and international influences

The 1995 UN Conference on Women and its pressures for women's leadership were reinforced by the passage of the 2000 UN Security Council Resolution 1325, which helped bring women's representation language into some peace talks and onto the agendas of gender advisors or gender focal points within peacekeeping forces as well as the work of the United Nations Development Fund for Women (UNIFEM), UN Women and the United Nations Development Programme (UNDP). These agencies provided technical assistance to advance these goals. Anderson and Swiss (2014) found

---

[5] Interview with 1.34, Kampala, June 19, 1992.

that "countries where any peace accord is present more rapidly adopt electoral quotas for women than those without a peace accord. Further, those countries that experience a peace accord with specific women's rights provisions are likely to adopt quotas even more rapidly." While it true that many peace agreements set the stage for women's increased representation, only one peace agreement in Africa mentioned quotas explicitly, and five mentioned equal representation of women in the transition process and beyond. Three of the peace agreements that mention seats for women in the national assembly (DRC, Togo, and Liberia) did not make good on their commitments. Other countries like Angola (2005) and Uganda (1986), which did adopt quotas, did not have a comprehensive peace agreement at the end of their conflicts.

Thus, as mentioned in Chapter 6, it is unlikely that the link between the peace agreements and electoral outcomes for women is a direct one and more likely that the link is mediated by UN agencies that are involved in processes where agreements have been negotiated. They are active more generally in advancing women's rights objectives in the postconflict context. The goals of UN agencies like UN Women, Department of Peacekeeping Operations (DPKO), and the women's desk of the UN peacekeeping troops regarding women's rights became much more focused after the passage of UNSCR 1325 in 2000, which is partly why we see an increase in quotas after 2000 in many postconflict countries.

These organizations and agencies have several key objectives. The Department of Political Affairs of the UN, which helps organize elections after conflict, for example, advocates for carrying out an assessment to see if there are legal regulations that limit women's participation. They and other UN agencies may help fund electoral management bodies (EMB) or electoral commissions that administer and supervise the elections. These bodies implement election laws, issue policy guidelines, arbitrate complaints, and oversee the processes of campaigning, voting, and counting. The independence of the EMBs is crucial to the smooth running of an election and building confidence in the electoral process. They may help pass legislation to get a quota system implemented. Having women represented on the EMBs is key to ensuring that women's interests are protected. This is sometimes provided for in the peace agreement.

The UN agencies may assist EMBs in formulating an election law that is transparent so that it does not discriminate against women directly or indirectly: through literacy or educational requirements that set additional hurdles for women who may be less educated than men, limited polling stations that make it difficult for women with small children to reach or make them wait for long periods of time to vote.[6] For example,

---

[6] www.un.org/womenwatch/osagi/wps/publication/WomenAndElections.pdf.

clear and accurate registration systems are key to getting women to vote. Self-initiated systems may disadvantage women if they have limited hours, making it difficult for women with small children to register. Botswana, Burkina Faso, Cape Verde, Lesotho, Mozambique, and Namibia all require voters to register at *registration offices* or through a *mobile registrar* (Mozambique, Namibia, Uganda). Other such systems include *Internet registration* or *registration by mail,* which may disadvantage poor women. State-initiated systems work better for women, although they don't guarantee that they actually vote. They also require regular maintenance. These include voter registration *links to applications for government services* used by Cape Verde and Seychelles, door-to-door registration campaigns, which are employed by Seychelles and South Africa, or *links to national population records,* which Botswana and Seychelles employ.[7] UN agencies like DPKO advise on such practices to make them more clear, transparent, and accurate for both men and women.

But even with all this external support, there are no guarantees that women's rights will be protected, and often it takes pressure from the women's movement to ensure that women activists' demands are represented in the electoral system. In the case of Liberia after the signing of the CPA in 2003, even after aggressive lobbying by women's organizations for female representation, the transitional government that was instituted had only four women in a legislature of seventy-six members and only three women in a cabinet of twenty-one. Women saw this as major problem that required attention (Massaquoi 2007). The women's movement criticized this low level of female representation and pressured the National Electoral Commission (NEC) to take action.

Three out of the five members of the NEC were women, and the head of the commission was Chief Justice Frances Johnson-Morris. Mary Brownell, one of the leaders of the women's movement, was also on the Commission, as was Elizabeth Boryenneh, a leader of the Association of Female Liberian Lawyers (AFELL). A draft electoral reform law was submitted by the NEC to the Transitional Legislature that included a 30 percent quota for women. Legislators could not see why women required special treatment. Many felt that the constitution gave women equal rights, and they thought that should suffice. Thus, even though the electoral guidelines were passed that required parties and coalitions to select one-third women as candidates, the regulation was not adhered to, and there were no consequences for noncompliance. The amended law of March 2011 dropped the provision, which was later revived for debate in the context of the constitutional deliberations.

Women adopted multiple strategies to improve political leadership. They encouraged women to register to vote and carried out a massive voter registration campaign, especially between the first and second rounds of the 2005 presidential election. As a result of registration efforts by the Liberia Women Initiative, the Association of Female Liberian Lawyers, the Liberian Marketing Association, Women in Peacebuilding Network and the Gender Ministry, slightly more women than men registered to vote, and overall 50 percent of the electorate were women. This in no small part helped in the election of Ellen Johnson Sirleaf to the presidency in the second round of the elections.

Some have argued that foreign aid influences female representation, especially because donors are a major conduit through which the diffusion of gender norms occurs. It would also seem that the most donor-dependent countries, such as those coming out of conflict, would be the most inclined to comply with international norms. But this assumes that donors are more effective in postconflict countries than elsewhere even though they tend to provide more funds to nonpostconflict countries. They frequently withdraw humanitarian funds at the end of a conflict and do not replace them with other forms of support (see Chapter 2). Moreover, Hughes and I (Hughes and Tripp 2015) were unable to find a correlation between Organisation for Economic Co-operation and Development (OECD) foreign aid (net Overseas Development Assistance [ODA] received per capita) and women's representation within any of our models.

Sarah Bush (2011) did, however, find that the amount of foreign aid, the presence of a UN peace operation supporting political liberalization, and whether a country had international election monitors was positively and significantly correlated with the adoption of gender quotas. However, the sample was limited to countries with national legal quotas because, as she explained, "They are the quotas advocated by the democracy establishment and that signal a country's commitment to gender equality." She includes a few cases of voluntary party quotas, where the party was an incumbent in an election. This selection of cases eliminates a large number of African and postconflict cases, which have reserved seats and voluntary quotas, making it challenging to apply these findings to sub-Saharan Africa.

Hughes' and my inability to find a correlation between female representation and foreign aid in Africa suggests that there may be other dimensions along which international pressures assert themselves (Hughes and Tripp 2015). It also suggests that donor aid influences alone cannot make this kind of difference. Their influence involves a combination of their efforts together with local women's rights activists and other external influences (e.g., support from UN agencies) that have been critical in bringing about change. It also should be pointed out that even though countries might be heavily under donor influence when it comes to women's rights, they may have also been adversely impacted by the ways in which funds were disbursed. For example, a study of UNSCR 1325 implementation in Liberia found that while funders made a difference, their orientation to short-term and medium projects sometimes limited the capacity of local organizations to plan and forced them into ad hoc activities. Local activists constantly had to worry about donor fatigue and fads (Caesar et al. 2010).

Targeted aid to women's rights and especially to quota adoption may also influence rates of female representation, but this should be tested empirically. The countries providing the greatest proportion of gender equality funding included (in proportion of amount) New Zealand, Germany, Sweden, France, and Belgium. The fragile states receiving the largest amount of aid addressing gender equality include Pakistan, Afghanistan, Ethiopia, DRC, Nigeria, Kenya, Uganda, Palestinian administration areas, Cameroon, and Nepal (OECD-DAC 2010).

One important source of regional pressure is SADC, which has set goals for its fourteen member states[8] to increase female representation. While many of them have relatively higher rates of female representation, when other factors are included in the model Hughes and I developed (Hughes and Tripp 2015), SADC membership did not appear to have independent effects. Nevertheless it does contribute to the increased levels of representation by reinforcing norms and facilitating diffusion. All of this is to say that international influences contribute to the changes we are seeing in female representation, but they are more indirect. They are evident in changing international norms that have influenced United Nations, donor, diplomatic, and international nongovernmental organizations to expand women's rights and representation (Strickland and Duvvury 2003).

Thus, any explanation of gender policy change in women's political leadership needs to account for the interplay between international and domestic forces. International funding alone is insufficient. Analysis of case studies shows that in many cases the engagement of UN agencies like UN Women with local women's rights coalitions was supported by donor funding, are critical to the adoption of effective quotas.

Democratization

While some scholars have found correlations between democracy and women's representation (Inglehart and Norris 2003; Inglehart, Norris, and Welzel 2002), others have argued that this relationship exists primarily in developed countries. Some, in fact, have found an inverse relationship between women's representation and democracy (Paxton 1997; Kunovich and Paxton 2005; Tripp and Kang 2008), while earlier studies did not find any correlation (Kenworthy and Malami 1999; Reynolds 1999). Alice Kang and I (Tripp and Kang 2008) found no relationship in cross-national comparative analysis,

---

[8] SADC member states include Angola, Botswana, Democratic Republic of Congo, Lesotho, Madagascar, Malawi, Mauritius, Mozambique, Namibia, Seychelles, South Africa, Swaziland, Tanzania, Zambia, and Zimbabwe.

TABLE 8.7 *Regime Type and Female Legislative Representation in Africa, 2015*

Regime Type	Average levels of female representation %
Democracy	24
Hybrid	19
Authoritarian	21

Source of data: Freedom House, https://www.freedomhouse. org; Inter-Parliamentary Union, www.ipu.org/wmn-e/classif. htm.

in part, because there are so many nondemocratic countries that have adopted quotas, thus increasing female representation.

Nevertheless most of the literature on women and political representation in Africa claims that women's representation is correlated with democratization (Lindberg 2004; Viterna, Fallon, and Beckfield 2008; Yoon 2004). However, if one looks at levels of average female representation by regime type in Africa, the differences are unremarkable (see Table 8.7). Some have argued more generally that democratization matters over time (Fallon et al. 2012; Paxton, Hughes, and Painter 2010). How does one explain these possibly contradictory findings? Partly it may relate to the models in which democratization is tested and the selection of cases. Paxton, Hughes, and Painter (2010) found in a longitudinal study that democracy does not influence *levels* of women's political representation at the start of political liberalization, but it does affect the *growth* of women's representation over time by creating conditions under which women can mobilize to improve their status by increasing representation. Hughes and myself similarly found in Africa that political opening early on was important to later increases in female representation, allowing sufficient space for women to mobilize to allow for quotas and for change (Hughes and Tripp 2015), thus even though women's representation is not correlated with levels of democracy, some modicum of political space early on makes a difference for later increases in female representation, particularly when it comes to civil liberties.

Fallon et al. (2012) found that women's representation increased in democratic countries that adopted quotas and ended conflict before 1995, but found that with time the transition from conflict was no longer a distinct pattern. However, the focus on democratic countries does not capture the majority of countries coming out of conflict, most of which remained authoritarian or semiauthoritarian/hybrid (see Table 8.8). Some of the highest rates of female representation are found in these contexts. Moreover, the countries that have not gone through conflict are much more likely to be democracies and hybrid regimes when compared to the conflict and limited conflict countries.

TABLE 8.8 *Regime Type and Conflict in Africa, 2015 (# countries)*

	Past conflict	Ongoing conflict	No conflict	Total
Democracy	2	0	9	11
Hybrid	5	1	14	20
Authoritarian	9	5	9	23

Source of data: Freedom House, https://www.freedomhouse.org; Inter-Parliamentary Union, www.ipu.org/wmn-e/classif.htm.

In Africa, most postconflict countries today are authoritarian regimes. A large number are also hybrid regimes. Between 1975 and 2005, hybrid states increased by 17 percent in Africa, while authoritarian countries decreased by 36 percent. In both hybrid and authoritarian regimes we have witnessed the adoption of quotas and increases in the representation of women, so that today there is little difference in outcomes based on regime type (see Tables 8.3 and 8.7).

Additional explanations of women's legislative representation in postconflict countries

When postconflict considerations are factored into models along with quotas, other popular explanations for female representation diminish in importance, including the role of proportional representation, left-leaning parties, GDP, female education, the influence of oil, and cultural considerations (Hughes and Tripp 2015; Tripp and Kang 2008). The following section briefly looks at how these factors interact with and are influenced by postconflict dynamics.

Proportional representation

Proportional representation (PR), which has generally been shown to be strongly correlated with female representation in cross-national analysis, did not emerge as an important explanatory factor in our longitudinal study in Africa, especially when postconflict and quota effects were factored into our model (Hughes and Tripp 2015). However, all three countries that adopted PR after 1990 were postconflict countries (Rwanda, Namibia, and South Africa). In PR systems women average 24 percent of legislative seats, 30 percent in mixed systems, and 16 percent in plurality systems (Tripp 2014). Overall, the influence of PR for women's representation is relatively weak in Africa compared with other parts of the world and compared with other factors, challenging the literature that claims that PR is always a central predictor of female representation. In Africa there are a significant number of plurality electoral systems that have produced through the use of reserved seats rather high rates of female representation (e.g., Uganda and Tanzania).

Colonial influences

It is difficult to generalize too much about the colonial legacy because the numbers are so small, but on balance, the Belgian former colonies in the major conflict category seem to have done the best in terms of female representation, while the former Portuguese colonies came second followed by the British, with the French having the lowest rates of female representation. The patterns change over time. The French started out in 1985–1990 with rates similar to the British, but fell behind until 2010 and today are basically on par (see Figure 8.2). I would attribute this, in part, to the fact that the former French colonies proportionately had the least countries experiencing major conflict, which suppressed levels of female representation. As the postconflict effects

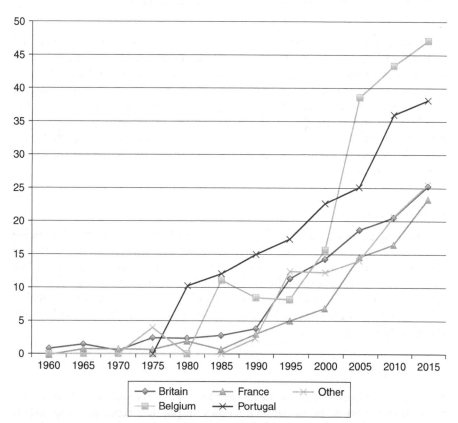

FIGURE 8.2 Former Colonial Power and Rates of Female Representation since Independence in Post-Major Conflict African Countries

TABLE 8.9 *Former Colonial Power and African Countries in Conflict, 2015*

	British	French	Portuguese	Belgian	Other
Post-major conflict	4	4	2	2	4
No conflict	11	16	3	0	2
Ongoing conflict	3	1	0	1	1
Total	18	21	5	3	7

Source of data: PRIO.

TABLE 8.10 *Rates of Female Legislative Representation in Former African Colonies, 2015 (%)*

	British	French	Portuguese	Belgian	Other
Female legislative representation	25	23	38	47	26

Source of data: Inter-Parliamentary Union, www.ipu.org/wmn-e/classif.htm.

diminished in the former British colonies after 2010, the countries converged in levels of representation. The former Portuguese colonies had increasingly higher rates of female representation than the British colonies between 1975 and 1995, mainly due to the left-leaning orientation of their ruling parties. But as the left-wing influences diminished in importance over time, the gap between the Portuguese and other countries diminished somewhat. The postconflict influences are extremely strong in Rwanda, which together with Burundi, explains much of the steep trajectory of the former Belgian colonies, especially after 1995.

Left-leaning parties

Left-leaning parties tended to have stronger influences on female legislative representation in the 1980s, when they were the only countries that had somewhat elevated rates of female legislative representation. But this effect diminished over time, especially with the end of the Cold War, the demise of Afro-Marxist regimes, and the decline of Cold War–related conflicts. Diffusion effects meant that countries with nonleft parties in power also adopted quotas (Hughes and Tripp 2015).

Economic growth

Economic conditions also influence gender equality outcomes. This comes through in almost all cross-national studies on political representation, which show that countries with higher levels of economic growth tend to do better in terms of women's rights (Hughes 2009; Inglehart and Norris 2003; Paxton,

Hughes, and Green 2006; Reynolds 1999; Tripp and Kang 2008; Viterna et al. 2008). This has implications for postconflict countries, which tend to have lower GDP levels by virtue of having recently come out of conflict. This reality, along with unmet expectations of change, may act as a constraint on advancing women's rights.

However, postconflict countries also have some of the fastest economic growth rates in their regions because of the baseline from which they generally have started. According to the World Bank in 2013, ten of the twenty fastest-growing economies in the world were fairly recent postconflict countries. Eleven of these countries were in Africa, and seven of them were African postconflict countries. Liberia's economy, for example, prior to the Ebola crisis, had experienced a strong recovery, recording an 8.9 percent growth rate in 2012, according to African Economic Outlook. GDP levels had more than doubled between 2003 and 2008. The country had enjoyed single-digit inflation, the lowest rates in three decades. The government's national budget had grown by 400 percent since 2006. The same pattern was evident outside Africa as well. It is true of postconflict Nepal, which doubled its GDP in that same period as did postconflict Sri Lanka and East Timor, according to World Bank indicators.

While one cannot make assumptions about growth being equally enjoyed across the population nor of wealth trickling down, nevertheless greater relative security and stability generally create conditions for improved economic welfare. Economic well-being also provides states with resources with which to implement gender policies. How these influence women's rights in postconflict countries is largely not understood, particularly when oil and other valuable natural resources are factored into the equation.

The mechanisms linking economic development with positive gender outcomes in nonpostconflict countries may not necessarily apply in postconflict and fragile countries. Inglehart and Norris (2003), however, argue that modernization, economic development, and the emergence of a postindustrial society lead to cultural changes, which in turn transform gender roles, resulting in greater female political representation together with the development of democratic institutions. It appears that postconflict countries have followed a different trajectory in adopting gender policies that are not tied in the same way to democracy and economic development, as had been the case in many OECD countries. Thus, regional considerations need to be accounted for in explaining trajectories of gender regime transformation. Along these same lines, Alice Kang and myself found that region was a powerful influence on women's legislative representation (Tripp and Kang 2008).

Education, labor force participation, and oil

Although some studies have found education and labor force participation to matter in developing countries (Fallon et al. 2012), studies in Africa have generally not found significant positive effects for women's adult literacy, secondary education, and labor force participation on women's legislative representation (Lindberg 2004; Yoon 2004). Hughes and I (Hughes and Tripp 2015) similarly did not find that female labor force participation had a significant impact in Africa over time. This is not surprising, given that most women participate in agricultural production and the informal sector. We also found weak effects for education in 2004 and 2010 and found that it does not interact with civil war in any way to influence female representation (Hughes and Tripp 2015).

Michael Ross (2008) has shown the importance of oil production in negatively influencing female representation, arguing that the existence of oil rents reduces the number of women in the workforce, which impacts fertility rates, educational levels of females, and ultimately women's political representation and participation. Because many African countries are oil producers, including Algeria, Nigeria, Angola, Sudan, Equatorial Guinea, Chad, Congo Brazzaville, Gabon, Libya, and most recently Uganda, this argument has bearing on our study. However, Alice Kang (2009) has demonstrated that when quotas are introduced, the impact of oil rents on female representation is not statistically significant, suggesting that there are other more salient factors to consider in understanding female legislative representation. In Africa, there does not seem to be any particular pattern linking oil to women's representation because many of the intervening variables like labor force participation are not relevant in explaining women's representation. The pressures for changing women's status have emerged in the absence of weak labor force pressures. At the same time, other explanatory factors tied to women's movements, such as postconflict effects and quotas, have been more salient, and none of these are accounted for in Ross's model.

Cultural influences

Some cross-national studies have shown that cultural attitudes influence gender equity indirectly by changing attitudes as a result of democratization. Democratic countries have higher rates of female representation because democracy is linked to more egalitarian attitudes (Inglehart and Norris 2003; Inglehart, Norris, and Welzel 2002). However, given that postconflict influences and quotas have such a powerful influence on female legislative representation and have trumped cultural factors, it is unlikely that cultural arguments can account for the rate of change we have seen in Africa in this area.

Moreover, if one looks at cultural values in Africa, the only consistent pattern one can discern from the twenty-nine countries surveyed in Round 5 of 2010–12 in answering the question "Women should have the same chance of being elected to political office as men" was a gender gap (see Table 8.11). The question was not included in earlier rounds, so there is no baseline for comparison. The gender gap was the highest for Swaziland (22%),

TABLE 8.11 *Gender Gap in Strong Support for Women Leaders in Postconflict African Countries**

		Total (%)	Men (%)	Women (%)	Gender gap (%)	Female representation in legislature (%)
Burundi	N = 1,200	43	40	46	6	30.5
Liberia	N = 1,199	45	45	46	1	11.0
Mozambique	N = 2,400	44	40	47	7	39.2
Namibia	N = 1,200	25	16	34	18	25.6
Sierra Leone	N = 1,190	32	30	34	4	12.1
South Africa	N = 2,399	41	34	47	13	40.8
Uganda	N = 2,400	56	47	64	17	35.0
Average		39	35	44	9	25.45

*Response "strongly agree" to statement: Women should have the same chance of being elected to political office as men.
Source: Afrobarometer (2012).

Mauritius (22%), Namibia (18%), Uganda (17%), and Benin (16%), with women uniformly agreeing more with the statement than men. There was no gender gap in Burkina Faso and Malawi. There is some difference in views between the postconflict and nonpostconflict countries, with postconflict countries exhibiting less support for women as leaders (see Tables 8.11 and 8.12).

However, the countries with the highest and lowest approval ratings tell us nothing about female legislative outcomes nor do they reflect religious affiliations, colonial legacy, levels of education, postconflict affects, or other factors that might influence such attitudes. This is because female legislative representation is largely shaped by an institutional innovation, namely the introduction of quotas, which are adopted precisely to sidestep cultural and religious objections to women's leadership. Therefore, it is unlikely that there would be a correlation between these attitudes and actual levels of female legislative representation as might have been predicted in earlier studies.

Religiosity is similarly thought of as a constraint on women's political leadership. The Afrobarometer survey (Chingwete et al. 2014) suggests that countries with predominantly Muslim populations have more conservative attitudes toward women as leaders. However, as with cultural values more generally, the introduction of institutional innovations such as quotas override such considerations. Predominantly Muslim countries in Africa, including the Maghreb, have on average only slightly lower rates of female legislative representation (20%) compared with non-Muslim countries (22%). This is because some of the countries most likely to adopt quotas in Africa have significant Muslim populations, such as Tanzania, Senegal, and Sudan. The same patterns visible in nonpostconflict countries are evident in postconflict

TABLE 8.12 *Gender Gap in Support for Women Leaders in Nonpostconflict African Countries**

		Total (%)	Men (%)	Women (%)	Gender gap (%)	Female representation in legislature (%)
Benin	N = 1,200	49	43	54	11	8.4
Botswana	N = 1,200	59	57	61	4	9.5
Burkina Faso	N = 1,200	41	41	41	0	18.9
Cameroon	N = 1,200	39	32	46	14	31.1
Cape Verde	N = 1,208	55	51	58	7	20.8
Ghana	N = 2,400	49	42	55	13	10.9
Guinea	N = 1,200	38	36	40	4	21.9
Lesotho	N = 1,197	52	49	55	6	26.7
Madagascar	N = 1,200	24	23	26	3	23.1
Malawi	N = 2,407	66	66	66	0	16.7
Mali	N = 1,200	38	36	40	4	9.5
Mauritius	N = 1,200	42	31	52	21	18.8
Niger	N = 1,200	25	20	31	11	13.3
Nigeria	N = 1,200	27	21	32	11	6.7
Swaziland	N = 1,200	42	31	53	22	6.2
Tanzania	N = 2,400	59	56	62	6	36.0
Togo	N = 1,200	55	52	58	6	17.6
Zambia	N = 1,200	53	47	58	5	10.8
Zimbabwe	N = 2,400	46	38	54	16	31.5
Average	N = 27,612	45	41	50	9	17.9

*Response to question: Women should have the same chance of being elected to political office as men.
Source: Afrobarometer (2012).

countries. One of the reasons these countries adopt quotas is because there is a concern that other cultural factors might hinder female representation. They have also been motivated at various times by pressures from female elites, the need to comply with changing international norms, to win female votes and sometimes to demarcate themselves from Islamicist political influences.

CONCLUSIONS

This chapter looked primarily at two outcomes of the end of conflict: the adoption of gender legislative quotas and the related increase in female representation. It showed how strongly the end of conflict and women's political representation are connected as a result of the disruptions in gender relations during war. The changes that take place in gender relations during war are reflected in the changing sex ratio and its strong correlation to women's legislative representation. This chapter has shown how these patterns are also related to the rise of women's movements, a modicum of democratization, and the role of international actors in the aftermath of war. It also explored some of the other factors that have been used to explain women's political representation in light of the postconflict dynamics. The chapter demonstrated that the patterns evident in rates of legislative representation for women are replicated in the executive, local government, judiciary, and other areas of public leadership, suggesting that the gender regime change is occurring along multiple dimensions simultaneously.

The chapter also showed how other factors that have traditionally been important in explaining women's legislative representation are not as influential or matter in different ways when postconflict factors are considered. These include proportional representation electoral systems, colonial legacies, left-leaning party influences, economic growth, levels of education of women, labor force participation of women, the presence of oil as a natural resource, cultural and religious factors, and more general attitudes toward women's leadership.

Women's Rights and Postconflict Legislative Reforms

As long as we take the view that these are problems for women alone to solve, we cannot expect to reverse the high incidence of rape and child abuse. Domestic violence will not be eradicated. We will not defeat this scourge that affects each and every one of us, until we succeed in mobilizing the whole of our society to fight it.

– Nelson Mandela

Previous chapters looked at two key opportunity structures or transitional processes that women's rights activists sought to influence: peace negotiations and constitution-making exercises. The outcomes of these processes included peace agreements (Chapter 6) and revised constitutions (Chapter 7) that incorporated provisions for increased women's representation and stronger women's rights. These paved the way for legislative changes and other policy reforms affecting women's rights. The main areas of legislative reform influencing women in postconflict contexts have been in the areas of violence against women, family law, land, and quotas to promote women's representation in legislatures and other bodies, which was already discussed in Chapter 8. This chapter looks at legislation around women's rights in the areas of gender-based violence and family law and discusses some of the challenges in focusing on legal solutions in postconflict contexts.

As with constitutional changes, there are large differences between countries that have experienced major conflict and those that have not when it comes to legislative reform. This was already evident in the Chapter 8 discussion of quota law adoption, where we saw that 76 percent of postconflict countries had adopted quotas while only 58 percent of nonconflict countries had done so. After the 1990s, women's rights activists in postconflict countries were beginning to see many of their aspirations for greater rights addressed through the passage of legislation. In discussing legislation as an outcome of the processes described in this book, there is no assumption that once legislation is enacted that it is always enforced or that it radically changes women's lives. However, it does establish the normative ground rules for society and what is regarded as acceptable societal practices and behavior. It creates the legal basis from which women can demand their rights and enforce change. Thus, these legal changes are a way of measuring where a society stands in relation to women's rights, but they are insufficient as a measure of their actual impact on women's lives. Nevertheless, lack of enforcement does not invalidate the importance of the effort of establishing a legal framework as a starting point.

UGANDA'S LEGAL FRAMEWORK FOR WOMEN'S RIGHTS

Uganda serves as a case in point, demonstrating how constitutional changes manifested themselves in legislative and other policy reforms. In Uganda, policy changes were spearheaded by the women's movement together with the Uganda Women Parliamentary Association (UWOPA), which has allowed women to work across party lines (Wang 2013b). They have been instrumental in passing a steady stream of legislation affecting women with respect to land (1997, 2010 amended), refugee rights (2006), maternity leave (increasing days off; 2006), employment (2006), sexual harassment (2006), equal opportunities (2007), defilement (2009), disability rights (2008), trafficking (2009), domestic violence (2010) and its regulations (2011), female genital cutting (2010), and many other concerns. An International Criminal Court Act (2010) criminalized sexual exploitation of women during conflict. In 2006 a law was passed to establish the Equal Opportunities Commission, which was mandated by the 1995 constitution to oversee the implementation of policies regarding women's rights. In July 2010, Uganda's Parliament ratified the Protocol to the African Charter on the Rights of Women in Africa (the Maputo Protocol), having faced powerful opposition by the Roman Catholic Church and the Uganda Joint Christian Council. There are still important gaps in legislation, particularly with respect to marriage, divorce, and land inheritance, but the legislature has continued to be active in passing laws affecting women.

The first National Gender Policy was passed in 1997, and the second Uganda Gender Policy was launched in 2007 along with a National Action Plan in response to the UNSCR 1325 requirement that countries develop policies to set their priorities in peacemaking and conflict resolution as they relate to women and girls.

The courts have also played a role in promoting women's rights. For example, in 2007, a constitutional court struck down key provisions of the Succession Act regarding women's right to inherit property, the Divorce Act, and the Penal Code Act and made a ruling that decriminalized adultery for women (it had not been criminalized for men).

GENDER-BASED VIOLENCE

At least 75 percent of postconflict countries have legislation around violence against women compared with 50 percent of countries that have not experienced conflict in sub-Saharan Africa (See Table 9.1). This is a very rough calculation because it does not address the content of the legislation. I made a similar calculation five years ago and found the difference between the two groups of countries to be even larger on the order of a 2:1 ratio (Tripp 2010b). This suggests that the gap is closing between the two sets of countries as a result of diffusion. Nevertheless, the postconflict trajectory has been faster than that of nonconflict countries, while taking place in the same time period. This is *because most of the conflict countries in question were not in any position to pass legislation until fairly recently because of instability* (Tables 9.1 and 9.2).

Much of the change in thinking regarding gender-based violence (GBV) in Africa overall came out of experiences within conflict that heightened awareness of the severity of the problem. For example, one of the most important rulings that helped shatter prevailing norms about gender violence, not only in Africa, but globally, was the judgment against former mayor Jean-Paul Akayesu delivered by the Trial Chamber of the International Criminal Tribunal for Rwanda (ICTR) in 1998. For the first time in history, rape and sexual violence were explicitly recognized as "an act of genocide and a crime against humanity." It was the first ruling to consider a broad definition of rape involving a sexual physical invasion beyond merely a narrow description of penile penetration of the vagina and to regard rape as a form of torture (Copelon 2000, 227). This ruling has made it possible for countries like Burundi to introduce laws like the 2003 Law (No 1/004/2003), which penalizes the crime

TABLE 9.1 *Gender-Based Violence Laws Passed in African Countries (% of total for category), 2014*

Sub-Saharan African countries	Sexual harassment	Sexual violence	Domestic violence	Marital rape	Trafficking	FGM*	Total
Post-major conflict	66	73	86	60	73	86	75
No major conflict	46	40	40	36	80	46	50
% Difference between conflict and no conflict	20	33	46	24	−13	40	25
All countries	56	56.5	63	48	76.5	66	62.5

*Figures only for countries that practice female genital mutilation (FGM).

TABLE 9.2 *Median Year Laws Passed in African Countries, 2014*

Sub-Saharan African countries	Sexual harassment	Sexual violence	Domestic violence	Marital rape	Trafficking	FGM*
Post-major conflict	2006	2002	2007	2008	2008	2002
No major conflict	2003	2002	2006	2007	2007	1998

*Figures only for countries that practice female genital mutilation (FGM).
Source: UN Secretary General's Database on Violence against Women: http://webapps01.un.org/
vawdatabase/searchDetail.action?measureId=10221 (Womanstats; LexisNexis). DR Congo,
Somalia, and Central African Republic are removed from the list because they have had ongoing
conflict.

of genocide, war crimes, and crimes against humanity, including rape, sexual slavery, enforced sterilization, or any other form of sexual violence. The ICTR Akayesu ruling helped irreversibly change the way people thought about GBV during conflict (Copelon 2000). It was part of a long series of legal efforts to shift the normative ground regarding women and their rights to bodily integrity both during and also after civil conflict.

GBV has been a central issue emerging out of conflict, as large numbers of women faced rape, kidnapping, and sexual abuse. There is no direct connection between resources and GBV, and it is far too simplistic to argue that the use of coltan in cell phones is causing rape in Eastern Congo (Turner 2014). Nevertheless, the increased reliance on diamonds, oil, and other resources in African conflicts has exacerbated levels of violence against civilians, including GBV. Jeremy Weinstein (2007) has shown how rebel groups that rely on external or readily available resources to support their insurgency are far more violent in their tactics than those that rely on the local population to sustain them. In such countries, one often finds extreme human rights violations, abductions, use of child soldiers, child sex slavery, decapitations, amputations, and sexual violence.

Domestic violence: The area where there is the greatest discrepancy between conflict and postconflict countries is in legislation on domestic violence. Only 40 percent of countries without major conflict have legislation in this area compared with as many as 86 percent of the postconflict countries. This suggests enormous stresses on families during wartime, resulting in domestic abuse. Gradually, perceptions of domestic violence have begun to change throughout Africa. Women's organizations, and now increasingly the legislature and courts, are challenging the view that it is simply a private family matter that does not necessitate public scrutiny. In some countries, wife battery had been justified on cultural grounds and had even been justified as a sign of a husband's devotion to his wife. Women's experiences during conflict helped foster an awareness of the need to end domestic violence and to use legal means as one tool to end such violence.

Women in Sierra Leone won a major victory in 2007 when a new law made wife beating a criminal offense. The law applies a broad definition of domestic violence. It includes "physical or sexual abuse, economic abuse, emotional, verbal or psychological abuse, harassment, conduct that harms, endangers the safety, health or well-being of another person or undermines the privacy and dignity of another person" (Domestic Violence Act 2007, Sierra Leone). The law also establishes family support units to educate police on sexual and domestic violence, work with rape survivors, ensure forensic testing, and help process cases. A Commonwealth police team has provided training to help police work with the community to carry out mediation and to support women who decide to press charges. Local women's organizations are regarded as key to ensuring that the new law is implemented ("Human Rights Problems ..." 2007).

Female genital mutilation (FGM): Almost all postconflict countries that practice FGM have passed legislation in this area with two exceptions, while only 46 percent of nonconflict countries have passed this legislation. Women activists have also sought to eradicate female genital cutting through a variety of strategies, not only the passage of laws but also the adoption of educational, health, and income generation campaigns. Even though female genital cutting pertains to family, clan, and community influences, it is an area where there has been considerable progress even in countries where other legislation regarding women has been slow in coming. The issue has garnered considerable attention at the national and regional level. The 2003 Protocol to the African Charter on Human and Peoples' Rights on the Rights of Women is the first international treaty to mention female genital cutting. In 2005, an African Parliamentary Conference held in Dakar focused on female genital cutting, and speakers and members of twenty African national parliamentary assemblies unanimously adopted a declaration calling for an end to the practice, arguing that "culture is not immutable and that it is subject to perpetual change, adaptations and reforms" ("Violence against Women ..." 2005). They pledged to work with civil society, traditional chiefs and religious leaders, women's and youth movements, and governments to adopt strategies to end the practice, drawing on a human rights framework by taking into consideration the education, health, development, and poverty dimensions of the problem. While most acknowledge that legislation alone can do little to eradicate the practice, it sets a normative bar and reflects a consensus on how societal leaders regard the practice. Education and the provision of incentives to circumcisers for alternate sources of income, in addition to other locally driven strategies, are key to eradicating the practice.

Sexual violence: All countries in Africa have antirape legislation, although in some countries it is fairly nonspecific, and the high penalty involved often prohibits arrests, charges, and convictions. In Uganda, one of the first laws regarding women enacted after the cessation of civil conflict in 1986 had to do with rape (called "defilement") of girls under the age of eighteen. The penalty of death that the crime carries has not only been challenged by human rights organizations, but has resulted in few convictions.

Since 2000, at least 73 percent of all postconflict countries have adopted new legislation specifically addressing sexual violence in contrast to non-conflict countries, where only 40 percent had such legislation. During and after the conflict in Liberia, rape was a relatively common form of violence, and rape legislation was adopted in 2005. Prior to this, only gang rape had been considered a crime. Members of Association of Female Lawyers of Liberia (AFELL) drafted the legislation, which strengthened penalties for rape, making it a nonbailable offense, carrying a sentence of ten years for rape of a woman and life imprisonment for rape of a minor. It raised the age limit for statutory rape to seventeen and recognized that rape is not perpetrated only against females. It defined rape beyond penile penetration to account for the use of gun butts and other such forms of violence. AFELL organized radio programs and held public forums to publicize the bill (International Crisis Group 2006).

Médecins Sans Frontières reported in 2009 that the incidence of rape was increasing in Liberia in the aftermath of war and was affecting girls in particular. Approximately 85 percent of the 658 reported rape cases at a Monrovia hospital were under eighteen, and 48 percent were between five and twelve. Even baby girls were being targeted. Over 90 percent of the children were raped by an acquaintance. Both women's organizations and the government have been concerned about the lack of prosecutions, which are related to a number of factors. Alleged rapists were sometimes put in jail cells without being charged, and the courts would free them because they had failed to prosecute them within the required 48-hour period. Sometimes poverty, cultural norms, and stigma relating to rape led parents to extort money from the alleged rapists to settle the matter. Another possible reason for the lack of prosecutions is that the penalty of conviction of rape of a minor is too high from a societal perspective. Rape of a minor carries a life sentence. Few rape survivors report cases due to the stigma associated with it, not to mention the fact that most abuse involves acquaintances and family members. Moreover, there is no guarantee that the police will treat the rape survivors with dignity and respect, creating additional disincentives to report ("Government, Women's Groups ..." 2007). Finally, the weakness of the security apparatus and justice system has resulted in cases of mob justice and excessive violence by security officers being directed at suspects. These weaknesses in the criminal system have led women's rights activists to point out that more community education is required regarding sexual assault.

Trafficking: The amount of legislation in nonpostconflict countries regarding trafficking exceeded legislation passed in postconflict countries. Unlike the other categories of violence against women, this one has little to do with cultural practices and existing norms and therefore may be easier to pass in nonconflict countries. In major conflict countries, other categories of violence are more important in terms of passing legislation, including sexual violence, domestic violence, marriage of girls eighteen and over, and FGM.

ACTIVISM AROUND GBV LEGISLATION

Violence against women has resulted in considerable domestic, regional, and international mobilization, especially after the 1995 Fourth World Conference on Women in Beijing. United Nations agencies also put pressure on governments to address women's rights in a concerted manner. At a regional level, the 2006 Southern African Development Community (SADC) protocol on gender and development sets targets relating to GBV to be met by 2020.[1] All member states were to have in place legislation on GBV, domestic violence, human trafficking, and sexual offences by 2008, and this legislation was to be enacted by 2010. Perpetrators of domestic violence, marital rape, femicide, and other forms of GBV were required to be brought to justice in a court of competent jurisdiction. Those in the criminal justice system were required to be educated about these laws, and steps would be taken to eradicate traditional customs that perpetuate violence against women and children.

In many countries, women parliamentarians have spearheaded GBV legislation. Rwanda is a well-documented case. The Rwandan 2009 GBV Act was drafted by the women's parliamentary caucus, known as the Forum of Rwandan Women Parliamentarians (Forum des Femmes Rwandaises Parliamentaires – FFRP), in a country where laws generally are drafted by the executive branch. The parliamentarians received support from the United Nations Development Programme (UNDP), Department for International Cooperation (DFID), Women Waging Peace, Swedish International Development Cooperation Agency (SIDA), United Nations Development Fund for Women (UNIFEM), and the African Development Bank in drafting the legislation (Pearson 2007). The FFRP's experiences in enacting this legislation reflect many of the challenges found with similar legislation in other parts of Africa. The parliamentarians initiated this legislation, in part, to address the high rates of rape, battery, and murder of women by their husbands. One study by the Rwanda National Police found that between 2005 and 2008, 259 wives were murdered by their husbands, over 2,000 rapes were reported to the police, and there were over 10,000 cases of rape of children below the age of eighteen (Kwibuka 2009). Amnesty International (Hillier and Wood 2003) attributed the heightened violence partly to an increased presence of small arms in the country.

---

[1] SADC Protocol on Gender and Development, 2006. www.sadc.int/index/browse/page/465.

According to the Rwandan Ministry of Gender and Family Promotion (RMGFP; cited in Pearson 2007), one in three women had been physically or verbally abused, and in the previous year one out of every two experienced domestic violence. Another Human Rights Watch study (cited in Pearson 2007) revealed that complaints of sexual violence against girls exceeded the number of complaints filed by adult women in 2003–2004. As a result of such figures, women activists were able to successfully lobby for a GBV desk in the national police force and also for the creation of a national GBV hotline (Pearson 2007, 31).

The ability of the women parliamentarians to enlist the support of men at every stage of the process was a key factor in explaining the passage of Rwanda's GBV Act. The women parliamentarians wanted men to feel ownership of the bill. Male parliamentarians were involved in field trips to consult with constituents; they participated in a national conference held in Kigali in 2005 to discuss the bill; FFRP shared early drafts with male colleagues; they got equal numbers of men and women to sponsor the bill; and male parliamentarians and men more generally were involved in public discussions of the bill. As one male parliamentarian put it:

I was in charge of delivering this particular message [on gender sensitivity]. At the end of the meetings, local leaders, local *male* leaders, were shaken up. Hearing the message format was an added value, [they were] more convinced, more able to take the message seriously. But if the message should come from a woman you [would have] found them saying, "Oh, yes we know the story," but they [wouldn't have] given it much weight. They tend to be more concerned with gender issues when a man delivers the message. (Powley and Pearson 2007, 17)

FFRP encountered some resistance from men who refused to cosponsor the bill or objected to some of the provisions within the bill, for example, they felt it overlooked men's experiences as victims of domestic violence. To counter these objections, FFRP cited studies that showed that although men were also affected by GBV, it was primarily women who were affected. They also were able to demonstrate that they had pursued a broad process in writing the bill, which underscored the fact that these were concerns prevalent within the population and therefore worthy of being addressed through legislation (Powley and Pearson 2007, 17–18).

FAMILY LAW

While GBV is one important area of concern for women activists in postconflict contexts, another important area relates to family law. In this area, postconflict countries rank higher on average (0.45) compared to nonconflict countries (0.55), with 1 being the lowest score in the Social Institutions and Gender Index. In all categories of family law, countries that experience major conflict do better than countries that have not experienced major conflict (Table 9.3).

TABLE 9.3 *Discriminatory Family Code*

	Postconflict	Nonconflict
Legal age of marriage	0.50	0.64
Early marriage	0.23	0.26
Parental authority in marriage	0.46	0.56
Parental authority after divorce	0.28	0.46
Inheritance: Daughters	0.63	0.68
Inheritance: Widows	0.60	0.70
Overall score	0.45	0.55

Ranking: 1 = lowest, 0 = highest.

Explanation of categories:

Legal age of marriage: Measures whether women have the same rights with respect to the legal minimum age of marriage.

Early marriage: Measures the prevalence of early and forced marriage. Percentage of women married between 15–19 years of age.

Parental authority in marriage: Measures whether women have the same right to be a legal guardian of a child during marriage.

Parental authority after divorce: Measures whether women have custody rights over a child after divorce.

Inheritance: Daughters: Measures whether widows have equal rights to their male counterparts as heirs.

Inheritance: Widows: Measures whether daughters have equal rights to their male counterparts as heirs.

Source: OECD Gender, Institutions and Development Database 2012.

Property and land

Only eleven countries in sub-Saharan Africa have eliminated laws that discriminate against women in the acquisition of property or basic legal transactions such as signing contracts or even getting a passport.[2] Seven of these are postconflict countries. One of the areas where women's movements in Africa are facing the most resistance with respect to customary authorities and practices is in the area of land ownership. New land laws were enacted in Uganda, Tanzania (and Zanzibar separately), Mozambique, Zambia, Eritrea, Namibia, Rwanda, Sierra Leone, Liberia, and South Africa after the 1990s incorporating women's rights concerns. All but two of these – Tanzania and Zambia – are postconflict countries. Women were active and in leadership of a variety of land alliances and coalitions – from Uganda, to Rwanda, Mozambique, and Namibia – which have fought for the land rights of women, pastoralists, the landless, and other marginalized people. The disruptions in property have

[2] Gender and Land Rights Database www.fao.org/gender/landrights/home/en/.

been more extreme in postconflict countries, making it more urgent to address women's need to control their means of livelihood and support for the household.

In Uganda, the Land Act of 1997 granted women the right to own and control land. As a result, women's ownership of land either on their own or jointly with their spouse increased from 7 percent in 1995 to 39 percent in 2011. More women participated in land administration, constituting 33 percent of the Land Boards, which manage and control land in the Districts and 34 percent of Land Committees that advise the Board on area concerns regarding land rights, ownership, customary, and third-party interests (MGLSD 2014).

In this context, women's movements in Africa, particularly in postconflict countries, have increasingly been adopting rights-based approaches that challenge customary land tenure arrangements. Feminist lawyers working with these movements have argued that customary law in the present-day context has been used to selectively preserve practices that subordinate women. Women's attempts to assert their rights in ways that challenge customary land tenure systems are often perceived as an attempt to disrupt gender relations and society, more generally. This explains why so much is at stake in these battles over women's rights to land and why women's gains in this area have been so slow.

CHALLENGES OF IMPLEMENTING THE LAW

The adoption of legislation is only a first step in the process of addressing problems like GBV or female inheritance. The implementation of these laws is challenging in postconflict contexts because the legal systems and infrastructure have been undermined, while customary laws and traditional authorities prevail in ways that often discriminate against women. Poor treatment of rape survivors at the hands of the police also serves as a disincentive to report GBV incidents. One of the legacies of years of civil conflict has been the erosion of the justice system (Medie 2013; Yacob-Haliso 2012).

In a country like Liberia, the perpetuation of a culture of corruption and impunity that led to fourteen years of civil war continues to paralyze the justice system and threatens the peace, according to the International Crisis Group. Its 2006 study of Liberia's justice system found that the temporary measures that have been adopted to revive the legal system cannot preempt the need for a major overhaul of the legal system (International Crisis Group 2006). In 2003, the Security Council gave the Legal and Judicial System Support Division of the UN Mission in Liberia authority to oversee judicial reform during the transition.

Many of the requirements for reviving the legal system are fairly mundane but absolutely essential. Courts, police stations, and prisons need supplies of basic equipment for improved file management and record keeping to ensure fair trial standards. Presently detainees remain imprisoned for lengthy periods due to a lack of personnel and proper documentation. The conditions in jails and prisons also need significant improvement ("Human Rights Problems ..." 2007). Lack of funds has meant that courts have stopped functioning in many parts of the country or hearings are held in alternative locations because the court buildings have been destroyed. Low salaries for judges lead to corruption. They often lack the necessary legal texts to carry out their work. Beyond this, women and men in Liberia and elsewhere need to be educated about their rights and given the means by which to exercise them. Legislative changes are inadequate when women lack the knowledge and capacities to make use of existing laws. These challenges facing Liberia's legal system are typical of postconflict countries in Africa.

New research has shown that where the state is weak, these limitations can potentially be circumvented through concerted efforts by international legal teams. In parts of eastern Congo, which has been severely affected by sexual violence, Milli Lake has shown that primarily international, but also domestic, NGOs working on sexual and gender-based violence have often been able to assume direct responsibility for administering justice. Despite weaknesses in Congolese law, the prosecutors have been able to use some of the most progressive international human rights protections to convict the accused. The NGOs have also helped shape national and local-level legislation and policy both through formal and informal means. As a result, survivors of sexual violence are tried under conditions that respect their privacy, while the conviction rates are unusually high. Nevertheless, the same problems mentioned previously influence outcomes even in these situations: Victims are often forced to pay bribes to police, while convicted prisoners are able to bribe their way out of prison or out of jail time and frequently fail to pay court-mandated damages to the victims (Lake 2014).

Current pressures for legislative change have also had to contend with some of the peculiarities of contemporary African legal systems, which are the product of a plurality of legal legacies originating during colonial rule. These legal legacies have shaped efforts at legislative reform in postconflict countries. Contemporary laws build on colonial common law traditions in former British colonies and civil law traditions in former French, Portuguese, Belgian, German, Italian, and Spanish colonies. These legal systems have coexisted at different levels of compatibility with customary law, including the laws of particular religious communities (see Chapter 8).

Beyond what is codified in terms of the relationship between formal and customary law, legal practice may diverge to an even greater extent so that even where there is a clear demarcation of jurisdiction between customary and general law, traditional authorities, customary local councils, informal local courts, and Sharia courts may prevail beyond their legal bounds. The decline of formal courts and the erosion of the rule of law as a result of civil war exacerbated this problem.

For example, a study in Sierra Leone showed that chiefs ruled on a wide range of cases that went well beyond their jurisdiction. They systematically ruled against women in matters of personal status, marriage, and inheritance, even though since the Courts Act, 1963, the local courts, which are under the statutory court, are the only institutions allowed to adjudicate in matters of customary law. The local courts were to replace the chiefs in this role after independence. There frequently has been collusion between parties and chiefs that works against women who are not connected to or do not have the resources to pay off the chiefs. Women are often treated as minors to be protected by their fathers, sons, or other male family members. Customary law, which is largely unwritten in Sierra Leone, is protected by the 1991 Constitution; however, the constitution also prohibits discriminatory law. Moreover, in the event that there is a conflict between customary law and common law, common law takes precedence. Sierra Leone's constitution limits the areas where the chiefs can adjudicate, particularly the extent to which they can influence matters of adoption, marriage, divorce, inheritance, and property. However, the chiefs, local authorities, and the litigants themselves are often unclear on the jurisdiction of the chiefs. Paralegal and legal aid organizations provide some legal assistance and mediation between family members and in holding education workshops for communities. But the larger problem of harmonizing customary and statutory laws and courts remains (Amnesty International 2006).

Thus, although some progress has been made in many postconflict countries, there is still a long way to go in reforming the legal system. There is a need to reconcile legal systems to allow appeals from the customary courts to be heard in the statutory courts, provide executive oversight of customary law, and support the training of judges. The aim is to eliminate various tiers of rights accorded women who have differential access to education, knowledge of legal rights, and resources. While some of the arrangements, like the three categories of marriage contracts in Rwanda, may be unavoidable as temporary transition provisions, ultimately women are not served by creating multiple systems of differential access to rights. These historical legacies pose enormous challenges for women's rights activists, who now are trying to find ways to harmonize mixed legal systems so that all women can enjoy the same rights. The central challenge is to create laws that respect culture without violating women's rights and discriminating against women.

While it has been of critical importance to pass legislation regarding violence against women, it has also become apparent that laws alone are insufficient and cannot replace community-based strategies, especially in countries with weak and poorly paid/corruptible judiciaries and police forces. One debate regarding the legal dimensions of tackling GBV is that legislation and criminalizing GBV alone does not begin to address the structural, systemic, and cultural factors underlying violence that are related to gender inequality. Moreover, women victims themselves may wish to adopt other, nonlegal methods to deal with

GBV and may not wish to have their partners arrested, as it brings the family into unwanted scrutiny by the police enforcement system. It is often minority and poor communities that disproportionately come under such scrutiny in many societies. Thus, the overemphasis on legal strategies is seen to remove agency from the woman and treats her only as a victim (Bumiller 2008; Garland 2001; Römkens 2001). Social policy and community-based strategies are required to address GBV structurally and systemically, for example, providing funding for shelters and support for changing societal attitudes and stereotypes regarding gender. This is why organizations like AFELL in Liberia place a lot of emphasis not only on providing women with legal advice and legal options, but also on alternative dispute mechanisms involving dialogue between conflicting parties.

The Uganda Association of Women Lawyers (FIDA) has made important gains, even in its most remote offices. A lawyer, Judith Adong, in Gulu talked in 2011 about how even in her war-ridden community, "Trends are changing, and the organization has had an impact on the ground, ... now wives have their voices." FIDA carries out mediations, trains the magistrates and others, partners with human rights organizations, conducts radio programs to educate the population, and promotes economic empowerment, and various legal education strategies. The main cases they took up have to do with GBV, land, and inheritance. About half their clients were widows facing landlessness in northern Uganda. Adong emphasized how the new legal framework assisted their work immensely. But much of their activity involved offering legal aid services to those seeking mediation of interpersonal conflict within the family.[3]

Thus, a balance between legal and social policy strategies and developing supportive policies is needed, including mediation, the creation of shelters, community support for domestic violence, and efforts to change societal attitudes and stereotypes through education.

Another limitation of policy in many countries is the persistence of steep penalties for rape and other forms of GBV. This makes victims reluctant to report rape, especially if family members are involved, and it results in few prosecutions and even fewer convictions. Human rights advocates are increasingly challenging death penalties for rape on the grounds that the use of violence to punish and deter violence is counterproductive and inhumane. The weakness of the security apparatus may result in excessive violence by security officers being directed at suspects.

Finally, in countries coming out of conflict there are particular challenges due to the erosion of the judicial and criminal system. The basic infrastructure of courts, police stations, and prisons needs drastic improvement to ensure fair trial standards. Corruption often remains rampant in situations where judges and other personnel are poorly paid.

---

[3] Interview with Judith Adong, Gulu, January 6, 2011.

CONCLUSION

We have witnessed some important developments in women's rights with the end of conflict in Africa, especially after the 1990s, when the number of conflicts began to decline significantly. The passage of GBV legislation is one of these developments, representing a normative shift that is taking place regarding women's rights across the continent. Postconflict countries led the way in adopting key GBV legislation, which then diffused to nonconflict countries. While the gap is narrowing between postconflict and nonconflict countries in the adoption of legislation, postconflict countries remain on a distinct and more rapid trajectory of reform. This is also evident in legislation around quotas, family law, and land law. It remains to be seen whether these advances in legal reform will result in changes in people's daily lives and whether they can be sustained.

PART V

FUTURE RESEARCH

10

New Frontiers in the Study of Women, Conflict, and Peace

> *I remember the leaders of the Women's Movement saying,*
> *we must stop dancing from the side*
> *we are done with*
> *begging*
> *lobbying*
> *talking*
> *negotiating.*
> *We are tired of being children of a lesser god*
> *we must operate from the centre*
> *we must live our dreams, they said*
> *I remember the leaders saying*
> *we must negotiate the double covenant*
> *we must decide on*
> *our destiny and that of our people.*
> *I remember that was the day the lord hath made*
> *the women rejoiced and were glad in her*
> *from that day henceforth the women moved to the centre, their centre*
> *it is now time for harvest.*
>
> — Wanjiku Kabira, excerpted from "Grandma Remembers,"
> *Time for Harvest,* 2012

This book has pursued one key question: Why are women's rights and rates of leadership improving more rapidly in postconflict countries in Africa than elsewhere on the continent, particularly in countries that have experienced major conflict? This chapter takes the key findings and situates them in a broader frame of gender regime change. It points to where this study takes us and what new unexplored issues emerge from this study.

At one level, the book argues that a combination of factors needs to be considered in linking postconflict dynamics with women's rights in Africa after the 1990s. They include disruptions in gender roles during conflict, the role of autonomous women's movements enabled by political opening, and changing international norms and UN pressures on governments.

Changing opportunity structures that limit or, in this case, facilitate social movements – in the form of peace negotiations and constitutional and electoral processes – allowed women's organizations to intervene in new ways to assert their interests, particularly a gender agenda. This was because the end of conflict shook up leadership structures, thus necessitating institutional change. Gaining power was at the core of the strategy of women activists because it was key to realizing their other demands.

At another level, this book is about a much bigger story that has to do with how gender regime change occurs. Laura Shepherd (2008) has argued that violence in war is gendered but it also creates gender. This book has shown that violence in the context of war, depending on other circumstances, can also disrupt and transform gender power relations. The most important disruptions have to do with women's altered economic status, women's newfound political voice, and symbolic changes in what became imaginable to women in their aspirations.

In the case studies explored in this book we saw disruptions within families, where women and men reversed roles, although more often women took on previously male roles of creating a livelihood, driving cars, and going outside the home in wartime to obtain food. We also saw at the community level how women found their voice and became more active in community affairs, both in terms of participation and leadership, but also in physically taking care of their marketplaces, neighborhoods, towns, and cities. At the national level, these types of disruptions translated into demands for a seat at the peace talks, in constitutional assemblies, in parliaments, and in government. Finally, the unthinkable all of a sudden became thinkable, and women began to envision for themselves new and more powerful roles as legislators, cabinet ministers, supreme court justices, businesswomen, bank directors, heads of universities, race car drivers, newspaper editors, and even presidents.

The beginnings of transformations in gender power relations were evident in all cases, if one takes the perspectives of Liberian men as any indication of these transformations (see Chapter 4). While these perspectives suggest that changes in power relations are not always easy for men to come to terms with, there has been nevertheless an acceptance of the changes. There was very little evidence of backlash in the cases examined in this manuscript. It is of concern, however, that in each case, men seemed to have had a more difficult time than women in adjusting to their new roles in peacetime, creating tensions that often led to gender-based violence, alcohol abuse, and other manifestations of an inability to cope. These challenges forced women to take even more responsibility in their homes, communities, and societies more generally. And while added responsibility may involve more power, it does not necessarily mean relief from duties and may create new hardships for women.

The changes one saw in the gender regimes were neither smooth nor straight-forward. Even though women were making considerable headway into key political and economic institutions, they were only beginning to make inroads into the military and police and into the leadership of religions, sports, and traditional institutions, as well as other key loci of power. Thus, there still are critical areas of power from which women remain almost totally excluded. As long as this is the case, the project of gender regime change will remain incomplete. This is not surprising, because change is uneven and although it permeates more than one institution and can diffuse from one institution to another, it does not take place in a predictable and orderly fashion.

The study, however, did find some important patterns: *The relationship between the end of conflict and women's rights in Africa is temporally confined to the post-1990 period* because this was when changes in international norms around women's rights intensified along with women's mobilization in Africa. The patterns, nevertheless, had their antecedents in the granting of suffrage to women in many countries that had been involved in World War I and are found in other parts of the world for many of the same reasons (Hughes 2009). We do not have the benefit of hindsight to know when this temporal period will end and how far out from conflict these patterns continue.

The relationship between conflict and women's representation was especially evident in intense conflicts and in conflicts long in duration because it required a major reordering of society to bring about change in the gender regime. The violent and/or deep ruptures within postconflict societies sped up these pro-cesses of change and helps explain why the postconflict countries embraced women's rights reforms faster than other countries. Prolonged conflict dis-rupted gender roles, launching women into new activities in the absence of men.

Civil wars and national liberation wars had a greater chance of creating possibilities for negotiating women's rights than other forms of conflict because they required a renegotiation of the terms of governance for the polity as a whole. Conflicts that were more localized in one part of the country also did not have these same sweeping effects as major civil war and therefore did not result in significant changes in women's status. Here the contrast between Uganda's 1980–86 Bush War and the conflict in northern Uganda, which was both a proxy interstate war and a localized conflict, illustrates these differences in types of war and how they resulted in very different outcomes for women in Uganda. Unlike the war ending in 1986, the conflict in northern Uganda did not result in the overthrow of the national government and elite and therefore did not necessitate a restructuring of the polity in ways that would have allowed for changes in women's rights and leadership through, for example, constitutional reforms. The postconflict dynamics were least evident in countries experiencing ongoing conflict, where the situation generally was too volatile or unsettled to sustain and respond to pressures for legal reform.

The conflicts where the war ended in a negotiated settlement were more conducive to women's rights because they allowed for the participation of civil society actors, not just in peace talks, but also in the reconstruction of society. Wars that ended abruptly with one side vanquishing the other, as in Angola, did not allow for such a process, and the role of civil society and women's organizations was minimized.

Finally, the fact that women were perceived as new actors untainted by war also contributed to their appeal as political actors in many cases. The reality was never that simple because many women participated in fomenting war in a variety of ways, but popular tropes linking women to motherhood and peace-making often helped women claim a new legitimacy as political actors in postwar contexts.

FUTURE RESEARCH ON WOMEN, CONFLICT, AND PEACEMAKING

Numerous questions emerge from this study that warrant further investigation.

Women's voices

There has been little commentary on or appreciation in the academic literature of women's own experiences, perhaps because international relations specialists have dominated the field of conflict and security. We are gradually beginning to hear from women whose voices had been previously erased. Women are now writing memoirs in the postconflict context to describe their wartime experiences. In fact, a whole new and exciting genre of women's war memoirs has emerged in Africa in recent years that reflects on civil war. These autobiographies are being written throughout the continent, from Liberia to South Sudan, and Burundi. Women are writing about their experiences as child soldiers and as combatants (Akallo 2007; Ball 2009; Kamara-Umunna 2011; Keitetsi 2004; Mehari 2008; Stone 2011), as refugees and internally displaced people (Birabiro 2004; Umutesi 2000), as wives of guerrilla fighters (Amony and Baines 2015), as doctors and nurses helping the wounded and dying (Bashir and Lewis 2008; Chishugi 2010), as peace negotiators (Johnson Sirleaf 2009), as activists in peace movements (Duany 2003; Gbowee 2011), as survivors of violence (D'Awol 2011; Hariir 2004), as economic actors (Elmi 2004; Osman 2004), as political actors (Arabi 2011; Isse 2004; Mariano 2004), and as witnesses of the horrors of conflict and how women have coped (Cooper 2008; Davies 2011; Diggs 2012; Forna 2002; Abdi and Robbins 2013; Ilibagiza and Irwin 2006; Iteka 2012; Shaw 2008). The sheer volume of this new genre is noteworthy in and of itself.

This new genre of female wartime memoir has come to be a dominant theme in the overall African autobiographical landscape. Even male authors writing about these experiences are few and far between compared with the number of women authors. There are a few notable exceptions, such as Sierra Leone's Ishmael Beah's *A Long Way Gone: Memoirs of a Boy Soldier* (2007), which gained popular acclaim. But unlike the autobiographies that were written primarily by men in Europe and the United States after World War I and II, interestingly in Africa this genre of wartime memoir has been claimed by women. I suspect this has to do with the fact that women were more directly involved with and affected by the violence. Unlike the earlier wars of liberation and independence in Africa in which men and women fought as nationalists and unlike the women who wrote about their roles in World War I and II as patriots, the women in the more recent African conflicts opposed the wars, even the combatant women authors.

Another way these voices are being expressed is through the media and social media. The role of Facebook, YouTube, Twitter, blogs, and Instagram, combined with the ease with which photos can be taken and posted online using new technologies, have irreversibly changed the levels of awareness of atrocities against women around the world. There is a big difference between the lack of attention given to the Lord's Resistance Army abduction of the 156 Aboke girls in northern Uganda in 1996 compared with the global attention given to the abduction of 276 girls in Chibok in northern Nigeria in 2014 and the response, especially of Nigerian women activists, to the abductions. The media has made it harder to ignore such events. Whether the world cares to take action is another matter.

Thus, to fully appreciate the changes that have taken place in war-torn countries, we need to pay more attention to the voices of those who have been left out of the conversation and pay particular attention to the various new ways women are expressing themselves. We also need more focus on the way in which women's experiences in war are framed.

Framing women in peacemaking

Generally when we do hear about women in peacemaking, they are still often framed as victims, survivors, saints, mothers, and other reductionist tropes. These tropes are often based on simplistic assumptions suggesting that women, often because of innate qualities, are key to peace. While the critique of these tropes is not new, the persistence of such frames has increasingly captured the popular imagination, influencing donors, development practitioners, policy makers, journalists, and even military strategists. Such assumptions matter in addressing donor priorities. They drive the financing of aid and determine which policy strategies gain traction for women's rights actors. The interest in gender policy has even made its way into unexpected corners, such as the U.S. Joint Chiefs of Staff and international security specialists who pondered how to increase girls' education in countries like Afghanistan and Pakistan. Women's education is being described as an essential component in the fight against global terrorism, as evident in the popularity of the books like *I Am Malala: The Girl Who Stood Up for Education and Was Shot by the Taliban* by Malala Yousafzai (2013) and *Three Cups of Tea* by Greg Mortenson (2007).

It would be useful to ask which frames do women adopt in their political engagements in peacemaking? While the critiques against essentialized notions of women and men appear to have been exhausted, there remains a conundrum that has not been adequately tackled in the literature. Motherhood tropes tied to peacemaking are extremely popular in Africa and elsewhere within movements themselves. Notions of political motherhood have often formed the basis for women's mobilization and for claims to political authority. Only a handful of authors seem to be willing to deal with this reality, particularly those writing in the West.

Another gap in the literature has to do with the extent to which women's mobilization has been shaped by religious influences. Religion played complex and multiple roles in shaping resistance to conflict on the part of women. In Liberia, women mobilized across contentious religious lines in demanding peace. This is true outside Africa as well. In East Timor women were actively involved in peaceful nonviolent protest and activism inspired by their Catholic roots (Mason 2005). The marginalization of lower Hindu castes has had a profound influence on the conflict in Nepal (Geiser 2005), while Buddhist influences played a role in Sri Lanka. Yet religion has featured in only a few studies (e.g., Skidmore and Lawrence 2007) and in ways that minimize its role relative to its influence and importance. Women's involvement in the spread of Pentecostalism and independent churches in Central and West Africa, particularly in contexts of conflict, for example, deserves greater investigation.

Feminist frames have also not been discussed much in the literature on peacemaking in Africa. The ascendance, redefinition of, and new acceptability of African feminism has profoundly shaped the ways in which women's rights are being adopted and pursued today. While feminism informs much of the theoretical framing of the literature on conflict, it is also part of the activist landscape, yet this rarely receives the recognition it deserves.

Finally, there could be more attention given to comparing various security frames and how effective they have been in addressing gender concerns. While feminists have gone far in critiquing realist and other existing frames, less has been done to discuss and compare frames that emerge from or intersect with women's rights concerns, for example, human security, mother politics, just peace, moral and religious frames, and gendered war and peace frames. Are some more useful than others in shaping policy interventions in particular contexts?

Women's movements, peacemaking, and peacebuilding

Perhaps the most frustrating aspect of studying women in conflict has been the lack of data. Few journalists have covered women in war, and when they have, they have not accounted for the peacemaking activities of women. Academics have written even less. Some filmmakers like Abigail Disney have given voice to women through documentaries like *Pray the Devil Back to Hell,* based on the activities of Liberian women peace activists. The awarding of Nobel Prizes to Leymah Gbowee and Ellen Johnson Sirleaf in 2010 gave new international recognition to the almost completely unheard of struggles of women in postconflict contexts. But for the most part, the experiences of women peacemakers and peacebuilders remain untold and untheorized except for the aforementioned memoirs of women themselves.

The literature on women and conflict has shifted the discussion away from women simply as passive victims of conflict to treating them as agents (Enloe 2000; Jacobs, Jacobson, and Marchbank 2000; Jetter, Orleck, and Taylor 1997; Kumar 2001; Lahai 2010; Moser and Clark 2001; Waller and Rycenga 2000). Curiously, much of the emphasis on agency has focused on women as fighters.[1] Surprisingly, the quality and quantity of the work on women as fighters has far outstripped that of women engaged in peacemaking, which has had more direct impacts on women's status in the postconflict period.

Women and peace movements

Within countries there are almost no histories of the post-1990s women's peace movements and initiatives. It would be important to analyze these movements as social movements. There are few in-depth accounts of how these movements engaged formal processes or were limited by them. How did they work with other movements, parties, interest groups, elites, the military, warlords, religious leaders, peacekeeping troops, and other social and state actors? What factors and forces facilitated or impeded their efforts? How did they engage international actors? What were the constraints they faced?

Some of the literature borders on the romantic, yet war makes people act in ways they would never dream of doing under normal circumstances in order to stay alive. As this book has shown, even peace activists – more often than is often acknowledged – cut unholy deals and collaborate with "the enemy" to survive. Opportunism, careerism, nepotism, corruption, self-aggrandizement, and deceit are rampant during conflict, and peacemakers are not immune to these tendencies. Agency is often described as a positive in the literature, but the realities of conflict may make agency a more ambiguous concept. These kinds of realities need to be incorporated in understanding the constraints peace movements face. Insider accounts, which are more commonly found than academic accounts, are often very useful and serve their own political and

---

[1] See, for example, work by Chris Coulter, Rachel Brett, Irma Specht, Dyan Mazurana, Khristopher Carlson, Jeannie Annan, Christopher Blattman, Megan MacKenzie, Myriam Denov, Richard Maclure, Susan McKay, Carol Thompson, Beth Verhey, Marie Vlachova, and Christine Gervais.

human interest purposes, but they often do not engage in the kind of hard-nosed objective analysis required in scholarship.

Women and peace negotiations

There are virtually no studies of attempts by women to engage and influence peace negotiations except for a few firsthand accounts and news reports as well as some aggregated data on women's rights language in the texts of peace agreements. Yet women have actively tried to influence talks from Somalia to DRC, Liberia, Uganda, and Burundi. All the basic questions still need to be answered: How did UNSCR 1325 affect peace negotiations? How have women been involved with international nongovernmental organizations (NGOs) that carry out behind-the-scenes diplomacy? For those women who were involved in official peace talks, did they work with women's organizations, and what interests did they see themselves representing? What impact did women have on negotiations, and which strategies worked best? Why was women's rights language left out of peace agreements? Was it, for example, the result of oversight, lack of expertise, commitment, or because it would make the overall agreement more difficult (see Bell and O'Rourke 2011)? What have been the impacts of women's mobilization on the talks? What evidence do we have that they made a difference?

Informal peacemaking

The literature on women's role in informal peacemaking is very anecdotal and descriptive. There has been almost no analysis that is comparative and theoretical. How important were the grassroots movements relative to other factors in bringing about an end to conflict? Which strategies worked best under which conditions? What conditions gave rise to these strategies? How were the strategies used to influence women's formal participation in peace negotiations? There should be more effort to understand these informal quotidian strategies of peace in addition to the formal processes.

The aftermath of war

There is also a need to look at what happens after the conflict in terms of peace building and state reconstruction. Women who went into forced or self-imposed exile returned with new skills and knowledge. While sometimes this created tensions between the returnees and those who had endured the hardships of war, it also resulted in an influx of new talent, resources, and leadership capacity. What were the impacts of these returnees on women's status and women activists' agendas?

During the wars, South Sudanese women were involved in grassroots mobilization and peacemaking activities. After 2005 and the signing of the

Comprehensive Peace Agreement (CPA), the majority of leading women took posts with the government and within as Sudan People's Liberation Movement (SPLM) structures. This meant that the women's movement was bereft of its leadership (Ali 2011). The same happened in Liberia after the 2003 Accra Accords were signed. Most of the leaders of the peace movement took better-paid positions with international NGOs or in government. In Angola, the peace movement similarly died down after the war and international funders pulled out. While one cannot necessarily expect a peace movement to continue in the same form after the conflict has subsided, the withdrawal of leaders from civil society has important implications for building democracy. It makes it harder for organizations to challenge the state, advocate for women's rights, play a watchdog role, continue with peace building, and ensure state accountability.

Building bridges across difference

One of the most interesting aspects of this study for me was to discover how women who were philosophically, politically, sometimes ethnically, or religiously at odds with one another transcended those differences to articulate a politics of strategic unity in a bid for peace. In the case of Liberia, the differences were not only based on ethnic and religious differences, but also on class and education. In Uganda, the differences were partly ethnic and religious.

These patterns extended well beyond the case studies. They took place at peace negotiations and in grassroots mobilization. Peace activists formed networks of peacemaking organizations like Dushirehamwe ("Let's Reconcile") that works in ten provinces in Burundi and initiated interethnic dialogues and engaged in conflict resolution. In DR Congo, women on opposite sides of the conflict held prayer vigils to pressure the militias to honor the 2002 peace accords in Ituri (Kapinga 2003, 25–26).

The fact that these alliances were built so consistently, especially when male peace negotiators and activists had a much harder time building such alliances, raises important questions about what gave rise to this type of unity from Burundi to Rwanda, Somalia, South Sudan, Liberia, Sierra Leone, DR Congo, and elsewhere. It would be naïve to think that these were based on some essentialist peace-loving commonality that women shared, even if women themselves frequently described it in this way. The tenuousness of some of these linkages speaks to how fragile the coalitions were. But the alliances were real, and they were consciously built. Given the divides in society, these linkages speak more to the urgency of forging a common women's rights agenda than to innate qualities of women. As Davidetta Brown, a Liberian radio producer, explained to me:

Women came together to prevent the religious and ethnic dimension from becoming salient. Men stuck with their own ethnic group. Women sat down, regardless of whether they were Christian or Muslim and strove to go above religious affiliation to discuss the situation affecting women as a whole.

Mary Brownell, one of the first leaders of the Liberian peace movement, also talked about how

The cross-cutting ties were built across religious difference, particularly Muslim and Christian women worked together, they included women of all classes although most were illiterate. All women were tired of war and had suffered from the violence, particularly sexual violence. Children were deprived of schooling; houses had been destroyed. Starvation affected women. They shared a common cause that brought them together.[2]

Another reason that women activists came together across these differences had to do with the fact that women generally had been marginalized from most forms of power, and therefore they collectively had less at stake in preserving a status quo that had brought them considerable suffering. They were not likely to reap any material benefits from continued fighting either. Women, therefore, found it easier than men to build alliances to de-escalate conflict and promote stability (Benderly 2000).

However, marginalization was also at times a double-edged sword. While women activists were able to engage in extraordinary efforts to broker peace at many levels, their marginalization and participation in informal peacemaking also relegated them to less-visible forms of negotiation. They operated from the sidelines in ways that were important, but less effective than if they had been thoroughly incorporated in all aspects of peacemaking. Thus, while exclusion from patronage and power may have provided women with common cause and helped unite them, it also had limiting aspects.

The question then remains, to what extent do women's peacemaking strategies simultaneously lock them into limited forms of peacemaking and keep them excluded from other roles? To what extent does their participation in these gendered structures perpetuate institutions that marginalize women rather than challenge them? How do they operate from a position of power while marginalized and excluded? Does power come from numbers? Or does power come from the moral authority of political motherhood, of not having participated in fighting, or of peaceful protest tactics? This study points to all of the preceding, but it is worth further investigation in multiple contexts.

Peacemaking as a process

Another striking difference in the way that women activists engaged in peacemaking related to their understanding of peace as a starting point, rather than an endpoint or an agreement to be achieved at the end of talks, resulting in a

---

[2] Interview with 2.13, Monrovia, September 12, 2007.

signature on a piece of paper. Rather than seeing peace as something that had to be achieved to carry out reconstruction, for the women activists the process of reconstruction itself was the way to peace. The working out together of problems of access to water, food distribution, garbage disposal, and town cleanliness *was* the process through which peace was built. The rebuilding of society became the means through which peace was built. This is a radically different notion of peacemaking and departs fundamentally from the way peace negotiations were framed. These negotiations often ended up being reduced to a discussion about how political spoils would be divided and who would get what ministries and positions. Yet the fact that women were so consistently excluded from talks suggests that the international community and political leaders in so many contexts did not seriously value this more constructive way of building and thinking about peace.

OTHER ACTORS

Multiple social relations and conflict

If conflict disrupts gender relations, as we have seen in this book, does it also disrupt other social relations? The disability movement is one that has become quite active in recent years in Africa, particularly in postconflict countries where large numbers of people suffered from serious injuries. Like women, this movement is demanding legislative, ministerial, and other forms of representation. They are also demanding legislation to address their particular needs.

In the past, disability in Liberia was regarded as a consequence of witchcraft and a curse. There is still enormous stigma surrounding disability, and discrimination is rampant, resulting in the disabled being kept inside and out of view. The war created new sensibilities regarding disability because of the large numbers of people injured as a result of armed conflict and landmines. A disability movement emerged in the late 1990s and started advocating for a commission for disability in 2000. In 2005, an act was passed to create the Commission. Liberia also ratified the UN Convention on the Rights of Persons with Disabilities in 2007 as a result of pressure from disability groups. Their main concerns had to do with access to education, jobs, public buildings, technologies to assist with mobility, and government funding for programs and activities related to disability.[3]

In Uganda, as result of pressure from disability advocacy groups, the 1996 Parliamentary Elections Statute set aside five seats for the disabled in parliament (including one for a woman) and there was also a minister of state for disability and the elderly. Disabled local councilors (one male and one female) must be represented at each level of local government. The statute

[3] Interview with 2.33, Monrovia, May 2012.

ensures that disabled persons do not have to wait in line to vote. Sign language facilities must be provided for civic education and information about voting procedures. In 2006 women's organizations played a key role in passing the Disability Act in Uganda, which was moved as a private member bill to provide for equal opportunities in education and employment for people with disabilities. There are many such synergies between the women's movement and the disabilities movement in Uganda. Kenya also adopted seats for the disabled in parliament and has quotas in other public spheres after its 2010 constitution that emerged in part as a response to the electoral violence of 2008.

The question, then, is whether there are parallels between the women's movement and movements of other marginalized people such as the disabled. LGBT activism expanded in South Africa and Namibia after the end of apartheid and enjoyed greater success in South Africa, which since 2006 has allowed for gay marriage. In Uganda, the LGBT movement also expanded after the conflict, but is now experiencing a backlash. To what extent is the expansion of LGBT activism in Africa linked to the end of conflict? My sense is that there is a connection, but it is not as strong as it is with women's rights reform, partly because the cultural hurdles are even greater. But in countries like Uganda, the LGBT movement was supported by key organizations and leaders in the women's movement, and so in some respects it benefited from the conflict indirectly as well as from political opening.

Youth were especially affected by the conflict, having been conscripted into fighting and denied an education and the capacity to build their lives. Given the youthfulness of the continent, with 62 percent of the population in Africa under the age of twenty-five (World Bank 2009), to what extent did the end of conflict open up new opportunities for them and for their mobilization? Did their shared interests coalesce in the same way that it did for women and if not, why not?

Thus, the success of women's mobilization in the postconflict context raises questions about whether the disability, LGBT, youth, landless, and other movements were also energized as a result of conflict because of the ways in which conflict affected them and gave them common cause and also because of some of the opportunity structures that emerged.

Changes in men's roles

While women's roles expanded after conflict and women were better positioned to demand further rights, it is less clear the extent to which men's roles changed. Did men also take on new roles and start doing more of the care work as women took on new roles outside the home? Did women continue to remain subordinate to men in the household even when their roles expanded outside the home? Certainly subordination does not disappear overnight, and it may take generations to undo, but if one sees change as a process, then the expansion of female roles is a first step in this direction. Some of the case studies pointed to difficulties men faced as they attempted to cope with the changes in gender relations. They are surprisingly reminiscent of the difficulties men confronted coming out of World War I. How should we think of these negative by-products of major social disruptions? Are they inevitable, or can they be ameliorated through greater attentiveness to these consequences?

The gender disruptions were not regarded nor experienced as entirely positive by men, as discussed in the case studies. Men often found it difficult to respond to the challenges of war through constructive community building and survival activities. In northern Uganda, Annan et al. (2011) found that unlike men, most women returning from armed groups were able to reintegrate socially and were more psychologically resilient. They exhibited little aggression and violence, even those who had been forcibly married and had borne children. Similar patterns were evident earlier in Uganda after the conflict which ended in 1986, not just among combatants, but in the population more generally (Liebling-Kalifani 2004). This raises important questions about why women have been more resilient and why men have found it harder to rebuild their lives after war. Moreover, as the case studies in this volume show, men sometimes responded by withdrawing, engaging in self-defeating behavior such as drinking, or inflicting violence on intimate partners.

Studies from other postconflict countries uncover other problematic patterns. In Rwanda, for example, Jennie Burnet (2011) describes a situation where new inheritance laws that benefited women created tensions between women and their brothers, while the rise of women in politics caused some men to withdraw from politics because they felt that all the good positions were going to women. She also found that women's improved status had created discord in the family. How should we think of these negative by-products of major social disruptions? Are they inevitable, or can they be ameliorated through greater attentiveness to these consequences?

Having raised all these questions, it is worth noting that some men have been very involved in women's rights activism in the contexts mentioned in this book. There is considerable discussion about how to bring men on board on women's issues in countries like Liberia and Uganda. Men and women worked actively together during the war around peace issues. Men are often very engaged in academic gender studies departments and in conferences and projects regarding women's rights. Cynics argue that men are taking advantage of perceived opportunities for funding and study, but the phenomenon is too widespread to be attributed to opportunism. This is yet another question among many that would require further more systematic investigation.

International actors

The relationship with international actors has proven to be the most complicated aspect of this study. Postconflict countries have sometimes been more easily influenced than other countries by international influences and new norms relating to gender due to the visible presence and influence of external actors, especially UN agencies, but also other multilateral actors and bilateral donors, which have put pressure on governments to address women's rights in a concerted manner. New international norms had embraced the need for women's empowerment in postconflict contexts through constitutional, legislative, and policy reforms as well as other measures. However, as this book shows, particularly in Chapter 6 in the discussion of peace agreements, the relationship between the international actors and gender outcomes is complex, indirect, nonlinear, and uneven. As a result, I am skeptical of claims regarding the direct impacts of foreign aid (both general and targeted at women's empowerment), peace agreements, peace negotiations, and peace-keeping troops, all of which have been associated with the changes described. This is not because the international factors don't matter, but because they are generally mediated by local women's movements, governmental actors, femo-crats, and other domestic considerations. The relationship between internal and external influences would require greater attention through case studies rather than simply the cross-national statistical studies that have been conducted. Thus, to what extent do donor funds and international actors set the gender agenda or interfere with it, and to what extent do they complement women's movement activities and goals?

For some time now China has been increasing its interest in Africa, and today China is the largest bilateral trading partner of African countries. China's political interest in Africa does not give consideration to democratic reform and human rights, and therefore it is unlikely that this growing relationship will have a positive influence on gender agendas on the continent, particu-larly in postconflict countries, as evident in Angola. Moreover, as countries in Africa are placing more emphasis on trade rather than aid as a development strategy, the extent to which external actors will have influence in promoting a women's rights agenda may become circumscribed. This requires further investigation.

Another issue relating to international influences has to do with Western domestic constituencies. Given the intense interest in Joseph Kony of the Lord's Resistance Army in Uganda generated by Invisible Children in the United States and globally in 2012, albeit brief, the campaign raised complex questions about the ways in which international social movements, religious organizations, and the media relate to conflicts in developing countries. The campaign was premised on militarism and simplistic understandings of the conflict in Uganda. It was virtually devoid of Ugandan agency, not to mention gender perspectives. Yet it touched deeply something in the psyche of Americans and in their basic desire for justice. More recently, the 2014 abduction of the Chibok girls in northern Nigeria provoked another kind of international response that was less problematic, but highlighted once again the issue of international mobilization around women's rights in conflict situations. There is a need to better under-stand such transnational movements and the moral and ethical questions they raise about how concern for others in conflicts is generated and expressed. Looking at the gender dimensions would be an important aspect of this.

Women combatants

It appears that it has been much easier to parlay women's peacemaking roles into political power than their combatant roles. Women served as combatants, for example, in the Algerian war of independence; the struggle for liberation in Mozambique, Angola, Eritrea, and Zimbabwe; as well as the guerrilla wars in Liberia and Sierra Leone. In the earlier wars prior to 1985, women and women fighters experienced backlash after the war. In the more recent wars, it has been difficult to see how women's wartime roles were leveraged into positions of power other than in a few instances. They may have helped in transforming gender relations because they challenged conventional gender norms. But only a handful of the fighters in the Ugandan war became postconflict leaders. Liberian women combatants did not play any significant leadership roles in the postconflict period, and the numbers of women in the security sector diminished considerably after the war compared with the numbers of women combatants in the various militias. Their level of education served as the most important constraint on their capacity to assume leadership roles. However, this subject would be worth investigating further to better understand why certain wartime roles have greater impact on women's advancement than others in the postconflict period.

Importance of region

Much of the literature on women and politics first emerged in relation to the Organisation for Economic Co-operation and Development (OECD) countries and the Nordic countries were historically regarded as leaders in advancing women as political leaders. Cross-national studies were initially circumscribed to the OECD countries by data limitations and only later were they expanded to the entire globe. Yet, there are important *regional* dynamics that got swallowed up in the eagerness to conduct global cross-national studies, which tried to explain multiple trajectories for change through the impact of the 1995 UN Beijing conference, the role of electoral systems, the adoption of quotas, the presence of peacekeeping troops, the adoption of peace agreements, cultural values, and so on. Yet some of these factors have mattered more than others in different parts of the world, and this has not been adequately explored.

The importance of civil war is one such factor that has mattered more in Africa than in many other parts of the world. Little research has been carried out to understand regional dynamics in Africa in the area of women's rights. The relationship between the end of conflict and women's rights regimes, for example, is found primarily in Africa. This is not because there is something unique about Africa because, in fact, the correlation is a global one

(Hughes 2009). But it is especially evident in Africa because so many conflicts ended on the continent after the 1990s and especially after 2000. Regional impacts are important but have not been sufficiently studied, even though there is awareness that the Nordic countries have generally enjoyed significantly higher rates of female political leadership and stronger women's rights policies than other parts of the world. Similarly, the Eastern European and Eurasian countries declined dramatically in rates of female representation after the collapse of communism in the region. Today, the Maghreb countries lead in the Middle East and North Africa in rates of female legislative representation. Thus, region matters in understanding changing norms. This is partly because of a shared colonial history, commonalities in struggles over economic status and governance, similar engagements with foreign donors and multilateral institutions, and common experiences with state collapse and economic decline. The regional diffusion of ideas, norms, and practices in women's mobilization and policy making around women's rights also contributed to the shared regional dynamics one finds today in so many postconflict countries. Thus, future research should pay more attention to regional dynamics in examining gender and politics. While cross-national research is important, there is a lot that is missed in trying to aggregate trends that are specific to region and are shaped by historical, socioeconomic, and geographic factors.

At the same time, I don't want to overstate the similarities within regions. Even in postconflict countries in Africa there are vast differences. The case of Angola in this book has highlighted the difference that the relative absence of women's movements and international pressures make in advancing women's rights. In Africa, the role of regional organizations like the Southern African Development Association has been more important in southern Africa than such organizations have been in other parts of the continent in influencing gender norms. Similarly, Islam has served as a constraint on women's rights in Sudan, but less so in Tanzania or Senegal. In Sudan, religion combined with a repressive authoritarian regime has resulted in onerous challenges for women's rights activists. Even in Somalia, mobilized women have had an unusually difficult slog, but there it is not state strength or religion as much as state weakness and the strength of clans that creates enormous challenges for women activists. Some governments in Africa use their women's rights credentials to create an impression of modernity and progressive-mindedness, while others thumb their noses at the international community and primarily respond to internal challenges. These are all differences that influence outcomes in the same region that would also need to be accounted for. But this does not negate the need to also highlight the congruence in experience.

Moreover, some of these dynamics have a *temporal* dimension to them that is not always recognized in the pursuit of cross-sectional explanations for women's representation. The influences of the end of the Cold War in the late 1980s, the decline of conflict in Africa in the 1990s, the end of communism in Eastern Europe and Eurasia in the late 1980s, the turn toward the right in

Europe and the Nordic countries in the 2000s, and the rise of Islamic fundamentalism after the 1980s but especially after the 2000s all influence the openness to women's rights and the ways in which women's rights policies are adopted. Thus, understanding better the regional aspects of gender and politics as well as differences within regions is crucial.

Regime type

One of the main debates in the postconflict literature has to do with the extent to which the lack of democratic constrains what women elected to office can do once in office. Much of this debate has focused on Rwanda. Some have suggested that the large numbers of women in the Rwandan legislature have improved prospects for both democracy and for women's rights. Others, like Carey Hogg (2009), argue that the ruling party, Revolutionary Patriotic Front (RPF), has created a situation in which the women parliamentarians are there to represent women in what she considers an essentialist manner. She argues that this construction has contributed to an ethnic equation that privileges Tutsi over Hutu. Still others are concerned about ways in which the legislative quotas have become part of an RPF strategy to maintain political power (Longman 2006; Reyntjens 2011).

Devlin and Elgie (2008) argue that the high rates of female representation in Rwanda have not had commensurate impact on gender policy. The Forum of Women Parliamentarians succeeded in getting a 1998 inheritance law and gender-based violence bill passed in 2008, along with legislation to expand the rights of pregnant and breast-feeding mothers in the workplace (1997) and to protect children from violence (2001). They also were successful in getting the gender quotas mentioned in the 2003 constitution. Nevertheless, the parliament passed a labor code that reduced paid maternity leave from eight to two weeks and increased the workweek from five to six days and from forty-five to fifty hours. During the debates around the 2004 Land Bill, the Forum for Women's Policy and the Ministry of Gender and Women in Development argued that land was not of specific concern to women as an issue. Jennie Burnet has been concerned that the female parliamentarians were more interested in the consequences of sexual violence rather than its causes, which relate to poverty, land conflict, hostile civil–military relationships, disorganization of the army and the police, weakness of the justice system, physical and economic insecurity, and oppressive gender norms. Thus, Burnet (2008, 2011) observes that as women's representation has increased, their ability to influence policy has decreased.

At the same time, Bauer and Burnet (2013) have also argued that because of the female-dominated parliament, issues are more likely to be raised for debate that primarily concern women, such as gender-based violence and abortion. National budgets are examined for their sensitivity to women's needs. Women are listened to at the local level in village councils (*umudugudu*), where a decade earlier they would have been ignored. Women are seen as competent decision makers in their households as a result of the fact that so many women have become household heads during and after the war. Thus, Burnet (2011) argues that the symbolic effects of female representation are palpable as a result of the upheaval in gender roles.

As in Rwanda, research in Sudan has shown similar limitations of the lack of democracy on women's ability to use their representation to advance a women's rights agenda. Liv Tønnessen and Al Nagar (2013) found that the 25 percent quota introduced in 2008 was the result of advocacy by women activists and international NGOs. They seized on the 2005 Comprehensive Peace Agreement and the language of UNSCR 1325 as an opportunity to push for quotas and were able to get it into the 2005 Interim Constitution. Women engaged the media, participated in protests, and submitted a memo to the constitutional review panel with their demands. The constitution ultimately included support for women's rights and a provision for affirmative action for women.[4] There were differences over the form the quota would take, with the government and progovernment women wanting a separate list for women and other women activists advocating for parties to include women on their lists.

The 2008 National Elections Act gave women 25 percent of separate closed women's lists in which one votes for the entire list. Women activists were concerned that by having a separate women's list, the parties would have little incentive to nominate them for the main party lists and constituencies. It would also create a situation where women would be beholden to the male party leaders who put them on the list. Thus, even though the outcome was not what most activists had wanted, the women's movement was able to rally around a common goal of the quota. As Sara Abbas (2010, 107) argues, the legacy of the quota is not likely to be so much the increase in the numbers of women parliamentarians as "the way in which it mobilized Sudanese women and propelled them into the political sphere." Clearly, even the leaders of the most authoritarian state of Sudan had to pay attention to its female constituency. However, the lack of democracy has acted as a serious constraint on the advancement of any pro-women's rights measures following these gains. Tønnessen argues that Sudan not only opened up for women's mobilization, but the same opening allowed for the emergence of conservative Salafi forces that worked to suppress women's rights (Abbas 2010; Tønnessen 2011; Tønnessen and al-Nagar 2013).

---

[4] 15 (2) The State shall protect motherhood and women from injustice, promote gender equality and the role of women in family, and empower them in public life; 32 (1) The State shall guarantee equal right of men and women to the enjoyment of all civil, political, social, cultural and economic rights, including the right to equal pay for equal work and other related benefits. (2) The State shall promote woman rights through affirmative action. (3) The State shall combat harmful customs and traditions which undermine the dignity and the status of women.

Even in adopting policies, authoritarian and hybrid regimes can be quite inconsistent. Uganda has adopted many pro-women pieces of legislation, yet the top leadership has been resistant to the Marriage and Divorce Bill, which was first introduced in 1965. Some human rights legislation has been passed, and the constitution is very clear on human rights, yet a highly problematic Anti-Homosexuality Act was passed in 2014 (and later repealed), threatening the human rights of LGBT people and anyone who knows an LGBT person, which would have meant that virtually everyone would have been at risk and could have been targeted by this sweeping legislation. The legislation was bitterly resisted by women activists and other human rights advocates. Yet, Uganda continues also to adopt other policies and legislation that favor women's rights.

These studies from Rwanda, Sudan and Uganda point to the need to better understand the ways in which authoritarianism constrains women's rights as well as what is possible within these constraints. And while authoritarianism poses its own challenges, these obstacles cannot be understood without reference to conservative forces that influence the state and impose their own limitations on women. Such conservative elements are apparent even in established democracies, as we find, for example, in the United States when it comes to reproductive rights or the rights of poor women and minority women.

SEXUAL VIOLENCE

There is an ongoing debate among scholars and activists over the occurrence of rape both during and after the conflict. Some have argued that it has reached alarming proportions, while others have argued that these figures are exaggerated. In recent years, *New York Times* journalist Nicolas Kristof (2009), the UN Population Fund (2006), the UN High Commission on Refugees, Amnesty International, International Rescue Committee, McKay (2009), Bannerman (2008), and others have cited a statistic that 60 to 75 percent of women in Liberia experienced sexual violence, and some have even produced a figure of 92 percent. The most frequently cited statistic about the prevalence of sexual violence in the Liberian conflict was that 75 percent of women were raped (e.g., Kristof 2009; United Nations Population Fund 2006). Rape rates are often inflated not just by consultants, NGOs, and journalists, but also by women themselves who seek to attract attention to their cause (Medie 2012).

However, evidence from two peer-reviewed, survey-based studies regarding sexual violence during the Liberian civil war (Swiss et al. 1998; Johnson et al. 2008), as well as from the Demographic and Health Survey (DHS 2007) produced much more modest results. The Swiss et al. survey found the rate to be closer to 15 percent, and the DHS survey found that 17 percent of women had experienced sexual violence at some time in their life. In Liberia, the DHS study showed that the majority (37%) named a partner as the perpetrator, and only 8 percent of those reporting sexual violence were victims of perpetrators who were "soldiers" or "police'"(Cohen and Green 2012; DHS 2007). It is interesting to note that there is no difference between rural and urban areas in rates of sexual violence. Women with primary, secondary, or higher education (18.5%) are at greater risk that those with no education (16.3%). Moreover, women in the fourth-highest wealth quintile experienced steeper rates of sexual violence (20.5%) than those in the lowest and second quintile (16%). This data challenges many of the assumptions that have been made about women coming out of conflict. This is not to minimize the problem, but, rather, to show that the need for accurate data in these contexts is paramount.

Related to this publicity, in recent years, the extreme sexual violence in the eastern Congo conflict has gained international attention and greater scrutiny, almost to the exclusion of other problems in the country, but also in narrow ways that have not looked at the broader causes of the problem relating to a void in governance institutions and the historical roots of such violence. Some argue that the heavy emphasis on sexual violence has had problematic implications (Bouta et al. 2005). Severine Autesserre (2012), for example, claims that an overly simplified narrative of sexual abuse of women and girls in Eastern Congo has emerged from advocacy groups, journalists, and policy makers that has created its own set of problems. Policy makers have focused on sexual violence to draw attention to the crisis in Congo in counterproductive ways. More attention is paid to sexual violence to the exclusion of other forms of violence that may be more prevalent. The narrative problematically feeds into an already existing stereotypical image of African "savagery." Funds are available for victims of sexual abuse to the exclusion of other forms of violence or other issues that require attention. Most disturbingly, militia find that the intense focus on sexual violence makes it even more forbidden, creating additional incentives to exploit it resulting in even greater increases in sexual violence. The focus also overlooks the fact that 4 to 10 percent of rape victims are men and boys. Autesserre's critique has gained considerable traction among scholars of Congo.

This critique was amplified by the Human Security Report 2012, which subsequently has come under sharp criticism from feminist international relations scholars. It argues that a series of prominent UN reports associated with the Security Council's Women, Peace and Security policy agenda has not only brought attention to issues of sexual violence, but they have also helped foster a narrative based on partial, misleading, and sometimes inaccurate assumptions. The report argues that sexual violence in the worst affected countries is treated as typical of all conflict-affected countries, whereas there is considerable variation in the extent of violence. It neglects domestic sexual violence even though it is more pervasive than conflict-related sexual violence. The report also concludes that "conflicts with extreme sexual violence are the exception rather than the rule," and that claims otherwise are not evidence based. Strategic rape is less common than purported.

Critics take issue with the Human Security Report's claim that conflicts in Congo, Rwanda, Sudan, Sierra Leone, Liberia, and Bosnia are exceptional cases, arguing that all wars feature sexual violence. They argue that there is insufficient data to know whether rape is increasing or decreasing or whether strategic rape is common (see, e.g., MacKenzie 2012).

It seems that rather than critique the intense focus on sexual violence, which seems warranted after decades of neglect, that it would be more appropriate to call for more attention in scholarship and policy making to other forms of violence against women and men and to the links between sexual and other forms of violence. The high levels of interest in sexual violence do raise real concerns that need to be considered by researchers. Already interesting work is being conducted on the variance in levels of sexual violence against women in different conflicts. However, as Eva Ayiera (2010) has argued, the scholarship and policy interventions have tended to separate sexual violence against women from the broader culture of violence that view it as an abnormality that will end when the conflict ends. It is not sufficiently linked to preexisting gender relations and other forms of gendered violence prior to the conflict. Even sexual violence against men is tied to existing norms in which the assertion of male dominance is used to humiliate men by feminizing them. What is missing in this literature is an examination of the roots of gendered violence within broader political, social, and economic dynamics and its links to weak institutions.

FUTURE TRENDS

Substantive impacts of women's representation

This book is about gender regime change. Such change is always painstakingly slow for the actors involved. It is incomplete, uneven, and often compromised. While this study has focused on the changes in norms as well as constitutional and legislative changes, more research is needed into the actual implementation of these laws. Postconflict states are usually weak; most are not democratic; and they are often unwilling to allocate resources to gender-based reforms. Their capacity and willingness for implementation cannot be counted on. Thus, it is necessary to further examine the real-world impacts of legal reform.

There are also a handful of studies that have looked at women legislators' impact on legislation in postconflict countries, for example, Disney (2008), Luciak and Olmos (2005), Pearson and Powley (2008), Tamale (1999), and Tripp (2000). There are others that look at important symbolic impacts (Burnet 2012; Tripp 2000), but the extent to which the new legislation actually changes practice needs further empirically work, particularly in places where the political will and state capacity is lacking and where opposition has been mobilized against reforms.

Duration and diffusion of postconflict impacts

I have argued that the phenomena described in this book are temporal, starting in the early 1990s. It is unclear how long this period of gender-related reform in postconflict countries will continue. Some activists in the Ugandan opposition claim that the momentum for women's rights reform died in 2000 as democracy became curtailed. They focus on the many gains yet to be made. Others point to the continued mobilization of women in new forms, the many pieces of woman-friendly legislation in the Eighth Parliament (2006–2011), and the increasing rates of female political representation. How does one determine when a movement has run its course, particularly in a nondemocratic context, where outcomes by definition are uneven and unpredictable? This study has focused on Africa, but the patterns clearly extend beyond this region to other postconflict contexts. It would be useful to take this study to a more broadly comparative level to see how the patterns play out. Looking at historic parallels with other relevant time periods, for example, the period after World War I, might also be useful.

Looking at the patterns over time to see if they change would also be important. It seems that the postconflict trajectories have started converging and influencing other nonpostconflict patterns. For example, quota adoption is quite widespread these days and extends even to some of the nonpostconflict laggards in Africa. Such patterns of diffusion would warrant further investigation.

Changing nature of conflict

The changing nature of conflict in Africa, and the fact that conflict today is found primarily in the activities of terrorist groups and in election violence, will need to be accounted for in future research. The rise, for example, of Boko Haram in Nigeria, Al Shabaab in Somalia, Ansar Dine in Mali, Al-Qaeda in the Islamic Maghreb (AQUIM) in Algeria and Mali, Movement for Monotheism, and Jihad in West Africa in Mali (MUJAO) and elsewhere, and other Islamic groups influenced by Salafism and other conservative ideologies is posing new challenges to these societies but also to women's rights.

It is unclear how these tendencies and conflicts will influence women's rights. If Algeria, which experienced over a decade of conflict involving radical Islamists between 1991 and 2002, is any indication, the patterns should be much the same as what has been described in this manuscript. Algeria fits the sub-Saharan trends described in this book very closely. Since the conflict, women in Algeria have experienced fairly radical changes in many aspects of their lives. Algeria today has the highest rates of female legislative representation in the Middle East (32%). The percentage of women in Algerian universities today exceeds that of men by 12 percent. The number of women graduates in the STEM (science, technology, engineering, and math) fields is almost the same as men, while women make up 70 percent of the country's lawyers, 60 percent of judges (up from 18% in 1988), and the majority of doctors. Women are moving into areas traditionally dominated by men such as driving buses and taxicabs, pumping gas, and waiting tables.

However, it is unclear how conflict will change in the future. According to the 2011 World Development Report of the World Bank, forms of violence are changing away from civil conflict and shifting toward criminal violence, terrorism, and civil unrest. As types of conflicts change, so too will forms of conflict resolution. The causes of conflicts will be different as well. In Africa, for example, conflicts will probably be related more to land grabbing, climate change, and the phenomenon of newfound oil in countries like Uganda, Ghana, Liberia, and Sierra Leone. Conflicts may be more localized. They may also entail, in addition to election-related violence and incidents of terrorism, coup d'états, low-grade violence, and widespread sexual violence as we have witnessed in eastern Congo. The phenomenon of state building will become more important than it has been, while peacemaking will need to be redefined if the present terrorist trends continue. What implications these changes have for women will require greater attention.

These are just a few of the areas that would require scholarly attention. More scholarly basic research is needed by people from the affected regions themselves based on empirical evidence. More comparative research is needed. This would assist greatly in policy making, in helping understand these societies and how they are transforming themselves, and in helping guide the work of those advocating for increased opportunities for women and men.

References

"Government, Women's Groups Decry Post-War Sexual Violence." *UN Integrated Regional Information Networks,* 15 January 2007.

"Human Rights Problems Persist, Says UN Report." 22 March 2007.

"Officials Adopt Legislation on Land, Property Ownership," *UN Integrated Regional Information Networks,* 8 September 2006.

"Paper Hails Liberian Women for Holding Peace Talks Delegates 'Hostage'." *Accra Mail, BBC Worldwide Monitoring,* 24 July 2003.

"Speaker Wants Women Bill Passed – Proposes Citizens Political Covenant." *The News,* 15 January 2003.

"Uganda Women to Form Lobby against War." *Africa Network News Bulletin* 9 October 1996.

"UIA in New Push for Women Investors." *The Monitor,* 21 June 2001.

"UN Informed About Government's Measures on Women (Angola)." *Angola Press* 12 March 2014.

"Violence against Women, Abandoning Female Genital Mutilation: The Role of National Parliaments." *African Parliamentary Conference.* 2005.

"Women Want International Force Deployed ...Concerned About Escalating Crisis." *The News (Monrovia),* 4 April 2003.

"Women in Uganda Stage March for Peace," *Globe and Mail* 7 September 1985.

"Women, Speaker Fuss over Appointment ...As WIPNET Presents Position to Lawmakers." *The News* 17, April 2003.

Abbas, Sara. "The Sudanese Women's Movement and the Mobilisation for the 2008 Legislative Quota and Its Aftermath." *IDS Bulletin* 41.5 (2010): 100–08.

Abdi, Hawa, and Sarah J. Robbins. *Keeping Hope Alive: One Woman, 90,000 Lives Changed.* New York: Grand Central Pub., 2013.

Action Against Hunger. *Food Security Assessment Gulu IDP Camps,* 2003.

Abdullah, Hussaina J., and Aisha Fofana-Ibrahim. "The Meaning and Practice of Women's Empowerment in Post-Conflict Sierra Leone." *Development* 53.2 (2010): 259–66.

Abdullahi, Abdurahman M. "Women and the Constitutional Debate in Somalia." Unpublished paper. 2009.

Abramowitz, Sharon, and Mary H. Moran. "International Human Rights, Gender-Based Violence, and Local Discourses of Abuse in Post-conflict Liberia: A Problem of "Culture"?" *African Studies Review* 55.2 (2012): 119–46.

Ahmed, Leila. "Feminism and Feminist Movements in the Middle East, a Preliminary Exploration: Turkey, Egypt, Algeria, People's Democratic Republic of Yemen'." *Women's Studies International Forum* 5.2 (1982): 153–68.

Akallo, Grace, and Faith J. H. McDonnell. *Girl Soldier: A Story of Hope for Northern Uganda's Children.* Grand Rapids, MI: Chosen, 2007.

Akello, Grace. *Self Twice-Removed: Ugandan Women (Change (UK) International Reports: Women and Society)* London: CHANGE International 1982.

Akesson, Lisa. *Angola Country Gender Analysis*: Prepared for the Swedish International Development Authority (SIDA), Luanda, Angola, 1992.

Ali, Nada Mustafa. *Gender and Statebuilding in South Sudan.* Washington. DC: U.S. Institute of Peace, 2011.

All-Party Burundi Women's Peace Conference. *Final Declaration.* Arusha. 2000.

Amnesty International. *Sierra Leone: Women Face Human Rights Abuses in the Informal Legal Sector.* Amnesty International, 2006.

Amony, Evelyn, and Erin Baines (editor). *I Am Evelyn Amony: Reclaiming My Life from the Lord's Resistance Army.* Madison: University of Wisconsin-Press, 2015.

Amundsen, Inge, and Cesaltina Abreu. *Civil Society in Angola: Inroads, Space and Accountability.* Bergen: Chr. Michelsen Institute, 2006.

Anderlini, Sanam Naraghi. "Translating Global Agreement into National and Local Commitments." *Women and War: Power and Protection in the 21st Century.* Eds. Kuehnast, Kathleen R., Chantal de Jonge Oudraat, and Helga Maria Hernes. Washington, DC: United States Institute of Peace Press, 2011. 19–36.

Anderson, Miriam. "Considering Local Versus International Norms on Women's Rights in Contemporary Peace Processes." Presented at Conference on *Gender, Peace and Security: Local Interpretations of International Norms.* Davis Institute, Hebrew University, Israel. 2010.

Anderson, Miriam J., and Liam Swiss. "Peace Accords and the Adoption of Electoral Quotas for Women in the Developing World, 1990–2006." *Politics & Gender* 10 (2014): 33–61.

Aning, Emmanuel Kwesi. "Women and Civil Conflict: Liberia and Sierra Leone." *African Journal of International Affairs* 1.2 (1998): 45–58.

Ankrah, Maxine E. "Conflict: The Experience of Ugandan Women in Revolution and Reconstruction." Unpublished paper. 1987.

Annan, Jeannie, Christopher Blattman, Dyan Mazurana, and Khristopher Carlson. "Civil War, Reintegration, and Gender in Northern Uganda." *Journal of Conflict Resolution* 55.6 (2011): 877–908.

Arabi, Asha. "'In Power without Power': Women in Politics and Leadership Positions in South Sudan." *Hope, Pain & Patience: The Lives of Women in South Sudan.* Eds. Bubenzer, Friederike and Orly Stern. Auckland Park, South Africa: Jacana Media, 2011.

Association for Women's Rights in Development. *Association of Women in Development 2011 Global Survey: Where Is the Money for Women's Rights?* 2011.

Autesserre, Severine. "Dangerous Tales: Dominant Narratives on the Congo and Their Unintended Consequences." *African Affairs* 111.443 (2012): 202–22.

AWPSG, African Women and Peace Support Group. *Liberian Women Peacemakers.* Trenton, NJ: Africa World Press, 2004.

Ayiera, Eva. "Sexual Violence in Conflict: A Problematic International Discourse." *Feminist Africa* 14 (2010): 7–20.

Badmus, Isiaka Alani. "Explaining Women's Roles in the West African Tragic Triplet: Sierra Leone, Liberia, and Côte D'Ivoire in Comparative Perspective." *Journal of Alternative Perspectives in the Social Sciences* 1.3 (2009): 808–39.

Bainomugisha, A. "The Empowerment of Women." *Uganda's Age of Reforms: A Critical Overview.* Ed. Mugaju, Justus. Kampala, Uganda: Fountain Publishers, 1999.

Ball, Jennifer. *In Their Own Voices: Learning from Women Peacebuilders in Uganda.* Guelph, ON: University of Guelph, 2009.

Banda, Fareda. *Women, Law and Human Rights: An African Perspective.* Oxford; Portland, OR: Hart Publishing, 2005.

Bannerman, Lucy. "We Are Women, Hear Us Roar." *Time Magazine* 12 January 2008.

Barnes, Catherine. *Owning the Process: Mechanisms for Political Participation of the Public in Peacemaking.* London: Conciliation Resources, 2002.

Bashir, Halima, and Damien Lewis. *Tears of the Desert: A Memoir of Survival in Darfur.* New York: One World Ballantine Books, 2008.

Bath, Tony. "Civil Society Take Maternal Mortality Fight to Supreme Court." URN 20 September 2013.

Bauer, Gretchen, and Hannah Evelyn Britton. *Women in African Parliaments.* Boulder, CO: Lynne Rienner Publishers, 2006.

Bauer, Gretchen, and Jennie E. Burnet. "Gender Quotas, Democracy, and Women's Representation in Africa: Some Insights from Democratic Botswana and Autocratic Rwanda." *Women's Studies International Forum* 41.2(2013): 103–12.

Bauer, Gretchen. "'What Is Wrong with a Woman Being Chief?' Women Chiefs and Symbolic and Substantive Representation in Botswana." *Journal of Asian and African Studies*: August 21 (2014).

Bauer, Jacqui. "Women and the 2005 Election in Liberia." *Journal of Modern African Studies* 47.2 (2009): 193–211.

Beah, Ishmael. *A Long Way Gone: Memoirs of a Boy Soldier.* New York: Farrar, Straus and Giroux, 2007.

Beckwith, Karen. "Gendered Competitive Interaction and Women's Executive Electoral Success." *Annual Meeting of the American Political Science Association.* 2009.

Bell, Christine, and Catherine O'Rourke. "Does Feminism Need a Theory of Transitional Justice? An Introductory Essay." *International Journal of Transitional Justice* 1.1 (2007): 23–44.

Belloni, Roberto. "Civil Society and Peacebuilding in Bosnia and Herzegovina." *Journal of Peace Research* 38.2 (2001): 163–80.

Benderly, Jill. "A Women's Place Is at the Peace Table." *SAIS Review* 20.2 (2000): 79–83.

Bennett, Elizabeth. "Rwanda Strides Towards Gender Equality in Government." *Kennedy School Review* (2014).

Bennett, T. W., and T. Vermeulen. "Codification of Customary Law." *Journal of African Law* 24.2 (1980): 206–19.

Binder, Christina, Karin Lukas, and Romana Schweiger. "Empty Words or Real Achievement? The Impact of Security Council Resolution 1325 on Women in Armed Conflicts." *Radical History Review* 101 (2008): 22–41.

Birabiro, Meti. *Blue Daughter of the Red Sea: A Memoir.* Madison: University of Wisconsin Press, 2004.

Black, Renee. "Mainstreaming Resolution 1325? Evaluating the Impact on Security Council Resolution 1325 on Country-Specific UN Resolutions." *Journal of Military and Strategic Studies* 11.4 (2009): 1–30.

Böhme, Jeannette. *Literature Research on the Implementation of UN Security Council Resolution 1325.* Berlin, Germany: Heinrich Böll Stiftung, 2011.

Bouta, Tsjeard, Ian Bannon, and Georg Frerks. *Gender, Conflict, and Development.* Washington, DC: World Bank, 2005.

Boyd, Rosalind. "Empowerment of Women in Contemporary Uganda: Real or Symbolic?" *Labour, Capital and Society* 22.1 (1989).

Boye, Abd-el K., Kathleen Hill, Stephen Isaacs, and Deborah Gordis. "Marriage Law and Practice in the Sahel." *Studies in Family Planning* 22.6 (1991): 343–9.

Brassard, Geneviève. "From Private Story to Public History: Irene Rathbone Revises the War in the Thirties." *NWSA Journal (Special Issue: Gender and Modernism between the Wars, 1918–1939)* 15.3 (2003): 43–63.

Britton, Hannah Evelyn. *Women in the South African Parliament: From Resistance to Governance.* Urbana: University of Illinois Press, 2005.

Bruthus, Lois Lewis. *Expert Group Meeting On Gender Equality and Ensuring Participation of Women.* Ottawa, Canada: United Nations Division for the Advancement of Women (DAW), 2003.

Bumiller, Kristin. *In an Abusive State: How Neoliberalism Appropriated the Feminist Movement against Sexual Violence.* Durham: Duke University Press, 2008.

Burnet, Jennie E. "Gender Balance and the Meanings of Women in Governance in Post-Genocide Rwanda." *African Affairs* 107.428 (2008): 361–86.

Genocide Lives in Us: Women, Memory, and Silence in Rwanda. Madison: University of Wisconsin Press, 2012.

"Women Have Found Respect: Gender Quotas, Symbolic Representation, and Female Empowerment in Rwanda." *Politics & Gender* 7.3 (2011): 303–34.

Bush, Sarah Sunn. "International Politics and the Spread of Quotas for Women in Legislatures." *International Organization* 65.1 (2011): 103–37.

Busharizi, Paul, and Alice Emasu. "Tilting the Balance." *Women's Vision* (1995): 1.

Caesar, Ruth, Cerue Konah Garlo, Chitra Nagarajan and Steven Schoofs. "Implementing Resolution 1325 in Liberia: Reflections of Women's Associations." International Alert, IFP GenderCluster, 2010.

Campbell, Horace. *Militarism, Warfare, and the Search for Peace in Angola: The Contribution of Angolan Women.* Pretoria: African Institute of South Africa. 2001.

Campbell-Nelson, Karen. *Liberia Is Not Just a Man-Thing: Transitional Justice Lessons for Women, Peace and Security.* London: International Center for Transitional Justice. 2008.

Candia, Steven. "Ugandan Appointed Interpol Boss for Africa." *New Vision* 12 January 2012.

Carroll, Rory. "'Everyone's Afraid of Her'." *The Guardian* 23 August 2003.

Castillejo, Clare. *Strengthening Women's Citizenship in the Context of State-Building: The Experience of Sierra Leone.* Fundación para las Relaciones Internacionales y el Diálogo Exterior (FRIDE), 2008.

Chatham House. "Angola: Drivers of Change." *Civil Society.* London: Chatham House, 2005.

Chibita, Monica Balya. "On God's Call." *Women's Vision* 30 January 1996.

Chingwete, A., S. Richmond, and C. Alpin. *Support for African Women's Equality Rises: Education, Jobs & Political Participation Still Unequal.* 2014, Afrobarometer.

Chishugi, Leah. *A Long Way from Paradise: Surviving the Rwandan Genocide.* London: Hachette Digital, Little, Brown Book Group, 2010.

Coalition for International Justice. *Following Taylor's Money: A Path of War and Destruction.* Washington, DC: Coalition for International Justice. 2005.

Cohen, Dara K., and Amelia H. Green. "Dueling Incentives: Sexual Violence in Liberia and the Politics of Human Rights Advocacy." *Journal of Peace Research* 49.3 (2012): 445–58.

Collier, Paul, et al. *Breaking the Conflict Trap: Civil War and Development Policy.* Washington, DC; Oxford: World Bank; Oxford University Press, 2003.

Comerford, Michael G. *The Peaceful Face of Angola: Biography of a Peace Process (1991 to 2002).* Windhoek, Namibia: John Meinert Printing, 2005.

Conaway, Camille Pampell, and Jolynn Shoemaker. *Women in United Nations Peace Operations: Increasing the Leadership Opportunities.* Washington, DC: Women in International Security, Georgetown University, 2008.

Connell, Raewyn. *Gender.* Cambridge, UK: Polity Press, 2002.

Cooper, Barbara. "The Politics of Difference and Women's Associations in Niger: Of 'Prostitutes,' the Public and Politics." *Signs* 20.4 (1995): 851–82.

Cooper, Helene. *The House at Sugar Beach: In Search of a Lost African Childhood.* New York: Simon & Schuster, 2008.

Copelon, Rhonda. "Gender Crimes as War Crimes: Integrating Crimes against Women into International Criminal Law." *McGill Law Journal* 46 (2000): 217–40.

Corrin, Chris. "Developing Democracy in Kosova: From Grass Roots to Government." *Women, Politics, and Change.* Ed. Ross, Karen. New York: Oxford University Press, 2002. 99–108.

D'Awol, Anyieth M. "'Sibu Ana, Sibu Ana' ('Leave Me, Leave Me'): Survivors of Sexual Violence in South Sudan." *Hope, Pain & Patience: The Lives of Women in South Sudan.* Eds. Bubenzer, Friederike and Orly Stern. Auckland Park, South Africa: Fanele/Jacana Media, 2011. xxxi, 259p.

Dahlerup, Drude. *Women, Quotas and Politics.* New York: Routledge, 2006.

Dallaire, Roméo. *Shake Hands with the Devil: The Failure of Humanity in Rwanda.* Cambridge, MA: Da Capo Press, 2004.

Dann, Philipp, and Zaid Al-Ali. "The Internationalized Pouvoir Constituant – Constitution-Making under External Influence in Iraq, Sudan and East Timor." *Max Planck Yearbook of United Nations Law, Volume 10.* Eds. von Bogdandy, A. and R. Wolfrum. Netherlands: Koninklijke Brill, 2006. 423–63.

Daoud, Zakya. *Féminisme et Politique au Maghreb: Sept Décennies De Lutte.* Casablanca: Editions Eddif, 1996.

Davies, Alberta. *Raw Edge of Purgatory: I Survived the Liberian Pogrom.* Xlibris, 2011.

de Watteville, Nathalie. *Addressing Gender Issues in Demobilization and Reintegration Programs.* World Bank, 2002.

Decker, Alicia C. *In Idi Amin's Shadow: Women, Gender, and Militarism in Uganda.* Athens: Ohio University Press, 2014.

Demographic and Health Survey (DHS). Monrovia, Liberia: Liberia Institute of Statistics and Geo-Information Services (LISGIS) Monrovia, Liberia. 2007. Ministry of Health and Social Welfare Monrovia, Liberia. National AIDS Control

Program Monrovia, Liberia. Macro International Inc. Calverton, Maryland, USA, 2007.

Denzer, LaRay. "Women in Freetown Politics, 1914–61: A Preliminary Study." *Africa: Journal of the International African Institute* 57.4 (1987): 439–56.

Devlin, Claire, and Robert Elgie. "The Effect of Increased Women's Representation in Parliament: The Case of Rwanda." *Parliamentary Affairs* 61.2 (2008): 237–54.

Diggs, Mwamini Thambwe Mwamba. *The Untold Story of the Women and Children of the Democratic Republic of the Congo: Analysis of Violence in Eastern DRC.* Houston, TX: Strategic Book Publishing, 2012.

Dini, Shukria. *Clan Leaders: Major Obstacle to Somali Women's Political Participation,* 2012.

Dirasse, Laketch. "The Gender Dimension of Making Peace in Africa." *Disarmament Diplomacy* 48. July (2000).

Disney, Jennifer. *Women's Activism and Feminist Agency in Mozambique and Nicaragua.* Philadelphia: Temple University Press, 2008.

Dolan, Kerry. "Daddy's Girl: How an African 'Princess' Banked $3 Billion in a Country Living on $2 a Day." *Forbes* 2 September 2013.

Doyle, Michael W., and Nicholas Sambanis. "International Peacebuilding: A Theoretical and Quantitative Analysis." *American Political Science Review* 94.4 (2000): 779–801.

DPA, United Nations Department of Political Affairs. *Women & Elections: Guide to Promoting the Participation of Women in Elections,* 2004.

Duany, Julia Aker. *Making Peace and Nurturing Life: An African Woman's Journey of Struggle and Hope.* Bloomington, IN: 1st Books, 2003.

Ducados, Henda. "An All Men's Show? Angolan Women's Survival in the 30-Year War." *Agenda Feminist Media* 43 (2000): 11–22.

Dukulé, Abdoulaye W. "Ellen Johnson Sirleaf Speaks on Governance, Elections and Other Issues (Interview)." *The Perspective* 6 May 2005.

Ebila, Florence. "Women Watering the Literary Desert." *The Women's Movement in Uganda.* Eds. Tripp, Aili Mari and Joy Kwesiga. Kampala, Uganda: Fountain Publishers, 2002.

El-Bushra, Judy. "Fused in Combat: Gender Relations and Armed Conflict." *Development in Practice* 13.2/3 (2003): 252–65.

Elmi, Halimo. "Testimony 5." *Somalia–the Untold Story: The War through the Eyes of Somali Women.* Eds. Gardner, Judith and Judy El-Bushra. London; Sterling, VA: CIIR; Pluto Press; Catholic Institute for International Relations, 2004. 127–38.

Enloe, Cynthia. *Maneuvers: The International Politics of Militarizing Women's Lives.* Austin, TX: Women's International News Gathering Service, 2000.

Essof, Shereen. "She-Murenga: Challenges, Opportunities and Setbacks of the Women's Movement in Zimbabwe." *Feminist Africa.* 4 (2005).

Fallon, Kathleen, Liam Swiss, and Jocelyn Viterna. "Resolving the Democracy Paradox: Democratization and Women's Legislative Representation in Developing Nations, 1975 to 2009." *American Sociological Review* 77.3 (2012): 380–408.

Farah, Ahmed Y., and Ioan M. Lewis. *Somalia, the Roots of Reconciliation: Peace Making Endeavors of Contemporary Lineage Leaders: A Survey of Grassroots Peace Conferences in Somaliland,* 1993.

Fearon, James D., Macartan Humphreys, and Jeremy M. Weinstein. "Can Development Aid Contribute to Social Cohesion after Civil War? Evidence from a Field

Experiment in Post-Conflict Liberia." *American Economic Review: Papers & Proceedings* 99.2 (2009): 287–91.

Femmes Africa Solidarité. *Peace Agreements as a Means for Promoting Gender Equality and Ensuring Participation of Women.* 10–13 November 2003. United Nations Division for the Advancement of Women (DAW) Expert Group Meeting.

Fernando, Pacheco. "Civil Society in Angola: Fiction or Agent of Change?" *Southern Africa. Civil Society, Politics and Donor Strategies* Eds. Vidal, Nuno and Patrick Chabal. Brussels & Luanda: Media XXI & Firmamento with Angolan Catholic University, University of Coimbra & Wageningen University, 2009. 123–34.

Forna, Aminatta. *The Devil That Danced on the Water: A Daughter's Quest.* New York: Atlantic Monthly Press, 2002.

Fortna, Virginia Page. *Peace Time: Cease-Fire Agreements and the Durability of Peace.* Princeton: Princeton University Press, 2004.

Friedrich Ebert Foundation. *Women's Landmarks in the Democratisation Process in Uganda.* Kampala, Uganda, 1995.

Fuest, Veronika. "'This Is the Time to Get in Front': Changing Roles and Opportunities for Women in Liberia." *African Affairs* 107.427 (2008): 201–24.

"Contested Inclusions: Pitfalls of NGO Peace-Building Activities in Liberia." *Afrika Spectrum* 45.2 (2010): 3–33.

Galtung, Johann. "Preface." *Communication and Culture in War and Peace.* Ed. Roach, C. London: Sage Publications, 1993.

Garland, David. *The Culture of Control: Crime and Social Order in Contemporary Society.* Chicago: University of Chicago Press, 2001.

Gayflor, Hon. Vabah. "Comments Made." *Women and Political Participation in Africa: Lessons from Southern and Eastern Africa.* International IDEA, Abantu for Development, Centre Pour Gouvernance Democratique, Burkina Faso, 2005.

Gbowee, Leymah, and Carol Lynn Mithers. *Mighty Be Our Powers: How Sisterhood, Prayer, and Sex Changed a Nation at War: A Memoir.* New York, London: Beast, 2011.

Geiser, Alexandra. *Social Exclusion and Conflict Transformation in Nepal: Women, Dalit and Ethnic Groups.* Swiss Peace, 2005.

Geisler, Gisela. "Sisters Under the Skin: Women and the Women's League in Zambia." *Journal of Modern African Studies* 25.1 (1987): 43–66.

Geisler, Gisela G. *Women and the Remaking of Politics in Southern Africa: Negotiating Autonomy, Incorporation and Representation.* Uppsala, Sweden: Nordiska Afrikainstitutet, 2004.

Gilbert, Sandra M. "Soldier's Heart: Literary Men, Literary Women, and the Great War." *Signs (Special issue: Women and Violence)* 8.3 (1983): 422–50.

Gilman, Lisa. "Purchasing Praise: Women, Dancing, and Patronage in Malawi Party Politics." *Africa Today* 48.4 (2001): 43–64.

Glassmyer, Katherine, and Nicholas Sambanis. "Rebel–Military Integration and Civil War Termination." *Journal of Peace Research* 45.3 (2008): 365–84.

Gleditsch, Kristian. "A Revised List of Wars between and within Independent States, 1816–2002." *International Interactions* 30 (2004): 231–62.

Global Network of Women Peacebuilders. *Women Count: Security Council Resolution 1325: Civil Society Monitoring Report.* 2012.

Goetz, Anne-Marie. "No Shortcuts to Power: Constraints on Women's Political Effectiveness in Uganda." *Journal of Modern African Studies* 40.4 (2002): 549–75.

Goetz, Anne-Marie, and Shireen Hassim. *No Shortcuts to Power: African Women in Politics and Policy Making*. Democratic Transition in Conflict-Torn Societies; V. 3. London: Zed Books, 2003.

Gogineni, Roopa. "Rwandan Parliament's Female Majority Focuses on Equality." *Voice of America* 26 September 2013.

Goldstein, Joshua. *Winning the War on War: The Decline of Armed Conflict Worldwide*. New York: Dutton/Penguin, 2011.

Government of Liberia. *State Party Report on the Convention to Eliminate All Forms of Discrimination against Women (CEDAW)*. Monrovia: Minister of Gender Development, 2008.

2008. *Poverty Reduction Strategy.*

Government of Somalia. *Implementation of The Beijing Platform for Action Beijing+20 Review: Somalia Country Report 2014*, United Nations Committee on the Status of Women.

Government of South Sudan. *National Evaluation Report on the Implementation of the Beijing Declaration and Platform for Action (1995) and the United Nations General Assembly (2000): South Sudan April 2014*, United Nations Committee on the Status of Women.

Grill, Bartholomäus. "Culture in Angola: Luanda Is Luminous." Website of the Goethe Institut, May 22, 2012. Accessed June 19, 2015, http://mucz-lbv-002.goethe.de/uun/bdu/en9329686.htm

Gray, L., and M. Kevane. "Diminished Access, Diverted Exclusion: Women and Land Tenure in Sub-Saharan Africa." *African Studies Review* 42.2 (1999): 15–39.

Grobbelaar, Neuma, and Elizabeth Sidiropoulos. *Observer or Participant? The Role of Civil Society in Angola*. Pretoria: South African Institute of International Affairs, 2002.

Guwatudde, Christine R. N. *"Church Affiliated NGOs Addressing Rural Women in Uganda: A Case of Two Development Projects."* M.A. Development Studies, Institute of Social Studies, 1987.

Hari, Daoud. *The Translator: A Tribesman's Memoir of Darfur*. New York: Random House, 2008.

Hariir, Shukri. "Testimony 4." *Somalia–the Untold Story: The War through the Eyes of Somali Women*. Eds. Gardner, Judith and Judy El-Bushra. Sterling, VA: CIIR; Pluto Press; Catholic Institute for International Relations, 2004. 142–52.

Hassim, Shireen. "Terms of Engagement: South African Challenges." *Feminist Africa*. 4 (2005): 10–28.

Heywood, Linda. "Angola and the Violent Years 1975–2008: Civilian Casualties." *Portuguese Studies Review* 19.1–2 (2011): 311–32.

Hillier, Debbie, and Brian Wood. *Shattered Lives: The Case for Tough International Arms Control*. London and Oxford: Amnesty International and Oxfam, 2003. http://controlarms.org/wordpress/wp-content/uploads/2011/02/Shattered-lives-the-case-for-tough-international-arms-control.pdf

Hogg, Carey Leigh. "Women's Political Representation in Post-Conflict Rwanda: A Politics of Inclusion or Exclusion?" *Journal of International Women's Studies* 11.3 (2009): 34–54.

Hughes, Melanie M. "Armed Conflict, International Linkages, and Women's Parliamentary Representation in Developing Nations." *Social Problems* 56.1 (2009): 174–204.

Hughes, Melanie, and Aili Mari Tripp. "Civil War and Trajectories of Change in Women's Political Representation in Africa, 1985–2010." *Social Forces* 93.4 (2015): 1513–1540.

Human Rights Watch. *Struggling to Survive: Barriers to Justice to Rape Victims in Rwanda.* New York, 2004.

Human Security Centre. *Human Security Report.* Vancouver, BC: Simon Fraser University, 2005.

Human Security Report Project. *Human Security Report.* Vancouver, BC: Human Security Report Project, Simon Fraser University, 2006.

I Am Malala: The Girl Who Stood Up for Education and Was Shot by the Taliban by Malala Yousafzai (2013) New York: Little, Brown and Company.

Ibrahim, Jibrin. "The First Lady Syndrome and the Marginalisation of Women from Power: Opportunities or Compromises for Gender Equality?" *Feminist Africa* 3 (2004).

Ilibagiza, Immaculée, and Steve Erwin. *Left to Tell: Discovering God Amidst the Rwandan Holocaust.* Carlsbad, CA: Hay House, Inc., 2006.

Inglehart, Ronald, and Pippa Norris. *Rising Tide: Gender Equality and Cultural Change around the World.* Cambridge, UK; New York: Cambridge University Press, 2003.

Inglehart, Ronald, Pippa Norris, and Chris Welzel. "Gender Equality and Democracy." *Comparative Sociology* 1.3–4 (2002): 321–45.

International Crisis Group. "Liberia: Resurrecting the Justice System." *Africa Report* 107.6 (2006).

Interparliamentary Union. *Women in Politics: 2015.* www.ipu.org/pdf/publications/wmnmap15_en.pdf

Isse, Dahabo. "Testimony 6." *Somalia–the Untold Story: The War through the Eyes of Somali Women.* Eds. Gardner, Judith and Judy El-Bushra. Sterling, VA: CIIR; Pluto Press; Catholic Institute for International Relations, 2004. 179–89.

Itano, Nicole. "The Sisters-in-Arms of Liberia's War." *Christian Science Monitor* 23 August 2003.

Iteka, Blaire Marcel. *Mother in My Mind: Memoir of a Teen Girl in the Killing Fields of Africa.* Amazon Digital Services, 2012.

Jacobs, Susie, Ruth Jacobson, and Jennifer Marchbank, eds. *States of Conflict: Gender, Violence and Resistance.* London and New York: Zed Books, 2000.

Jacobson, Ruth. "Mozambique and the Construction of Gendered Agency in War." *Women's Studies International Forum* 29 (2006): 499–509.

Jalalzai, Farida. "Women Rule: Shattering the Executive Glass Ceiling." *Politics & Gender* 4.2 (2008): 205–31.

Jarkloh, Bill K. "Liberia: Gov't Stays Away from Peace Rally – as Women Vent out Anger." *The News* 16 April 2003.

Jennings, Yves-Renée. *The Impact of Gender Mainstreaming on Men: The Case of Liberia.* PhD Dissertation, George Mason University, 2012.

Jetter, Alexis, Annelise Orleck, and Diana Taylor. *The Politics of Motherhood: Activist Voices from Left to Right.* Hanover and London: University Press of New England, 1997.

Jirira, Ona. "Gender, Politics and Democracy: Kuvaka Patsva (Reconstructing) the Discourse." *Safere* 1.2 (1995): 1–29.

Johnson, K. J. Asher, S. Rosborough, A. Raja, R. Panjabi, C. Beadling, and L. Lawry. "Association of Combatant Status and Sexual Violence with Health and Mental

Health Outcomes in Postconflict Liberia." *Journal of the American Medical Association* 300.6 (2008): 676–90.

Johnson Sirleaf, Ellen. *This Child Will Be Great: Memoir of a Remarkable Life by Africa's First Woman President.* New York: Harper, 2009.

Kabira, Wanjiku. *Time for Harvest: Women and Constitution Making in Kenya.* Nairobi: University of Nairobi Press, 2012.

Kafeero, Stephen. "Women Who Defined 2013." *The Independent* 15 November 2013.

Kakwenzire, Joan. "Ugandan Women Suffer Discrimination." *New Vision* 26 September 1990.

Kamara, Tom. "Carter's Sad Liberia Goodbye." *The Perspective* 9 November 2000.

Kamara-Umunna, Agnes, and Emily Holland. *And Still Peace Did Not Come: A Memoir of Reconciliation.* New York: Hyperion, 2011.

Kamau, Jean Njeri. *Assessment Report on Women's Participation in the Peace Process: Mid-Decade Review of the Implementation of the Dakar and Beijing Platforms for Action in the African Region.* Addis Ababa: Economic Commission for Africa, Sixth African Regional Conference on Women, 1999.

Kamau-Rutenberg, Wanjiru N., *Feuding in the Family: Ethnic Politics and the Struggle for Women's Rights Legislation.* PhD Dissertation, University of Minnesota, Minneapolis, 2008.

Kang, Alice. "Studying Oil, Islam and Women As If Political Institutions Mattered." *Politics & Gender* 5.4 (2009): 560–68.

Kanyeihamba, G. W. "What Others Say." *Gender, Politics, and Constitution Making in Uganda.* Ed. Matembe, Miria. Kampala, Uganda: Fountain Publishers, 2002. 198–208.

Kapinga, Marithe. "Africa: Women in Congo Form Common Front for Peace." *Ms. Magazine* 13.1 (2003): 25–26.

Karmo, Henry. "Liberian Women Hold Conference on Constitutional Review." *FrontPage Africa* 6 June 2014.

Katumba, Rebecca. "Woman Leader Answers Critics." *Uganda Times* 2 August 1979.

Keitetsi, China. *Child Soldier.* London: Souvenir Press, 2004.

Kellow, Tim. *Women, Elections and Violence in West Africa: Assessing Women's Political Participation in Liberia and Sierra Leone.* International Alert, 2010.

Kelly, Liz. "Wars against Women: Sexual Violence, Sexual Politics and the Militarised State." *States of Conflict: Gender, Violence and Resistance.* Eds. Jacobs, S., R. Jacobson, and J. Marchbank. London: Zed Books, 2000.

Kenworthy, Lane, and Melissa Malami. "Gender Inequality in Political Representation: A Worldwide Comparative Analysis." *Social Forces* 78.1 (1999): 235–68.

Kindervater, Lisa. *Seize the Day: Gender Politics in Liberia's Transition to Peace and Democracy.* MA Dissertation, Dalhousie University, 2013.

Kiplagat, Bethuel. "Reaching the 1985 Nairobi Agreement. Protracted Conflict, Elusive Peace: Initiatives to End the Violence in Northern Uganda." 2010.

Kitschelt, Herbert. "Political Opportunity Structures and Political Protest: Anti-Nuclear Movements in Four Democracies." *British Journal of Political Science* 16.1 (1986): 57–85.

Kristof, Nicholas. "After Wars, Mass Rapes Persist." *New York Times* 20 May 2009.

Krook, Mona. *Quotas for Women in Politics: Gender and Candidate Selection Reform Worldwide.* New York: Oxford University Press, 2009.

  "Reforming Representation: The Diffusion of Candidate Gender Quotas Worldwide." *Politics & Gender* 2.3 (2006): 303–27.

Kumar, Krishna, ed. *Women and Civil War: Impact, Organizations and Action*. Boulder, CO: Lynne Rienner Publishers, 2001.

Kunovich, Sheri, and Pamela Paxton. "Pathways to Power: The Role of Political Parties in Women's National Political Representation." *American Journal of Sociology* 111.2 (2005): 505–52.

Kwibuka, Eugene. "Gender Violence Law to Be Passed in Two Weeks." *New York Times* 11 February 2009.

Lacy, Marc. "A Mother's Bitter Choice: Telling Kidnappers No." *New York Times* 25 January 2003.

Ladu, Ismail Mus. "Uganda's First Female Bank Md Bows Out." *Daily Monitor* 15 April 2014.

Lahai, John Idriss. "Gendered Battlefields: A Contextual and Comparative Analysis of Women's Participation in Armed Conflicts in Africa." *Peace & Conflict Review* 4.2 (2010): 1–16.

Lake, Milli. *Building the Rule of Law in Fragile States: The Role of External Actors in Shaping Institutional Responses to Mass Violence in the Democratic Republic of Congo and South Africa*. PhD Dissertation, Political Science, University of Washington, Seattle, WA, 2014.

Levitsky, Steven, and Lucan Way. "The Rise of Competitive Authoritarianism." *Journal of Democracy* 13.2 (2002): 51–65.

Liebling-Kalifani, Helen Jane. *A Gendered Analysis of the Experiences of Ugandan Women War Survivors*. PhD Dissertation, University of Warwick, 2004.

Lindberg, Staffan I. "Women's Empowerment and Democratization: The Effects of Electoral Systems, Participation and Experience in Africa." *Studies in Comparative International Development* 39.1 (2004): 28–53.

Logan, Carolyn. "Selected Chiefs, Elected Councillors and Hybrid Democrats: Popular Perspectives on the Co-Existence of Democracy and Traditional Authority." *Journal of Modern African Studies* 47.1 (2009): 101–28.

Longman, Timothy. "Rwanda: Achieving Equality or Serving an Authoritarian State?" *Women in African Parliaments*. Eds. Bauer, Gretchen and Hannah Britton. Boulder, CO: Lynne Rienner, 2006. 133–50.

Luciak, Ilja A. *Conflict and a Gendered Parliamentary Response*. UNDP Initiative on Parliaments, Crisis Prevention and Recovery, 2006.

Luciak, Ilja A., and Cecilia Olmos. "The Guatemalan Peace Accords: Critical Reflections." *Gender, Conflict, and Peacekeeping*. Eds. Mazurana, Dyan E., Angela Raven-Roberts, and Jane Parpart. Lanham, MD: Rowman & Littlefield, 2005. 42–62.

Lueker, Lorna L. "Fighting for Human Rights: Women, War, and Social Change in Zimbabwe." *Instraw News* 28 (1998): 34–44.

Lyons, Tanya. *Guns and Guerrilla Girls: Women in the Zimbabwean National Liberation Struggle*. Trenton, NJ: Africa World Press, 2004.

MacKenzie, Megan. "War Rape Is Not Declining." Duck of Minerva 2012. Web. 15 November 2012.

Macauley, Cameron. "Women after the Rwandan Genocide: Making the Most of Survival." *Journal of ERW and Mine Action* 171 (2013): 35–38.

Mahoney, James. "The Logic of Process Tracing Tests in the Social Sciences." *Sociological Methods & Research* 41.4 (2012): 570–97.

"Tentative Answers to Questions About Causal Mechanisms." *Annual Meeting of the American Political Science Association*. 2003.

Mariano, Noreen. "Testimony 7." *Somalia–the Untold Story: The War through the Eyes of Somali Women.* Eds. Gardner, Judith and Judy El-Bushra. London; Sterling, VA: CIIR; Pluto Press, Catholic Institute for International Relations, 2004. 142–52.

Marques de Morais, Rafael. *Diamantes De Sangue: Tortura E Corrupção Em Angola (Blood Diamonds: Torture and Corruption in Angola).* Lisbon: Tinta da China, 2011.

Mason, Christina. "Women, Violence and Nonviolent Resistance in East Timor." *Journal of Peace Research* 42.6 (2005): 737–49.

Massaquoi, William N. *Women and Post-Conflict Development: A Case Study on Liberia.* MA Dissertation in City Planning, Massachusetts Institute of Technology, 2007.

Matembe, Miria. *Gender, Politics, and Constitution Making in Uganda.* Kampala, Uganda: Fountain Publishers, 2002.

"How Far Have the Women of Uganda Gone in Realising Their Rights." 1991.

McKay, Susan. "Civil War's Painful Legacy for the Women of Liberia." *Irish Times* (2009).

McKeon, Celia. "Civil Society: Participating in Peace Processes." In *People Building Peace II: Successful Stories of Civil Society.* Eds. Tongeren, Paul van, et al. Boulder, CO: Lynne Rienner, 2005.

Medie, Peace. "Fighting Gender-Based Violence: The Women's Movement and the Enforcement of Rape Law in Liberia." *African Affairs* 112.448 (2013): 377–97.

Police Behavior in Post-Conflict States: Explaining Variation in Responses to Domestic Violence, Internal Human Trafficking, and Rape. PhD Dissertation, University of Pittsburgh, 2012.

Meena, Ruth. "The Politics of Quotas in Tanzania." *A paper presented at the International Institute for Democracy and Electoral Assistance (IDEA)/Electoral Institute of Southern Africa (EISA)/Southern African Development Community (SADC) Parliamentary Forum Conference "The Implementation of Quotas: African Experiences."* 2003.

Mehari, Senait. *Heart of Fire: One Girl's Extraordinary Journey from Child Soldier to Soul Singer.* London: Profile Books, 2008.

Meintjes, Sheila, Anu Pillay, and Meredeth Turshen. *The Aftermath Women in Post-Conflict Transformation.* London: Zed Books, 2002.

Messiant, Christine. "The Eduardo Dos Santos Foundation: Or, How Angola's Regime Is Taking over Civil Society." *African Affairs* 100.399 (2001): 287–309.

Ministry of Gender, Labour and Social Development (Uganda). "National Report on Implementation of the Beijing Platform for Action (1995) and the Outcome of the Twenty Third Special Session of the United Nations General Assembly (2000) in the Context of the 20th Anniversary of the Fourth World Conference on Women and the Adoption of the Beijing Declaration and Platform for Action 2015," June 2014.

Mohamed, Faiza Jama. "Somali Women's Role in Building Peace and Security." *The ARRIA Formula Meeting On Women, Peace and Security, United Nations Security Council.* 2000.

Moran, Mary. "Our Mothers Have Spoken: Synthesizing Old and New Forms of Women's Political Authority in Liberia." *Journal of International Women's Studies* 13.4 (2012): 51–66.

Mortenson, Greg. *Three Cups of Tea: One Man's Mission to Promote Peace ... One School at a Time.* New York: Penguin Books, 2007.

Moser, Caroline N. O., and Fiona Clark, eds. *Victims, Perpetrators or Actors? Gender, Armed Conflict and Political Violence*. London and New York: Zed Books, 2001.

Mpoumou, Doris. "Women's Participation in Peace Negotiations: Discourse in the Democratic Republic of the Congo." *The Implementation of Quotas: African Experiences*. Stockholm: International IDEA, 2004.

Msimang, Sisonke. "The Backlash against African Women." *New York Times* 10 January 2015.

Mueller, John. "War Has Almost Ceased to Exist: An Assessment." *Political Science Quarterly* 124.2 (2009): 297-321.

Mugabe, Robert. *An Opening Address by the President of Zanu (PF) Women's League Conference*. March 15-17, 1984.

Muriaas, Ragnhild L., Liv Tønnessen, and Vibeke Wang. "Exploring the Relationship between Democratization and Quota Policies in Africa." *Women's Studies International Forum* 41 (2013).

Muriaas, Ragnhild L., and Vibeke Wang. "Executive Dominance and the Politics of Quota Representation in Uganda." *Journal of Modern African Studies* 50.2 (2012): 309-38.

Nduka-Agwua, Adibeli. "'Doing Gender' after the War: Dealing with Gender Mainstreaming and Sexual Exploitation and Abuse in Un Peace Support Operations in Liberia and Sierra Leone." *Civil Wars* 11.2 (2009): 179-99.

Nilsson, Desirée. "Anchoring the Peace: Civil Society Actors in Peace Accords and Durable Peace." *International Interactions* 38.2 (2012): 243-66.

Nossiter, Adam. "Woman Chosen to Lead Central African Republic out of Mayhem." *New York Times* 20 January 2014.

Nsambu, Hillary. "Laetitia Kikonyogo: A Lady of Many Firsts." *New Vision* 8 January 2013.

Nyanzi, Peter. "Looking Back at 1985 Peace Talks and Why Nothing Came Out of Them." *Uganda Journal* 19-25 December 2004.

O'Connell, Helen. "What Are the Opportunities to Promote Gender Equity and Equality in Conflict-Affected and Fragile States? Insights from a Review of Evidence." *Gender & Development* 19.3 (2011): 455-66.

Odoki, Benjamin J. *The Search for a National Consensus: The Making of the 1995 Uganda Constitution*. Kampala, Uganda: Fountain Press, 2005.

OECD-DAC. *Aid in Support of Gender Equality in Fragile and Conflict-Affected States*, 2010.

Ollek, Maya Oza. *Forgotten Females: Women and Girls in Post Conflict Disarmament, Demobilisation and Reintegration Programs*. MA thesis. McGill University, 2007.

Onyejekwe, C. J. "Women, War, Peace-Building and Reconstruction." *International Social Science Journal* 57.2 (2005): 277-283.

Ormhaug, C. M., O. Meier, and Helga Maria Hernes. *Armed Conflict Deaths Disaggregated by Gender*. Oslo: PRIO; A Report for the Norwegian Ministry of Foreign Affairs, 2009.

Osman, Habiba. "Testimony 1." *Somalia–the Untold Story: The War through the Eyes of Somali Women*. Eds. Gardner, Judith and Judy El-Bushra. Sterling, VA: CIIR; Pluto Press; Catholic Institute for International Relations, 2004. 41-50.

"Women's Work in Peace: Lessons from Training Projects in the Horn of Africa," Training to Promote Conflict Management, Ed. David Smock. Washington, DC: US Institute for Peace, 1999.

Otto, Dianne. "The Exile of Inclusion: Reflections on Gender Issues in International Law over the Last Decade." *Melbourne Journal of International Law* 10.1 (2009): 11–26.

Pankhurst, Donna. "Post-War Backlash Violence against Women: What Can "Masculinity" Explain?" *Gendered Peace: Women's Struggles for Reconciliation and Justice,*. Ed. Pankhurst, Donna. Oxon: Routledge, 2007. 293–320.

"The 'Sex War' and Other Wars: Towards a Feminist Approach to Peacebuilding." *Development in Practice* 13.2/3 (2003): 154–77

"Women and Politics in Africa: The Case of Uganda." *Parliamentary Affairs* 55.1 (2002): 119–28.

Pankhurst, Donna, and Jenny Pearce. "Engendering the Analysis of Conflict: Perspectives from the South." *Women and Empowerment*. Ed. Afshar, Haleh. London: Routledge, 1997.

Pasquali, Valentina. "Country Report: Angola: Moving Forward in Fits and Starts." *Global Finance Magazine* 2 March 2014.

Pawson, Lara. "The 27th May in Angola: A View from Below." *Revista Relações Internationais* 4 (2007).

Paxton, Pamela. "Women in National Legislatures: A Cross-National Analysis." *Social Science Research* 26 (1997): 442–64.

Melanie M. Hughes, and Jennifer Green. "The International Women's Movement and Women's Political Representation, 1893–2003." *American Sociological Review* 71.6 (2006): 898–920.

Paxton, Pamela, Sheri Kunovich, and Melanie M. Hughes. "Gender in Politics." *Annual Review of Sociology* 33 (2007): 263–84.

Paxton, Pamela, Melanie M. Hughes, and Matthew Painter. "The Difference Time Makes: Latent Growth Curve Models of Women's Political Representation." *European Journal of Political Research* 49.1 (2010): 25–52.

Pearson, Elizabeth. *Gender, Power, and Policymaking: Developing Gender-Based Violence Legislation in Rwanda*. M.Phil. thesis, Oxford: University of Oxford, 2007.

Pearson, Elizabeth, and Elizabeth Powley. *Demonstrating Legislative Leadership: The Introduction of Rwanda's Gender-Based Violence Bill*. The Initiative for Inclusive Security, 2008.

Pehrsson, Kajsa in in collaboration with Gabriela Cohen, Henda Ducados and Paulette Lopes. *Angola Country Gender Analysis*: Prepared for the Swedish International Development Authority (SIDA), Luanda, Angola, 2000.

Powley, Elizabeth. *Strengthening Governance: The Role of Women in Rwanda's Transition*. Women Waging Peace Policy Commission, 2003.

Strengthening Governance: The Role of Women in Rwanda's Transition a Summary United Nations. Office of the Special Adviser on Gender Issues and Advancement of Women (OSAGI) Expert Group Meeting on "Enhancing Women's Participation in Electoral Processes in Post-Conflict Countries" 19–22 January 2004, Glen Cove: United Nations, 2004.

Pratt, Nicola, and Sophie Richter-Devroe. "Critically Examining UNSCR 1325 on Women, Peace and Security." *International Feminist Journal of Politics* 13.4 (2011): 489–503.

Puechguirbal, Nadine. "Gender and Peacebuilding in Africa: Analysis of Some Structural Obstacles." *Gender and Peacebuilding in Africa*. Eds. Rodríguez, Dina and Edith Natukunda-Togboa. Ciudad Colón, Costa Rica: University for Peace, 2005.

Quinn, Michael, David Mason, and Mehmet Gurses. "Sustaining the Peace: Determinants of Civil War Recurrence." *International Interactions* 32.2 (2007): 167–93.

Ranchod-Nilsson, Sita. "Gender Politics and the Pendulum of Political and Social Transformation in Zimbabwe." *Journal of Southern African Studies* 32.1 (2006): 49–67.

Reynolds, Andrew. "Women in the Legislatures and Executives of the World: Knocking at the Highest Glass Ceiling." *World Politics* 51.4 (1999): 547–72.

Reyntjens, Filip. "Constructing the Truth, Dealing with Dissent, Domesticating the World: Governance in Post-Genocide Rwanda." *African Affairs* 110.438 (2011): 1–34.

Römkens, Renée. "Law as a Trojan Horse: Unintended Consequences of Rights-Based Interventions to Support Battered Women." *Yale Journal of Law* 13 (2001): 265–90.

Ross, Michael. "Oil, Islam, and Women." *American Political Science Review* 102 (2008): 107–23.

Rubimbwa, Robinah. *Uganda UNSCR 1325 Monitoring Report*. Kampala, Uganda: CEWIGO, 2010.

Rwandan Ministry of Gender and Family Promotion. *Violence against Women*. Kigali, 2004.

Salhi, Zahia Smail. "The Algerian Feminist Movement between Nationalism, Patriarchy and Islamism." *Women's Studies International Forum* 33 (2010): 113–24.

Sambanis, Nicholas. "A Review of Recent Advances and Future Directions in the Literature on Civil War." *Defense and Peace Economics* 13.2 (2002): 215–43.

Sanya, Samuel. "First Women's Commercial Bank Launched in Uganda." *New Vision* 17 January 2014a.

"What Makes Allen Kagina Tick." *New Vision* 25 October 2014b.

Schedler, Andreas. 2006. *Electoral Authoritarianism: The Dynamics of Unfree Competition*. Boulder, CO: Lynne Rienner Publishers.

Sewell, Jr., William H. *Logics of History: Social Theory and Social Transformation*. Chicago: University of Chicago Press, 2009.

Shaw, Elma. *Redemption Road: The Quest for Peace and Justice in Liberia*. Washington DC: Cotton Tree Press, 2008.

Shella, Kimberly. *Interparty Competition, Political Risk, and the Decline of Women's Representation in Africa*, in *Annual European Political Science Association Annual Conference*. Barcelona, Spain, 2013.

Shepherd, Laura J. "Power and Authority in the Production of United Nations Security Council Resolution 1325." *International Studies Quarterly*. 52.2 (2008): 383–404.

SIGI Index, Social Institutions & Gender. "Angola." 2014. Web. 15 July 2014.

Sinclair, Michael and Janet Place eds. *Women and Children in Southern Africa: An Introduction*. Women and Children at Risk in Southern Africa. April 1, 1990. Southern Africa Grantmakers Affinity Group of the Council on Foundations.

Skidmore, Monique, and Patricia Lawrence. *Women and the Contested State: Religion, Violence, and Agency in South and Southeast Asia*. Notre Dame: University of Notre Dame Press, 2007.

Smith, Dakota. "Spice Girls Power up for Pavarotti's Liberia Charity Show." *MTV News* 10 April 1998.

Snyder, Anna. "Peace Profile: Federation of African Women's Peace Networks." *Peace Review* 12.1 (2000): 147–53.

Snyder, Margaret. "Unlikely Godmother: The UN and the Global Women's Movement." *Global Feminism: Transnational Women's Activism, Organizing, and Human Rights* Eds. Ferree, Myra Marx and Aili Mari Tripp. New York: New York University Press, 2006. 24–50.

Women in African Economies: From Burning Sun to Boardroom. Kampala, Uganda: Fountain Publishers, 2000.

Soares de Oliveira, Ricardo. *Magnificent and Beggar Land: Angola Since the Civil War.* Oxford: Oxford University Press, 2015.

Staunton, Irene. *Mothers of the Revolution: The War Experiences of Thirty Zimbabwean Women.* London: James Currey, 1990.

Steady, Filomina Chioma. *Women and Leadership in West Africa: Mothering the Nation and Humanizing the State.* New York: Palgrave Macmillan, 2011.

Stedman, Stephen, Donald Rothchild, and Elizabeth M. Cousens, eds. *Ending Civil Wars: The Implementation of Peace Agreements.* Boulder, CO: Lynne Rienner Publishers, 2002.

Steinberg, Donald. *Beyond Words and Resolutions: An Agenda for UNSCR 1325.* Chapter from the forthcoming book "Women and War: Power and Protection", United States Institute of Peace, 2010a.

The United Nations and Women: Walking the Walk on Empowerment? Submission to the "Together for Transformation" *Conference of the International Fellowship of Reconciliation's Women Peacemakers Program,* The Hague, Netherlands, 2010b.

"Failing to Empower Women Peacebuilders: A Cautionary Tale from Angola." *PeaceWomen E-News* 25 April 2007.

Stone, Lydia. "We Were All Soldiers': Female Combatants in South Sudan's Civil War." *Hope, Pain & Patience: The Lives of Women in South Sudan.* Eds. Bubenzer, Friederike and Orly Stern. Auckland Park, South Africa: Fanele/Jacana Media, 2011.

Straus, Scott. "Wars Do End! Changing Patterns of Political Violence in Sub-Saharan Africa." *African Affairs* 111.443 (2012): 179–201.

Strickland, Richard, and Nata Duvvury. *Gender Equity and Peacebuilding: From Rhetoric to Reality: Finding the Way.* Washington DC: International Center for Research on Women, 2003.

Swiss, Shana, et al. "Violence against Women During the Liberian Civil Conflict." *Journal of the American Medical Association* 279.8 (1998): 625–29.

Sylvester, Christine. "Patriarchy, Peace, and Women Warriors." *Peace: Meanings, Politics, Strategies.* Ed. Forcey, Linda Rennie. New York: Praeger, 1989. 97–112.

Tachou-Sipowo, Alain-Guy. "The Security Council on Women in War: Between Peacebuilding and Humanitarian Protection." *International Review of the Red Cross* 92.877 (2010): 197–219.

Tamale, Sylvia. *When Hens Begin to Crow: Gender and Parliamentary Politics in Uganda.* Boulder, CO: Westview Press, 1999.

Temmerman, Els. *Aboke Girls: Children Abducted in Northern Uganda.* Kampala, Uganda: Fountain Publishers, 2001.

Tinde, Gry Tina. "Top United Nations Peacebuilders and Advocacy for Women, Peace, and Security." *Refugee Survey Quarterly* 28.1 (2009): 140–50.

Tønnessen, Liv. "Beyond Numbers? Women's 25% Parliamentary Quota in Post-Conflict Sudan." *Journal of Peace, Conflict and Development* 17 (2011): 43–62.

Tønnessen, Liv, and Samia al-Nagar. "The Women's Quota in Conflict Ridden Sudan: Ideological Battles for and against Gender Equality." *Women's Studies International Forum* (2013).

Tripp, Aili Mari. Women's Political Participation in Sub-Saharan Africa, Conflict Prevention and Peace Forum, CPPF Working Papers on Women in Politics: No. 1. 2014. Social Science Research Council. http://webarchive.ssrc.org/working-papers/CPPF_WorkingPapers_WomenInPolitics_01_Tripp.pdf

Museveni's Uganda: Paradoxes of Power in a Hybrid Regime. Boulder, CO: Lynne Rienner, 2010a.

"Legislating Gender Based Violence in Post-Conflict Africa," *Journal of Peacebuilding and Development.* 5.3 2010b: 7–20.

"Conflicting Agendas: Women's Rights and Customary Law in Africa Today," *Constituting Equality*, Ed. Susan Williams. Cambridge, UK: Cambridge University Press, 2009. 173–94.

"Women and Democracy: The New Political Activism in Africa." *Journal of Democracy* 12.3 (2001): 141–55.

Women and Politics in Uganda. Madison: University of Wisconsin Press, 2000.

Tripp, Aili Mari, and Alice Kang. "The Global Impact of Quotas: On the Fast Track to Increased Female Legislative Representation." *Comparative Political Studies* 41.3 (2008): 338–61.

Tripp, Aili Mari, and Isabel Casimiro, Joy Kwesiga, and Alice Mungwa. *African Women's Movements: Transforming Political Landscapes.* New York: Cambridge University Press, 2009.

Tryggestad, Torunn L. "The UN Peacebuilding Commission and Gender: A Case of Norm Reinforcement." *International Peacekeeping* 17.2 (2010): 159–71.

Turrittin, Jane. "Aoua Kéita and the Nascent Women's Movement in the French Soudan." *African Studies Review* 36.1 (1993): 59–89.

Turner, Tom. "Does Your Cell Phone Cause Rape?" *Women's Leadership, Supporting Peace and Building Sustainable Livelihoods in the Democratic Republic of Congo and Region.* Centre for Global Women's Studies, National University of Ireland, Mary Robinson Centre, and Georgetown Institute on Women, Peace and Security, 2014.

Turshen, Meredith. "Engendering Relations of State to Society in the Aftermath." *The Aftermath: Women in Post-Conflict Transformation*, Eds. Meintjes, S., A. Pillay, and M. Turshen. London: Zed Books, 2001.

Tvedten, Inge. *Angola 2000/2001. Key Development Issues and the Role of NGOs.* Bergen: Chr. Michelsen Institute, 2001.

Uganda Constitutional Commission. *The Report of the Uganda Constitutional Commission* Kampala, Uganda: Uganda Constitutional Commission, 1993.

Umutesi, Marie Béatrice. *Fuir ou mourir au Zaïre: Le vécu d'une réfugiée Rwandaise.* Mémoires Lieux De Savoir Archive Congolaise. Paris: L'Harmattan, 2000.

UNIFEM. *Celebrating 20 Years of Commitment to the World's Women, Annual Report.* New York: UNIFEM, 1996.

Engendering Peace: Reflections on the Burundi Peace Process. New York: UNIFEM, 2001.

United Nations Population Fund. *Liberian Men and Women Unite to Fight Rape.* 2006.

UN Women. *Women's Participation in Peace Negotiations: Connections between Presence and Influence.* 2012.

Urdang, Stephanie. ""Precondition for Victory": Women's Liberation in Mozambique and Guinea-Bissau." *A Journal of Opinion* 8.1 (1978): 25–31.

U.S. Department of State. *Human Rights Report: Angola.* 2013.

Viterna, Jocelyn, Kathleen M. Fallon, and Jason Beckfield. "How Development Matters: A Research Note on the Relationship between Development, Democracy, and Women's Political Representation." *International Journal of Comparative Sociology* 49.6 (2008): 455–77.

Waliggo, Rev. Fr. John Mary. "Did Women Get a Raw Deal?" *Arise* 17 (1996): 37–43. "What Others Say." *Gender, Politics, and Constitution Making in Uganda.* Ed. Matembe, Miria. Kampala, Uganda: Fountain Publishers, 2002. 143–58.

Waller, Marguerite, and Jennifer Rycenga, eds. *Frontline Feminisms: Women, War, and Resistance.* New York and London: Garland Publishing, 2000.

Walter, Barbara E. *Committing to Peace: The Successful Settlement of Civil Wars.* Princeton, NJ: Princeton University Press, 2002.

Walusimbe, Deo. "Brig Nalweyiso: I Can't Support Muhoozi When Museveni Points at Him." *The Monitor* 1 December 2013.

Wang, Vibeke. *Women's Substantive Representation in Uganda's Legislature.* PhD Dissertation, University of Bergen, 2013a.

Wang, Vibeke. "Women Changing Policy Outcomes: Learning from Pro-Women Legislation in the Ugandan Parliament," *Women's Studies International Forum* 41 (2013b): 113–21.

Watson, Catherine. "Uganda's Women: A Ray of Hope." *Africa Report* July-August (1988).

Weinstein, Jeremy M. *Inside Rebellion: The Politics of Insurgent Violence.* New York: Cambridge University Press, 2007.

White, Carolyn Day. The Role of Women as an Interest Group in the Ugandan Political System. MA thesis, Makerere University, 1973.

Whitman, Shelly. "Women and Peace-Building in the Democratic Republic of the Congo: An Assessment of Their Role in the Inter-Congolese Dialogue." *Southern African Universities Social Sciences Conference (SAUSSC).* 2005.

Wiliarty, Sarah Elise. "Chancellor Angela Merkel — a Sign of Hope or the Exception That Proves the Rule?" *Politics & Gender* 4.3 (2008): 485–95.

Willett, Susan. "Introduction: Security Council Resolution 1325: Assessing the Impact on Women, Peace and Security." *International Peacekeeping* 17.2 (2010): 142–58.

Williams, Jody. "UK Summit on Sexualized Violence: 'A Time Warp in the Wrong Direction'." 2014. Web.

Williams, Korto R. *Beyond Mass Action: A Study of Collective Organizing among Liberian Women Using Feminist Movement Perspectives.* Capstone Collection: School for International Training, 2008.

Wilson, Woodrow. *Address to the Senate.* 30 September 1918.

World Bank. *Africa Development Indicators: The Potential, the Problem, the Promise. Youth and Employment in Africa.* 2008/09. Washington, DC: World Bank, 2009.

Yacob-Haliso, Olajumoke. "Investigating the Role of Government Legislation and Its Implementation in Addressing Gender-Based Violence among Returnee Refugee Women in Liberia." *Wagadu* 10 (2012): 132–49.

Yoon, Mi Yung. "Explaining Women's Legislative Representation in Sub-Saharan Africa." *Legislative Studies Quarterly* 29.3 (2004): 447–68.

Zakaria, Fareed. "The Rise of Illiberal Democracy." *Foreign Affairs* 76.6 (1997): 22–43.

Zuckerman, Elaine, and Marcia Greenberg. "The Gender Dimensions of Post-Conflict Reconstruction: An Analytical Framework for Policymakers." *Gender and Development* 12.3 (2004): 70–82.

Zziwa, Hassan Badru. "Women Soccer Should Be Supported." *Monitor* 29 April–1 May 1996: 15.

Index